Understanding the New Testament and Its Message

An Introduction

by

Vincent P. Branick

PAULIST PRESS
New York/Mahwah, N.J.

The Publisher gratefully acknowledges the use of photographs taken by the author for inclusion in this book; excerpts from *The Documents of Vatican II,* Abbott-Gallagher edition, are reprinted with permission of America Press, Inc., 106 West 56th Street, New York, N.Y. 10019, © 1966, all rights reserved; reproduction of Rylands Greek Papyrus 457 is by courtesy of the Director and University Librarian, the John Rylands University Library of Manchester (England). Reproduction of Codex B is by courtesy of the Biblioteca Apostolica Vaticana (Vatican City).

Book design by Theresa M. Sparacio

Cover design by Irving Freeman

Copyright © 1998 by Vincent P. Branick

Library of Congress Cataloging-in-Publication Data

Branick, Vincent P.
    Understanding the New Testament and its message : an introduction /
by Vincent P. Branick.
        p.   cm.
    Includes bibliographical references and index.
    ISBN 0–8091–3780–1 (alk. paper)
    1. Bible. N.T.—Introductions. I. Title.
BS2330.2.B73   1998
225.6´1—dc21   97–47026
                                                                    CIP

Published by Paulist Press
997 Macarthur Boulevard
Mahwah, New Jersey 07430

Printed and bound in the
United States of America

Contents

To Arlene

Introduction

"What makes the New Testament special for you?" I ask the students on the first day of class.

Some responses point to the age and historical character of the books. "The Bible and the New Testament have influenced our world a lot." Two thousand years of influencing people and cultures are in fact nothing to sneeze at, even if you do not believe it was a good influence. Other responses focus on information *about* Jesus— "a very influential person"—or information *from* Jesus—"a great teacher of spiritual things." These responses impress me. They exhibited no small academic sensitivity.

Among the student responses, however, are also responses of faith, faith in some transforming or strengthening power of the text. "I read the New Testament to be close to God," one student wrote without adding how that can happen. "The New Testament is special because it helps us believe that Jesus came to save us," another stated.

For some of the students, it is clear, the New Testament is sacred. It is a holy book. For others it is simply a historical book, a classic of our culture. And both groups are attending the same university class, which is mandated to be a rigorous or scientific study of the texts. The study is not to be a prayerful Bible study. Rather, the method of investigation is to be the same as for any classic text. It is to be analytical and empirical. We are to draw our conclusions from the evidence of the text.

To some degree this modern scientific approach to scripture forces a certain schizophrenia on religious students. On the one hand, the analytical and empirical approach of the modern methods focuses on the Bible as a human work emerging from human history, expressing "the all too human." On the other hand, Christian faith holds the Bible to be a revelation from God, as a personal message of divine love. Reading scripture as scholars and believers, the

1

religious students may find their spirit split in two—one half for the classroom, the other half later for church. Schizoid lives are livable, but they are not very pleasant. Thus, many students opt for one side of the split or the other, either reading the Bible simply as a testimony of ancient human endeavors and aspirations—sometimes not too lofty—or reading the Bible as God's personal message demanding an adherence that cannot be compromised by any scholarly prerequisite or academic canon.

Yet we believe that God gave us an intellect to use. We believe that the God who reveals himself also holds in existence all true evidence. If both revelation and history have their origin in God, the study of both should lead to him. The study of both should lead to a sense of unity and coherence, not division of the spirit.

This book will attempt to lead to that coherence or at least will attempt a few steps in that direction. The key will be to focus on the faith of the historical writers. The New Testament as a historical collection testifies to the faith of the earliest Christians, which in turn is rooted in God. That faith can and must be studied with the tools of history, language analysis, and other forms of scientific study. God is not subject to scientific analysis, but human faith is. God may be approached in art, poetry, song, and mystical contemplation—all beyond scientific precision. But once the artistic or mystical endeavor comes to religious expression, a human phenomenon falls under the many scopes of science. The faith of Luke or Paul, as expressed in the New Testament, can be observed, quantified, analyzed, reformulated, and tested for consistency. While the God of their faith cannot be so manipulated, we can glimpse that God as we study those human expressions of faith. Even as scientifically analyzed, the biblical texts can become the springboard of our own artistic, poetic, and contemplative leap.

What I describe here is theology. This is "faith seeking understanding," as the medieval universities called theological reflection. This is a move beyond "religious studies," the careful study of the human phenomena, toward an attempt to integrate intellectual insight and faith—without compromising either.

In the "religious studies" approach to scripture, attention is given to the diverse historical and social background out of which the text and the religious faith of the text arise. This approach is descriptive. It eschews any endeavor to discover a "normative" essence to biblical faith. The results are extremely valuable. Nuances, subtle differences of position, as well as decisively diverse approaches in scripture become apparent. These aspects have often been crushed down in a steamroller approach to find the unchanging and essential truth of the text.

Unfortunately the practitioner of the "religious studies" approach often defends his or her studies by ridiculing an "essentialist" approach, according to the presupposition—sometimes expressed—that religion, and Christian faith in particular, has no essential core but is fully identical to its diverse forms as a function of historical and sociological pressures.

The approach of this book, on the other hand, is unabashedly theological. In no way, however, do I want to ridicule or play down the importance of the descriptive approach with its concerns for the historical and sociological functions in the text. This book could not have been written without the training I received in the descriptive approach. My presupposition lies in the faith that religion is indeed something more than human, that it is a response to a divine initiative. Religious faith, even biblical faith, will always be found in diverse, historically conditioned realizations. In and through those historical realizations, however, an idea can be abstracted that moves us to what is beyond history.

The real methodological choice, it seems to me, is not between the descriptive documentation of religious studies and the prescriptive intuitions of theology to the disdain of the other. The choice is to be a specialist in religious studies leaving the theological challenge to someone else or to attempt to do a little of both, to find theological truth in and through the particular historical phenomenon. My choice is to embrace the descriptive, phenomenological method of biblical studies and to start the intuitive theological process by sorting out aspects that correspond to modern issues of faith, to seek the religious faith of the biblical authors as it may respond to questions common to the author and to us. After this difficult work, at once descriptive and intuitive, I will attempt theological reflections whereby the results speak to us today. That is, I will seek a normative, summoning truth expressed in the text and by the text.

For the believer today, ready to see the summoning truth of a biblical text, the principal difficulty is to let the text speak. The believer possesses a larger picture. This is the picture produced by a lifetime of learning and synthesis in which the reality of Jesus, salvation, and eschatology is understood. When we want to read the message of Mark, we must put that larger picture aside and let the text of Mark speak by itself. The larger picture remains in our minds as question, but the answer must come from the text. Like some of the original readers, we must read the text as if it were the first time we heard many of these elements described. The lack of response to some of our faith questions disappoints, but the delicate nuances apparent only by detailed and sensitive description often enrich and correct answers we may have given to some of those questions.

In this method we lose material. Descriptions of God, of Jesus, or of salvation that do not correspond to our questions will fall through the cracks of our study. In fact we are not the original readers. Our questions are different. While this difference should alert us to the constant need to enlarge our views, we need also, I believe, to accept the concerns in our heart as *our* concerns. Future generations will have yet other questions, and therefore the text becomes an inexhaustible source of interpretation.

I have included sets of questions and exercises at the end of each chapter. The "Exercises" are geared for those of you who want to do more than what I have covered in the text. By working through these exercises you should be able to probe additional background material or other aspects of the biblical text at hand. At times an exercise consists in your trying to work out the religious ideas of the text before reading my explanation. The "Review Questions" are questions that a careful reading of this text should prepare you to answer. They are rather factual and could form a test of how well you learned the main points of the chapter. The questions "For Further Reflection and Discussion" lead immediately into the theological dimension of the text. They are attempts to link the issues of the text to those of today's reader.

The translations of biblical and ancient texts are mine unless otherwise indicated. Modern translations with their insistence on good English often lose nuances that I want to bring out. Please excuse the wooden quality of my translations. For this study accuracy is far more important than readability.

My sincere thanks to the University of Dayton for the time to complete this book, to all my students from whom I have learned so much. I want to thank in a special way Arlene Branick, my wife, and Mary-Margaret Melanson, a student of mine and a professor of English, who proofread this whole book and provided precise and accurate improvements in the composition. Deep thanks also to Larry Boadt, C.S.P. He worked with me in the development of this study. Much of his advice is in fact now part of this book.

Dayton, 1997

1

A Problematic Method

I. The New Testament as the Word of God

Individuals speak of finding life in the New Testament writings, discovering the word of God, or attaining some guidance from above concerning the tough issues of this life. The New Testament and the Bible in general operate in the life of a believer as a source of strength, a guide for decisions, a personal expression of love from the God of faith. To the Christian, the New Testament along with the whole Bible, means something related to God, something sacred. When Christians pick up the New Testament, they usually anticipate some contact with God.

It is clear, however, from the briefest reading of the New Testament that these writings are the product of human beings writing to each other. The author of the Third Gospel, whom we call Luke, describes his work of investigating and writing down the story of Jesus (Lk 1:1–4). Even the "heavenly" sounding book of Revelation includes an account of the human being, John of Patmos, as he achieved his visions and wrote them down (Rv 1:1–2; 4–5).

A. Inspiration and Biblical Revelation

Christian faith has traditionally expressed this combination of divine power and human writing in terms of *inspiration*. This term alludes to the breath or spirit of God filling an author and raising that author to a divine level. The concept of inspiration appears to be borrowed from Jewish theology to describe the presence of the word of God in the writings of the prophets and eventually of the entire Jewish scriptures. During the centuries just before Jesus, Jews pictured the first five books of the Bible as actually more than inspired, as an actual product handed over to Moses from God—something in the manner of the Hollywood picture of God's finger carving out the Ten Commandments. The pictures differ somewhat, but the basic thrust is to describe a synergy between God and human authors. Behind the various images are attempts to describe how God and a human author can work together to produce a writing that can appropriately be called God's word.

The result of inspiration, according to Christian faith, is divine *revelation,* God "unveiling" or manifesting some reality of himself that would otherwise be hidden or inaccessible. For the Christian, God reveals himself in the Bible. In the New Testament God reveals his ultimate plan of love and salvation through God's ultimate word and Son, Jesus of Nazareth (Heb 1:1–4; Jn 1:1–18). According to Christian faith, Jesus is the ultimate revelation of God. The inspired accounts about him and his work extend this revelation through the centuries into times when Christians can no longer see, hear, and touch Jesus as his earliest disciples could (1 Jn 1:1).

B. A Catholic Position

Christian churches have expressed their faith in biblical inspiration in different ways but have always insisted on the divine character of the Bible. In Catholic circles the clearest and most significant expression is a paragraph in the document *Dei Verbum,* written in 1965 by the ecumenical council Vatican II.

> Those divinely revealed realities which are contained and presented in sacred Scripture have been committed to writing under the inspiration of the Holy Spirit. Holy Mother Church, relying on the belief of the apostles, holds that the books of both the Old and New Testament in their entirety, with all their parts, are sacred and canonical because, having been written under the inspiration of the Holy Spirit (cf. Jn 20:31; 2 Tim 3:16; 2 Pet 1:19–21; 3:15–16) they have God as their author and have been handed on as such to the Church herself. In composing the sacred books, God chose men and while employed by Him they made use of their powers and abilities, so that with Him acting in them and through them, they, as true authors, consigned to writing everything and only those things which He wanted.

> Therefore, since everything asserted by the inspired authors or sacred writers must be held to be asserted by the Holy Spirit, it follows that the books of Scripture must be acknowledged as teaching firmly, faithfully, and without error that truth which God wanted put into the sacred writings for the sake of our salvation. Therefore "all Scripture is inspired by God and useful for teaching, for reproving, for correcting, for instruction in justice; that the man of God may be perfect, equipped for every good work" (2 Tim 3:16–17, Greek text). (*Dei Verbum*, #11)

This council insists on the Bible as the word of God. The biblical books "have God as their author." Even though human authors such as Luke or Paul wrote the physical texts, we can attribute everything that these texts say to God himself, as we attribute the statements of a book to its author.

Moreover, the Catholic Church here insists that this inspiration applies to the biblical books "in their entirety, with all their parts." They are therefore attributable to God as author. In this perspective of faith, we cannot materially divide the Bible into texts that are the word of God and others that are not. Inspiration involves the whole Bible.

The council then draws the conclusion regarding the *inerrancy* of the Bible. If God is the author of the books of scripture, then a person of faith must see these books as "teaching firmly, faithfully, and without error that truth which God wanted put into the sacred writings for the sake of our salvation."

The council chose the wording here with great care. On the one hand, it did not want to say that the biblical books give us accurate paleontological truth or even inerrant information about the political history of nations. On the other hand, the council would not say that we could separate texts dealing with religion or salvation from other texts treating other matters, holding to one and rejecting the other. In some way inerrancy had to apply to the whole Bible. To say this the council chose to link the inerrancy of the Bible to a quality that could be present *more or less* in every statement of scripture, namely, the way in which that text concerns our salvation. We are talking about "that truth which God wanted put into the sacred writings for the sake of our salvation." In some way that truth is present in every word in every statement of the Bible, in some places marginally and in other places intensely. *To the degree* that a text expresses a saving truth, to that degree the text is "inerrant."

C. A Protestant Position

Most Protestant churches stress the divine character of the Bible with even greater emphasis. No one expression of this faith in the Bible sums up the teachings of all Protestant churches, but the *Book of Confessions* of the United Presbyterian Church in the United States articulates a mainline Christian position toward the Bible very similar to that of most Protestant churches. The Westminster Confession, adopted in 1958, again speaks of God as the author of the Bible:

> The authority of the Holy Scripture, for which it ought to be believed and obeyed, dependeth not upon the testimony of any man or church, but wholly upon God (who is truth itself), the author thereof; and therefore it is to be received because it is the Word of God. (*Book of Confessions,* 6.004)

Roughly a decade later the Confession of 1967 again insists on the authority of the Bible, both as a witness to revelation of God in Jesus and as the word of God itself:

> The one sufficient revelation of God is Jesus Christ, the Word of God incarnate, to whom the Holy Spirit bears unique and authoritative witness through the Holy Scriptures, which are received and obeyed as the word of God written. The Scriptures are not a witness among others, but the witness without parallel. The church has received the books of the Old and New Testaments as prophetic and apostolic testimony in which it hears the word of God and by which its faith and obedience are nourished and regulated. (*Book of Confessions,* 9.27)

In other Protestant circles the concern centers more on the transformation of individuals. Pastors generally focus on the *life-giving* character of the Bible. Private testimonies abound of substance abusers and unfaithful spouses finding in the Bible the higher power to turn their lives around. For these believers the Bible is no ordinary book. God and his saving power are experienced in the text itself.

D. The Analogy of the Incarnation

In the human words of the Bible, Christians thus see a special presence of God. Of course Christian theology speaks of God's presence on many levels. On the broadest level, God is present everywhere by his power continually creating and governing all things and every event. God is present in a more intense way to the person who addresses him in prayer. Christians see the presence of God in the Bible as yet even more intense.

The one analogy that seems to capture for Christians the special presence of God in biblical texts is the presence of God in Jesus. In and through the humanity of Jesus, God is present in the world. According to a Christian teaching that stems from the Council of Nicea in A.D. 325, the human and the divine in Jesus form a single entity so that the deeds of Jesus can be called the deeds of God. The Second Vatican Council returned to this analogy in its description of the human and the divine in the Bible:

> For the words of God, expressed in human language, have been made like human discourse, just as of old the Word of the eternal Father, when he took to Himself the weak flesh of humanity, became like other men. (*Dei Verbum,* #13)

(See exercise 1.)

II. The Challenge and the Response

A. The Challenge of the Enlightenment

In the eighteenth century, an epoch-making challenge to this Christian faith arose. This was the challenge of the Deists, who saw God "too busy" to be inspiring gospels and letters. The Deists conceived of God operating on the level of ultimate origins and universal totalities, but neither knowing nor caring about individuals. This was the age of *enlightenment* and of an understandable effort to free people from abusive church powers. Individual Deists studied the Bible to show blatant inconsistencies, wholesale incorporation of contemporary ideas, copying from one document to another, the inaccuracy of alleged authorship—in short, to debunk the Bible.

The tendentious approach of the Deists led to exaggerations and outright falsifications of data. However, many of their discoveries about the Bible and the New Testament would not simply go away by some revitalization of piety. The scientific method was in the air, and for a religious scholar that meant looking at the data without fear of where the data might lead. It meant especially tracing the historical development of an idea—even if it was an article of faith. History became a countervailing authority even to religious office within a church.

The scientific method of reading the Bible was welcomed by those tired of the subjective arbitrariness found in many spiritual readings of the biblical texts. Unfortunately we can, and often do, approach scripture already convinced of what it will say to us. We can have our minds so set in our preconceived ideas that we find in the Bible only what we want to find. Throughout history people have misused and abused the Bible, digging through it to find weapons and ammunition to defend their positions and to attack others. Anti-Semitic programs frequently allude to the Gospel of Matthew with its insistence on the role of the Jews in the death of Jesus. Modern fundamentalists often cite the epistles of Paul to justify the subordination of women to male leaders.

The method developed by the Deists became a remarkable tool for overcoming this subjectivism and uncovering meaning in the biblical texts. The method was basically an attempt to see the texts in their own historical setting, speaking to people of the time and culture of the writer, drawing on contemporary ideas and events. In this sense the method was a *historical* reading. On a more profound and problematic level, the method involved reading the Bible in a detached way, not seeking how the text puts the reader in question and summons the reader to a response, but rather seeking to put the text in question and asking what in the text justifies any conclusion about the presumed meaning of the text. In this sense the method involved a *critical* reading. Thus, the *historical-critical method* became an umbrella term describing the various techniques of modern biblical scholarship.

B. The Christian Response

The nineteenth and early twentieth centuries were marked by intense discussions about these new theological developments. Efforts were made to understand how the Genesis creation account could be "true," yet leave room for the work of the paleontologist who was discovering origins irreconcilable with the biblical account. Theories appeared to explain how the Gospels could be historical and yet contain multiple and apparently contradictory descriptions of the same events. Apprehensive pastors and faithful caucused to plan denunciations of these "modernist heresies."

Most mainline Christian churches recognized the need to analyze scientifically the texts of the Bible and attempted to come to grips with this theological ferment. In 1943 Pope Pius XII explicitly instructed Catholic scholars to make use of "history, archaeology, ethnology and other sciences" to determine the meaning of the sacred texts. Only in this way can the human modes of expression be understood (*Divino afflante spiritu,* 35).

Expressing its faith in the Bible the Presbyterian Confession of 1967 declared:

> The Bible is to be interpreted in the light of its witness to God's work of reconciliation in Christ. The Scriptures, given under the guidance of the Holy Spirit, are nevertheless the words of men, conditioned by the language, thought forms, and literary fashions of the places and times at which they were written. They reflect views of life, history, and the cosmos which were then current. The church, therefore, has an obligation to approach the Scriptures with literary and historical understanding. (*Book of Confessions,* 9.29)

Two years earlier, in 1965, the Second Vatican Council of the Catholic Church turned its attention to the human authors of the Bible and expressed a requirement on the part of believers to engage in historical and literary scholarship:

> However, since God speaks in sacred Scripture through men in human fashion, the interpreter of sacred Scripture, in order to see clearly what God wanted to communicate to us, should carefully investigate what meaning the sacred writers really intended, and what God wanted to manifest by means of their words.

> Those who search out the intention of the sacred writers must, among other things, have regard for "literary forms." For truth is proposed and expressed in a variety of ways, depending on whether a text is history of one kind or another, or whether its form is that of prophecy, poetry, or some other type of speech. The interpreter must investigate what meaning the sacred writer intended to express and actually expressed in particular

circumstances as he used contemporary literary forms in accordance with the situation of his own time and culture. For the correct understanding of what the sacred author wanted to assert, due attention must be paid to the customary and characteristic styles of perceiving, speaking, and narrating which prevailed at the time of the sacred writer, and to the customs men normally followed at that period in their everyday dealings with one another. (*Dei Verbum*, #12)

Here again the council carefully selected its wording. We see here the need to investigate the intention of the human author. "The interpreter of sacred Scripture...should carefully investigate what meaning the sacred writers really intended." And again, "the interpreter must investigate what meaning the sacred writer *intended to express* and actually expressed." This direction means looking for clues in the text and in the historical context of the writing for what an author could have meant by a statement. This means recognizing the limits inherent in human intentions as a constraint to the meaning of the Bible. By focusing on the intention of the human author, the council endorses the attempt to look objectively at the text. That intention is a given fact, and it will not change with our changing subjective desires and positions. Searching for that intention means focusing on data that can be observed by others from other perspectives and subjective orientations.

The council leaves the door open for truth that may surpass the human intention. Biblical scholars should investigate "what the sacred writer intended to express *and actually expressed.*" The final words of this sentence recognize that a text once written attains a certain independence from its human author and can in fact contain truth that the human author may not have explicitly envisioned. But again this focus of investigation can be expressed objectively, looking at the words of the texts and their meanings as generated from contemporary linguistic backgrounds.

This council of Catholic bishops based much of its conclusions on a document produced a year earlier by an official commission of Catholic biblical scholars. In 1964 the Pontifical Biblical Commission issued an instruction pointing out the three stages of tradition that readers must attend to if they are to understand what kind of truth exists in the Gospels. The first stage is that of Jesus in his preaching, accommodating himself to the mentality of his listeners. The second stage is that of the first Christians proclaiming the message of Jesus, interpreting the words and deeds of Jesus according to their faith in Jesus' resurrection and according to the needs of their listeners, using various literary forms. The third stage is that of the Gospel writers who adapted their narrations by careful selections, synthetic reductions, and other explications, changing the sayings of Jesus while preserving their sense.

Both the Catholic Council and the Presbyterian Confessions acknowledge a fundamental insight in modern biblical scholarship, namely, the need to recognize the *literary form* or "the thought forms and literary fashions" of a biblical text. We recognize literary forms all day long when we read any texts, whether it be a telephone directory, the front page of a newspaper, an advertisement, or a comic strip. We know what kind of questions to ask a text. We know what kind of truth to look for depending on the identification of the text's literary form. We make this identification by certain writing conventions that immediately clue us in to what to expect. If we hear the words, "Once upon a time...," we have the clue that sets our mind in the direction of the possible truth the text might express. Problems arise when we no longer understand the literary conventions of a past culture and presume, for example, that some narration about past people has as a literary form something like modern critical history. Truth, however, is proposed and expressed in a variety of ways, as the Catholic Council insists. And we must investigate *the way* a biblical text expresses its truth before we ask what truth it is expressing. If we misunderstand the literary form actually present, we will probably misunderstand the message of the text. The whole thrust of these church instructions is to endorse the hard work of the historical-critical method.

The investigation of a biblical author's intention does not come easily. First, it requires understanding the historical setting in which the biblical author wrote, a historical setting that may be completely foreign to our own, a historical setting where even the way of perceiving things differs from ours. Second, such a method precludes presupposing that words necessarily have the same meaning for the biblical author as they do for us. We must, therefore, attempt to understand key words, such as *God* or *sin,* from the way an author uses that word, not by consulting a modern dictionary. Third, such a method requires understanding the modes of writing or literary forms chosen by the author to express his thoughts. Modes of writing may vary from pure fiction to newspaper reporting. The literary form the author chose may not be the one we would have chosen.

(See exercise 2.)

III. Remaining Difficulties and Challenges

In effect this method requires approaching the Bible without adverting to the doctrines of our faith, allowing the author to express his faith without presupposing that it is exactly like our own. If we are to draw conclusions only from the evidence of the text, if we are to apply the rigorous procedures of empirical scientific research, we must take a somewhat neutral position. We are talking here about a certain gap of detachment that would allow the various possible positions of the text an equal opportunity to speak. Focusing on the doctrinal positions of our faith with one eye while trying to read the text with the other not only leads to a headache but tends to filter out any statement that would disagree with our position. Methodological detachment is at the heart of scientific observation.

A. How Much Neutral Detachment?

We face a serious problem here. This type of detachment is appropriate for scientific studies such as research into smoking and lung cancer, where we would not want a tobacco company to do the observations. But what about research into a Christian text? Are scholars of faith thereby disqualified?

No scientific method demands an abandonment of all interest and related positions. Neither does the scientific study of a sacred text require an abandonment of all religious faith and sensitivity. Such an abandonment would prevent us from seeing any religious meaning in the text, even that of the author. We must have an intense sensitivity to the questions that the text deals with. A scientific method insists only that this sensitivity take the form of a questioning. We must be willing to look at the text and question the text in the light of our religious sensitivity, while not demanding an answer that conforms to a position of faith we have already taken.

Our approach will be to raise questions of faith that might mean a great deal to us: Who is Jesus of Nazareth? What was he announcing when he proclaimed the coming of the kingdom? How could his death save us? In fact these questions have meant a great deal to the New Testament authors we will be studying. In these questions of faith we have a bond that can unite us to the text and let the text speak to us. Our approach, however, will then be to let the text answer: to look for direct statements as well as presuppositions and implications based on the text and from this observable data form the answer that seems to be that of the biblical author.

Other questions of faith could be raised. We are starting, however, with questions that appear from the evidence of the text to be the important questions of the New Testament authors.

We will be looking at how individual authors answered those questions while avoiding for the time being how we answer those questions. As we will see, not only do the answers of the biblical authors differ from our answers; they differ from each other. Yet as we see these differences, we must not race into the question, Who's right?—although such a delay may run counter to a basic urge of our heart.

B. Can Meaning Be Separated from Truth?

Expressed another way, our method will focus at first on the *meaning* of the text rather than the *truth* of the text. The meaning of a text is not the same as the truth of a text. The distinction lies in the power that truth has over us. When we propose something as true, we imply that we have discovered something that exists independently of our discovery and therefore resists our arbitrary manipulation, something we therefore propose for acceptance or rejection. If I say something as simple as "It is raining," I am implying a weather condition that exists independent of my discovery. I am also calling on someone to accept this situation—or reject it if it appears I am wrong. A statement of truth is meant to have an impact on the listener. Thus, a statement of possible truth—for example, the utterance "God calls you to a life of selfless love"—implies acceptance or rejection on the part of the listener as one recognizes the utterance as true or false.

The study of *meaning,* on the other hand, involves a clarification of a position taken by a writer or speaker, how the elements of the utterance cohere, or how the utterance relates to the context of the writer. When I search for the meaning of a text, a text as important as "the Word became flesh and dwelt among us," I am not immediately asked to react personally to the proposition. I look to see where the fourth evangelist stands on the matter, without my having to accept or reject it.

The question of truth, however, is unavoidable, and every Christian must deal with the truth of a religious statement. Without the willingness to consider the truth of the matter, any investigation tends to degenerate into something like a game.

For this reason most of the subsequent chapters in this book will conclude with "theological reflections." Here we need to look beyond the restricted scope of historical criticism or exegesis to see where the potential truth of the material might have an impact on us. This extended view is the work of theology properly so called. In academic circles we are familiar with the need to specialize, where theologians do their thing and exegetes do theirs. It probably has to be that way, despite the violence done to the subject matter. The purpose of the "theological reflections" is to facilitate the articulation of the two disciplines. By showing the organic flow from one to the other, we hope to show in the first place how historical exegesis involves a gripping investigation of serious matters with which we already have intense lived connections. Second, the organic flow should also indicate how good theology develops from the complex lived experiences manifested in the biblical texts—not just from systematizing data isolated from the Bible.

In other words the justification of our scientific approach with its initial methodological neutrality lies in seeing the approach as only one part of the full investigation of the New Testament. Our approach is based on the conviction that the truth of a text must be carried by the meaning of the text, and sometimes it is worthwhile to move slowly, to investigate with patience the meaning before posing the question of truth. In matters as complicated and profound as those of religious faith, to rush the question of truth, to demand a hurried answer to Who's right?, is to run the risk of missing the point.

C. Can a Sacred Text Be Objectified?

On the deepest and most comprehensive level, many would still object that the drawback of this method lies in the way it objectifies the text. Instead of the biblical text putting us on the spot, instead of the text questioning us, we question the text. We lay the text out in front of us as a biologist might examine an object of analysis. Such analysis can be offensive to one who sees the Bible as sacred. It may seem wrong to dissect something holy. It may seem like an arrogant claim to dominate the word of God. Can someone study scripture from an objective point of view and still see it as scripture, that is, as a holy text?

We cannot answer these questions convincingly at the start of this study. The proof of the pudding lies in the final product. Some people have found this approach terribly sterile and have abandoned it. Others have found hidden treasures in the religious themes and views uncovered by objective analysis.

Paradoxically, while avoiding at first the question of the truth of the sacred text as conceived by the author, this historical-critical method demands a fierce commitment to truth on another level, namely, to the facts of the physical text. If we are to engage in this study we must be open to "the way things are" in the text, even if that truth is unpleasant, even if that truth upsets our most cherished positions. The truth of historical data and literary fact is a different kind of truth from that intended to be expressed by the author. At the root, then, a religious practitioner of this method must be convinced that all truth coheres and leads to God, whether that truth be historical and scientific or religious and interior.

Anticipating this contact with God in and through the Bible, a person of faith desires to read the Bible in a spiritual way, that is, to hear a living word. Were scripture not to function in this way, there would be little reason for the believer ever to open the Bible. In a context of any believing community, this spiritual reading of scripture is in many ways the goal of all biblical study and research.

Can we achieve this goal through study and research? To achieve this goal requires three steps, starting with a simple reading of the New Testament as the word of God calling us to faith, turning to an analytic and critical examination of the biblical meanings, and then returning to allow the text to summon us with a powerful call. The possibility of such a cycle may well require a dynamism beyond the scope of this study, a dynamism of the heart that has less to do with reason than with reverent contemplation.

D. The Interpretation of the Bible in the Church

The challenge we have set up here parallels the concerns expressed by a commission of Catholic scholars in 1993. The Pontifical Biblical Commission issued an extended reflection on the tasks and difficulties of balancing scientific and ecclesial responsibilities. The document is entitled "The Interpretation of the Bible in the Church."[1]

In it the commission stressed again the importance of the historical-critical method as we outlined it above:

> The very nature of biblical texts means that interpreting them will require continued use of the *historical-critical method,* at least in its principal procedures.[2]

At the same time, the commission stressed the need for biblical studies to articulate with systematic theology, with various forms of prayer, and with faith in general. Using the "critical method" a scholar "operates with the help of scientific criteria that seek to be as objective as possible."[3] Yet, following the insights of modern hermeneutics, good interpretation requires "that there be a lived affinity between the interpreter and the object, an affinity which constitutes, in fact, one of the conditions that makes the entire exegetical enterprise possible."[4]

The Pontifical Biblical Commission suggests a method for exegetes to ease the interchange between objective historical study and systematic theology. If exegetes want their work to be "as it were the soul of theology (*Dei Verbum,* #24)...they ought pay particular attention to the religious content of the biblical writings."[5]

Our study is geared toward the religious questions of the biblical authors, primarily their questions of christology, soteriology, and eschatology. Our goal is to seek out and express how the authors answered those questions, to grasp the religious faith of the authors and of the communities to whom the authors were writing. Our hope is that we might contribute to the interpretation of the Bible in the church.

(See exercises 3, 4.)

NOTES

[1] Published in *Origins: CNS Documentary Service* 23/29 (January 6, 1994): 498–524.
[2] Ibid., 524.
[3] Ibid., 501.
[4] Ibid., 513.
[5] Ibid., 519.

EXERCISES

Exercise 1. (see pages 5–9): Try to express in writing as clearly as you can what the New Testament means to you. What, if anything, for you is the most important or precious aspect of these texts? Answer in writing as accurately as you can. Would you agree without qualification that the texts of the New Testament have God as their author? Do you have any difficulties with this description of the New Testament?

Exercise 2. (see pages 10–13): Imagine you have just received a letter from a close friend and parts of this letter do not seem to make sense. In your attempt to make sense of these parts, what questions would you pose? What would you try to search out in order to find the meaning of the letter?

Exercise 3. (see pages 17–18): If interpreting scripture involves so many aspects and tasks, how would you delegate the various tasks in your church? Who would do what so that the community would fully understand the Bible? Consider the people you know in your local church, in the church of our country, and in the world as a whole.

Exercise 4. (see pages 17–18): Describe how one interprets a work of fine art. How objective and historical should the interpretation be? What kind of love or lived involvement with the art should the interpreter have? What parallels do you find between the study of art and the study of scripture?

REVIEW QUESTIONS

1. According to traditional Christian teaching, what is meant by the inspiration of scripture? Where can we find this traditional teaching?

2. What is the meaning of *biblical inerrancy*? How is it a consequence of inspiration? To what does it extend in the text of scripture?

3. What is the goal of historical-critical studies of the Bible? What position have Christian churches taken in regard to historical-critical studies?

FOR FURTHER REFLECTION AND DISCUSSION

1. Christian groups and churches have disagreed—sometimes violently—about the meaning of the Bible. How do you think they should resolve their differences? Should they even try? Why?

2. Should there be an authority to say what a biblical passage means? Should individuals decide for themselves what a biblical text means? Should a church decide? If so, who in your church should decide? Why?

3. How important is it to understand a biblical text in an intelligent manner? Do we have to be intelligent to be saved?

2

Origins of the Text

I. The Canon

When we turn to the New Testament, the first question we ask deals with its origin. Where do we get the New Testament? We are asking about the very selection of the books that form our New Testament, the list of books that Christians have traditionally used to decide the composition of the New Testament collection. Who made this selection? What were the bases or criteria of the selection?

The list of New Testament books—which we find in the table of contents in our Bibles—forms the standard by which writings from the first two centuries are included or excluded from the official New Testament. In Greek the word for "standard" is *kanōn*. Thus, an inquiry of this type is generally described as one about "the canon" of the New Testament.

An empirical study of the New Testament canon remains shrouded in much ignorance. We know little about the way in which the early Christians made their choice of the New Testament books. Certain milestones, however, appear in the historical evidence as it comes down to us. From these milestones we catch a glimpse of the historical process, a process that seems to have taken up to three centuries, during which time the canon remained in flux.

A. 2 Peter

The first milestone in the development of the canon is a statement by an early Christian author which presupposes the kickoff of the whole process. The statement is found in 2 Pt 3:15–16:

And consider the patience of our Lord as salvation, as our beloved brother Paul, according to the wisdom given

20

to him, also writes to you, speaking of these things as he does in all his letters. In them there are some things hard to understand that the ignorant and unstable distort to their own destruction, just as they do the other scriptures.

In this text an early Christian writer, probably not St. Peter as we will see, alludes to the letters of Paul with two implications that for our purposes are more important than the explicit statements about difficulty and distortions. The first implication occurs in the phrase "all his letters." Recall that Paul wrote letters to the Christians of Rome, Corinth, and other specific communities, addressing the particular concerns of the people he *wrote* to. Outside of one instance when Paul suggested an interchange of letters (see Col 4:16), Paul probably did not expect any letter to go beyond the church to which it was addressed.

That the author of 2 Peter referred to "all his letters" suggests that these letters had been collected. Churches probably exchanged letters, copied them, and preserved them as writings, no longer as letters to specific audiences but as essays that could be considered addressed to anyone who read them. In this way, 2 Peter, which itself is an essay addressed to all believers (see 1:1), refers paradoxically to what Paul "wrote *you*" (3:15). Paul's letters now collected are read not as letters but as essays.

The second implication appears when 2 Peter compares the letters of Paul to "other scriptures" (3:16). The term *scriptures (graphai)* without further qualification was a technical term in early Christian vocabulary for what Christians call today the Old Testament. By placing the distorted interpretations of Paul's letters on the same level as distorted interpretations of the scriptures, the author of 2 Peter is in effect placing Paul on the level of the inspired writings of the Jewish faith. Moreover, the fact that 2 Peter can simply imply this inclusion of Paul's letters among scripture without explaining or defending it suggests that the inclusion was made and accepted some time before 2 Peter was written.

Jewish theology at the time of 2 Peter had yet to determine its biblical canon. A Greek canon was circulating which differed from the Hebrew—and Aramaic—canon. The differences involved the third major part of the Jewish scriptures, the Writings. The list of five books for the first major part, the Torah, was accepted almost universally by people of the Jewish faith or of related faiths. The list of books for the second major part, the Prophets, likewise seemed to elicit fairly universal consensus among those who were willing to go beyond the Torah in their recognition of sacred books. It was the last section, the Writings, that remained an open question among Jews. This was a section, given a rather nondescript name, that included the Psalms and Proverbs—generally accepted without controversy—as well as the books of Maccabees and the Wisdom of Solomon—accepted only by some Jews.

When the early Christians thus identified Paul's letters as scripture, what they appear to be doing is including these letters among the sacred Writings. We have here the earliest evidence of the process of collecting Christian writings considered to be the inspired word of God. The collection, however, was not a separate and distinct grouping; it was rather an extension of "the scriptures" to include some Christian writings.

B. Marcion

The next observable milestone in the development of the canon is the first list or canon itself. A man by the name of Marcion, writing in the middle of the second century, is reported to have developed a rather short New Testament. We do not have any copy of Marcion's canon, but we do have descriptions of it from early church writers such as Irenaeus and Tertullian, writing around the turn of the second century and the beginning of the third. From these descriptions it appears that Marcion accepted an edited form of Luke's Gospel and ten letters of Paul.

Marcion's motive for developing a New Testament is important. For Marcion, a leader of a Gnostic community (about which we will learn more later), material creation was essentially evil. Hence, the God of the Old Testament, as well as the Old Testament itself, were inherently evil. For Marcion, therefore, it was important to develop a new body of writings to replace the Jewish scriptures, which at the time of Marcion was the unique Holy Book or scripture for Christians and Jews alike.

Marcion therefore came up with the idea of a *separate* list of explicitly Christian writings, which he apparently called "the New Testament." Here is the origin of the now commonly accepted idea of two collections, the Jewish writings of the Old Testament and the Christian writings of the New. More than anything else, this idea of a separate list was Marcion's lasting contribution to the development of the New Testament canon.

C. The Muratorian Canon

The Gnostic ideas of Marcion met with stiff resistance. His short New Testament provoked others to develop more complete collections. Although some scholars today dispute its early dating, a manuscript exists today that appears to represent a larger canon developed only decades after Marcion, that is, toward the end of the second century. Today it is known as the Muratorian Canon from the discoverer of this fragment, Lodovico Muratori (d. 1750). The fragment begins with words that seem to refer to Mark's Gospel:

> ...but at some he was present, and so he set them down. The third book of the Gospel, that according to Luke, was compiled in his own name by Luke the physician, when after Christ's ascension Paul had taken him to be with him like a student of law....

> The fourth of the Gospels [was written] by John, one of the disciples. When exhorted by his fellow-disciples and bishops, he said, "Fast with me this day for three days; and what may be revealed to any of us, let us relate it to one another." The same night it was revealed to Andrew, one of the apostles, that John was to write all things in his own name, as all recognized....

> The Acts, however, of all the Apostles are written in one book. Luke puts it briefly to the most excellent Theophilus, that the several things were done in his own presence, as he also plainly shows by leaving out the passion of Peter, and also the departure of Paul from the City on his journey to Spain.

> The Epistles, however, of Paul themselves make plain to those who wish to understand it, what epistles were sent by him, and from what place or for what cause.... Since the blessed Apostle Paul himself, following the order of his predecessor John, writes only by name to seven churches in the following order—to the Corinthians a first, to the Ephesians a second, to the Philippians a third, to the Colossians a fourth, to the Galatians a fifth, to the Thessalonians a sixth, to the Romans a seventh; whereas although for the sake of admonition there is a second to the Corinthians and to the Thessalonians....To Philemon one, to Titus one, and to Timothy two were put

in writing from personal inclination and attachment.... There is currently also one to the Laodicenes, another to the Alexandrians, forged in Paul's name to suit the heresy of Marcion, and several others, which cannot be received into the Catholic Church; for it is not fitting that gall be mixed with honey.

The Epistle of Jude, no doubt, and the couple bearing the name of John, are accepted in the Catholic Church; and the Wisdom written by the friends of Solomon in his honour. The Apocalypse of John, and of Peter only we receive, and which some of our friends will not have read in the Church.[1]

In this canon we find allusion to four Gospels, with Luke and John named explicitly; thirteen letters of Paul, but not Hebrews; the letter of Jude; 1 and 2 John; the book of Revelation; and the *Apocalypse of Peter* as well as the book of Wisdom. The list is surprisingly close to our New Testament. Not all of the New Testament letters are included, and two books are included that will later be dropped, the book of Wisdom, which now appears in the Greek Old Testament and the *Apocalypse of Peter,* which Christians have now relegated to the apocrypha (also called pseudo-epigrapha), the rather extensive collection of early Christian writings no longer considered canonical.

D. Athanasius

We find the final form of the canon in a letter written in A.D. 367 by a man named Athanasius, bishop of Alexandria. The important paragraph of this letter reads as follows:

Concerning the New Testament: There are four Gospels, Matthew, Mark, Luke and John. Then the Acts of the Apostles. Then seven epistles, as follows: one of James, two of Peter, three of John. After these one of Jude. Fourteen of Paul follow in this order: first to the Romans, then two to the Corinthians, one to the Galatians, one to the Ephesians, one to the Philippians, one to the Colossians, two to the Thessalonians, later one to the Hebrews, then two to Timothy, one to Titus, and another to Philemon. Finally the Apocalypse of John. (*Epistola* 39, PG 26:1438)

The letter was Athanasius's *Paschal Epistle.* As we can see, he lists the very same books as our present New Testament. This is the earliest document that we possess that contains this list. This is the earliest hard evidence we have of the canon we use today:

> The Gospel according to Matthew
> The Gospel according to Mark
> The Gospel according to Luke
> The Gospel according to John
> The Acts of the Apostles
> The Letter to the Romans
> The First Letter to the Corinthians
> The Second Letter to the Corinthians
> The Letter to the Galatians
> The Letter to the Ephesians
> The Letter to the Philippians
> The Letter to the Colossians
> The First Letter to the Thessalonians
> The Second Letter to the Thessalonians
> The First Letter to Timothy
> The Second Letter to Timothy
> The Letter to Titus
> The Letter to Philemon
> The Letter to the Hebrews
> The Letter of James
> The First Letter of Peter
> The Second Letter of Peter
> The First Letter of John
> The Second Letter of John
> The Third Letter of John
> The Letter of Jude
> The Book of Revelation

Several other extant lists or discussions of individual books appear in the gap between the Muratorian Canon and that of Athanasius. These discussions either name books we no longer consider canonical or leave out books that are part of our canon. The best known are the following:

Irenaeus of Lyon (d. 202), *Against the Heresies,* 3.11.8–9; Tertullian (d. 220), *Against Marcion,* 5.17–21; Origen (d. 253), cited by Eusebius, *Church History,* 6.25.1–14; Eusebius of Caesarea (ca. 325), *Church History* 3.25.1–7; The canon of Codex Claromontanus (mid-fourth century); The Cheltenham canon (ca. 360).

After Athanasius, Christian leaders seemed to form a basic consensus about the Gospels and the Pauline Epistles. Some disagreements will still appear for several centuries, especially about such writings as Revelation and 2 Peter. Thus, the discussion continues in the *Apostolic Constitutions* (ca. 380), VIII, 47, can. 85; Cyril of Jerusalem (d. 387); and Gregory of Nazianzus (d. 390).

The regional councils of Hippo in 393 and that of Carthage in 397, the writings of Pope Innocent I in 405, as well as the work of Jerome (d. 420), were important steps in the gradual conformity of the Greek and Latin churches to the list of Athanasius. As late as the fifth century, however, the Syrian church (seen in the semiofficial Syriac translation call the Peshitta) omitted 2 Peter, 2 and 3 John, Jude, and Revelation.

THE DEVELOPMENT OF THE CANON OF SCRIPTURE

2 Peter (c. A.D. 110)
Marcion (c. A.D. 150)
Muratorian Canon (c. A.D. 190)
Irenaeus (2nd–3rd c.)
Tertullian (3rd and 4th c.)
Origen
Eusebius (4th c.)
Athanasius (A.D. 367)

Figure 1.

From the canons that we have studied we can begin to understand the situation of the early Christian community. We see, for example, how quickly this community arrived at a canon fairly close to the present one. Yet it is also clear that a great deal of flexibility remained for centuries. Books were added; others were dropped. The process appears as a human effort, probing in one direction, correcting itself, then making another effort, always searching. This picture of the canon's formation gives us a clue to understanding how the New Testament documents themselves were written.

E. Criteria for Inclusion

It is interesting to read the reasons given by these early Christians for their selection of canonical books. Over and over, the criterion mentioned as guiding their selection is that of apostolic authorship. The early Christians developing the canon saw the New Testament books as written either by apostles or by people associated with apostles. Thus, for example, the Gospels of Matthew and

John were connected with members of the Twelve. Luke was seen as a companion of Paul; Mark, a companion of Peter.

As viewed through the eyes of historical criticism, however, authorship of the New Testament does not appear so simple. As we will see in the examination of each book, the identification of the authors of the First and Fourth Gospels with apostles is very difficult. Moreover, serious doubts can be raised regarding the connection between Luke with Paul and Mark with Peter.

In effect, the actual criterion determining the inclusion or exclusion of a writing from the New Testament seems to have been much more subjective. The real criterion seems to have been simply a consensus among Christians about the way in which a work reflected their faith. Ancient works, even those purporting to be from apostles, were rejected because of their heterodox teaching. The canonical books, on the other hand, reflected the faith of the early Christians. In a very specific way, the faith the Christians thus precedes the New Testament. Although it later becomes a pillar and source of life for subsequent Christian communities, the New Testament itself appears to rest in turn on a believing community, a community that knew its faith and could recognize that faith expressed in contemporary writings.

(See exercise 1.)

II. Manuscripts

We need to deal briefly with one other question of origins, namely, the textual transmission of the New Testament from the biblical writers to the Bibles we have in our hands today. Our New Testaments are for the most part translations. These translations are made from critical editions of Greek New Testaments. These Greek editions are called *critical* because of the discerning work of dealing with a multitude of New Testament manuscripts and the *variants,* or differences, that exist among them. The scholars who deal with manuscripts and variants are called *text critics.* Their scientific techniques are called *text criticism.*

The most important group of these Greek manuscripts consists of booklike codices, folded and nested pages of parchments, that stem from the fourth century to the tenth. These are the so-called *uncials*—given that name because they were written entirely in uppercase letters. From the ninth century to the sixteenth the style of Greek handwriting shifted to lowercase letters. This later time period

**Codex B (Vaticanus), one of the most important manuscripts
of the Bible, from the 4th century. Here is the
beginning of the Gospel of John.**

has provided us with hundreds of important New Testament manuscripts *(minuscules),* which seem to depend on the earlier uncials.
On the other hand, before the uncials, history provides us with
papyrus fragments, sometimes small, broken, and decayed pieces,
other times almost whole pages of the New Testament. The earliest
of these fragments is a tiny piece of the Gospel of John, "Papyrus
Rylands Greek 457," discovered in Egypt and dated from before A.D.
125 (see next page).

What interests anyone studying the New Testament are the
variants that occur among the uncials and the methods of dealing
with these variants. When manuscripts differ, we must decide
which one more probably contains the text as the biblical writer
composed it. Sometimes the variants appear to be simple mis-

**Papyrus Rylands Greek 457, the oldest extant
fragment of the New Testament.**

takes—for example, omissions of a line of text that resulted from
the copyist's jumping from a word in one line of the source text to
the same word in another line. Other times the variants appear to
be deliberate, conscious attempts to "improve" the meaning of a difficult or obscure text believed by the copyist to have been already
corrupted.

We can find a good example of this deliberate change when we
compare manuscripts of the last verses of Mark's Gospel. The variant is so important that most good translations today include some
note or symbol to draw attention to the problem. The affected text is
Mk 16:9–20. The earliest uncial manuscripts simply do not have
these verses. In these manuscripts the text of the Gospel stops with
v. 8. In the sixth century vv. 9–20 began to appear and soon became
standard. How did Mark really end his Gospel, with v. 8 or with v.
20? (The numbering of verses started only after the Middle Ages.
The issue here is the text, not the numbering of verses.)

We could simply count the number of manuscripts giving us one
variant and compare that with the number giving us another, but
since manuscripts are copied from each other, a greater number of
physical manuscripts does not always or even usually imply a greater
number of independent witnesses. The age of the manuscripts in

question is far more important. The older the manuscript, the better, simply because we are closer to the source. A variant that
appears only in later manuscripts would suggest a variant introduced at a later date.

However, since centuries elapsed before our earliest textual
witnesses, the possibility still remains that a variant was introduced early enough to distort even our earliest manuscripts and
that a later manuscript might in fact reflect an independent link to
the original text. For this reason, other criteria also must be used,
often in tandem with the age of the textual witnesses.

If, for instance, we could understand why a copyist would
introduce a variant, we would have a reason for understanding the
variant as such. Looking again at the ending of Mark, we note that
the earlier ending concludes the Gospel very abruptly:

> [The angel said,] "Go now and tell his disciples and Peter,
> 'He is going ahead of you to Galilee, where you will see
> him just as he told you.'" They [the women] made their
> way out and fled from the tomb bewildered and trem-
> bling; and because of their great fear, they said nothing to
> anyone. (16:7–8)

It is relatively easy to hypothesize how an early copyist would
find this ending dissatisfying, even to the point of thinking something must have been lost from the Gospel. It is also easy to see
how the copyist could have gotten the materials for the next eleven
verses from the Gospels of Luke and John, where we have fuller
stories of the events. On the other hand, it is rather difficult to
hypothesize how and why an early copyist would have found a copy
of Mark that extended through 16:20 dissatisfying and thus would
have decided to drop the last twelve verses. The shorter version
ending with v. 8 is much more difficult to understand than the
longer version.

In effect, then, along with the age of the manuscripts testifying
to a variant, a second criterion can help us. This criterion has been
called "the more difficult reading." When choosing between two
variants of a text, probably the more difficult reading is the original.

Another example of an important variant where this criterion
of "the more difficult reading" seems to help is the end of Paul's Letter to the Colossians, where Paul sends greetings by name to the
people he knows. According to some manuscripts Col 5:15 reads:

> Give our best wishes to the brothers at Laodicea and to
> Nymphas and the assembly that meets at his house.

Another group of manuscripts of the same text reads:

> Give our best wishes to the brothers at Laodicea and to
> Nympha and the assembly that meets in her house.

We can ask which reading would be the more difficult for an early copyist? That which refers to a man, Nymphas, who hosts and therefore probably presides at a Christian assembly? Or that which refers to a woman, Nympha, who hosts and therefore probably presides at a Christian assembly? Which is more likely in a period characterized by a general depreciation of women and a blanket exclusion of women from leadership roles in the church? Would an early copyist (the variants appear in the sixth century) have seen reference to a man in his source and transformed Nymphas into a woman? Or would an early copyist have seen reference to a woman in his source and transformed Nympha into a man?

Scholars continue to discuss these questions, and thus even today we find different English versions of Col 5:15 and other texts affected by significant variants. However, scientific scholarship will seek criteria to decide the more probable alternative. Here again the scientist needs to put aside his or her personal preference or even cherished belief. The criterion of the more difficult reading is a dramatic example of how important it is for the scholar to avoid a personal faith to determine meaning, at least until the text can be established.

(See exercise 2.)

III. Theological Reflections

Important questions of faith should arise as we briefly glance at these questions of textual origins. The history of the canon is surprisingly human. In the first chapter we looked at the church's faith in the divine interventions giving us the inspired word in scripture. How does this faith mesh with the view of a very human, almost haphazard recognition of that inspiration? Consider, for example, that the very idea of a New Testament canon was begun in a Gnostic environment, one later vigorously rejected by the church as "heresy."

Instead of miraculous guidance, we find natural human consensus building. Instead of an immediate recognition getting the

New Testament on the market as soon as possible, we see apparently three centuries of development. Could this pattern be a clue to understanding the nature of the New Testament in general?

Our study of the canon is clearly a study of the church. Any faith in the present list of New Testament books is a faith in the church—at least the church of the first three centuries. That community discussed, argued, and gradually came to a consensus about the list. If we would anticipate divine guidance in the development of the canon—however historical and otherwise integrated into human nature that guidance might be—we are anticipating divine guidance in the church. Of course this ecclesial perspective is just another way of formulating the perplexing question of divine grace in history.

The history of the New Testament manuscripts likewise poses serious questions. Again, where is the divine protection against errors in transmission that we could expect if God took the effort to have the original text speak his word "without error"? Any text is only as good as its transmission. Is God less concerned or less active in favor of the later generations?

If we would answer this question by asserting a divine plan to place more personal responsibility on the later generations to preserve and correct the text, we have a good answer if we like doing theology by an *ethical transformation* of the question. This may be the only way of handling a divine mystery.

But note the consequences of this approach. Human responsibility here comes down to the science of text criticism with its basically secular and empirical techniques. Are we in effect subjecting "the word of God" to science? Maybe the word *subjecting* distorts the question. Maybe we are dealing with a *synergy,* where science is removing obstacles for us to hear divine revelation. The formulation of the question goes a long way toward theological understanding. When the Revised Standard Version came out differing from the old King James Version—mostly from the discovery and use of older and better manuscripts, the anger and bitterness expressed by those cherishing the older version seem to have arisen from a poor formulation of the problem. The objections were formulated in terms of the superiority of the Bible over science.

Still we cannot expect every Christian who wants to use the Bible to be an expert in text criticism. How can the average Christian be assured of access to the real text? Somehow the word *synergy* comes back as an answer. In the church there are many gifts, as Paul would say. For some the Spirit gives the gift of text criticism; for others, the gift of interpreting text criticism. We see here a picture of a gathering or "church" of people sharing their gifts. Again the glimpse into the origins of the New Testament underlines the importance of seeing this collection as a church collection.

An objection still rings: Do Christians therefore have to wait for the text critics to do their work before they can read the text of scripture? Well, yes, I guess we do have to wait. Just as we have to wait for the bookstore to open before we can buy our Bible. We have to wait for the printer to finish before we can read the word of God. Thus, we must insert ourselves into the network of human relationships of mutual dependencies before we can hear the word of God. The special aspect of text criticism lies in its ongoing nature. It is good to wait, but sooner or later you have to move with the imperfect state of the art.

There is a "myth," often expressed among fundamentalist Christians, of spiritual independence. "I don't need others to tell me what the word of God is. I've got my Bible." This myth is simply wrong. Carrying your Bible under your arm implies being inserted into a tradition and a network that ties us to the earliest Christian communities selecting the books of the Bible, the bleary-eyed copyists passing the books on, and the community of faith today reading and celebrating these texts.

NOTE

[1] Latin text from Henry M. Gwatkin, *Selections from Early Writers* (London: Macmillan, 1914), 82–87.

EXERCISES

Exercise 1. (see pages 20–27): Imagine yourself as a Christian living in the second century. What differences would exist in your use of the New Testament compared with that of a Christian of the twentieth century?

Exercise 2. (see pages 27–31): Imagine yourself a teacher. You have received essay assignments from two students, and the essays are about 95 percent word for word the same. One student apparently copied from the other. What clues would you look for to determine who copied from whom?

REVIEW QUESTIONS

1. What is meant by "the canon of scripture"? Trace its development as seen in historical documents and references. What is the earliest trace

we have of a New Testament collection? What is the earliest evidence we have of a collection that is identical to our present collection?

2. What caused the early Christian church to make a collection of Christian writings? What criteria did they appear to use for including a writing in this collection?

3. What is the manuscript problem with the ending of Mark? Name another manuscript problem with the text of the New Testament.

4. What is text criticism in biblical studies? Describe its purpose and some of its methods.

FOR FURTHER REFLECTION AND DISCUSSION

1. What does this short history of the New Testament canon suggest about the nature of the New Testament? Where is God and his inspiration in all of this?

2. Catholics and Protestants differ somewhat in what they include in the biblical canon. Should they try to resolve their differences? If so, how could they go about this?

3. What would have to happen for the church now to add another book to the New Testament canon? Or is this impossible?

4. Should individuals be allowed to decide for themselves what manuscripts to follow in the New Testament? If not, what authority should make this decision for them?

3

Behind the Gospels: Oral Tradition and the Two-Source Theory

How was the New Testament written? How did the words get from the actual preaching and actions of Jesus to the descriptions of that preaching and action that we have in the Gospels? Do the texts "betray" any hints of the human process in this composition? The Gospels of Matthew, Mark, and Luke, the *Synoptic Gospels,* are actually filled with hints about this process, but the hints are apparent only if you know what to look for. The hints stared readers in the face, but their significance was not apparent until someone asked the question, How did the evangelists actually write their texts?

These hints have pointed scholars toward two very important conclusions regarding the Gospels of Matthew, Mark, and Luke. Today a general consensus—by no means unanimous, however—leads scholars to reconstruct a process of word-of-mouth transmission as well as a period of intense copying among the evangelists.

I. Oral Tradition

The scientific process of reconstructing the composition of the Synoptics begins with some anomalies. Most science begins with anomalies, details that puzzle the careful observer. Instead of being frightened by the anomalies or trying to minimize their importance, a scientist—even in the humanities—focuses on those details in an effort to "get to the bottom" of them or at least offer a plausible hypothesis, an imagined scenario that could explain the anomalies. The hypothesis can then be tested with more observations, leading to either a revision of the hypothesis or its confirmation.

35

Two anomalies in the Synoptic Gospels have led scholars eventually to hypothesize a period of oral tradition behind the accounts we now have. We will look at these anomalies, develop a hypothesis, and test it.

A. Basic Data

1. Differences among the Accounts

(See exercise 1.)

When the manuscripts of the fourth century finally prevailed in correcting the critical editions of the New Testament, careful readers began to puzzle over the differences between Matthew's and Luke's accounts of the Lord's Prayer, as found in Mt 6:9–11 and Lk 11:2–4. These were precious words, and the anomaly entailed a certain urgency. The wording is similar enough to assure us that the two accounts are dealing with the same prayer. This was a prayer held in the highest esteem by the first Christians who learned it and passed it on. We would hardly expect any carelessness in transmitting these words. If this were the same prayer, then either the Christians transmitting the Matthean account added lines, or those transmitting the Lucan account deleted some. It is difficult to understand why anyone would delete the lines that are missing from the Lucan account. It is easier to hypothesize the addition of lines in the Matthean account, since these lines all serve to clarify the prayer. The "father" we are addressing is more clearly identified as "our father in heaven." The meaning of "your kingdom come" is more clearly identified as the accomplishment of God's will on earth as it is accomplished in heaven. But under what circumstances would a devout believer add words to the prayer Jesus himself taught us to use?

COMPARISON OF THE LORD'S PRAYER IN MATTHEW AND LUKE

Matthew	Luke
Our Father in the heavens,	Father,
may your name be held holy.	may your name be held holy.
May your kingdom come.	May your kingdom come.
May your will be done	
as in heaven so also on earth.	
Give us today	Give us each day
our daily bread,	our daily bread,
and forgive us our debts,	and forgive us our sins,

just as we have forgiven our debtors. And lead us not into temptation, but rescue us from the evil one.	for we ourselves forgive all who owe us. And lead us not into temptation.

Figure 2.

A similar situation arises in the examination of the words of Jesus at the Last Supper. Matthew 26:26–28 records the words at the blessing of the bread and wine:

> While they were eating, Jesus, taking bread and saying the blessing, broke it, and giving it to his disciples, he said, "Take, eat; this is my body." And taking a cup and giving thanks, he gave it to them, saying, "Drink of it, all of you; for this is my blood of the covenant, which is poured out for many for the forgiveness of sins. I tell you, however, I shall not drink again of this fruit of the vine until that day when I drink it new with you in my Father's kingdom."

The words are almost word for word the same in Mk 14:22–25, but in Lk 22:17–20 they are quite different:

> And taking a cup and giving thanks, he said, "Take this, and divide it among yourselves; for I tell you that from now on I shall not drink of the fruit of the vine until the kingdom of God comes." And taking bread and giving thanks, he broke it and gave it to them, saying, "This is my body which is given for you. Do this in my remembrance." And likewise the cup after supper saying, "This cup which is poured out for you is the new covenant in my blood."

Interestingly, Luke's account is remarkably close to that in Paul's first letter to the Corinthians (11:23–26):

> The Lord Jesus on the night in which he was betrayed took bread, and giving thanks, he broke it and said, "This is my body which is for you. Do this in my remembrance." In the same way also the cup, after supper, saying, "This cup is the new covenant in my blood. Do this, as often as you drink it, in my remembrance."

Again, these are words held in the highest esteem by the early

Christians. They were treasured and used at the early Christian eucharist. Yet we have two different versions of them.

Differences also appear in the way the Gospels describe the actions of Jesus and the disciples. A comparison of the story of Jesus walking on the water in Mk 6:45–52 with the story as given in Mt 14:22–33 illustrates these differences. Matthew includes more information about Peter. Even more striking are the differences at the end of the story. In the two accounts the reactions of the disciples are quite opposite. They could have reacted as Matthew writes or as Mark writes, but they could not have reacted as both write.

2. Short Episodes and Internal Patterns

Another less urgent but nevertheless puzzling characteristic lies in the forms of the stories themselves as recounted by the Synoptics. The stories are for the most part short, independent episodes about Jesus. Most of these stories are only five or ten verses long. They are loosely connected with the preceding and following stories. We usually do not need the preceding or following stories for an understanding of any particular episode.

(See exercise 2.)

These episodes, furthermore, tend to follow certain patterns or structures and can be classed according to those structures. We will look at two of these patterns, that of the miracle story and that of the pronouncement story. In these two classes of episodes the structure appears very clear.

A short miracle story appears in Mk 1:30–31. The story is told in three steps:

1. The need is presented to Jesus.

   Simon's mother-in-law lay ill with a fever, and the first thing they did was to tell him about her.

2. Jesus works the miracle.

   He went over to her and grasped her hand and helped her up, and the fever left her.

3. A detail assures the readers that the miracle took place.

She immediately began to wait on them.

Why do we identify these three steps? We do so because these three steps can be easily identified in other stories of Jesus working a miracle. In the other stories one or another of the steps may be much longer, much more developed. In the other stories the needs are different, the miracles are diverse and involve diverse gestures by Jesus, and the narrator's assurances or demonstrations take on different forms, but the three steps are almost always there.

(See exercises 3, 4.)

A very different kind of story and pattern appears in Mk 10:2–9 and 12:13–18. In both cases the narration, which lacks extensive details about the time and place, leads to a climactic verse. In the first example, this climactic verse is the saying, "Let no one separate what God has joined" (v. 9). These stories are therefore classified as *pronouncement stories*. Interestingly, in both of these pronouncement stories, the episode is developed similarly:

1. The adversaries of Jesus ask a hostile question.

   Then some of the Pharisees came up and as a test began to ask him whether it was permissible for a husband to divorce his wife.

2. Instead of answering the question Jesus counters with his own question.

   In reply he said, "What command did Moses give you?"

3. The adversaries answer this counterquestion.

   They answered, "Moses permitted divorce and the writing of a decree of divorce."

4. Jesus answers the original question, ending with a pronouncement in the form of a punch line.

   But Jesus told them: "He wrote that commandment for you because of your stubbornness. At the beginning of creation God made them male and female; for this reason a man shall leave his father and mother and the two shall become as one. They are no longer two but one flesh. Therefore let no one separate what God has joined."

After this punch line the scene abruptly ends.

(See exercise 5.)

B. Hypothesis: A Stage of Oral Tradition

Understanding these data means forming a hypothesis or a description of a possible larger picture in which these data cohere or make sense. A clue to this hypothesis comes from our knowledge of the world at the time of Jesus and the writers of the New Testament. This was not a world of disposable pens and scratch paper. This was a world where one sheet of parchment would cost a month's wage. Even cheaper papyrus was an expensive item, and ink had to be made by hand. This was a world where poorer people had to rely on memory and word of mouth for most information. As a result, people developed prodigious powers of retention, especially for matters of importance.

The hypothesis, therefore, that we will form and test will be that the stories of Jesus—now written down in the Synoptic Gospels—were passed down first by oral tradition. They may have been transmitted by people with excellent memories, people who also exercised great care regarding the precious message they were conveying, passing it down through the medium of oral transmission. Such a medium inevitably leads to changes in the way stories are told. We need to reflect on the ways oral tradition changes the content of a story.

First of all, oral transmission almost always involves clarifying. A person speaking face-to-face to others is concerned primarily with being understood. In a purely oral mode, the speaker can offer no backup text which the listener can later consult. The message must be understood at the point of hearing. A speaker will therefore adapt to the listener. Furthermore, in order to be understood a speaker must fully grasp what he or she is saying. Unlike reading from a text, a person speaking from memory must have personally assimilated the message. Even before the speaker opens his or her mouth, the process of clarification has begun.

If no text of the matter exists, the speakers become authorities unto themselves. If no one authoritative account exists, the oral accounts have nothing against which they are measured. The result is a freedom to develop the message—a freedom and a creativity that disappear when things are written down.

Second, oral transmission involves getting the material into memorizable form. Often this part of the digestive process means shortening and summarizing. It often means having some form of skeletal account in mind on which other details of a story can be affixed. Normally real-life events do not occur neatly organized. Oral transmission means using a variety of memory aids, or *mnemonics* to access the material.

Third, oral transmission from memory means random access to the material. Any memorable day in our life can be recalled in a variety of ways. We do not need always to start with the first thing that happened, then the next thing, and so on to the last. We can group the events in any way we want, or if we desire, we can isolate the events in any recall. The sequence and combinations, therefore, of an extended narration produced from oral transmission may very well be the result of the narrator's decisions rather than a reflection of the historical events.

THREE WAYS CHANGES OCCUR IN ORAL TRANSMISSION

1. Clarification

2. Memorizable form

3. Narrators' decision on sequence

Figure 3.

How do the data of the Gospels fit this hypothesis? First of all, we can now more easily understand the differences among the parallel stories. We can hypothesize a real freedom which the narrators enjoyed in telling the stories about Jesus. In the absence of an official version to which the narrators had to conform, such a freedom is understandable. In contrast, we today have official versions in the *written* texts of the Gospels and hence feel bound to these official versions.

We can better understand the short, episodic character of the Gospel stories. Because they are short episodes, the stories of Jesus in the Synoptic Gospels are relatively easy to remember. Long stories usually require a written text.

The internal structures and patterns of these stories likewise facilitate remembering them. By keeping in mind the three steps of a miracle story, we could fairly easily retell the story of either Peter's mother-in-law or that of the demoniac in the synagogue. Structures like those in the miracle stories or in the pronouncement stories are valuable crutches to tell and retell stories without referring to a written page.

(See exercise 6.)

Without proving the matter one way or another, the initial data strongly suggest that the stories of Jesus, recounting both his words and his actions, were first passed down by word of mouth. In this supposition, the first witnesses of Jesus did not write the stories of Jesus down but rather told them orally to those interested in listening. These listeners in turn told and retold the stories to others—all with great care but also with the changes that occur in oral transmission. Only later—some thirty years later, as we will see—did Christians write down these stories.

This conclusion is a hypothesis. It functions like the hypotheses in the natural sciences, giving an explanation of the data. Hypotheses are always a matter of probability. The more data they explain, the more probable they are. Because scientists never see all the data, they never arrive at absolute certitude. However, until a better hypothesis appears to explain the data better and more simply, a scientific method requires using the hypothesis at hand.

C. Confirmation of the Hypothesis

1. Mnemonics in the Text

The hypothesis of oral tradition receives confirmation from further examination of the texts. We will look first at Mk 9:35–42. This text contains an important clue of oral tradition. The clue, however, is often lost in translation. Below is a special translation that attempts to be faithful to the original Greek even where this leads to awkward English expressions:

> [35] And sitting down, [Jesus] called the Twelve and said to them: "If someone wishes to be first, let him be the last of all and the *servant* of all...." [36] And taking a *child,* he stood him in their midst and embracing him said to them: [37] "Whoever receives one of such *children* in my *name,* receives me. And whoever receives me, receives not me but the one sending me." [38] John said to him: "Teacher, we saw one in your *name* expelling demons, and we forbade him, because he was not following us." [39] Jesus, however,

said: "Do not forbid him; there is no one who performs won-
ders in my *name* and can quickly speak ill of me. [40] Who
then is not against us, is for us. [41] Whoever, then, gives
you a cup of water to drink in the *name* because you are
Christ's, amen I say to you that he will not lose his reward.
[42] And whoever *scandalizes* one of these *smallest* believers in me, would be better off with a millstone around his
neck and thrown into the sea. [43] And if ever your hand
scandalizes you, cut it off. You are better off entering life
maimed, than with two hands to go into Gehenna, into
unending fire. [45] And if your foot *scandalizes* you, cut it
off. You are better off entering life crippled than having two
feet being thrown into Gehenna. [47] And if your eye *scandalizes* you, throw it away. You are better off half blind,
entering the kingdom of God, than having two eyes being
thrown into Gehenna, where the worm never ends and the
fire never goes out. [49] All *fire* will be *salted*. [50] *Salt* is
good. If however *salt* becomes tasteless, for what use is it?
Have *salt* in yourselves and be at peace with one another."

Several things strike us about this passage. First, the selection
seems very disunified in its content. The selection appears to be a
loose collection of sayings about all sorts of things: humility, receiving children, performing miracles, scandal. However, the repeated
words (printed in italics above), *child, name, scandalize, fire,* and
salt hold the section together. Some of the sayings, in fact, have two
key words. Verse 37 contains *child* and *name*. Verse 49 contains *fire*
and *salt*. These verses thus function as hinges between two sets of
sayings tied together by the thread of a common word. The under-
lined words *servant* (v. 35) and *smallest* (v. 42) may originally have
been part of the key words. The Aramaic word *talya* could easily be
used for "servant," "child," and "small one."

As given here, these thirteen verses would be fairly easy to
memorize. (The better manuscripts omit vv. 44 and 46.) We would
first remember the key words: *child, name, scandalize, fire,* and *salt*.
The rest of the sayings would come to mind as we would later recall
the key words. Likewise, the repetitive style of several of the sayings,
especially those with *scandalize,* facilitates memorization.

The use of such memory aids or mnemonics makes sense only
if these sayings are being passed down orally. A selection like this in
a Gospel confirms our hypothesis that the Gospel stories were
passed down orally. A selection like this further indicates that this

oral transmission left a strong imprint on the final written form of this tradition.

2. Movable Contexts

Other texts that confirm the hypothesis include the parallels in Mt 21:26; Mk 4:22; and Lk 12:2, all giving the same proverb, "Nothing is hidden that will not be made known; nothing is concealed that will not be revealed." The double form of this proverb, known as parallelism, is typically Semitic. This could well be a proverb taught by Jesus.

What is not clear from the isolated proverb, however, is the meaning of the reality first concealed and then revealed. The proverb itself remains unspecific. It is only from the context of this proverb as given in each Gospel that we get some idea of this reality. Matthew's context deals with the preaching of the Gospel, even in the face of obstacles. Mark's story deals with the hidden meaning of Jesus' parables. Luke's account deals with the hypocrisy of the Pharisees. From the three contexts, the reality to be revealed is thus either the Gospel itself, the meaning of Jesus' parables, or inner thoughts.

It is possible that Jesus told this proverb on three different occasions with three different meanings in mind. This explanation, however, presupposes a puzzling lack of clarity on the part of Jesus as well as an extraordinary coincidence of each Gospel relating a different occasion.

A simpler hypothesis explains the common proverb and the diverse contexts by splitting the proverb from its context and suggesting that each had different lives in their transmission from Jesus. Only after Jesus did the proverb and the context come together. Such independent transmission and free combination could easily occur in oral tradition.

(See exercise 7.)

D. Some Consequences

The consequences of recognizing oral tradition behind the Gospel stories are enormous. No longer can we use the image of a stenographer taking notes during the preaching of Jesus and recording these notes for posterity. Now we have the picture of a community of people transmitting the message and only later writing it down. We begin to see, likewise, that the whole story of Jesus, the continuous narrative we have in the Gospels, is the result of later editors putting the episodes together. If we think of oral tradition, we must think of individual episodes being passed down independently of each other and only gradually being combined into a continuous story. This combination, moreover, need not follow the chronology of Jesus' life. The combination could be made on theological grounds or even on the basis of easy memorization.

In this hypothesis of oral transmission, we likewise see the reason for diversity among the accounts. We see Matthew—or better, the community in which the Matthean storytellers lived—modifying the episodes about Jesus so they could better understand them, shifting a story, for example, from the apostles lacking understanding to one describing them as filled with faith in Jesus as Son of God. We can understand better now the same community transmitting the Lord's Prayer and adding "thy will be done" because that community needed to understand better the meaning of "thy kingdom come."

The hypothesis of oral transmission includes accepting the role of the community forgetting some things, summarizing others, combining stories and sayings, shifting details, adding lines—all to make a story more relevant to their readers. These are all modifications typical of oral tradition. We can, however, presuppose a great concern by the storytellers to preserve "the essentials" of the story. The stories had intense importance for these people.

The hypothesis of oral transmission means, in effect, that we no longer have the actual words of Jesus, that we no longer can be sure he did exactly what the narrations describe him doing. The exact words and actions of Jesus are perhaps forever lost behind the screen of modifications and interpretations operating during the period of oral transmission.

On the positive side, this hypothesis means that we now have an interpreted view of Jesus, one that simultaneously tells us about Jesus and about the faith of the early Christians in Jesus. The hypothesis of oral transmission means reading the Gospel texts above all as testimonies of faith, rather than newspaper reports about Jesus.

II. The Two-Source Theory

A. The Basic Data

Early in this century scholars put the Gospels of Matthew, Mark, and Luke in parallel columns so that the three could be read in one glance. Such an edition of the Gospels is called a *synopsis,* a Greek word meaning "viewing together." Hence, the name *Synoptic* for these Gospels, which are so easily placed in parallel columns. The following stories are selected to show the various types of parallel stories:

The Parable of the Seed

Matthew 13:1–9	*Mark 4:1–9*	*Luke 8:4–8*
On that day Jesus going out of the house sat beside the sea. And great crowds gathered about him, so that he getting into a boat sat down; and the whole crowd stood on the beach. And he spoke to them much in parables, saying:	Again he began to teach beside the sea. And a large crowd gathered about him, so that he getting into a boat sat down on the sea; and the whole crowd was beside the sea on the land. And he taught them much in parables, and in his teaching he said to them: "Listen! A sower went	And when a great crowd came together and people from town after town journeyed to him, he said in a parable:
"A sower went out to sow. And as he sowed, some fell along the path, and the birds coming devoured them. Other fell on rocky ground, where it had not much soil and immediately it sprang up, since it had no depth of soil, but with the sun rising it were scorched; and since it had no root it withered away.	out to sow. And it happened as he sowed, some fell along the path, and the birds came and devoured it. Other fell on rocky ground, where it had not much soil and immediately it sprang up since it had no depth of soil; and when the sun rose it was scorched, and since it had no root it withered away.	"A sower went out to sow his seed; and as he sowed, some fell along the path, and was trodden on, and the birds of the air devoured it. And some fell on the rock; and as it grew up, it withered since it had no moisture.
Other seeds fell upon thorns and the thorns grew up and choked them. Other, however, fell on good soil and gave forth fruit, some a hundredfold, some sixty, some thirty.	Other seed fell among thorns and the thorns grew up and choked it, and it yielded no fruit. And other fell into good soil and gave forth fruit, growing up and increasing and yielding thirty-fold and sixtyfold and a hundredfold." And he said	And some fell amidst thorns; and the thorns growing with it choked it. And some other fell into fertile soil and grew and produced a hundredfold." Saying this, he called out, "He who has ears
"He who has ears let him hear."	"He who has ears to hear, let him hear."	to hear, let him hear."

John the Baptist's Preaching

Matthew 3:7–10	*Luke 3:7–9*
But seeing many of the Pharisees and Sadducees coming for baptism, he said to them, "Brood of vipers! Who directed you to flee from the coming wrath? Bear fruit worthy of repentance, and do not think to say to yourselves, 'We have Abraham as our father'; for I tell you, God is able from these stones to raise up children to Abraham. Even now the axe	He said therefore to the crowds coming out to be baptized by him, "Brood of vipers! Who directed you to flee from the coming wrath? Bear fruits worthy of repentance, and do not begin to say to yourselves, 'We have Abraham as our father'; for I tell you, God is able from these stones to raise up children to Abraham. Even now the axe

is close to the root of the trees; every
tree therefore that does not bear good
fruit is cut down and thrown into
the fire."

is close to the root of the trees; every
tree therefore that does not bear good
fruit is cut down and thrown into
the fire."

John's Preaching to Special Groups

Luke 3:10–14
And the multitudes asked him saying, "What
then shall we do?" And answering them he
said, "He who has two coats, let him share
with him who has none; and he who has food,
let him do likewise." Tax collectors then came
to be baptized, and said to him, "Teacher, what
shall we do?" And he said to them, "Collect no
more than is appointed for you." Soldiers then
asked him, "And we, what shall we do?" And
he said to them, "Do not extort or falsely
accuse anyone and be content with your
wages."

Such a synopsis immediately gives rise to very interesting observations. First of all, we can now classify the Gospel stories into those found in all three Gospels (triple-tradition stories), those in only two (double-tradition stories), and those in only one (single tradition). Almost all of Mark is triple tradition. Most of Mark can be found also in Matthew and Luke. On the other hand, only about half of Matthew's and Luke's stories are triple tradition, shared with Mark. Moreover, the triple-tradition stories are often word for word the same in all three and often maintain the same order in all three.

Most of the double-tradition stories are in Matthew and Luke, accounting for about a quarter of these Gospels. Many of these stories show verbatim similarities, but they are not at all in the same order. Matthew tends to group these double-tradition stories into five major speeches or sermons. Luke concentrates this material into a central section of his Gospel.

The single-tradition stories are also mostly in Matthew or Luke. These stories, special to each evangelist, account for a little less than a quarter of these Gospels.

We can summarize these results in five significant observations:

1. Mark's Gospel is the shortest. In terms of printed pages, Mark is only about two-thirds the size of Matthew and Luke. More significantly, Mark has only about half the stories of Matthew and Luke.
2. Most of Mark's material is also in Luke and Matthew. Luke repeats about 85 percent of Mark's stories; Matthew about 95 percent. Even more significant, these common stories in the different Gospels appear often with significant strings of text,

word for word the same. This verbatim similarity is very striking when we compare Mark and Matthew. It is a little less
when we compare Mark with Luke. But in all three we can
find expressions involving several words that are identical in
all three Gospels, and these verbatim strings appear in the
same order throughout the story.

3. Mark's material in Luke and Matthew is for the most part in
   Mark's order. Except for a few transpositions, especially in
   Luke, the stories in Matthew and Luke that are also in Mark
   follow each other as they do in Mark. As we will see in the next
   chapter, Mark's order of stories is a tight weave of repeated
   stories or themes spaced fairly regularly apart. If we looked
   just at the stories in Matthew or Luke which are shared with
   Mark, we can find that same tight weave. However, when we
   look at Matthew and Luke and include the other non-Marcan
   stories, that tight weave is now "distorted." The regularity of
   the repetitions is now broken by the non-Marcan material.
   (See appendix 1 for story-by-story comparisons of Mark and
   Matthew as well as Mark and Luke.)

4. Matthew and Luke have material common to each other. Many
   times this material has the same type of verbatim similarities
   as we saw in the stories they share with Mark—significant
   strings of text, word for word the same, and in the same order
   within the story. However, as mentioned above, these stories
   that Matthew and Luke share appear in a very different order.

5. Matthew and Luke have material special to themselves. Some
   of these stories are very beautiful and moving. Luke alone, for
   instance, has the story of the prodigal son (15:11–32). Matthew
   alone has the story of the final judgment based on caring for
   the needy (25:31–46).

To an observer trained to look for clues regarding the way compositions are written, these observations strongly suggest a hypothesis regarding the manner in which the Gospels were written.

B. The Hypothesis of the Two Sources

Under normal circumstances, two people independently writing the same story will do so in very individual ways. A writer's
vocabulary and use of words are as individual as his or her finger-
prints. Word-for-word similarity between two compositions means
copying went on. The compositions need not be completely the

same. However, a series of verbatim strings, especially if they occur in both compositions *in the same order,* under normal circumstances almost certainly means copying took place.

The word-for-word similarities in the Synoptic Gospels lead us to two possibilities. We have a divine miracle providing verbatim similarities (God miraculously providing the same words to each author), or these writers are copying in some way (either from each other or from common sources).

It is not for us to eliminate the possibility that God worked a miracle to bring about such accounts. Supposing a miracle, however, presents a methodological problem. It is too convenient. To refer to a miracle every time we run into something puzzling would be to abdicate the hard work of searching for natural causes. We could simply repeat the phrase, "God did it!" to all our questions, but in the end we would understand the data no more than when we started. Methodologically, recourse to miracle helps only as a last resort, when no natural cause can be found to explain the data. At that time we can pull a miracle out of our theological hat.

Hence, we must look seriously at the hypothesis that extensive copying or *literary dependence* took place in the writing of the Synoptic Gospels. The scientific method requires choosing the simplest hypothesis possible to explain the data. We have no need to multiply and complicate hypothetical causes when a simple one will do. The simplest hypothesis, now known as *the two-source theory,* is based on the five observations listed above and leads to three conclusions:

1. Luke and Matthew copied from Mark.

When we look at the five observations above, three of them clearly lend support to this conclusion. Number 2 again argues that copying took place. Numbers 1 and 3 argue that Luke and Matthew copied from Mark and not vice versa. To suppose that Mark copied from Matthew and Luke or from either requires us to see Mark dropping a great deal of material from his sources, that is, from Matthew and/or Luke. Some of this material ranks among the most precious material held by the early Christians, for instance, the Lord's Prayer. It is very difficult to see why Mark would have dropped that material. On the other hand, it is relatively easy to see why Luke and Matthew would have added material to Mark.

Number 3 of the data observations lends more support to the priority of Mark over Matthew and Luke. As number 3 observes, we can find Mark's sequence of stories in both Matthew and Luke but in distorted form, that is, with material separating things that are together in Mark. The "distortions," furthermore, differ considerably in Matthew and in Luke. To see Mark copying from Matthew and Luke together one would have to say that he selected only those things that were common to the two and in the same order. It is really not clear why he would have been so selective on such a very formal basis (that is, having nothing to do with the content but only with the arrangement of the material). To see Mark copying from only Matthew or Luke leads to the supposition of extraordinary coincidences, his choice of Matthew or Luke just happened to be exactly those stories in the other in the same order. It is much easier to see Matthew and Luke using Mark and building around Mark, much like a modern builder might use an ancient temple to build a modern church. The careful observer can still see the older temple, but now fitting into a newer, larger unit.

2. Matthew and Luke did not copy from each other.

A second conclusion is a key one and perhaps the most difficult for this hypothesis, namely, that Matthew and Luke did not copy from each other. For this conclusion we need to focus on the observations mentioned above that detail the differences between Matthew and Luke.

First, Matthew and Luke have stories special or unique to themselves, the "single-tradition" stories. These are stories that often would have fit very well with the special concerns of the other Gospel, which does not include it. Matthew, for instance, has the story of the last judgment based on care of the poor (25:31–46). Care for the poor, however, is one of the major concerns of Luke's Gospel, yet Luke does not have this Matthean story. Conversely, Luke has the story of the prodigal son (15:11–32). Matthew, who constantly emphasizes forgiveness and the mercy of God, does not have this story. If Matthew and Luke had depended on each other in any way, as we are supposing they depended on Mark, the absence of these stories becomes perplexing since we would have to suppose a deliberate choice to exclude them.

Second, Matthew and Luke use their common stories in very different manners. Matthew basically groups these common stories into five major discourses of Jesus (see chapters 5–7; 10; 13; 18; and parts of 24–25). Luke, on the other hand, groups most of these stories into one middle section of his Gospel (9:51–18:15). Thus, the material that would argue for the interdependence of Matthew and Luke, namely, the common stories, carries with it an aspect suggesting that each evangelist made use of the material without knowing how the other used it.

3. Matthew and Luke had a common written source.

The second conclusion, that Matthew and Luke did not copy from each other, leads to the third conclusion. If the material common to Luke and Matthew often in verbatim similarity cannot be explained by their copying from each other, then we are forced to see another written source behind their Gospels, a source that they both used independently of each other. It was a German scholar who first drew this conclusion. The word *source* in German is *Quelle;* hence, scholars today traditionally call this second source simply Q.

In schematic form, the above conclusions can be shown in figure 4.

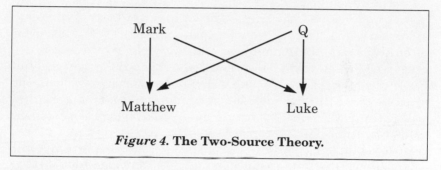

Figure 4. **The Two-Source Theory.**

The arrows here show the literary dependence among the Synoptic Gospels.

C. The Consequences

The consequences of this theory, if accepted, are important for analyzing the Gospels. We are warned, first of all, not simply to count the number of times a story occurs in the Synoptic Gospels to see how many times we have an independent testimony about some event in the life of Jesus. Copying multiplies an account. It does not multiply the testimony.

Second, and more positively, this theory gives us an important approach to understanding the Gospels of Luke and Matthew. We can study these Gospels by comparing them to their sources. The differences that exist between these Gospels and Mark or Q indicate deliberate changes. Observing a series of deliberate changes tells us a great deal about the particular theological interpretation that was guiding Matthew or Luke.

(See exercise 8.)

Working with Q is difficult. We have to reconstruct it from the combined accounts of Matthew and Luke, which can be very hypothetical. We can see, however, how Matthew and Luke modify Mark. From these changes, we can begin to suppose what they did to their other source(s). In this way we can begin to speculate about what the original Q might have looked like.

The two-source theory is not without weak points. Not all scholars are willing to work with it. Unfortunately, the alternatives proposed are often so complicated that they give little help for understanding the Gospel texts. (See appendix 2 for a schematic form of an alternative.)

The difficulties with the theory generally revolve around the nature of Q. For instance, why do we not have any trace of Q outside of Matthew and Luke? The early Christians preserved Mark, even after it was incorporated into the other Gospels. Why did they not preserve Q? Another difficulty more germane to the very use of the theory concerns the nature of Q. Q material sometimes is almost word for word the same in Matthew and Luke, for example, the story of John the Baptist's preaching in Mt 3:7–12 and Lk 3:7–9. (This verbatim similarity appears in the Greek and in very literal translations.) At other times the stories common to Matthew and Luke resemble each other only in broad lines, for example, the story of the great banquet in Mt 22:1–10 and Lk 14:16–24. Should Q then be considered a single source or many sources?

A second important difficulty with the theory deals with a section of Mark not found in Luke. If we see Luke copying from Mark, then we must ask why Luke omits Mk 6:45–8:27. No one has yet proposed a satisfactory answer in the confines of a strict two-source theory. Perhaps this difficulty of the "great Lucan omission" requires us to avoid presupposing that Luke (or Matthew) copied from a text of Mark identical to our Gospel of Mark. Perhaps a slightly shorter version of Mark circulated for a time.

These difficulties point to the hypothetical character of the two-source theory. We do not have all the answers. The research must continue. Yet we must work with what we have. In the rest of these studies, we will use this two-source theory, but we must be aware of the possible need in the future for revisions.

III. Theological Reflections

A person of faith, a person who reads the New Testament with a full adherence to the Christian doctrine of biblical inspiration and revelation, may find some difficulties reconciling that adherence with the scientific analysis above. In fact it becomes very difficult to understand or imagine how God is inspiring an author to write the Gospel stories if the stories are not the result of his "inspired" composition, but have been developed by a multitude of storytellers. The contribution of the actual Gospel writer may actually be only a fraction of the total product, perhaps the final arranging of stories. How does this arranging or other form of editing turn the preexistent material into inspired writing? Does the inspiration of Matthew and Luke turn the Q material into the word of God? On a deeper level, a difficulty may appear in the human manner by which the Gospels now seem to have evolved, people telling and developing stories and people copying from others. Where exactly is God in all this?

The question of how to imagine God's role, however, is not a question of faith; it is a question of theology. It is a question of understanding our faith, seeing how the elements of our faith fit together, and developing concepts and images that express that faith. The hypotheses of oral tradition and of literary dependence among the Gospels challenge a theology that developed without contact with these hypotheses. A theology, for instance, that conceived of God dictating each word into the ear of the inspired author is hardly compatible with these hypotheses. A theology that insists on inspiration and revelation as miraculous events, events that cannot be explained by natural human dynamisms, will need a great deal of adjustment if it wants to consider the historical-critical methods seriously.

If incompatibility between theology and science arises, however, the wise approach may not be to scream, "Heresy!" The wise approach may be silence before what is not yet understood and a willingness to reexamine both sides of the incompatibility. Could the scientific hypotheses be wrong? Of course. Science deals in probability, not certitude. A hundred years from now, scholars will probably ridicule the inadequacies of our scientific positions as they work from the inevitable revisions. Could the theology be wrong? Of course! Theology consists of human gropings toward the mystery of our faith. Scientific findings have already urged Christians to revise their theologies regarding human and cosmic origins or natural law. These theological revisions do not constitute the surrender of faith to science; they simply illustrate the human mind's dynamism to integrate and form a unified picture.

What possible revisions of theology could be envisioned by the hypotheses studied in this chapter? First of all, the details now seen in the reconstruction of the composition suggest the dominance of human dynamisms in the formation of the Gospels. This view thus urges a theology that could conceive of God operating within human processes, not short-circuiting these processes. This view urges a reluctance to demand miracles to mark the powerful action of God. This view presumes a willingness to see the everyday process of telling a story and copying a text as possible vehicles by which God brings about what he wants to accomplish.

A theological revision should probably also shift attention from "inspired authors" to the "inspired text." Who exactly is the author of the Gospel of Matthew, if in fact Matthew copied much from Mark, and Mark got his material from a multitude of storytellers? Instead of one writer being responsible for the text, we now have a whole community of people contributing various elements to the text. Our faith demands that we hold to the final product as the word of God. Our theology then should reflect on the various contributions and focus on an aspect or formality dispersed through the community contributions to the final product, for instance, "as contributing to the final product." We begin to conceive of a sort of communitarian inspiration, which involved individuals *to the extent* that they contributed to the final product. Obviously a written composition must be produced by real people. But we can conceive of the "inspired authors" only through the aspect or formality of "contributing to the final product," which in turn can be conceived only by starting with "the inspired text." The order of these thought steps is crucial.

One major difficulty remains in this theological revision. It becomes next to impossible to imagine God operating in this way. The image of God whispering into the ears of holy writers is fairly easy to imagine. The image has been the subject of many paintings—with angels in the place of God. However, to think of God operating within an autonomous human dynamism, to think of inspiration as spread among a multitude of persons according to some formality—all this surpasses our imagination. This theological revision requires a series of religious statements all carefully placed in a demanding sequence. But the step of pulling the revision together in a beautiful image escapes us. However, this lack of imagery may be the sign of good theology.

EXERCISES

Exercise 1. (see page 36): Read the following texts in the Gospel of Matthew along with their parallels in Mark or Luke. Note the similarities and the differences. Would you see the differences as very significant, not at all important, or somewhere in between?

Mt 6:9–11 compared with Lk 11:2–4

Mt 26:26–28 compared with Mk 14:22–24 and Lk 22:19–20

Mt 14:22–23 compared with Mk 6:45–52

Exercise 2. (see page 38): Read Mk 1; 10:2–9; 12:13–18. Identify the individual episodes in these readings. What are the words that link these episodes with the preceding and following ones? Look for relationships of time or place.

Exercise 3. (see pages 38–39): Identify the three steps in this short miracle story of Mk 1:30–31.

Exercise 4. (see pages 38–39): Identify the three steps in Mk 1:23–27. Note how 1:22 and 1:27b form a framework around this miracle story, giving it a particular meaning.

Exercise 5. (see pages 39–40): Identify the pattern in the text of Mk 12:13–18. What is the climactic verse of this story? Where are the questions and answers?

Exercise 6. (see pages 41–42): Explain how the internal structures of stories help us to remember enough to retell them. What stories do we normally conserve by memory? Jokes tend to follow specific patterns, which facilitates memorization. Can you identify these patterns?

Exercise 7. (see page 44): A proverb about placing a lamp on a lamp stand and not under a basket appears in Mk 4:21; Mt 5:15; and Lk 11:33. Develop a hypothesis based on evidence concerning the transmission of this proverb. What is its context in the three Gospels? How do these contexts change the meaning of "the lamp"?

Exercise 8. (see page 51): Reread the account of Jesus walking on the water first in Mk 6:45–52 and then in Mt 14:22–33. What exactly has Matthew done to his source? What possible significance do you see in these changes? What is on Matthew's mind as he makes these changes?

REVIEW QUESTIONS

1. What are the various ways in which the traces of oral tradition appear in the Gospel stories? Describe the structures and other various memory aids still apparent in the written texts. Give examples for each from the Gospel texts.

2. In what ways do stories and other teachings tend to change when passed down by memory rather than by writing? Which of these changes would still occur if the storyteller's memory is very powerful?

3. How can oral tradition explain the shifts in meaning in the teaching of Jesus as it appears in Mt 10:26; Mk 4:22; and Lk 12:2?

4. Diagram the two-source theory and explain the data that argue for (a) Matthew and Luke copying from Mark, (b) Matthew and Luke independent of each other, and (c) Matthew and Luke copying from Q.

5. What arguments in favor of the two-source theory consist of verifiable data, and what arguments are probable conclusions? What are the weak points of the two-source theory?

FOR FURTHER REFLECTION AND DISCUSSION

1. *How would you explain to a devout but uneducated person the idea of Gospels being copied from each other, as held by the two-source theory? Should you even try to make this explanation?*

2. *Imagine yourself a traveling "evangelist" of the year* A.D. *40. No Gospels have been written. Christians want to hear the good news of and about Jesus. What do you tell them? What stories can you relate? What stories do you want to relate? How much detail can you give?*

3. *Has a* hidden *miracle ever occurred to you, an event where you felt God acted dramatically in your favor but where everything in the event was explainable as the result of natural causes? What made you think God was there for you?*

4

The Gospel According to Mark

We now turn to the texts of the New Testament. The first one we will study is the Gospel according to Mark. This is by no means the earliest writing of the New Testament, but, as we have seen, it is probably the earliest Gospel. Since the Gospels bring us into contact with the central figure of the New Testament, Jesus of Nazareth, this is a good place to start.

We will examine this Gospel first for such overall issues as authorship, readership, dating, and overall organization. We will then examine this Gospel for the specific faith of the author as it influenced the telling of the story. We will look especially at those expressions of faith that deal with the author's understanding of Jesus, his understanding of the death of Jesus as saving, and his understanding of the end of the world.

I. Historical Background and Overview

A. The Author

When we ask the question, Who wrote this Gospel? we find two conflicting answers. The first answer comes from tradition. The second answer comes from a critical analysis of the text.

1. The Traditional Answer

A fourth-century church historian, Eusebius of Caesarea, gives us the traditional identification of the author. The key text is from Eusebius's *Ecclesiastical History,* in which he quotes or reproduces the writings of many earlier Christian authors. When he deals with the writing of the Gospels, Eusebius cites a second-century writer named Papias:

Mark became Peter's interpreter, he wrote down accurately, although not in order, all that he remembered of what was said or done by the Lord. For he had not heard the Lord nor followed Him, but later, as I have said, he did follow Peter, who made his teaching fit his needs without, as it were, making any arrangement of the Lord's oracles, so that Mark made no mistake in thus writing some things down as he remembered them. (3.39)

Following Papias, Eusebius thus identifies the author as a man named Mark, a companion of Peter. By associating the author with Peter, this traditional answer corresponds to one of the important criteria used by the early Christians for accepting a writing into the canon of scripture, namely, being written by an apostle or by someone associated with the apostles.

Another version of this traditional answer goes somewhat further and identifies the author with the John Mark of the Acts of the Apostles. This person is mentioned in Acts 12:12 as a member of a rather wealthy Christian family in Jerusalem. Later the same person appears as a companion of Paul and Barnabas for a short part of their missionary journey (Acts 13:5, 13). Such an identification would probably make the author an eyewitness to the Jerusalem ministry of Jesus.

2. The Critical Answer

The greatest difficulty with this traditional answer arises from the data we have looked at in the last chapter. We have seen strong evidence for oral tradition behind the Gospels, an oral tradition in which the stories of Jesus were passed down, molded, and then finally written. Because the Gospel of Mark has the quality of written oral tradition, it does not look like the dictated memoirs of an eyewitness, much less an account written by an eyewitness himself.

Rather, the Gospel of Mark looks like the product of a community effort, in which one member recorded the memories of the community. We can call him *Mark,* but we should remember how little we know about him.

B. The Original Readers

The one important clue that we have about the readership of this Gospel is found in the text. In Mk 7:2–5 we see the author carefully explaining Jewish customs:

> [The Pharisees] had observed a few of his disciples eating meals without having purified—that is to say, washed—their hands. The Pharisees and in fact all Jews, cling to the custom of their ancestors and never eat without scrupulously washing their hands. Moreover, they never eat anything from the market without first sprinkling it. There are many other traditions they observe—for example, the washing of cups and jugs and kettles. So the Pharisees and the scribes questioned him....

With these explanations the author interrupts his story and addresses his readers. Such an effort by the author would probably not be necessary unless the audience was Gentile, unfamiliar with these Jewish customs.

C. The Date of the Writing

The clue to the dating of this Gospel is found in chapter 13, where the end of the world is described and is closely associated with the destruction of Jerusalem, as we will see later in this chapter when we study Mark's view of the end of the world. In fact, the Roman armies destroyed the city of Jerusalem in A.D. 70 in the process of crushing a Jewish rebellion.

Mark 13 reads like a speech given by Jesus close to his death around A.D. 30. The historical-critical approach, however, requires us to examine this chapter on the level of Mark's writing down the account rather than on the level of Jesus' speaking. From this perspective, Mark's willingness to see the end of the world as following closely the destruction of Jerusalem strongly suggests two things: (1) the collapse of the city's defense is imminent, and (2) it has not yet happened or has happened not long before the writing of the Gospel. The imminence of Jerusalem's destruction would explain Mark's great interest in the event and in its theological significance. On the other hand, had the collapse already taken place some time before, Mark most probably would have interpreted the reported speech by Jesus in such a way as to avoid having Jesus appear to predict something that did not take place, namely, the end of the world coming on the heels of the war. Hence, our best guess for dating this Gospel is somewhere around A.D. 69. At that time, the end could still possibly occur as Jesus was reported to have predicted.

D. The Structure of the Gospel

Searching for the literary structure of a Gospel means attempting to find the internal development of the narration in its present form. Seeing such an internal development is vital for understanding the Gospel as a whole. It entails especially understanding the sequence of pericopes that Mark, as the final editor, gave to the independent stories passed down to him. It is an attempt see how Mark understood the articulation of the pericopes in some outline form.

To work out such an outline, we need observable literary indications in the text itself of the major divisions and the subdivisions. Without such indications, we run the risk of imposing our organization on the Gospel. Attempting to find major parts simply by noting what appear to be major shifts of topics is risky because the "major shift" might appear to be major only because it corresponds to our concerns, not necessarily the concerns of the author. On the other hand, a proposed outline should provide us with insight into the ideas and concerns of the author. If it does so, we have a confirmation that our outline may be that of the author. However, the first step must be to seek out the literary indicators.

Very often ancient writers developed their accounts by means of cycles rather than step-by-step progression. Hence, repetitions become one of the key literary indications to the internal organization. Often repetitions of similar scenes, ideas, or even words occur at the beginning and at the end of a work or a section of a work. Such a repetition, called an *inclusion,* functions as a frame for the work or section and provides a particular perspective from which to view the material included within this repetition. Similarly, repetitions of several parallel items form a common literary indication of structure. For example, an author might develop a section by three elements: a, b, and c. The next section could have three similar elements in the same (or sometimes reverse) order: a´, b´, and c´. The result is a cyclical development where each cycle resembles the other but usually involves some improved perspective.

Such an inclusion and such parallelism together, in fact, distinguish a central section of the Gospel of Mark, thus effectively dividing the Gospel into three parts. This section begins and ends with a cure of a blind man, 8:22–26 and 10:46–52.

The first cure of the blind man is curious. It involves a two-stage miracle and it ends with the strange admonition of Jesus not to publicize the cure. Immediately following this cure is the story of Peter and the disciples at Caesarea Philippi, where they discuss the identity of Jesus. We see a parallel two-stage drama, two interventions by Jesus each followed by progressively better responses. The story ends with an admonition to silence. Also like the story of the blind man, the real issue is *seeing clearly*. These two stories belong together and in that way introduce the middle section of the Gospel.

STRUCTURE OF "INCLUSION" AND "PARALLELISM"

Inclusion	Parallelism
A	A
B	B
C	C
D	A´
E	B´
A´	C´

Figure 5.

Immediately after this introduction, Jesus predicts his suffering and death (8:31–32a). Peter then appears in the role of opposing this plan of God (8:32b–33). After this pair of stories, we see a series of episodes about Jesus on his "way" to Jerusalem. At 9:30 we have a repetition of the preceding pattern. Jesus predicts his suffering and death (9:30–31). Then occurs a mention of the disciples' failure to understand along with the story of their ambition (9:32–34). Again at 10:32 the pattern occurs. Jesus predicts his passion

**Capernaum: An early Christian church
thought to mark Peter's house.**

(10:32–34). Then comes the unflattering story of James and John and their request for the best places in the kingdom (10:35–41). The parallel pattern is evident: (a) the necessity of Jesus' suffering and death and (b) the blindness of the disciples.

The section ends with the cure of Bartimaeus, a cure that happens in one step and ends with the man following Jesus (10:46–52).

By analyzing the patterns of sequencing in this way we can spot the main ideas of the evangelist. From the examination of the central section of the Gospel, we can clearly see Mark's interest in blindness and seeing. We can likewise note the particular blindness of the disciples regarding the suffering and death of Jesus. All in all the disciples look very dull in regard to grasping the words of Jesus. Yet we see Jesus portrayed here as a savior who cures blindness.

A similar analysis can be made on the first part of the Gospel, Mk 1:1–8:21. After an introductory section in 1:1–13, Mark stops to give us a summary of Jesus' words and activity:

> Jesus appeared in Galilee proclaiming the good news of God: "This is the time of fulfillment. The reign of God is at hand! Reform your lives and believe in the gospel." (1:14–15)

The description here is one of Jesus' general activity. It is not meant to recount his preaching at any particular place or time. A longer summary occurs in 3:7–12 and a very short one in 6:6b (the *b* refers to the second part of the verse).

What makes these summaries appear to be literary indications of structure is the way each one is followed by a story about the disciples: 1:16–19 describes the call of the first disciples; 3:13–19, the appointment of the Twelve; 6:7–13, the mission of the Twelve. If we take this parallelism of paired stories as organizing this first third of the Gospel into smaller units, we then can note how each unit ends with a form of blindness: the Pharisees plot to kill Jesus (3:5–6); Jesus' kin at Nazareth reject him (6:1–6a); his own disciples fail to understand his words (8:14–21). The blindness draws progressively closer to Jesus.

The third part of the Gospel (11:1–16:8) describes the final climactic week in Jerusalem. Inclusions and parallelisms are more difficult to find. Chapter 13 stands out by itself as a discourse about the end of the world. Chapters 14 and 15 recount the passion and death of Jesus followed by a brief account, 16:1–8, of the empty tomb. Chapters 11 and 12 describe the climax of the conflict between Jesus and the leaders in Jerusalem. More work is needed on this section to develop its literary structure, but the theme of Jesus' death is clear throughout this section.

The proportionally extensive treatment of the final days of Jesus in his suffering along with the constant reminder we have throughout the Gospel of Jesus moving toward his death have led some commentators to see the whole Gospel as basically a passion narrative with a long introduction.

Thus, the outline we will follow in studying Mark is the following:

I. Prelude (1:1–13)

II. Part One: The Progressive Revelation of Jesus as Messiah (1:14–8:21)

   A. Jesus with the crowd and the leaders (1:14–3:6)
     1. Summary and call of the first disciples (1:14–20)
     2. Episodes of Jesus' teaching and healing (1:21–3:5)
     3. Blindness: The Pharisees' plot to kill Jesus (3:5–6)

   B. Jesus with his disciples (3:7–6:6a)
     1. Summary and appointment of the Twelve (3:7–19)
     2. Episodes of Jesus' teaching and healing (3:20–5:43)
     3. Blindness: The disbelief at Nazareth (6:1–6a)

   C. Jesus manifests himself to his disciples (6:6b–8:21)
     1. Summary and mission of the Twelve (6:6b–13)
     2. Episodes about Jesus (6:14–8:13)
     3. Blindness: The disciples' lack of understanding (8:14–21)

III. Part Two: "The Way" of the Suffering Son of Man (8:22–10:52)

   A. The cure of the blind man and Peter's confession (8:22–10:52)

   B. First passion prediction and Peter's blindness (8:31–33)
     —Episodes (8:34–9:29)

   C. Second passion prediction and the disciples ambition (9:30–37)
     —Episodes (9:38–10:32)

E. The Text of the Gospel

As we saw in chapter 2, the text of Mark's Gospel based on the manuscript evidence poses a particularly perplexing problem, that of its ending. The earliest manuscripts of this Gospel, including two of the most reliable manuscripts of the New Testament from the fourth century, omit 16:9–20. Furthermore, these verses now added to our text look like summaries of the resurrection appearances of Jesus found in other Gospels. A few late manuscripts replace 16:9–20 with still other endings. All of them appear to be very late.

The earliest forms of Mark's Gospel, therefore, apparently ended with 16:8, a very somber and negative verse. Some have suggested that the original ending Mark wrote was simply lost. The sole basis for this hypothesis, however, lies in the feeling that 16:8 is not a proper way to end a gospel. That feeling, however, might stem from our modern mentality, not from Mark, who insists on the somber and the negative all through his Gospel. If the earliest forms of Mark's Gospel ended with 16:8, then our job must be first of all an attempt to make sense of this form before we have recourse to the hypothetical lost sheet.

II. The Faith of Mark

With these overall perspectives now in mind, we can read the Gospel of Mark. The outline of Mark should help us both to see the development of the Gospel and to allow us to divide the Gospel into digestible units.

Our reading will search especially for Mark's portrayal of Jesus (Mark's christology), his view of Jesus' work and death as saving (Mark's soteriology), and his presentation of the end of the world (Mark's eschatology). We must be careful to let Mark speak on these topics, to allow him to develop these themes as he saw them. Our tendency is to search the Gospels for what we already believe about these matters. Often such a tendency prevents us from seeing what is really there. Our task is to read the text as though this were the first time we had ever seen it, as though this were the only source of information we had about Jesus, the end of the world, and Jesus' work of salvation.

A. Mark's Christology

(See exercise 1.)

Mark's christology is complex. If we read this Gospel simply looking for a confirmation of traditional christological doctrine, we end up confused and disappointed. Instead of the univocal clarity of such later formulated christological doctrines as "one person at once God and man," we find paradoxical descriptions of a man nobody understood. To use a phrase now popular among scholars, Mark's christology comes in the form of *narrative theology*. If we are to understand these narrations, however, we must digest and translate stories in an intellectual probe toward a more unified view. One simple method of such intellectual probing is to classify the narrations according to categories that arise from the text but also correspond to our questions.

As we read Mark, we find that the descriptions of Jesus seem to fall into general categories. At times the categories seem to conflict. For instance, one group of descriptions pictures Jesus as limited; another group pictures Jesus as a divine-like Son of God. Closely connected to these two categories are also descriptions of Jesus as Son of Man and as mystery. In our analysis here we will often refer to a text or provide some key wording. A full understanding requires reading the whole gospel story from which the text or key wording is cited.

1. Jesus as a Limited Human Being

In several places throughout his Gospel, Mark dramatizes the limits of Jesus. At Nazareth confronted with his compatriots' lack of faith, Jesus is unable to work miracles. In 6:5–6 Mark writes, "He *could* work no miracles there, apart from curing a few who were sick...so much did their lack of faith distress him." The significance of this statement becomes clear when it is compared with its parallel in Mt 13:58: "And he *did* not work many miracles there because of their lack of faith" (italics mine). Matthew softens the description to a statement of fact, not one about Jesus' power.

Again in 10:40 the Marcan Jesus refers to an important limitation about his authority. It is not for him to assign places in the kingdom. In 13:32, Jesus states, "As to the exact day or hour, no one knows it, neither the angels in heaven *nor even the Son,* but only the Father" (italics mine). Both of these limits deal with matters central to Jesus' very mission.

Related to these limits is another aspect of Jesus that Mark frequently mentions and is conspicuously absent from the other Gospels—Jesus' emotions. According to Mark, the scene at Nazareth involved Jesus being deeply distressed. Other emotions described by Mark include Jesus' anger (3:5) and annoyance (1:14) as well as his love (10:21). Mark describes Jesus as embracing the children who come to him (9:36; 10:16). These details all contribute to the general impression of a person who is fully human, a real flesh-and-blood human being.

The humanity and even weakness of Jesus appear, however, with even greater intensity during the passion narrative, Mark 14–15. These chapters are filled with details of Jesus being humiliated, tortured, and dragged to his death. They climax with the cry on the cross, "My God, my God, why have you forsaken me?" (15:34).

2. Jesus, the Powerful Son of God

(See exercise 2.)

Parallel to this portrayal of the limited human being is another, almost directly contrary aspect of Jesus. Mark signals this with the opening line of the Gospel, "Here begins the Gospel of Jesus Christ, the Son of God" (1:1).

This title is not used with great frequency in the Gospel, but it is used at strategic parts. At the baptism of Jesus we hear the voice of God address Jesus, "You are my beloved Son" (1:11). A similar heavenly declaration is repeated at the transfiguration (9:7). Meanwhile an occasional demon will remind us of Jesus as Son of God (3:11; 5:7). These supernatural voices will be joined by a human confession of Jesus as Son of God only at the crucifixion. At the darkest hour of Jesus' career, the Gentile centurion declares, "Clearly this man was the Son of God!" (15:39). If we combine this human confession at the end of the Gospel with the opening confession by the evangelist himself, we find an inclusion framing the whole Gospel.

Like the title *Son of Man,* which we will consider next, the title *Son of God* is originally a Hebraism for a person close to God or like God. In some texts of the Old Testament, we can find the use of "son of God" meaning simply a "godly" person (see Wis 2:18). When the king was called "son of God" (1 Sm 7:14; cf. Ps 2:7; 110:3), the writers probably meant to express some special closeness to God. The kings of the Old Testament were by no means considered divine. Ancient Hebrew was poor in adjectives, especially proper adjectives. Hebrew compensated for this paucity by different circumlocutions including the "son of ____" expression. An Israelite was a son of Israel. A wicked man was a son of iniquity.

If we consider the confession of the centurion on Calvary as part of the historical event, we cannot presuppose a great deal of significance in his words. We can presume that the historical Roman soldier would have understood the expression "son of God" simply as describing a pious or innocent man. If, however, we consider the confession of the centurion from the point of view of Mark writing the Gospel, then we must see very special significance in this expression. By its placement in the Gospel, this title appears to be the key to understanding Mark's christology. Yet Mark here gives us no explanation at all of what he means by the title.

In the same line, Mark tantalizes us by his use of the Old Testament in the opening lines of the Gospel. Although he attributes the citation to Isaiah, Mark cites a text from Malachi before he cites one from Deutero-Isaiah. A close comparison of Mark's citation with that of Malachi reveals a significant change:

Mark 1:2	*Malachi 3:1*
I send my messenger	I send my messenger
before you	to prepare the way
to prepare your way.	before me.

In Malachi as in Mark, the "I" is God. The messenger in Mark is John the Baptist; in Malachi, Elijah. The "you" in Mark, however, is Jesus, a word Mark has changed from the divine "me" in Malachi. By so doing Mark has taken a text referring to God and applied it to Jesus.

A similar shift occurs in the second citation of Mark from Deutero-Isaiah. Again, Mark reproduces the text with some word changes:

Mark 1:3	*Isaiah 40:3*
A herald's voice	A voice cries out:
in the desert crying,	in the desert
Make ready the way of the Lord	prepare the way of the Lord
clear him a straight path.	Make straight in the waste-
	land a highway for our God!

Mark first of all shifts "the desert" from indicating the place of the new highway to indicating the place of the voice. In this way Mark identifies the voice with John the Baptist. Thus in Mark "the Lord" for whom the path is prepared is Jesus. For Deutero-Isaiah, "the Lord" is clearly God. This is apparent from the parallelism of the text. Mark again has taken a text referring to God and without any explanation applied it to Jesus.

Throughout the Gospel, Mark insists on Jesus' divine-like character also by recounting the miracle stories. Jesus has power over illness and over the forces of nature. For Mark this power is more than that of a wonder-worker or superman. From the start, Mark associates the miracles of Jesus with his teaching. Mark 1:21–28 in particular shows this association. Here Mark frames the cure of the demoniac with a description of Jesus teaching authority. The miracle story begins with the scene of Jesus teaching (1:21). After the miracle, the crowd is amazed at his teaching (1:27). In the same way Mark begins the miracle of the bread for the five thousand with Jesus teaching the crowd "at great length" (6:34–44).

In another early story the miracles evidence the power of Jesus to forgive sins (2:5–12). When the people brought a paralyzed man to Jesus through the roof, Jesus begins with the words, "Your sins are forgiven" (2:5). These words could be understood as a declaration by Jesus that God had forgiven the man's sins. The passive voice was a common way of speaking of divine activity without having to use the name of God. However, in the form that Mark now presents the story, the declaration of forgiveness is interpreted as proclamation of Jesus' power to forgive sins. (The scribes in the story function as an interpreting chorus to give us this new understanding.) The miracle that Jesus then works is meant to assure that Jesus has this power. Jesus, as Mark declares, shares God's "authority" to forgive sins, an authority that he demonstrates by his "power" to heal.

For Mark, Jesus is clearly no ordinary human being. He is no ordinary prophet or teacher of the law. He is a man of extraordinary authority. The Greek word used by Mark to indicate this authority is *exousia,* a word that means both authorization to teach and power to effect great things. Jesus, for Mark, is the Son of God filled with this *exousia*.

3. Jesus as the Son of Man

We thus have two contrasting aspects of Jesus, both stressed by Mark: Jesus as the limited man of emotion and suffering and Jesus as the powerful Son of God. This contrast appears in the title for Jesus which in Mark is the one consistently on Jesus' own lips, namely, Son of Man.

In its original sense the title was simply a Hebraism for "human being." Sometime in the two hundred years before Jesus, however, the title began to take on a special sense indicating a glorious and powerful figure. The first time we see this meaning is in the book of Daniel, written around 170 B.C. In his visions, Daniel sees

> One like a son of man coming on the clouds of heaven;
> When he reached the Ancient One and was presented
> before him, he received dominion, glory, and kingship;
> nations and peoples of every language serve him. His
> dominion is an everlasting dominion that shall not be
> taken away, his kingship shall not be destroyed. (Dn
> 7:13–14)

It is not clear who this figure is or represents. In Daniel it could be an angel (cf. Dn 8:15), or perhaps it represents Israel (cf. Dn 7:37). The next time we see this figure in Jewish writings, it seems more clearly to designate a messianic instrument of God, again with divine-like power. Such is the figure that appears in *1 Enoch* 37–71, as well as *4 Ezra* 13. These are religious works more or less contemporary with the New Testament but which show no signs of Christian influence. These works, therefore, give evidence of a way of picturing and naming a glorious and powerful messianic figure among Jews at the time of Jesus.

A number of times in Mark, Jesus seems to identify himself with this glorious Son of Man. When describing his return in power at the end of the world, the Marcan Jesus uses words from Daniel:

> Then men will see the Son of Man coming in the clouds
> with great power and glory. He will dispatch his angels
> and assemble his chosen from the four winds, from the
> farthest bounds of earth and sky. (13:26–27)

Looking across the Kedron Valley to the Garden of Olives.

When responding to the high priest's accusation "Are you the Christ?" Jesus states:

> I am; and you will see the Son of Man seated at the right hand of the Power and coming with the clouds of heaven. (Mk 15:62)

The title here seems to be a way of correcting the high priest's concept of "the Christ."

Adding to and changing this glorious image, however, Mark identifies Jesus as a suffering and victimized Son of Man. Three times in Mark Jesus predicts his suffering and death. Each time Jesus uses the title Son of Man:

> He began to teach them that the Son of Man had to suffer much, be rejected by the elders, the chief priests, and the scribes, be put to death, and rise three days later (Mk 8:31; cf. 9:31; 10:33–34)

4. Jesus as Mystery

(See exercise 3.)

Who then is this Jesus? In various ways throughout his Gospel, Mark insists on this person at once glorious and powerful while suffering and powerless unto death. How do these contrasting aspects come together? Mark does not give any clear answer to these questions.

A scene in Mark, in fact, epitomizes the difficulty. The scene is that of the storm on the lake and Jesus sleeping like a tired human being. After being awakened by the disciples, he then calms the storm with a command. The scene ends with a question, "Who can this be that the wind and the sea obey him?" (4:41). The question in effect dominates the whole Gospel, but a clear answer is not given.

In place of clarity, we have lack of understanding. We have seen this lack of understanding especially in those who were closest to Jesus, his disciples. We see a blindness on the part of almost all who deal with Jesus. Yet Mark points out that the lack of understanding was not just the fault of the disciples. There was something deliberately obscure about Jesus himself. By describing Jesus in this way, Mark in effect points in the direction toward which the above conflicting descriptions converge.

The Marcan Jesus, for example, taught in ways that were deliberately obscure. Normally parables function to make a spiritual message more understandable. Parables are stories involving matters of daily life: sweeping the house, fishing with a net, sowing a field. Parables function as examples do in a classroom lecture. Jesus historically used parables in this way. When, however, we read the Marcan interpreted picture of Jesus using parables, we see just the opposite. The discussion about the purpose of parables occurs in 4:10–12, immediately after the parable of the seed. The text is very clear. Jesus speaks to the crowd in parables "so that they will look intently and not see, listen carefully and not understand." On the level of the historical Jesus, this explanation does not make sense. On the level of Mark writing his Gospel, however, this explanation fits well into the theme of Jesus the mystery: "To you the mystery of the reign of God has been confided" (4:11).

Similarly, the Marcan Jesus frequently commands secrecy after working a miracle. The miracles were clear demonstrations of who Jesus was, yet in this Gospel Jesus prevents the miracles from functioning in this way. It may be that the historical Jesus was very discreet about publicity, perhaps in view of Roman suspicions. In the Gospel of Mark, however, this secrecy and discretion become unrealistic. In 5:21–24, 35–43 we have the story of Jesus restoring life to a little girl. The girl is dead. The neighborhood knows about this. The funeral has started. Jesus raises her to life and then commands the father and mother "not to let anyone know about it." Such an impossible command does not make sense on the level of the historical Jesus. We can view this *messianic secrecy,* however, as part of a plan of Mark to portray Jesus as an enigma, as one objectively veiled to the eyes of those around him.

If then we are perplexed by the way Jesus appears in this Gospel, at once as a limited human being and as a powerful Son of God, if we leave this Gospel asking ourselves the question, Who can this man be? this is perhaps exactly what Mark wishes to convey. Mark is allowing us to experience the mystery of Jesus, to experience the difficulty that the closest disciples themselves had in understanding Jesus. To us, as to the disciples, "the mystery is given," but it is given as mystery.

(See exercise 4.)

B. Mark's Soteriology

An aspect of faith that we can trace through the New Testament authors concerns the death of Jesus and how that death can be considered saving. How can a Roman execution bring forth life? What type of salvation can come from a murder? The Greek word for "salvation" is *sōtēria;* hence, the name coined for this study is *soteriology.*

The suffering and death of Jesus for Mark constitute in effect the heart of the "mystery" surrounding Jesus. The topic of the death of Jesus appears for the first time at the end of the first subsection of the Gospel (3:6). These subsections (1:14–3:6; 3:7–6:6a; 6:6b–8:21) all end with stories of incomprehension. In the first such story, where Jesus is presented with the power to heal and to interpret the meaning of divine law, but also as a man with intense human emotion, the authorities decide "to destroy him."

In the central section of the Gospel, 8:22–10:52, with its triple prediction by Jesus of his suffering and death, a section bracketed by Jesus curing physical blindness, Mark insists on both the necessity of Jesus to suffer and die and on the disciples' impossibility of grasping this necessity. In the first prediction, Jesus speaks of a divine necessity binding him to his death. "He began to teach them that the Son of Man had to (*dei*) suffer...and be put to death" (8:31). Although Peter can recognize Jesus as the Christ, he cannot recognize Jesus as the Christ who must suffer and die (8:29, 33–34). In their concern for personal advantage and glory, the other disciples also appear incapable of understanding this paradox of a suffering Messiah (9:32–34; 10:35–36).

The death of Jesus is portrayed as a moment of great darkness (15:33–37). But this is the moment in which it is possible for a human being to confess Jesus as the "Son of God" (15:39). No accompanying miracles are portrayed (contrast Mt 28:52–53), other than the tearing of the Temple veil—which the confessing centurion would not have seen. It is as if the very darkness and mystery of the crucifixion become the medium of divine revelation. What was proclaimed from heaven with light (1:10–11; 9:2–8) now finally can be accepted and confessed in darkness.

Mark briefly alludes to the death of Jesus as a "ransom" (*lytron*, 10:45). Paul will develop this concept. Mark gives no further explanation. The allusion occurs in the setting of the story of James's and John's incomprehension and the ensuing instruction on humble service (10:35–44). Since he gives us no explanation or development of this extraordinary image, Mark appears to be repeating a trace of developing tradition rather than developing a "ransom" or "redemption" theology.

C. Mark's Eschatology

The third major theme to examine in Mark is his view of the end of the world. The study about the end of the world is called *eschatology,* from the Greek word *eschaton,* which means the "end" or "final thing."

(See exercise 5.)

1. Expectations of an End Coming Soon

Concern for the end of the world, both on the part of Jesus and on the part of the early Christians, fits into a general picture of apocalyptic expectations at the time. Matthew reflects this interest in the words of John the Baptist (3:7–10). 2 Peter, a letter written probably at the turn of the second century, shows the embarrassment such apocalyptic expectations had for the early Christians (2 Pt 3:3–9). Numerous other noncanonical works testify to the same mentality (see *4 Ezra* 4:26ff., 40ff.). It was a time, apparently, of intense hope and concern for God's ultimate triumph over evil.

Mark expressly deals with the end of the world in chapter 13 of his Gospel. This *eschatological discourse,* however, begins with a discussion about the Temple and Jesus' prediction about the coming destruction of that Temple. Throughout the rest of the chapter, the instruction about the end of the world is closely connected with that about the destruction of the Temple.

It is quite probable that Jesus historically predicted the destruction of the Temple. In several different and independent places in the Gospels, we hear echoes of this prediction. At his trial his adversaries accuse him of threatening the Temple (see Mk 14:58). The words "not a stone upon a stone," as recorded in Mk 13:2, may well be the very words of Jesus.

On the other hand, the full discourse in Mark 13 has the earmarks of a *written* composition developed by Christians after Jesus' death (see 13:14). With its running citations and allusions to the book of Daniel, this discourse appears as a carefully composed essay.

In any case the discourse brings together two events, the destruction that would take place at the hands of the Romans in A.D. 70 and the destruction of the whole universe as pictured in apocalyptic circles. Some verses in this discourse clearly refer to one or the other event. The admonition, for example, to leave Judea and "flee to the mountains" makes sense against the backdrop of the Roman invasion. It does not make a great deal of sense against that of the end of the world. The descriptions of the wars, persecutions, and false messiahs—even the horrors of 13:18–20—could well fit into the picture of the war, although apocalyptic traits color the whole description. On the other hand, vv. 24–27 clearly refer to the end of the world. Here we see cosmic catastrophes and the climax of Jesus, the glorious Son of Man, coming on the clouds.

When we look for words that relate the two events to each other, we see such expressions as "this is but the onset" (v. 8) and "during that period after trials of every sort" (v. 24). These expressions indicate a view of the end coming on the tails of the Roman war. Even the questions of the disciples in v. 4 place the two events together. Mark therefore seems to see the Roman war and the end of the world as two separate events but as coming one after the other. Apparently Mark took quite seriously the words of Jesus in v. 30, "I assure you, this generation will not pass away until all these things take place." Mark appears to have expected an end of this world and an inauguration in power of the kingdom of God in this generation.

2. The End and the Mystery

This expectation of a quick end to the world will demand thorough reinterpretations on the part of other New Testament writers.

It is important, however, to see how this expectation fits into Mark's general perspective about Jesus and salvation.

A clue to the overall importance of this expectation appears in words of Jesus to the high priest during the trial (14:60–62). The high priest demands an answer to his question, "Are you the Messiah, the Son of the Blessed One?" Jesus answers, "I am," but then explains that his adversaries will recognize him as "the Son of Man seated at the right hand of the Power and coming with the clouds of heaven." This matches the description of the end of the world, "Then men will see the Son of Man coming in the clouds with great power and glory" (13:26). Jesus is explaining to his adversaries how they eventually will come to recognize him, how the obscurity veiling Jesus will finally be lifted. He is saying that this end of the mystery will take place only at the end of the world.

Similarly in chapter 13, Jesus predicts great suffering for his disciples. Not only will the future include wars, famines, and natural disasters for all humanity (13:7–8), but in addition the disciples will have to face hatred and persecution (13:9–13). All this suffering is to continue to the very end.

Such a condition for the disciples is a very strange form of salvation. Years after the death and resurrection of Jesus, a Christian might object, What in effect has Jesus accomplished? Where is salvation? The Christians at the time of Mark believed that Jesus rose from the dead, that he had conquered death, not just for himself but for all. From this faith in Jesus' resurrection, it would be easy to think that death, suffering, and illness should not exist for the Christian. It would be easy to think that a suffering or sick Christian simply did not believe intensely enough in Jesus. Mark may well be writing for Christians who thought exactly in this way, Christians fascinated with the resurrection of Jesus, forgetting the mystery of Jesus' suffering and death.

Mark's answer to these Christians is found in his eschatology. Mark says, in effect, that the clarity of Jesus' glory will appear only on the last day. Up to that point, suffering and persecution will be the normal condition of the disciple. Up to that point, Christian life must be lived in obscurity.

Perhaps for this reason Mark insisted on the passion and death of Jesus and on the obscurity that shrouded Jesus during his healing ministry. Mystery and darkness are not signs of lack of faith but rather an essential part of Christ and Christian discipleship. Perhaps for this reason Mark deliberately ended his Gospel on the obscure note of 16:8, "They made their way out and fled from the tomb bewildered and trembling; and because of their great fear, they said nothing to anyone."

Mark clearly deemphasizes the resurrection of Jesus, although he obviously believes in it—"He has been raised up; he is not here" (16:6). Rather than pointing to the past resurrection of Jesus, Mark points to the future return of Jesus. "Then people will see the Son of Man coming in the clouds with great power and glory" (13:26). Then finally the mystery will be lifted.

III. Theological Reflections

Can these meanings we have uncovered in the analysis of Mark speak to us today? Can we see this historical text as a statement of truth? We have examined three major aspects of Mark's faith: his faith in Jesus' identity, his faith in the return of Jesus, and his faith in salvation through suffering and mystery. Christians of later centuries will pick up the New Testament writings to find a continuity between their faith and that expressed in the texts. Can we find a continuity between our christology, our eschatology, or our soteriology and those of Mark?

Mark's christology ends with an open-ended question, Who can this man be? Can this question still summon us to a position? If we think of Christian theology as answering the question, via the texts of the Fourth Gospel or via Christian theological reflection, then it would seem that Mark's christology no longer needs to be taken seriously.

We must, however, always measure theory by experience. We must measure christology by the concrete reality of Jesus. Unfortunately we cannot repeat the experience of the disciples of Jesus. We cannot repeat this lived immediacy. But Mark's Gospel gives us a "lively" account. Mark's Gospel is not without mediating theory. No human experience comes to us without some interpretation. But Mark's christology still holds a certain simplicity. The question of Jesus is still a question.

Furthermore if we see the later theological precisions as themselves probes into a mystery, expressions about Jesus in which the words used no longer mean the same as they do in expressions about mundane matters, if we understand the metaphorical and poetic character of all theology, then it becomes important to return to the mystery of Jesus as mystery. Later theology about one *person* and two *natures* help the human mind think through this mystery, but such new vocabulary does not resolve it. We in fact do not really know what *person* and *nature* mean. Designating the individual in his or her radical uniqueness, the word *person* was practically coined by Christians to deal with the mystery of Jesus. It was coined basically to point to the mystery, not to provide more information. Theologians must constantly remember that they really do not understand what they are talking about. Mark's christology is a reminder of this important realization.

Mark's eschatology poses a special problem for a theology that insists on the *inerrancy* of the New Testament. The link in Mark between the glorious coming of the Son of Man and the war of A.D. 70 was wrong. The apparently erroneous picture of the end poses a stumbling block to the potential truth in this Gospel. Furthermore, this link cannot be dismissed as are the cosmological or paleontological presuppositions in the Bible which scholars now describe as simply outside of the truths in scripture God communicated "for the sake of our salvation." We are in fact talking about the coming of God's kingdom.

As we will see in later chapters, this stumbling block posed major problems for Christians for the next half century and was taken seriously by later writers, who devised ingenious ways around it. 2 Peter 3:3–4 testifies to those problems, and 2 Pt 3:8–9 testifies to the ingenious solutions.

One approach to this eschatological "error" is to wait for the later reinterpretations by biblical writers of the meaning of this end of the world and its delay. Both Luke and John will try to show how this end in some way did come in Jesus' generation.

Another approach is to understand this imminence of the end as again a presupposition stemming from the apocalyptic fervor of the time. We will look at this apocalyptic movement in a coming chapter, where we glance at the Jewish background of the times. With his announcement "The kingdom of God is at hand!" Jesus entered a powerful current of his day and developed his message from within that current. Such a current became the backdrop for contemplating the Roman forces bearing down on the city of God, preparing to destroy the very Temple of God on earth. The appearances here fit too well the symbolism of apocalyptic in its description of the final battle between good and evil.

Any text, including this one, is fraught with presuppositions, presuppositions that may become clear only when the text is transposed into another milieu. The intention of an author, where the issue of truth has its primary locus, usually bypasses these presuppositions precisely because they are presupposed. The intention of an author speaks out from within those presuppositions to express a new development. Even where the development is a reflection on presuppositions—like this one, not every presupposition is reflected, and those that are not reflected might be the most powerful.

The link between the war of A.D. 70 and the end of the world is certainly a powerful determinant of the meaning of Mark 13. We would be remiss to overlook this link. However, the truth content might lie beyond this link. The truth might lie perhaps in the *qualitative nearness* of the kingdom in any situation of intense conflict and suffering. The truth might lie perhaps in the *inevitability* of the kingdom implied in the link found in Mark 13. Perhaps the truth might lie in this text as an apocalyptic elaboration of the simple statement of Jesus, "The kingdom of God is at hand."

Mark's picture of suffering and darkness continuing up to the day of the return of Jesus in power, in any case, speaks directly to us. Jesus spoke of the divine necessity according to which he had to suffer and die. Jesus required of his disciples that they follow him in this way of suffering. The suffering of Jesus and that of the disciple are brought together. Suffering and weakness, even the experience of abandonment by God, are not a sign of a weak faith. According to Mark this suffering is part of God's mysterious plan of salvation. The believer must follow Jesus' way of the cross even up to the final day—no promises of economic success, of healings, or of special strength mediated through faith. Mark offers only one promise, "During that period after trials of every sort...then men will see the Son of Man coming in the clouds with great power and glory" (13:24–26).

EXERCISES

Exercise 1. (see page 65): Read Mk 3:5; 6:5; 10:16, 21, 40; 13:32; 14–15. What general impression do you get about Jesus from these texts? Read Mk 1:1, 11, 21–28; 2:5–12; 9:7; 15:39. What general impression do you get about Jesus from these texts?

Exercise 2. (see page 66): Compare Mk 1:2–3 with Mal 3:1 and Is 40:3. What remains the same in Mark's citation of the Old Testament? What differences are there in wording or in the meaning of words?

Exercise 3. (see page 70): Read Mk 4:10–12, 41; 5:43. What common theme do you find in these texts?

Exercise 4. (see pages 65–72): List the significant stories about Jesus that you can now remember. Which three would you see as most important for identifying Jesus?

Exercise 5. (see page 73): Examine Mark 13. Some details, such as cosmic upheavals, clearly refer to a great cosmic "end of the world." Other details, such as the need to get out of the city into the mountains, seem to refer to a historical war. Try to assign the verses of Mark 13 to one or the other of these events; then look for any correlation between the two events.

REVIEW QUESTIONS

1. According to Christian tradition, who wrote the Gospel of Mark? What is the major difficulty with that identification?

2. Give a possible outline or structure of Mk 8:22–10:52 based on inclusions and elements repeated in three parallel cycles.

3. Give a possible outline or structure of Mk 1:14–8:21 based on elements repeated in three parallel cycles.

4. How does Mark present Jesus? How does he present him as powerful? As limited and human? In what way does Mark leave Jesus as a great mystery? Illustrate these aspects with specific texts.

5. How does the theme of Jesus as mystery show up in the stories of Jesus' parables and miracles?

6. Where and how does Mark deal with the end of the world? What does he presume or presuppose about its timing? Cite specific texts.

7. In what way does Mark's picture of the end fit into the apocalyptic movement of his time? How does Mark 13 connect this end with the war of A.D. 70? How does Mark 13 help in dating this Gospel?

8. What for Mark is the major significance of the death of Jesus?

FOR FURTHER REFLECTION AND DISCUSSION

1. *With its stress on darkness and suffering, the Gospel of Mark appears very somber and perhaps even depressing. Can you find the Good News here? Is there a message of joy here?*

2. *Which image of Jesus speaks more directly to you, that of the powerful Lord in glory or that of the suffering Son of Man at times limited and irritated?*

3. *Mark develops his Gospel around mystery and many unanswered questions. Where in your life do you experience mystery and question? Can it ever appear as an offer of God's love?*

5

Historical Background—
A Political Sketch

The New Testament grew out of a historical period and reflects that period. Even if they were not the immediate concerns of the New Testament authors, the historical events occurring at their time form a presupposed bedrock on which the authors stand. In our effort to understand the intentions of the authors, we must recreate in our imaginations those historical events.

We will start with the politics of the time, the governments that vied with one another and eventually placed their armies in Israel. The world we are talking about is that of the Roman Empire, which itself mastered a Greek empire as it took control of the land of Jesus.

The complexities should not daunt us. For our purpose we need only grasp the broadest strokes of this history. In effect the historical picture jumps into focus around three broad strokes of the picture which interact and overlap. These strokes consist of the movements of three successive reigns in Israel: the Greek or Hellenistic empire, the Jewish kingdom, and the Roman Empire. These three movements intensely influenced each other. They were fully interdependent. Studying each one separately, however, helps us understand the complex political world behind the New Testament. We will take them in the order in which they appeared in the world.

(See exercise 1.)

I. The Hellenistic Empires (336 B.C.–167 B.C.)

We move back to the middle of the fourth century B.C. to a turning point in world history. The geographical areas are Greece and the Middle East. From the drama unfolding at this time, our Western world will be born.

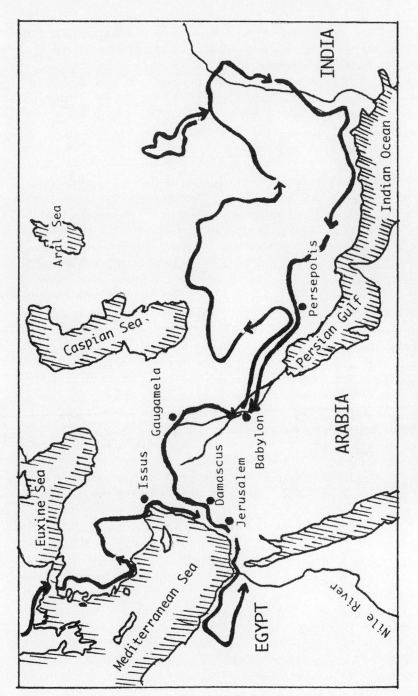

Figure 6. The route of Alexander's armies.

Like a superpower in its day, Persia had been dominating the world. Persia ruled the Middle East and was expanding into Europe. For some time the city-states of Greece had been battling to stop Persian expansionism.

At Pellas, Macedonia, just north of Greece, a young prince succeeded to throne of his father, Philip of Macedonia. Philip had recently forced the reluctant city-states of Greece into a unified power. At twenty-one years of age the son of Philip inherited a small but disciplined army directed by clever military leaders. His name was Alexander.

Alexander's ambition was no less than the world as he knew it. He would destroy the power of Persia and replace it with the power of Greece. It would be a world united under his rule and cemented by Greek culture. He loved that culture. His teacher, Aristotle, had inculcated a love for the Greek way of thinking and living.

Alexander's army numbered around thirty-five thousand, no match for the much larger Grand Army of the Persians, numbering perhaps in the millions, especially in classic warfare, where armies lined up against each other and began hacking away to see who would run out of soldiers first. Alexander's generals realized their hopelessness in this form of battle and devised a new strategy, not one of killing the greatest number of soldiers but of penetrating behind the enemy lies and attacking the headquarters. In this strategy the size of the Persian army would be its weakness.

At Issus in 333 B.C., at the northeast corner of the Mediterranean, the two armies met. Alexander's forces charged through the Persian lines in self-directed, wedge-shaped units called "phalanxes." As several phalanxes neared the Persian headquarters, the Persian king, Darius III, fled from the field. The huge Persian army now without a head became a clumsy giant, easy prey for the disciplined Greeks.

The scene was repeated at Gaugamela, on the banks of the Tigris River. This time Darius committed suicide. From that day on, Alexander began mopping up the world. He entered Palestine in 331 B.C. Roughly twelve years later, his armies crossed into India. (See figure 6.)

Alexander not only secured political control; he commanded the adoption of the Greek culture. The Greek language spread, at least among those wanting to share in the new power structure. Fluency in Greek meant access to business markets, a career in political administration, or at least some form of social status above landed peasants. Colonies of Greek army veterans took root across the Middle

East. The Greek system of education became the standard for the upper class of all the ethnic groups in the new empire. Greek architects constructed cities according to the Greek plan of orderly streets, running parallel to each other or crossing at right angles, and including, of course, the theaters, stadiums, and gymnasiums no self-respecting Greek city could do without. Clarity and regularity were the order of the day according to the Greek ideal of reason.

With surprising acceptance, this culture spread. Apparently the Persian empire had left a cultural vacuum. Greece quickly filled this void. The resulting world culture became an amalgam of the pure *Hellenic* culture of classical Greece along with the Middle Eastern cultures of the old Persian world. This new amalgam is known today as *Hellenistic* culture. This was something of a watered-down Greek culture. It shows up in the simpler grammar of Hellenistic Greek as well as in the strange mixture of Oriental love for entanglements with Greek passion for clarity. We will examine this Hellenistic culture later (chapter 10) with special attention to its religions.

After fifteen years in the field, the soldiers of Alexander demanded an end to the conquests. They wanted to return home. Alexander, who now had earned his title, "the Great," acquiesced. On the return, however, as the armies were bivouacking at the ancient city of Babylon, Alexander the Great became sick and died. The year was 323 B.C.

Like vultures over a corpse, the generals of Alexander began dividing the empire into several kingdoms. For the background of the New Testament, two of these kingdoms are important because at one time or another they controlled Palestine. General Ptolemy at first seized both Egypt and Palestine. General Seleucus grabbed the rest of the Middle East from Syria eastward. (See figure 7.)

Little is known about the political life of the Jewish people under the Ptolemies. Biblical archaeology finds a clear demarcation between the Hellenistic Period and the preceding Persian Period around 323 B.C. by the forms of pottery and some architectural remains. However, the Ptolemies apparently ruled Israel with a certain benign tolerance for Jewish ways. Israel continued to function as a theocracy, as it had under the Persians. The high priest in Jerusalem controlled the internal affairs of the Jews. According to our best guesses, it was during this period that Jews wrote the books of Chronicles, Qoheleth, and Tobit. During this period the scribes and scholars responsible for the preservation of Proverbs added the speculations about Wisdom and the origins of the universe that eventually became the first nine chapters of this biblical book.

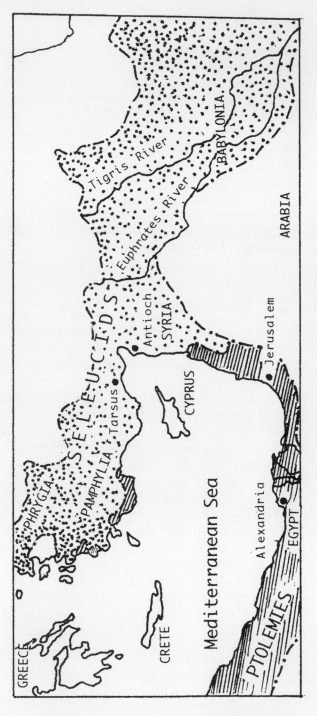

Figure 7. The division of Alexander's empire.

Eventually, however, the Ptolemies lost control of Palestine to the rival Seleucids, now ruling from Antioch in Syria. With this switch of masters, Israel was to undergo a traumatic struggle.

The Seleucids had little respect for the Jewish ways. Furthermore, pressures were building up from the West requiring the Seleucids to secure a firm base of power in their own empire. Reacting to these pressures one of the Seleucids, Antiochus IV, known also as Antiochus Epiphanes, demanded that all Jews abandon their traditional religion and adopt the official state religion of the Greeks. For those who refused, the penalty was death. A highly romanticized account of Antiochus IV and his religious persecution comes down to us in the First and Second books of Maccabees. At this time the book of Daniel likewise appears, describing the anguish and hope of pious Jews living in a world apparently gone mad with evil.

TIMELINE OF POLITICAL CHANGE / BIBLICAL EVENTS AND WRITINGS

Alexander the Great	336	B.C.	
defeats Persia	333		
enters Palestine	331		
dies	323		
Ptolemies/Seleucids			Chronicles
			Qoheleth [no "u"]
			Tobit
			Proverbs 1–9
Roman power in West	201		
Antiochus IV	171		Repression of Jews/ Maccabean revolt
Roman domination	63		
Herod	37		
	6		Birth of Christ acc. to Matthew
dies	4		
Herod Antipas	4	B.C.	
Pontius Pilate	A.D. 26		Ministry of John the Baptist
	27		Baptism and Ministry of Jesus
	30		Death of Jesus
	35		Death of Stephen
Herod Agrippa I	39		
Herod Agrippa II	56		Paul's letters
Jewish revolt	67		
Temple destroyed	70		The Gospels
Bar Kochba revolt	135		

Figure 8.

Before following this story of the Hellenistic powers into the Jewish movement, we must first look to the West, to the power provoking Antiochus to his brutal repression of the Jews. We must now trace in broad strokes the power of Rome.

II. The Roman Empire (201 B.C.–A.D. 70)

Rome began as a city-state, founded on the Tiber River close to the west coast of Italy. Legend has it that the founders were the refugees from the destroyed city of Troy. As Rome gained power economically and militarily, it conquered and absorbed its Italian neighbors, particularly the Etruscans, from whom it learned much about architecture and design. Rome had a way of conquering and absorbing all it considered valuable in conquered people. Eventually, after a series of devastating wars (264–201 B.C.) with its rival, Carthage, Rome gained control of the western Mediterranean Sea. Soon Rome began moving eastward.

By 171 B.C., the armies of Rome were moving into Greece. It was at this time that the Hellenistic king Antiochus IV began his repression of the Jews. According to the proverb, "the enemy of my enemy is my friend," Rome and the Jews forged a special bond that would eventually turn into absolute disaster for Israel.

Wherever Rome went, it took over, sometimes by war of conquest, other times by political settlement. Seeing the irrepressible power of Rome, the last king of Galatia, Amyntas, simply bequeathed his kingdom of north central Turkey to Rome (25 B.C.). Where peaceful submission occurred, Rome left local kings on their thrones. These rulers were known as client kings. They would control internal affairs but forgo all foreign policy and, of course, pay heavy tribute. Where countries resisted in battle, Rome conquered by force and often established a direct rule by a Roman official in that land.

By the 60s Rome removed the remains of the Hellenistic rulers from Antioch and had penetrated as far as Damascus, where the Roman general Pompey established his military headquarters. From here the Romans would soon move south to absorb Israel, as we shall see below. (See figure 9.)

Shortly after this period of conquest in the Middle East, however, the city of Rome underwent serious political turmoil, which would leave its mark directly on the New Testament. In 49 B.C. Julius Caesar, the general who had conquered the Gauls and secured control over most of Europe, marched into Rome in defiance of the Roman Senate. The Commander—or *Imperator,* as the Latin-speaking Romans called him—crossed the Rubicon River just north of the city. Epoch-making events followed quickly. Julius Caesar was assassinated. Civil war broke out. The forces of the Senate were eventually defeated by the forces of the *Imperator.* The decisive battle was fought in Macedonia not far from Alexander's home, on the plains of Philippi. Rome thus became an empire. After a subsequent war, the former allies, Octavius and Mark Anthony, battled each other for power. Octavius won and became the first official emperor, in the image of Julius the *Imperator.* "Caesar" became his title, from the name of his mentor, Julius. "Augustus" ("Revered") became his designation. Caesar Augustus!

Rome. The forum along the Via Sacra.

Tiberius Caesar followed Octavius in A.D. 14 and ruled until A.D. 37. He in turn would be followed by Caligula (A.D. 37–41), Claudius (A.D. 41–54), and Nero (A.D. 54–68). The last years of Nero's reign would be marked by the rebellion of Judea and the military expeditions of Vespasian against the Jews, and turmoil in Rome. Before completely suppressing the revolt of the Jews, Vespasian would be invited back to Rome by the military to become emperor (A.D. 69–79). Titus his son would destroy Jerusalem and its Temple in A.D. 70 and return triumphant to Rome carrying the spoils of war. Eventually Titus succeeded his father as emperor (A.D. 79–81).

The list of emperors through New Testament times is as follows:

Caesar Augustus	27 B.C.–A.D. 14
Tiberius	A.D. 14–37
Caligula	A.D. 37–41
Claudius	A.D. 41–54
Nero	A.D. 54–68
Galba	A.D. 68
Otho and Vitellius	A.D. 69
Vespasian	A.D. 69–79
Titus	A.D. 79–81
Domitian	A.D. 81–96
Nerva	A.D. 96–98
Trajan	A.D. 98–117

III. The Jewish Kingdom (167 B.C.–A.D. 70)

This sketch of Roman history brings us almost to the end of New Testament times. We must, however, back up and look more carefully at the developments in Israel during this period.

In 167 B.C. Antiochus IV, the Seleucid ruler, underestimated the will of the Jews. Although some in Judea were happy to accept the Hellenistic way of life, others under the leadership of Mattathias Hasmoneus retreated to the hills to wage a guerrilla war against the Hellenistic armies. The story of this warfare comes to us in the accounts of 1 Maccabees 2–16 and 2 Maccabees 8–15.

Mattathias was killed in 166 B.C. and was succeeded by his son Judas Maccabeus, who gave his name to the movement, the Revolt of the Maccabees. For about six years Judas waged a successful guerrilla war, raiding and attacking the weak points of the Hellenistic army but refusing prolonged battle.

The Maccabees' success, however, rested a great deal on the role of Rome. It was the Roman armies in northern Syria that prevented Antiochus from dispatching his full forces against the Jews. Roman support apparently supplied the Maccabees with what they needed to fight Antiochus.

Judas was killed in battle in 160 B.C. and was succeeded by his brother Jonathan (160–142 B.C.). Jonathan turned from military force to skillful political maneuvering to consolidate the victories.

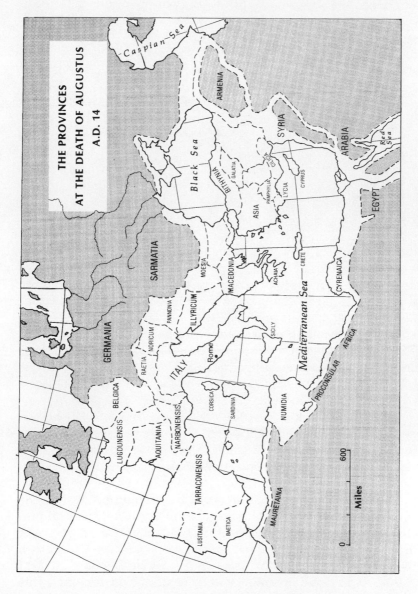

THE PROVINCES
AT THE DEATH OF AUGUSTUS
A.D. 14

Figure 9. The Roman Empire in the First Century.

Playing Hellenistic rivals off against each other, Jonathan gathered support from any source he could (see 1 Mc 9:23–12:53).

Against the traditions of his people, however, Jonathan sought and obtained the office of high priest. He was of neither the tribe of Levi nor the house of Aaron, in which the priesthood was scrupulously held and passed down. This arrogation of the high priesthood fit his plans, however, because this office held great political power in the theocracy of Israel. By this act, however, Jonathan alienated a group of Jews, called Essenes, who eventually broke off from the Jerusalem power structure and established themselves in the desert. While Jonathan is basically a hero to the authors of 1 and 2 Maccabees, he appears to be "the wicked priest" among the Essenes in the desert (see 1QpHab 9–12). In the next chapter we will look more closely at this group, along with their writings, which we now call the Dead Sea Scrolls.

Jonathan was eventually murdered by a trick. He accepted the hospitality of an enemy and was assassinated. The story is told in 1 Mc 12:39–53.

Jonathan was succeeded by his brother Simon as leader of the Jewish forces (141–135 B.C.). Simon, likewise, accepted the title high priest, to which he added also that of *ethnarch,* "leader of the nation." Like his brother, Simon eventually was murdered in a ruse (1 Mc 16:11–24). His son John Hyrcanus succeeded him (135–104 B.C.) and thus began the succession of power from father to son which later historians would call the Hasmonean dynasty, after the name of Jonathan's grandfather, Mattathias Hasmoneus.

The next son, Aristobulus, received the title *basileus,* "king," but he reigned as such only one year (104–103 B.C.). When his brother Alexander Janneus took over (103–76 B.C.), followed by Alexander's wife, Alexandra (76–67 B.C.), little of the original Maccabean idealism remained. Corruption had set in. In his hunger for power, Alexander did not scruple to use his mercenary army against his fellow Jews.

The sons of Alexander and Alexandra brought corruption to a deeper level. These sons, Hyrcanus II and Aristobulus II, fought each other over the throne. Civil war was about to break out in Jerusalem when a third faction requested Pompey, the Roman general quartered in nearby Damascus, to settle the dispute. The year was 63 B.C. Pompey accepted the invitation and marched into Jerusalem. At this point Rome took over control of Israel. From this period through the rest of the New Testament period, Rome would be the political power controlling Israel.

Pompey established Hyrcanus II on the throne of Jerusalem as a client ruler (63–40 B.C.). The Romans, likewise, provided Hyrcanus with a prime minister, an Edomite by the name of Antipater. Antipater would become famous because of his son, Herod.

Young Herod received enormous assistance for his political ambitions from his powerful father. Marriage was also a tool for his ambitions. He married a total of ten wives, women from the powerful Hasmonean family as well as from other prominent families in Judea. In particular, it was his marriage to Mariamne, granddaughter of Hyrcanus II and Aristobulus II, that strengthened Herod's political base and established acceptance in Judean circles. (He executed her eight years later.)

At the death of Hyrcanus II, Herod was named the new king by the Roman leader, Mark Anthony. It took Herod about three years to consolidate his power, which was recognized again by Octavius after his war with Mark Anthony. Herod's ability to switch patrons from Mark Anthony to Octavius without loss of power is an indication of his political cleverness.

A model of the Roman fortress Antonia at Jerusalem.

Herod ruled from 37 to 4 B.C. Under his reign, Israel attained a size comparable to the ancient kingdom of David. Herod began the rebuilding of the Temple, one that would surpass in splendor even that of King Solomon. This building campaign, as well as his general ability to control the land under the patronage of Rome, earned him the title "the Great." A contemporary historian, Josephus, tells the story of his murder of his two sons, whom he suspected of being too eager to succeed their father (see *Jewish Antiquities,* 16.10.6–16.11.8; see books 14–16 for more details about Herod). From these sketches, we get the picture of a cruel and clever monarch, a powerful man, and an extremely dangerous opponent. This picture is not unlike the portrayal Matthew 1–2 gives of this king—although no indiscriminate slaughter of children appears in historical accounts of his life.

The Romans often controlled the power of their client kings by dividing their kingdoms at the death of a ruler. Hence, when King Herod died in 4 B.C., the Romans divided his kingdom into three parts. One son, Archelaus (see Mt 2:22), received control of Judea. His brother, Herod Antipas (see Mk 6:14; Lk 3:1), received control of Galilee and a section east of the Jordan called Perea. A third son by another wife, Philip (see Lk 3:1), became the ruler of the northeastern part of the kingdom, the areas of Trachonitis and Iturea. (See figure 10.)

Archelaus's control of Judea lasted only until A.D. 6. His rule was apparently so incompetent, or at least so unacceptable to the Romans, that he was replaced by non-Jewish rulers sent from Rome. The Romans appointed prefects (later named procurators) to rule Judea. From the period of A.D. 6 to A.D. 66, fourteen prefects ruled this area. The most famous was Pontius Pilate (A.D. 26–36). For the most part these Roman prefects were cruel and corrupt officials, one worse than the other. The last, Florus (A.D. 64–66), was so intolerable that open rebellion broke out in Jerusalem. This was the revolt that would lead to the disaster of A.D. 70.

Herod Antipas ruled Galilee as *Tetrarch* ("ruler of a quarter") from 4 B.C. to A.D. 39. This was the Herod who frequently appears in the Gospels during the ministry of Jesus. He was succeeded by his nephew, Herod Agrippa I, who for a while replaced the prefects in Jerusalem. This Herod is best known for his murder of James the apostle and the arrest of Peter (see Acts 12:1–23). After Herod Agrippa's death in A.D. 44, his son Herod Agrippa II took over in Galilee (see Acts 25:13). (See appendix 3 for the family tree of Hasmonean and Herodian rulers from Mattathias to Agrippa II.)

The closing scene of this rapid review of history is that of Jerusalem in flames. This event began with the revolt in A.D. 66, much like the revolt of the Maccabees two hundred years earlier. Again, religious zeal motivated the fighting. The leaders were the Zealots, a fanatical group violently opposed to the rule of Rome. At first the revolt succeeded. The Roman garrisons in Israel were slaughtered. The Zealots took over and quickly fortified strongholds, as they waited for the inevitable response from Rome.

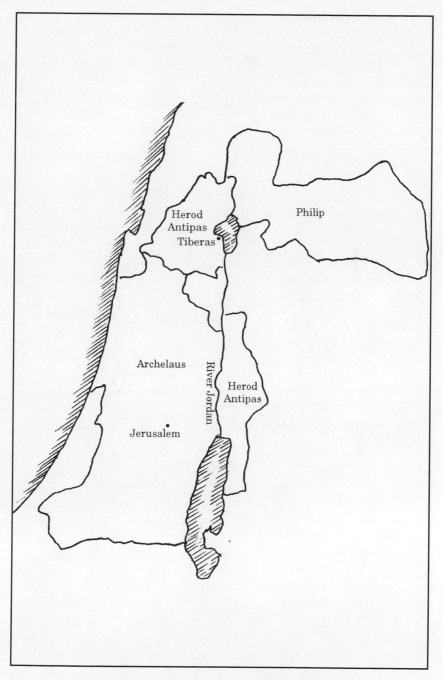

Figure 10. **The Division of Herod's Kingdom.**

The response came with General Vespasian, who brought the legions down through Syria, destroying one fortified town after another. According to the techniques learned from centuries of warfare, Vespasian then laid siege to Jerusalem. No one could enter or leave (see Lk 21:20). After two years and a change of command from Vespasian to his son Titus, the city fell.

With the fall of Jerusalem and the ensuing burning of the Temple, both Judaism and Christianity lost their mother city. A common bond disappeared, forcing both Christians and Jews into the outside Hellenistic world.

Rome. The Arch of Titus in the Roman Forum.

Quickly Christians and Jews separated more and more from each other. Soon even in the eye of the outsider, Christians and Jews appeared to be following different religions.

The interior relief on the Arch of Titus commemorating the reconquest of Jerusalem.

Sixty-five years later, another rebellion broke out in Judea under the leadership of man calling himself the Messiah and named by his followers as Bar-Kochba, "Son of the Star." The rebellion ended in even greater disaster for the Jews. Rome systematically razed the city of Jerusalem, rebuilt its own Aelia Capitolina on the spot, and forbade Jews from entering the city under pain of death.

In these dramatic years of political turmoil, Jesus of Nazareth appeared on the scene, and the followers of Jesus began preaching and recording their new faith.

(See exercise 2.)

IV. Theological Reflections

The New Testament is deeply rooted in history. It cannot be understood as some document springing from eternity and expressing only timeless truths. Like Jesus himself, the New Testament reflects its times. Any attempt to ignore its historical, earthly character leads to gross distortions. Such is the distortion that comes from reading the New Testament as simply a theological treatise or moral essay, attempting to jump immediately into timeless abstractions and ideas. In fact, whatever timeless message the New Testament has, that message comes to us as historical data. Like Jesus, the New Testament appears as God's word enfleshed in human, historical form.

Similarly, we distort the New Testament by reading the stories simply as "myths." As we have seen in the preceding chapter's study of Mark, the evangelist is intensely interested in "what happened." Although the Gospels give us a freely revised and interpreted account of the events, they are clearly concerned about the actions and words of the concrete Jesus whose life took place in history. As we will see in chapter 8, Luke in particular takes pains to situate the narration of Jesus in the context of world history. These accounts are anything but "timeless myths," good stories that serve to provide insight or straighten out our ideas but in no way inform us of historical truth.

Conversely, as we better understand this historical concern and the historical background of the New Testament, our faith perceives a dimension of history—incomprehensible outside of faith, namely, that history is the medium of God's action. Faith can see the events of the Greco-Roman world as leading to Jesus and from Jesus. The God of Christians—as well as the God of Jews—is a God who acts in and through history, not just in the interiority of one's heart.

By describing Jesus and his activity in a particular place at a particular time, the New Testament tells us to look to history first to see the salvation of God. Such a historical concern is not opposed to mystical interiority, but this concern insists that the mystical approach be open to reading history books and newspapers. For all its arbitrary meanderings, the temporal flow of this world is capable of sacramentality, of being an outward sign of divine grace.

EXERCISES

Exercise 1. (see page 80): Read Matthew 2–3 and Luke 1–2. List the figures of political importance mentioned in these accounts. What do you know about these figures?

Exercise 2. (see pages 88–95): 1 Maccabees 1–16 and 2 Maccabees 1–15 describe the events at the time of Antiochus IV and the successful revolt of the Maccabees. Read these texts for background. How many events and persons from these accounts do you recognize? How did the writers of these books understand the theological significance of these events?

REVIEW QUESTIONS

1. Describe the effect Alexander the Great had on the world of his time. When did he die? What happened to his empire at his death?

2. Describe the principal figures at the time of the Maccabean revolt. What is the dating of this revolt?

3. Describe how Rome gained control of Israel. Who was the leading Roman general? When did this happen?

4. Describe how Herod the Great became king of Israel. What are the dates of his rule? What happened to his kingdom at his death? Name his successors.

5. Who are the other Herods mentioned in the New Testament?

6. How and when were Jerusalem and the Temple destroyed?

FOR FURTHER REFLECTION AND DISCUSSION

1. If Jesus were born in the twentieth century, how would contemporary events probably change the nature and color of his preaching as well as what would have happened to him?

2. How did military power determine the events of the world at the time of Jesus? Contrast the ministry and environment of Jesus with that power. In particular, contrast the figures of Herod the Great and Jesus in terms of power and its forms.

6

Historical Background—
A Sketch of Jewish Culture

Parallel to the political and military history behind the New Testament is a history of the human spirit. The religious and cultural history behind the New Testament forms a powerful matrix out of which the New Testament takes shape. Even the most original idea must be expressed in a language that forms the thought. Even the truly unique individual grows up in a community of social and spiritual patterns that constitute a universe of reflected and unreflected presuppositions.

Jesus was a Jew. The first followers of Jesus and the first members of the church of Jesus were Jews. Their hopes were Jewish hopes; their image of God was a Jewish image; the opponents and followers whose concerns stimulate the first steps of the Christian faith were Jewish opponents and followers.

We are talking about the Jewish faith and culture of the Greco-Roman world. This is the faith and culture rooted in the Israelite faith of the Hebrew Scriptures, the Mosaic traditions gradually written down and gathered into documents stemming from the tenth century B.C. But this Jewish faith and culture are not the same as the classical Israelite religion. Rather, the faith and culture contemporary with Jesus and the New Testament writers are a faith and culture with their own proper color, characteristics, and institutions. The distinctiveness of Judaism as such begins with the return from exile of the Jews in 538 B.C. and their settling again the land of Judah. After the armies and ideas of Alexander invaded the land, Judaism began to show the gradual influence of Hellenism.

This later Judaism appears not only in the New Testament but also in the writings stemming from times just prior to and following the New Testament: the midrashim, the targumin, the mass of anonymous apocalypses of this time, contemporary Jewish writers

The Land of Jesus

Figure 11.

such as Philo and Josephus, as well as in the later Mishna and Talmuds. From these sources we see a faith and religion based on the ancient Hebrew Scriptures, yet one that freely interpreted those scriptures. It is this faith and religion that form the link between the New Testament and the Old.

For two distinct reasons, we need an overview of this faith in which at least the major traits can be illuminated. First of all, we need to have a fuller picture of the groups and institutions mentioned in the New Testament. For the writers of the New Testament, many of these groups and institutions were so dominant that little need existed to explain the nuances that give full color to their appearance in the New Testament. We, on the other hand, need to reestablish those nuances.

Second, we need to understand the spiritual and cultural presuppositions guiding Jesus and the New Testament writers, presuppositions they may not have even been aware of. The tools we need to think and act on a spiritual level are tools we start receiving from the time we are born. They enter our minds from the words and gestures of our parents, from the joys and anguish of the society we grow up in, from the praise and reprimands we hear all our lives—long before we are taught by religious authorities about which tools we need and how to use them. Immersed in these presuppositions, we normally have little reason to reflect on them. They are often silent partners in our spiritual development. Another culture studying us, however, would have to find and articulate those presuppositions. So we must understand the presuppositions of Mark and Matthew, Paul and John, and Jesus himself. To the degree we examine those spiritual and cultural presuppositions which they could not or simply did not examine, to that degree we might understand the thought of these persons better than they did themselves. This is not arrogance. This is just recognition of human history.

This Judaism was an incredibly complicated culture. Library shelves of books attempt to explain it. In a book of this nature, we must restrict ourselves to a brief sketch that traces the major aspects of the culture. Our attempt will be to look at four major institutions and movements of Judaism, which will give us at least a sense of the major pillars of this culture.

I. The Temple and the Priesthood

King Solomon built the first Temple in the tenth century B.C. That Temple eventually became the unique place of lawful sacrifice, the slaughtering of animals and burning of foodstuffs by which the Israelites worshiped God. The book of Leviticus details the forms and importance of such sacrifices.

Nebuchadnezzar and his Babylonian army destroyed the Temple in 586 B.C. A disappointing Second Temple arose from the ruins sometime after the return of the Jews from deportation. Around 20 B.C., Herod the Great took upon himself to rebuild this Second Temple and restore it to the legendary glory and splendor of Solomon's Temple. The rebuilding continued through A.D. 63.

A model of the Herodian Temple in Jerusalem.

The Temple consisted of a series of concentric courts and rooms, each with greater exclusivity. All groups were allowed into the outer court, the Court of the Gentiles. Within this court was a smaller one, that of the Israelites, into which Gentiles were forbidden to enter under pain of death. Dividing this court was a wall, forming an inner court into which only men could enter. In this Court of the Men stood the main building of the Temple, the Sanctuary or "Holies." Only priests were allowed into this building to offer incense. In the Holies stood the Altar of Incense and the seven-branched candlestick known as the *menorah.* Within the Holies was an inner sanctum, the "Holy of Holies," which in the Solomonic Temple housed the Ark of the Covenant. At the time of the New Testament, the Holy of Holies was an empty room. Into this empty room only the high priest could enter once a year on the Day of Atonement. (See figure 12.)

The officials of the Temple, the priests, had their offices by heredity. Presumably they were descendants of Aaron and of the tribe of Levi—until the Hasmoneans usurped the office. The high priest presided over the whole operation. Normally he had his office for life, although the Romans and Herod himself did not hesitate to depose high priests and install others in his place.

The more wealthy priests formed a powerful political party. Known as the Sadducees, this group constituted the clerical aristocracy mostly in Judea. The Sadducees accepted only the first five books of the Bible, the Torah, as authoritative. This made the Sadducees reluctant to accept any doctrine that developed in later Judaism, doctrines such as the resurrection of the dead or the existence of angels.

Next to the Herodian rulers, the high priest was perhaps the most powerful figure within Judaism at the time of the New Testament. At the destruction of the Temple, however, the Sadducees as well as the priests in general lost their base of power and ceased to exist as an influential group in Judaism.

(See exercises 1, 2.)

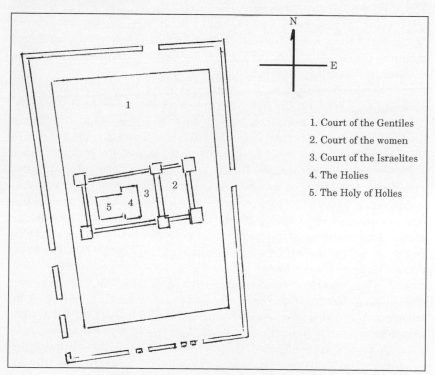

1. Court of the Gentiles
2. Court of the women
3. Court of the Israelites
4. The Holies
5. The Holy of Holies

Figure 12. The Temple of Jerusalem.

II. Scripture and the Lawyers

A second pillar of the Jewish religion was Holy Scripture, what Christians today call the Old Testament. These texts contain for the Jew the foundational stories of Israel's origins under God as well as the commandments of God for his people. The Jew sees these writings as inspired revelation, as God's communication to his people.

While the Sadducees accepted only the first five books as scripture, others took a wider view. In the wider view, scripture consisted of three groups of writings: the Torah, the Prophets, and the Writings. The Torah, which means in Hebrew "instruction," consists of the first five books of the Bible. The Greek-speaking Jews of the Greco-Roman world translated the word *Torah* by the Greek word *nomos*, "law." The Law for the Jew is thus not simply the Ten Commandments or even the elaborate social and religious codes of the Bible. The Law includes also the stories that establish the very identity of Israel. The translation of *Torah* as *Nomos* creates a confusion that runs even into the letters of Paul in his polemic against "the Law."

The second group of biblical books is called "the Prophets," in Hebrew, *ha Nabiim.* The prophetic books, such as Isaiah, Jeremiah, and the other prophets, are included in this group, but so are the historical books from Joshua through 2 Kings. While the Torah remains the heart of scripture, the Prophets constitute the first line of interpretation of the Torah.

The third group has the nondescript name "the Writings," in Hebrew, *ha Ketubim.* It is a collection of all the other books eventually included in the Jewish Bible. Whereas the list of the Torah books was apparently firm from the fifth century B.C., and the canon of the Prophets seemed to generate a consensus a century or so later—except for dissenters like the Sadducees—the official list of the Writings remained an open question even through New Testament times. It was the reverence for such books as the Psalms that opened most Jews to accept more than the Torah and the Prophets. However, local Jewish communities differed from one another in regard to accepting specific books, such as the Maccabees, the Wisdom of Solomon, and others.

Reflecting the very development of the Old Testament canon, this division is behind the traditional Jewish manner of referring to scripture as "the Law and the Prophets" (see Mt 7:12; 11:13; 22:40) or sometimes "the Law, the Prophets, and the Psalms" (Lk 24:44).

The synagogue service arose from and revolved around Holy Scripture. Only Jerusalem had a Temple for sacrifice, but almost every Jewish community had its synagogue, where the people could gather weekly and worship God through the Bible. The synagogue, a Greek word that means "gathering" or "assembly," may have started in the sixth century B.C., when the Jews were first deported from their Temple and needed another way of worshiping besides animal sacrifice. In the synagogue service, the scroll of the Torah received great reverence. A selection from it was read aloud, followed by a selection from the Prophets. In response to these readings the congregation sang psalms and listened to a homily or exposition of the biblical texts read. The goal of the homily was often to weave the passages of the texts together and create a meaning that spoke directly to the listening congregation.

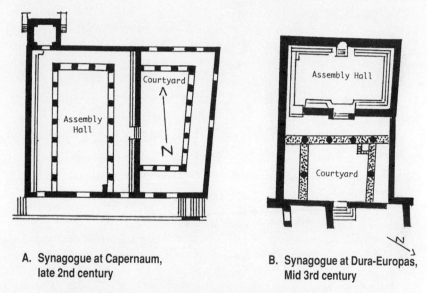

A. Synagogue at Capernaum,
   late 2nd century

B. Synagogue at Dura-Europas,
   Mid 3rd century

Figure 13. **Early Jewish Synagogues.**

The synagogue service was much more democratic than that of the Temple. Generally any adult male Jew could be invited to read or give the homily (see Lk 4:16–22). The distinction between clergy and laity did not appear here. Nevertheless, a special group of experts in the Law developed. These "lawyers," also known as "teachers" or "rabbis," were laymen dedicated to the study of the Torah. Such experts had great influence in the synagogue service and eventually assumed charge of it. (See figure 13.)

Among the rabbis one very important group was the Pharisees. These formed a type of religious political party parallel to the Sadducees. Unlike the Sadducees, however, the Pharisees were laymen.

Their work was not sacrifice but knowledge and observance of the Law. Their attitude toward scripture was much broader than that of the Sadducees. They accepted as inspired not only the Torah but also the Prophets, the Writings, as well as much of the oral tradition that stemmed from learned discussions about the Law. This oral tradition was codified centuries later in the Mishna and the Talmuds. Hence, the Pharisees were quite enthusiastic about doctrines such as the resurrection of the dead and the role of angels, doctrines that appear in later parts of the Jewish Scriptures and which receive great elaboration in later oral tradition. From this oral tradition, the Pharisees developed an elaborate system of rules that went far beyond the laws of the Torah. Some six hundred regulations, now codified in the Mishna and Talmuds, governed almost every aspect of life, forming as it were a hedge around the Torah. By observing these oral traditions, the Pharisee felt assured of observing the central Law of God and confident of doing almost everything in obedience to God.

The Pharisees saw themselves as being an elite group in God's people, and they sought to remain apart from others less dedicated to the Law. Their name apparently derives from the Hebrew word, *parash,* which means "to separate."

The synagogue at Capernaum from the 2nd century A.D.

The Pharisees and the rabbis in general did not draw their power from the Temple as did the Sadducees and priests. Hence the Pharisees and rabbis could maintain their influence after the destruction of the Temple in A.D. 70. It was this group that maintained the identity and vitality of the Jewish people after the loss of their Temple and holy city. It was this strand of Judaism that survived and became the typical form of Judaism into Christian times, known today as rabbinic Judaism.

(See exercise 3.)

III. Messianism and the Apocalyptic Enthusiasts

A. Royal Messiahs

A third important pillar of Judaism at the time of the New Testament was an intense interest in a new intervention of God to save his people. Groups differed as to the nature of this intervention. Some saw God intervening directly; others saw him operating through a human instrument, a special *anointed one.*

The image of being anointed comes from the traditions of the ancient kings of Judah and Israel. At first only the king was anointed. Later the high priest was anointed, after he had assumed kingly power in the Jewish theocracy. The *anointed one* thus originally connoted the idea of a king or political figure. The word for "anointed" in Hebrew is *mashiach;* in Greek *christos.* From these words respectively, we get our English words *messiah* and *Christ.* Thus in Ps 2:2 the king is described as God's *messiah* or *christ,* depending on whether our translations are based on the original Hebrew or Greek.

In fact the images of that "christ" took on various forms among different Jewish groups. Sometimes the image resembled that of the ancient kings; other times, that of the ancient priests. Shortly after Pompey had entered Jerusalem and established the corrupt Hyrcanus on the Hasmonean throne (64 B.C.), a group of pious Jews prayed:

> Behold, O Lord, and raise up unto [your people] their king, the son of David, at the time in which Thou seest, O God, that he may reign over Israel Thy servant. And that he may purge Jerusalem from nations that trample [her] down to destruction.... With a rod of iron he shall break in pieces all their substance. (*Psalms of Solomon* 17:23–24)

This prayer represents one specific form of messianic hope, looking forward to a Davidic Messiah.

Meanwhile, in the Judean desert another group of pious Jews, known as Essenes, men who had given up all hope in the religious and political establishment of Jerusalem, prayed for two anointed ones, one priestly, the other kingly, "the Messiahs of Aaron and Israel" (1QS 9:11). Concerning the kingly Messiah, these sectarians wrote:

> He is the Branch of David who shall arise with the Inter-preter of the Law [to rule] in Zion [at the end] of time. As it is written, "I will raise up the tent of David that is fallen" [Am 9:11]. That is to say the fallen "tent of David" is he who shall arise to save Israel. (4QFlor 1:11–12)

For all its variety within Judaism at the time of the New Testament, messianic hope looked essentially toward a political figure. His role was to function much like the great king David, who liberated his people from political oppression by means of military prowess. His strength and success would come not from the size of his fighting force but from God. Motivated by the memory of the Maccabees a little over a century earlier, this political messianic movement looked to God as the all-important and zealous ally.

GROUPS WITHIN JUDAISM AT THE TIME OF JESUS

Group	Status	Power Base	Sacred Documents
Sadduccees	priests	Temple & Sanhedrin, led by high priest	Torah only
Pharisees	rabbis	synagogue & Sanhedrin	Torah Prophets Writings Oral Tradition
Herodians	government officials	palace	
Scribes	laymen	courts schools?	Scripture & Wisdom literature
Essenes	"priests" & laymen	separate communities	Scripture & Community documents
Zealots	laymen	anti-establishment	Scripture & Apocalyptic writings

Figure 14.

From the time of Herod the Great, messianic unrest pervaded the land. Josephus describes repeated uprisings, where the leaders presented themselves with kingly trappings (*Jewish Wars* 2.4.1–2; 2.8.1). As the decades progressed after the time of Jesus, identifiable groups began to appear. The *Sicarii,* dagger fighters, appear to be urban terrorists who pursued the strategy of selective assassination, at times taking oaths not to eat anything until they had killed their targeted Roman official or Roman sympathizer. We can note the similar attack on Paul described in Acts 23:12–15. Zealots appear as an organized militant party only after the war of A.D. 67–70 broke out. The name may have referred earlier to various groups and persons who felt that zeal for God's Law would assure military success. The name that Josephus consistently uses in his own contemptuous way to identify the religious terrorists is "brigands," in Greek *lēstēs.* The name helps us understand better the character of Barabbas (Jn 18:40) or the two "thieves" crucified with Jesus (Mk 15:27), all called *lēstai* in the Gospels.

The Essenes, located in a tightly organized monastery by the side of the Dead Sea, do not directly appear in the New Testament but were very much defined by their expectation of God's holy war. They saw themselves as the unique group to be saved by God, and they uncompromisingly opposed the religious establishment of Jerusalem. We now know a great deal about this group from the discovery of their library in 1947 near the shores of the Dead Sea. Their dualistic views, their exclusivism, and their sense of privileged insights into God's plans remind us somewhat of the Gnostics. They witness to the way in which Hellenism had infiltrated the most conservative circles of Palestine.

Qumran caves.

The Essenes therefore indicate the real possibility that the Hellenistic elements of the New Testament may be rooted right within Judaism. Prior to the discovery of the Dead Sea Scrolls, scholars thought it necessary to trace Hellenistic elements to relatively late developments of the New Testament, developments that took place after Christianity spread from Palestine into the Hellenistic world. The Essenes' library now forces us to revise much of this historical reconstruction.

B. The Apocalyptic Movement

The Brigands and the Essenes are part of a much larger movement which viewed the world as rapidly coming to an end. This is the apocalyptic movement we looked at briefly in our study of Mark 13. With its roots in the writings of Ezekiel, apocalyptic Judaism began to flourish around the time of Antiochus IV, around 190 B.C., and continued its powerful current down to the second destruction of Jerusalem in A.D. 135. After that second terrible experience, the rabbinic leaders apparently began a systematic purge of apocalyptic from Jewish writing. So today we find hardly a trace of this movement in the Mishna or Talmuds.

At the time of the New Testament this Jewish movement could be summarized in a line out of the book of *4 Ezra,* "God did not create one world *(aiōn)* but two, the one that is present and the one to come" (7:50). The word for "world" in Greek, *aiōn,* can mean either a spatial world or a temporal epoch. The basic idea, however, lies in the view that this world, fraught with evil and suffering, is not God's last word in his creative discourse. God has prepared a new and better world, where his loving care will eliminate all tears. This salvation will be God's work, and it will be as radical a work as that of the first creation.

This view of salvation arises from a specific view of evil that must be grasped if apocalyptic is to make sense at all. This view differs from our modern personalist view of evil, in which evil exists as a powerful problem in our hearts ("I wish I weren't so selfish and greedy") or as a problem among people ("We need tougher laws to deal with criminals"). In apocalyptic, evil is a cosmic power. In some apocalyptic images, it is the power of Satan given loose leash on earth (Revelation 12). In other apocalyptic images, it is the power of death and corruption as a force that is larger than human attitudes and enslaves human beings. It is the power of darkness (see Rom 7:13–24; 1 Thes 5:4–8). For the believing Jew, this power has its origins in a creaturely rebellion against God, not in some eternal dark force or evil god. For the believing Jew, God made all things and made them good, but once the human being chooses against God, evil becomes larger than the human being.

While it is difficult for us to understand this cosmic sense of evil and thus understand the background of the Gospels, we have in our culture some experiences that help us enter the religious world of Judaism at the time of the New Testament. One of those experiences is war. A visit to memorials now standing on the sites of Nazi death camps or the memorial at Hiroshima can allow us to sense the power of an evil larger than human, a power that almost compels us to massive destruction. Modern writers have reflected on the mystery of this force, which, once unleashed, can no longer be controlled and ends up changing once compassionate human beings into vicious killers. Such an experience reminds us that our view of evil as a form of human "sickness" might be a bit narrow.

In apocalyptic this evil is under God's control. The countervailing power of God's Spirit can effortlessly triumph over evil—if and when God so chooses. The whole point of apocalyptic is to elicit hope—even in a hopeless situation. The hope of apocalyptic is in God, simply because the present evil rages beyond the power of human beings.

To deal with the apparent delay of God's triumph, apocalyptic presupposes an almost deterministic view of history. It pictures the course of events as though written on a scroll, on which the events of the past and the future are detailed. As in the script of a play, the ending is assured, but the painful scenes of the present and near future must be acted out. The scroll is an image of God's absolute control over history and of his mysterious decision to allow "evil times."

The prevailing presupposition of apocalyptic, however, is that these evil times cannot last long. The delay of God's triumph will be brief. When an angel interpreter responds to Ezra's questions about how soon, the angel responds "Go ask a woman in her ninth month of pregnancy if she can hold her child much longer" (4 Ezra 4:40). This generation, according to apocalyptic, is the last one.

When Jesus appears preaching, "The kingdom of God is at hand!" (Mt 4:17; Mk 1:15), we must hear the apocalyptic alarm of the day. This is not simply an enlightened ethical teacher but rather a prophet appealing to the sensitivities of his day and proclaiming God's imminent and cosmic intervention to save.

(See exercises 4, 5.)

IV. Diaspora Judaism

The Temple, the Sacred Scriptures, and messianic apocalypticism in many ways form the central structures of the Judaism at the time of Jesus and the New Testament. Yet there is another angle vital for understanding the connection between Judaism and the New Testament writers. This is the Judaism in cities such as Antioch of Syria, Alexandria of Egypt, Athens and Corinth, and Rome—the centers around the empire outside of Israel where the Christian communities first developed. These Christian communities frequently developed from Jewish synagogues or from the work of Christian Jewish leaders like Paul of Tarsus. The Jews of these centers outside of Israel referred to themselves as the Jews of the dispersion or the Diaspora.

The Diaspora Judaism was a Judaism deeply influenced by the surrounding Hellenism. Few Jews in these communities had any ability to understand the Hebrew Scriptures or even their Aramaic translations. As a result, there developed several translations of the Bible in Greek, the most famous of which is the Septuagint, a Bible named for a legend about seventy translators and often designated by the Roman numeral LXX.

The Septuagint—or at least some form of it—became the Christian Bible. This was the Bible most often cited or alluded to by the writers of the New Testament. We can see this when we compare the LXX as we have it today and the Hebrew text of the Bible that we have today. Sometimes the two versions are quite different.

The most obvious difference consists of the actual books included in the two. The LXX contains a number of books not included in today's Hebrew version, such as the books of the Maccabees, the Wisdom of Solomon, the book of Ben Sirach, Tobit, Judith, as well as parts of Esther and Daniel. This difference between the Hebrew canon and the Greek canon lies behind the difference between Protestant and Catholic Old Testaments.

Even among the books common to the Hebrew Bible and the Greek Bible, significant differences appear in the texts. At first most scholars felt that these textual differences resulted from a faulty translation into the Greek. That opinion was challenged by the discovery of two Isaiah scrolls among the Dead Sea Scrolls, scrolls almost a thousand years older than the extant manuscripts behind today's Hebrew Bible. Many times where a difference exists between the Greek and the Hebrew texts, those Dead Sea Scrolls agree with the Greek against the Hebrew. Such data suggest that the differences between the Greek and the Hebrew were not the result simply of faulty translation but rather attest to a Hebrew textual tradition different from that behind the present Hebrew text, an ancient Hebrew tradition that was lost except for a witness to it in the present Greek text.

BOOKS IN THE SEPTUAGINT BUT NOT THE HEBREW BIBLE

1 and 2 Maccabees
Wisdom
Sirach
Tobit
Judith
Esther (parts)
Daniel (parts)

Figure 15.

The influence of Hellenism on the Diaspora Jews shows up also in many new issues discussed and documented by their writers. Philo of Alexandria, a Jew more or less contemporary with Paul of Tarsus, wrote several long treatises comparing the Mosaic faith to Greek philosophy. Reflecting on the many personifications of "the Word of God" in the Bible (e.g., Is 55:10–11), Philo suggested that we could call this Word "the second God," much like the figure of the Demiurge in Plato's philosophy (*Questions and Answers on Genesis* 2.62). An unknown Jewish author speculating on the wisdom of Solomon speaks of divine Wisdom as "the artificer of all" (Wis 7:22) and then continues the description of Wisdom as the perfect image of God who "can do all things" (see Wis 7:22–8:1). The author of the Wisdom of Solomon is developing a theme in Hellenistic Judaism that had been brewing both in and away from Israel for several hundred years under the influence of Hellenistic speculations about the origins of the universe. We find similar descriptions of divine wisdom in the first nine chapters of the book of Proverbs, the last section to be included in the book.

This speculation on the wisdom and word of God will have profound influence on the attempts of Christian thinkers to understand Jesus. Writers such as Paul of Tarsus or the author of the Fourth Gospel appear to draw directly on this divine wisdom and word speculation to find vocabulary to express their faith.

(See exercises 6, 7.)

V. Theological Reflections

To see the way the study of the New Testament leads naturally to the study of contemporary Judaism is a reminder that even the religious message of the New Testament emerges from history. Again we glimpse God revealing himself in and through history rather than plopping a message down out of eternity.

For those who accept the divine revelation of the Old Testament, the Jewish roots of the New Testament seem understandable. But the Judaism at the time of Jesus is not the Old Testament; it is an extension of that Old Testament. Most importantly, it is a medium by which the Old Testament enters the New.

For the most part (with the exceptions of Daniel, 1–2 Maccabees, and Wisdom) the writings of this time were not accepted into any Old Testament canon. On the other hand, trying to carve up the writings into "biblical and nonbiblical," into divinely guided Israelite history and secular Jewish history is artificial. In Israelite history and in its extensions—even to the modern day—we are dealing with a divinely privileged culture. At the time of the New Testament we see a culture marked by sin and rejection of divine gifts, but that mark can be traced back to the time of David and Moses. In some mysterious way, this culture is special by its own roots in the great Mosaic revelations. As the apostle Paul writes of his contemporary kinsmen:

> Theirs is the sonship, the glory, the covenants, the Law,
> the worship and the promises. Theirs the patriarchs.
> (Rom 9:4–5)

In a Christian perspective, this culture becomes theologically more significant. This is the culture that allowed Jesus to be who he was and to preach the nearness of "the kingdom." Without this culture and its concepts, the gospel as we have it would be "unthinkable." Just as Jesus drew his body from a Jewish woman, he drew his message from a Jewish background. And that relationship to Jesus draws this culture deeper into divine revelation. As Paul concludes in his warning to respect the Jews of his time, "From them is Christ according to the flesh" (Rom 9:5).

EXERCISES

Exercise 1. (see pages 99–101): Read 1 Kings 6–7 for the description of Solomon's Temple. From the complicated descriptions in this text, picture in your mind or diagram on paper the Temple. Remember that a cubit is about a foot and a half.

Exercise 2. (see pages 99–101): Look for references to the Temple in Luke 1–2. How do these brief references fit our knowledge of the Temple as a whole?

Exercise 3. (see pages 102–105): Read Psalm 119. This long prayer celebrates the Law. Imagine what would have been in Jesus' mind as he prayed this Psalm.

Exercise 4. (see pages 108–109): Read Daniel 7–12 and note the typical apocalyptic elements of this text. What terms used in this Old Testament text are echoed in the preaching of Jesus?

Exercise 5. (see pages 108–109): John the Baptist, a contemporary of Jesus, is described in Mt 3:1–12. Comparing him to the groups we have studied as a grid, how would you identify John?

Exercise 6. (see pages 99–111): Read Matthew 22–23. List the Jewish groups in these chapters portrayed as questioning and challenging Jesus. How do their questions and challenges reflect their background?

Exercise 7. (see pages 102–111): Read Matthew 1–2. Note the places where this Gospel cites the Old Testament. Why does Matthew do this?

REVIEW QUESTIONS

1. Identify the Pharisees, the Sadducees, the Zealots, and the Essenes. Describe what we know—if anything—about their distinctive social status and their attitude toward the Bible.

2. Describe the positioning of the courts and buildings of the Jerusalem Temple at the time of Jesus.

3. Briefly describe the divisions of the Jewish Scriptures at the time of Jesus. What is the relative importance of those parts?

4. What is the Septuagint? Where does it fit in Jewish culture?

5. What are the various shades of meaning of the word *messiah* in terms of its historical origin and its function at the time of Jesus? What various forms did the image of a messiah have in New Testament times? What is the relationship between the words *christ* and *messiah?*

6. What are the main characteristics of Jewish apocalyptic?

FOR FURTHER REFLECTION AND DISCUSSION

1. We often refer to a Christian church as a temple. *What similarities exist between a church and the ancient Jerusalem Temple? What similarities do you think should exist? What differences exist or in your view should exist?*

2. What similarities exist or should exist between a Christian church and the Jewish synagogue? What differences?

3. What groups today appear to be expecting the end of the world quickly? How do their attitudes compare to the apocalyptic attitudes at the time of Jesus?

7

The Gospel of Matthew

We turn now to the Gospel of Matthew. After looking at the evidence to determine the historical situation of the text, we will look at the principal and distinctive themes of this Gospel. In this Gospel we will find a strong reflection of the Jewish background examined in the last chapter.

I. History and Overview

A. The Author

We run into the same complexity as we did for the Gospel of Mark when we ask, Who wrote this Gospel? Tradition gives us one answer; a critical examination gives us another.

1. The Traditional Answer

Early church writers traditionally identify the author of the first Gospel as Matthew the apostle of Jesus, a person who was with the Lord and later wrote down his memoirs. The earliest witness to this identification comes to us from Irenaeus, writing toward the end of the second century. Irenaeus writes of the apostles, "proclaiming the good things we have from God and announcing to men the heavenly peace." In this context he then writes:

> Matthew edited a writing of the Gospel among the Hebrews in their own language, while Peter and Paul were preaching the Gospel in Rome and founding the Church. (*Against Heresies* 3.1.1)

Some fifty years later the great Christian writer Origen wrote:

The first [Gospel] is written according to Matthew, the same that was once a publican, but afterwards an apostle of Jesus Christ, who having published it for the Jewish converts, wrote it in the Hebrew.

These words of Origen we have only through Eusebius (*History* 6.25), who apparently is quoting Origen's *Commentary on the Gospel of Matthew* at a part we no longer have.

2. *The Critical Answer*

If we accept the two-source theory (see above), we are confronted by a major difficulty with the traditional answer. Why would an eyewitness and apostle rely so heavily on written sources? Some 80 percent of Matthew's Gospel appears to be copied either from Mark or Q. Even the story of the call of Matthew (Mt 9:9–13) is copied almost word for word from Mk 2:14–17. An eyewitness and apostle would hardly tell the story of his experiences by copying from another account.

Were we not to accept the two-source theory, we would still be confronted with the same difficulties we saw in Mark—namely, the material still does not look like the account of an eyewitness. It has the earmarks of oral tradition.

The text of this Gospel does, however, contain an interesting connection with the apostle Matthew. The story of Jesus calling the tax collector to discipleship, which appears in all three Synoptic Gospels (Mt 9:9–13; Mk 2:14–17; and Lk 5:27–32) is virtually identical except for the name of the tax collector. Mark and Luke name him Levi. Matthew names him Matthew. All three Gospels include a list of the Twelve (Mt 10:2–5; Mk 3:16–19; Lk 6:13–16), and in all three lists we find the name Matthew. Matthew's list of the Twelve, however, is the only one to include the expression "Matthew the tax collector" (Mt 10:3). Mark and Luke generally give us the impression that Levi was a disciple along with the Twelve. Only Matthew clearly identifies this tax collector as one of the Twelve, and specifically as the apostle Matthew.

This special information about Matthew the apostle could indicate some link between the writer of this Gospel and the apostle. Some have suggested that this Gospel arose in a "school of interpretation" that developed around this apostle.

A simpler explanation, however, is available, and it is connected with role of the twelve apostles in this Gospel. In this first Gospel the twelve apostles are the only disciples of Jesus. Jesus surrounded by the Twelve appears to be a symbolic picture suggesting intense continuity with Israel and the twelve tribes. When Jesus later promises his disciples that they will "sit on twelve thrones to judge [i.e., govern] the twelve tribes of Israel" (Mt 19:28; also Lk 22:30), we see how the Twelve in this Gospel function to link the church to Israel. The presence of Levi among the disciples following Jesus in Mark and Luke, however, clearly shows the presence of more disciples than the Twelve—since there is no hint of an identification of this tax collector with any of the Twelve. The First Gospel appears to solve this problem by identifying the tax collector with Matthew.

The evidence leads us to see the actual writer of this Gospel as an unnamed Christian scribe—perhaps remotely connected with the apostle Matthew—who had Mark's Gospel and Q along with other sources and who elaborates his own interpreted picture of Jesus, a picture situating Jesus especially in the traditions of the Old Testament. Perhaps the description of Mt 13:32 is an autobiographical hint:

> Every scribe learned in the reign of God is like the head
> of a household who can bring from his storeroom both the
> new and the old.

We shall for simplicity's sake continue to call him Matthew.

B. The Readers

As we noted above, the explanation of Jewish customs in Mk 7:2–5 suggests that Mark's Gospel was destined for a Gentile audience. When we look at the parallel in Mt 15:2 we find the explanations deleted. Several other times Matthew refers to Jewish practices—the work of the priests on the Sabbath (12:3), the tithes (23:25), even the diverse dialects (26:73)—without a word of explanation. We also find Matthew deeply involved in Jewish issues: the fulfillment of the prophets (see especially 1:22–23; 2:15, 17–18, 23; 4:14–16; 8:17; 12:17–21; 13:35; 21:4–5; 27:9–10), the continuing validity of the Law even for Christians (5:17–19), and the practices of Jewish piety (6:1–8). Together these details argue strongly for a Jewish audience.

On the other hand, this Gospel does not look like an apologetic work, trying to prove the faith to nonbelievers. Matthew seems to presuppose faith in Jesus. We can therefore envisage the original readers addressed by this Gospel as a Jewish-Christian community, a conclusion that dovetails with the ancient tradition about this Gospel. If this is true, then Matthew's Gospel in effect gives us an insight into a branch of Christianity that died out as a separate branch, but which remains an authentic form of the faith, Jewish Christianity. This branch may also be responsible for an intense reappropriation into the Christian church in the next century of many Jewish practices, such as priesthood, sacrifice, and Temple.

The Gospel is written in a high-quality Greek, certainly superior to that of Mark. It does not look like a translation from an Aramaic document—despite the ancient tradition to that effect. When we look for a Greek-speaking Jewish-Christian community in the latter decades of the first century, the city of Antioch appears as a likely candidate. (See figure 16.) After the destruction of Jerusalem, this city and Syria in general became an important place of congregation for the Jewish Christians fleeing Judea.

(See exercise 1.)

C. The Date

Arguing from the two-source theory, we need to place the writing of this Gospel about ten years after Mark. A good decade would have allowed the Gospel of Mark to have been copied, published, and recognized as a trustworthy source. We thus place the writing of Matthew around A.D. 80.

When we look for references to the destruction of Jerusalem, we find ambiguous evidence. On the one hand, we seem to have a clear allusion to this destruction in Mt 22:7. The story of the great feast occurs in both Mt 22:1–10 and in Lk 14:16–24. From its simpler form, the Lucan version appears to be closer to the original Q. The Matthean detail about an army sent to burn the city thus appears as an addition. Such an addition would be very comprehensible after the disaster of A.D. 70.

On the other hand, Matthew's eschatological discourse in chapter 24 stays very close to Mark 13, even with its tight connection between the end of the world and the destruction of the Temple. We used this tight connection to argue that Mark was composed shortly before the destruction of A.D. 70. We could possibly argue the same with Matthew. In the case of Matthew, however, this argument is weakened by the fact that Matthew is repeating his source. Details added by an author generally form a better indication of his

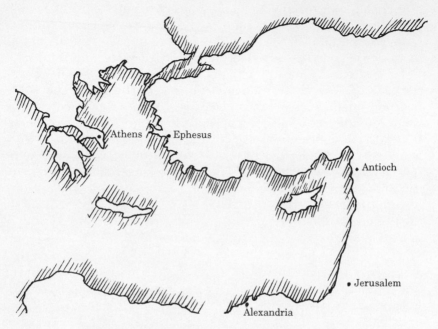

Figure 16. **Antioch in the ancient Near East.**

special viewpoint. Details repeated by an author from his source may indicate his viewpoint or may simply indicate his fidelity to a source. As we will see below, the parables that Matthew attached to this eschatological discourse after the Marcan material suggest a date sometime after the destruction of the Temple.

The evidence in general thus points to the 80s as the time of writing for this Gospel.

D. The Structure and Outline of the Gospel

Finding the structure or outline of this Gospel as the author intended it poses a special problem, which lies behind the wide variety of outline proposals found in modern studies of Matthew. The difficulty consists in the fact that Matthew used preexisting structured material instead of small bricks that can be incorporated easily into the plan of a builder.

This Gospel in a way reminds us of churches today found in places such as Rome or Athens, where ancient Roman and Greek temples—sometimes in ruins—were converted into churches. Parts of the peristyle still encircle the building, with the spaces between the columns now filled in to form outside walls. A Christian steeple rises above the triangular temple face. It does not, however, take too much training to identify the Christian architectural unity that incorporates the older, distorted temple unity.

If Matthew incorporated Mark into the new Gospel, we can expect to see traces of the old structure of Mark still appearing in Matthew, for example, the three predictions of the passion, but this old structure is now distorted from its original symmetry. We need to find the structure that gives an organization to the whole of Matthew, not just to the Marcan material. We need to find Matthew's symmetrical plan.

The clue to that structure lies in a refrain that occurs five times:

—"And it happened when Jesus finished those words..." (7:28).
—"And it happened when Jesus finished instructing his twelve disciples, he left from there..." (11:1).
—"And it happened when Jesus finished those parables, he left from there..." (13:53).
—"And it happened when Jesus finished those words, he left Galilee..." (19:1).

—"And it happened when Jesus finished all those words…" (26:1).

This refrain concludes five major discourses of Jesus in this Gospel: (1) the Sermon on the Mount (chapters 5–7), (2) the mission of the disciples (chapter 10), (3) the parables of the kingdom (chapter 13), (4) the community of the disciples (chapter 18), and (5) the eschatological discourse (chapters 24–25). While Jesus gives instructions throughout the Gospel, in these five sections Jesus only talks. Very little action occurs.

These five discourses function as the great pillars supporting the whole Gospel. Preceding and following these discourses is narrative material, mostly descriptions of Jesus' activities. Furthermore, both the discourses and the narratives relate to one another in an intricate form. The first discourse, for example, explaining the foundation of the kingdom, relates to the last discourse describing the climax of that kingdom. In the first, we pray that the kingdom come; in the last, it comes. The second discourse, about the activities of the disciples toward outsiders, corresponds to the second-last discourse, about the activities of the disciples toward each other. The third discourse stands in the center in a pivotal position. The five discourses relate to each other according to the pattern A, B, C, B´, A´. Scholars call this type of composition, common in ancient writings, a *chiasm* or a *chiastic structure,* from the Greek letter *chi* (X). It consists in a form of inverted symmetry, often with a central element that gives a focus to the whole composition.

CHIASTIC STRUCTURE

a

   b

      c

   b´

a´

Figure 17.

When examined closely, the narratives themselves appear to follow this chiastic structure. The opening narrative, chapters 1–4, deals especially with the infancy of Jesus. This infancy story is dominated by the figure of Herod, who attempts to destroy Jesus. Matthew adds the detail, "King Herod became greatly disturbed, and with him all Jerusalem" (2:3). This narrative thus anticipates and prepares us for the passion and death of Jesus in Jerusalem in the final narrative, chapters 26–28. Similarly, the only hint of the universalism proclaimed in the last lines of the Gospel can be found as an anticipation in the story of the Gentile magi of the opening narrative.

Thus Matthew appears to have composed his Gospel according to the following plan:

I. NARRATIVE: The Beginnings (1:1–4:25)
   A. The genealogy (1:1–17)
   B. The infancy narrative (1:18–2:23)
   C. John the Baptist, the baptism of Jesus, the temptation (3:1–4:11)
   D. The opening of the ministry and the first disciples (4:12–22)

II. DISCOURSE: The Sermon on the Mount (chapters 5–7)

III. NARRATIVE: The Miracles of Christ and the Following by the Apostles (8:1–9:35)

IV. DISCOURSE: The Mission of the Disciples (9:36–10:42)

V. NARRATIVE: The Rejection of the Pseudo-Israel (chapters 11–12)

VI. DISCOURSE: The Parables of the Kingdom (chapter 13)

V´. NARRATIVE: The Partial Faith and Understanding of the Disciples (13:53–17:27)

IV´. DISCOURSE: The Community of the Disciples (chapter 18)

III´. NARRATIVE: The Kingdom Taken Away and Given to Others (chapters 19–23)
   A. Moving to Jerusalem (chapters 19–20)
   B. In Jerusalem (chapters 21–23)
II´. DISCOURSE: The End of the World (chapters 24–25)
   A. The description of the end (24:1–31)
   B. Seven parables of vigilance (24:32–25:46)
I´. NARRATIVE: The Passion and Resurrection (chapters 26–28)

A. The conspiracy and the Last Supper (26:1–35)
B. The arrest, trials, and death of Jesus (26:36–27:61)
C. The resurrection (chapter 28)

II. The Faith of Matthew

A. Matthew's Christology

Matthew's christology is complex. It differs from Mark's in several important and distinctive ways. Our purpose in this introductory study is to get a sense of the unique character of this Gospel; hence, we will look at only two traits, Jesus as the Messiah and Jesus as Son of God.

1. Jesus, the Messiah

Matthew's Jewish character appears very clearly in his insistence that Jesus is the Messiah, the Christ or "anointed one," designated by God to save his people. Matthew uses the title Christ for Jesus far more frequently (fourteen times) than either of the other Synoptics. He applies this title especially with the article, "the Christ," thus preserving its function as a description of Jesus' role, not simply as a second name for Jesus (as in later writings).

A second clear designation of the Messiah, "son of David," is used only by Matthew. Not all the Jewish groups at the time of Jesus or before expected a Davidic messiah, an anointed one who would come from the lineage of David or according to the model of David. As we saw in the previous chapter, however, some clearly did expect such a messiah.

Matthew uses this title in the very opening line of his Gospel, along with Son of Abraham (1:1). He uses it on the lips of the crowd, acclaiming Jesus on "Palm Sunday" (21:9, 15). He uses it especially on the lips of little people, people of minor account in the eyes of contemporaries: the two blind men in Galilee (9:27), the Syro-Phoenician woman (15:22), the two blind men at Jericho (20:30–31), and the children in the Temple (21:15). As the new Davidic king, Jesus has a very humble constituency.

An interesting tension appears, however, when we look at the genealogy that Matthew gives. The purpose of this genealogy is clearly to show that Jesus is the Messiah. The designation forms an inclusion to the list of ancestors (1:1 and 17). Matthew emphasizes David's place in this genealogy (1:17) and therefore is explaining how

Jesus is truly Son of David (1:1). According to Matthew, however, Jesus is not begotten by Joseph, the last natural descendent of David in Jesus' line. In the genealogy Matthew avoids describing Joseph as the natural father of Jesus, and in the narration that follows, Matthew describes the virginal conception of Jesus. Matthew is dealing with two apparently conflicting traditions, Jesus as descendant of David, and Jesus as virginally conceived. Matthew reconciles the two traditions by a simple detail. He has Joseph, the son of David (1:20), name the child (1:21, 25). By so doing Joseph accepts the child as his and confers on the child all the rights of the Davidic family. By contrast, it is Mary in Luke's Gospel (Lk 1:31) and the "maiden mother" in the original prophecy of Isaiah (Is 7:14) who name the child.

A third way by which Matthew insists on Jesus as the Messiah appears in Matthew's use of the Old Testament. Matthew cites the Old Testament far more often (thirty-six times) than all the other Gospels combined. He is clearly insisting on the continuity between the story of Jesus and the story of Israel. Of those citations, ten stand out by their special form (1:22–23; 2:15, 17–18, 23; 4:14–16; 8:17; 12:17–21; 13:35; 21:4–5; 27:9–10). All ten begin with a formula something like, "This was to fulfill what was spoken...." In all ten the speaker is Matthew himself, who interrupts the narration to point out this fulfillment of prophecy. These *reflection citations,* as scholars call them, show Matthew's intense concern about situating Jesus in the current of the Old Testament and thus identifying him as the promised Messiah.

The use of the Old Testament by Matthew is a subject of much study. A brief comparison of the texts as cited by the evangelists and as found in the Old Testament (either in the Hebrew or the Greek) shows many discrepancies. Did Matthew have another version of these texts different from those we have? Did he freely modify the texts to bring out even greater correspondence between them and Jesus? Was there an accepted technique of scriptural study at the time of Matthew that involved both the free interpretation of a text and the incorporation of that interpretation back into the original text? Such a procedure, called *pesher,* was discovered among the Dead Sea scrolls at Qumran (see "The Habakkuk Scroll").

(See exercise 2.)

2. Jesus, the Majestic Son of God

The freedom with which Matthew uses his source, Mark, constitutes the method by which Matthew expresses a second—

although related—aspect of Jesus. Jesus is the recognized Son of God, not in the mysterious veiled mode of Mark, but in a manner by which his disciples can recognize this aspect. He is Son of God likewise in a powerful and majestic way.

Except at the opening of the Gospel, Matthew repeats the key texts of Mark that call Jesus "Son of God." At the baptism scene, however, the divine announcement is directed to the bystanders, not to Jesus alone, as in Mark. Compare the following parallel texts:

> And a voice came from heaven, "You are my Son, the Beloved; with you I am well pleased." (Mk 1:11)

> And a voice from heaven said, "This is my Son, the Beloved, with whom I am well pleased." (Mk 3:17)

If Matthew is receiving his information about this scene from Mark, he is changing an intimate communication of God to Jesus into a public proclamation of the identity of Jesus. This changes a communication presumably giving Jesus information he did not know before into a pronouncement to anyone willing to listen. In Matthew's Gospel Jesus presumably does not need this information.

In this Gospel we are not surprised to hear the disciples during the ministry of Jesus confess him as the Son of God:

> And those in the boat worshiped him, saying, "Truly you are the Son of God." (14:33)

> Simon Peter answered, "You are the Messiah, the Son of the living God." (16:16)

These confessions are not in Mark's Gospel, although Mark has these same stories. Outside of these confessions, Matthew shows complete dependence on Mark's Gospel for his knowledge of the stories.

In Matthew's Gospel we also hear Jesus refer to God as his Father. Some of these examples are in stories that only Matthew has:

> Do not despise one of these little ones; for, I tell you, in heaven their angels continually see the face of my Father in heaven. (18:10)

> Again, truly I tell you, if two of you agree on earth about anything you ask, it will be done for you by my Father in heaven. (18:19)

Do you not think that I cannot appeal to my Father, and he will at once send me more than twelve legions of angels? (26:53)

Others are in stories where this relationship is apparently added by Matthew:

Not everyone who says to me, "Lord, Lord," shall enter the kingdom of heaven, but he who does the will of my Father who is in heaven. (7:21)

Compare this text to the Q text as we have it in Luke:

Why do you call me "Lord, Lord," and not do what I tell you? (Luke 6:46)

Similarly, Matthew's Jesus at the Last Supper says,

I shall not drink again of this fruit of the vine until that day when I drink it new with you in my Father's kingdom. (26:29)

In Mark, the source of this text, we read,

I shall not drink again of the fruit of the vine until that day when I drink it new in the kingdom of God. (Mark 14:25)

Clearly Matthew wishes to stress this relationship of Jesus as Son of God.

Connected with this title are a special majesty and transcendence which radiate from the Matthean Jesus. Matthew consistently drops references to Jesus' emotions. Unlike the Marcan story, the account of Jesus healing the man with the withered hand (Mt 12:9–14) no longer refers to Jesus looking "around at them with anger, grieved at their hardness of heart" (Mk 3:5).

Similarly the Matthean Jesus questions less than does the Marcan Jesus. Instead, Matthew prefers to describe Jesus giving a command. This shift appears clearly in the contrast between the question in Mark and the command in Matthew regarding the preparation for the Jerusalem Passover:

The Teacher says, "Where is my guest room, where I am to eat the Passover with my disciples?" (Mk 14:14)

The Teacher says, "My time is at hand; I will keep the Passover at your house with my disciples." (Mt 26:18)

It is the grand finale of this Gospel, however, that epitomizes the majesty of this Son of God:

Full authority has been given to me both in heaven and on earth; go, therefore, and make disciples of all nations.... Teach them to carry out everything I have commanded you. And know that I am with you always, until the end of the world! (28:18–20)

The Matthean Jesus is somewhat less human than the Marcan Jesus, but a great deal more kingly. The magi had come seeking "the newborn king of the Jews" (2:2). When he appeared preaching and teaching the Law of God, the crowds were astonished at his authority (7:28–29).

B. Matthew's Soteriology: The Passion and Death of Jesus

Mark insisted, as we saw, on the passion and death of Jesus, underlining especially the darkness and hiddenness of this mystery. Matthew reproduces almost all of Mark's descriptions of these final scenes but adds a number of scenes and details where his particular interpretation of the events is expressed. To understand the mind of Matthew, we will focus on the descriptions special to this evangelist.

(See exercise 3.)

1. Judas and the Thirty Pieces of Silver

From Mark's Gospel, Matthew reproduces the meeting of Judas with the chief priests but adds the details of the chief priests actually paying Judas a sum of thirty pieces of silver (Mt 26:14–16; Mk 14:10–11). These details prepare for the scene unique to Matthew, that of Judas' death (27:3–10). In this second scene, Matthew mentions the sum of money five more times. Matthew describes Judas throwing the money into the Temple, refers to the Temple treasury, and adds a reflection citation curiously named as from Jeremiah, but which clearly paraphrases a story from Zechariah:

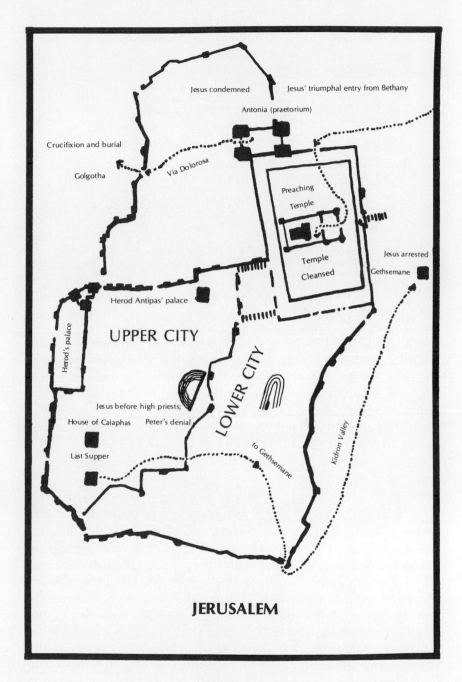

Figure 18.

And they took the thirty pieces of silver, the price of him
on whom a price had been set by some of the sons of
Israel, and they gave them for the potter's field, as the
Lord directed me. (27:9–10)

The extended text of Zechariah gives us the clue to the meaning of this scene for Matthew:

Then I took my staff "Favor" and snapped it asunder,
breaking off the covenant which I had made with all peoples; that day it was broken off. The sheep merchants
who were watching me understood that this was the
word of the Lord. I said to them, "If it seems good to you,
give me my wages; but if not, let it go." And they counted
out my wages, thirty pieces of silver. But the Lord said to
me, "Throw it in the treasury, the handsome price at
which they valued me." So I took the thirty pieces of silver and threw them into the treasury in the house of the
Lord. (Zec 11:10–13)

The influence of this text from Zechariah on Matthew's scene is
clear from a number of the common details. In Zechariah, the scene
describes the breaking of a covenant between God and his people;
both the snapping of the staff and the thirty pieces of silver represent that break. Matthew also saw in the story of Judas not just an
individual tragedy but a drama of national proportions, a breaking
of the covenant between God and his people.

2. The Roman Trial

After the death of Judas, Matthew rejoins the Marcan narrative and begins the Roman trial (Mt 27:11–26; Mk 15:2–15). The
additions of Matthew are striking and follow the same point, an
insistence on the Jewish responsibility for the death of Jesus:

(a) Matthew introduces the wife of Pilate, who intercedes for
Jesus, "Have nothing to do with that righteous man, for I have suffered much over him today in a dream" (27:19). Meanwhile "the
chief priests and the elders" outside are seeking to destroy Jesus
(27:20).

(b) Matthew adds the scene of Pilate washing his hands and
declaring "I am innocent of this man's blood" (27:24).

(c) Matthew adds the chilling response of the people to Pilate's gesture, "His blood be on us and on our children" (27:25). It is "all" who cry out, "Let him be crucified" (27:22).

Of all the Gospels, Matthew's is the most brutal in its portrayal of the Jews at the time of Jesus. This Gospel has been the basis for many of the lines in modern "passion plays" which today are seen as "anti-Semitic." In fact this Gospel has been cited more than any other text to justify oppression of the Jewish people. Often forgotten, however, is the fact that Matthew himself seems to have been a Jew writing for Jewish Christians.

3. The Theological Intention

Often forgotten also is the theological intention of this author. The details of the stories, whether historically accurate or not, are meant to lead us to understand God's dealings with humanity, to understand God's plan in history.

This theological intention of Matthew appears in one of the final arguments between Jesus and the Jewish leaders. After he has cleaned out the Temple (21:12–17), cursed the tree for not bearing fruit (21:18–22), and compared the leaders both to a son who is "all mouth" but does nothing (21:28–32) and to the vineyard tenants who murder and steal (21:33–42), Jesus then solemnly declares:

> For this reason, I tell you, the kingdom of God will be taken away from you and given to a nation that will yield a rich harvest. (21:43)

Earlier in the Gospel, Matthew insisted on the restricted scope of both Jesus' mission and that of his disciples. The disciples are instructed, "Do not visit pagan territory and do not enter a Samaritan town. Go instead after the lost sheep of the house of Israel" (10:5–6). Speaking to the Syro-Phoenician woman, he declares, "My mission is only to the lost sheep of the house of Israel" (15:24).

Yet the last scene of the Gospel describes the universal scope of the disciples new mission, "Go, therefore, and make disciples of all the nations" (28:19). After the death of Jesus, the mission has changed. Just as Jesus announced, no longer will the kingdom be the exclusive possession of Israel. Now the Gospel is for all nations.

In between these opposite positions occurs the narration of the passion and death of Jesus with its insistence on the Jewish role, now seen as a breaking of a covenant and a shift in "ownership" of the kingdom. Matthew, therefore, has a theological reason for insisting on the Jewish responsibility for the death of Jesus.

At first glance it would appear that the Jews are now excluded from this kingdom—"taken from you and given to a nation bearing fruit." Yet Matthew is a Jew writing to Jewish Christians. The line dividing insiders and outsiders is not so clearly drawn as dividing ethnic groups. In effect, the tragic rejection by the Jews of their Messiah has resulted in a great blessing on *all*. A previous exclusive covenant has been broken, but a new and greater one takes its place, one that is universal in scope: "Go teach all nations." No nation is excluded. We hear a tone of sadness in Matthew's description of his own people's tragedy, but we also hear him express his faith in God "writing straight with crooked lines."

C. Matthew's Eschatology

(See exercise 4.)

Matthew's actual description of the end of the world in 24:1–36 is very close to his presumed source in Mk 13:1–32. Some changes in this description, however, seem motivated by a shift of understanding regarding the end. Even more significant, however, Matthew adds a series of parables in the rest of chapters 24–25 that provide us with his own understanding. Two ideas stand out in these parables: vigilance and delay.

1. Changes to Mark 13

A number of changes occur in Matthew's copy of Mark 13 that appear as attempts simply to clarify the meaning of obscure Marcan statements. For instance, the question of the disciples in Mt 24:3 is clearly about the events for which information is sought. The disciples in Matthew want information about the destruction of the Temple, which Jesus has just predicted, and about "your coming and the close of the age." Compare this question to the vagueness in Mk 13:4. We see a similar clarification in the warning of Mt 24:4 compared with the parallel in Mk 13:6.

Other changes, however, seem to reflect the issue of the timing of the "end of the age." One such change occurs in Matthew's copy of Mk 13:9–13. In Mark these verses reflect the persecutions and other forms of hostility that lead up to the end. Matthew repeats that text of Mark, but he places it in chapter 10, where Jesus instructs his disciples as he sends them out to preach the Gospel. The wording is almost identical. The context is different. By changing the context,

Matthew changes the meaning of the description. No longer are these persecutions and hostilities signs of the approaching end. In Matthew 10 they are signs only that the disciples are doing what Jesus has instructed them to do. Matthew has "de-eschatologized" these persecutions. When these sufferings happen, we are no longer to look on them as signs of the end.

COMPARISON OF MATTHEW 24:3–4 WITH MARK 13:4–6

Mt 24:3	**Mk 13:4**
However, as he sat on	As he sat on
the Mount of Olives	the Mount of Olives
	facing the temple
the disciples approached	Peter and James and John and Andrew
him privately, saying,	asked him privately,
tell us when these things	tell us when these things
will be and what is the	will be and what is the
sign of your coming and	sign when all these things will
the end of the age.	come to an end.
Mt 24:5	**Mk 13:6**
For many will come	Many will come
in my name saying,	in my name saying,
I am the Christ.	I am he.
And many will be	And many will be
deceived.	deceived.

Figure 19.

---

2. The Parables of Vigilance Despite Delay

If we turn to the series of parables that now follow the description of the end, we see the consistent theme of vigilance. The first is the parable of the fig tree (24:32–33). Except for one important word, Matthew reproduces it almost verbatim from Mk 13:28–29. Matthew changes Mark's expression, "when you see these things," to "when you see *all* these things." As in Mark, the reference is to the signs preliminary to the end, except now the preliminary signs must include the cosmic upheavals, not just the wars and destruction of Jerusalem.

The second parable (Mt 24:37–41) consists of a comparison with the story of Noah. Matthew has this story as well as the next two from Q. The story stresses the suddenness of the end and how normal activity in this world can distract from preparations for this end.

The third parable (Mt 24:42–44) of the householder waiting for a thief points to the need for intense vigilance, precisely because the hour of arrival is unknown. Matthew adds a night setting, which heightens the concern for the unexpected.

The fourth parable (Mt 24:45–51), taken from Q (cf. Lk 12:42–46), begins the theme of delay by contrasting two servants waiting for their master to return. The wise servant cares for his master's household. The second does not because of a fatal miscalculation: "My master is delayed" (24:48).

The fifth parable (Mt 25:1–13) is unique to Matthew. It is the story of the ten maidens, five wise and five foolish. The foolish are manifested as such because of a critical detail in the story, "the bridegroom was delayed" (25:5).

The sixth parable (Mt 25:14–30), again from Q, is about the talents. It is the story about responsible and productive use of the master's goods while he is away. Matthew adds the detail that the master returned to settle accounts only "after a long time" (25:19).

In all of these parables thus far, we see the unmistakable lesson about vigilance. In the last three, however, a new theme is appearing, the element of delay. Matthew appears to be dealing with what is becoming more and more a serious problem for the early Christians: Why has Christ not come back? (see 2 Pt 3:3–9). Matthew gives no answer to this question, but he is clearly facing this problem. Christ has not come back as soon as expected. Those who think this delay justifies relaxing vigilance are mistaken. They must be vigilant, but they must also be ready for a wait.

3. The Interim Ethic

The final eschatological parable returns to a thought briefly touched on in some of the preceding parables but now developed with burning clarity. The wise servant or steward is distinguished by his care of the household while the master was away. The parable of the talents insisted on responsible and productive activity as the servants waited for the master. Now by constant repetition, this final parable will insist on the type of responsible and practical love that constitutes true vigilance. This is the parable of the sheep and goats at the last judgment, a parable unique to Matthew (25:31–46).

Four times Matthew names the type of care expected by the Lord:

> I was hungry and you gave me food, I was thirsty and you
> gave me drink, I was a stranger and you welcomed me, I
> was naked and you clothed me, I was sick and you visited
> me, I was in prison and you came to me. (25:35–36)

Surprisingly, nothing in the list deals directly with a religious attitude, nothing we would usually identify as an "eschatological vigil."

Furthermore, the sheep are surprised that this caring activity was in fact done to the Son of Man. Essential here is not the motive for the activity, whether it was explicitly religious or not, but the fact that it was done. "As you did it to one of the least of these my brothers, you did it to me.... As you did not do it to one of the least of these, you did not do it to me" (25:40, 45).

Scholars discuss the identity in Matthew's mind of "the least of my brothers." The disciples are called "brothers" by Jesus (28:10), and some of the members of the community are called "little ones" (18:6). However, the description of their needs in this parable leads us to think of all the poor.

Particularly in this last parable, Matthew is giving us a standard to live by, a standard to test what is a good life and what is a wicked life. Once the perspective of an extended life on earth before the Second Coming replaces that of an imminent return of Christ, such a standard becomes crucial. Where Christians see the end delayed, they must then ask what they are to do in the meantime. Christian ethics becomes important.

Matthew's standard reflects a practical attitude toward life. As later the Epistle of James would insist, don't just talk about your faith, show me it in action (Jas 2:14–17). This attitude is typically Jewish and is reflected throughout Matthew's Gospel. The Matthean Jesus teaches us to pray to God, "Your will be done" (6:10) and concludes the Sermon on the Mount with the admonition, "Anyone who hears my words and *puts them into practice* is like the wise man who built his house on rock" (7:24).

4. Calvary

When Matthew describes the death of Jesus on Calvary, he adds details that must be considered part of the eschatology of this Gospel. Matthew follows Mark carefully in his portrayal of the crucifixion and death of Jesus. After copying from Mark the mention of the Temple curtain's tear, Matthew adds the following details:

And the earth shook, and the rocks were split; the tombs also were opened, and many bodies of the saints who had fallen asleep were raised. And coming out of the tombs after his resurrection, they went into the holy city and appeared to many. (27:51–53)

Earthquakes and the resurrection of the dead are events scheduled for the end of the world. Matthew has them occur at the death of Jesus. Matthew thus provides an eschatological color to the crucifixion. This historical event becomes a brief anticipation of the end, a sudden flash of things to come.

Matthew knows that history continued after the death of Jesus. Those risen "saints who had fallen asleep" disappear in the story as mysteriously as they appeared. With this brief scene, however, Matthew begins an approach that will develop in later writers, an approach to the end that sees it as somehow already begun, already present in history without destroying history. The time after the crucifixion becomes in some way the "end-time" while continuing its course toward the great climax of Jesus return.

III. Theological Reflections

In the history of Christianity, Matthew's Gospel has been the favorite Gospel. It is cited by Christian writers far more often than the other Gospels. Its place as the First Gospel probably reflects that preference.

Matthew's is a conservative Gospel. Jesus here did not come to abolish the old ways but to fulfill them. Matthew's constant emphasis on the fulfillment of the scriptures is an appeal to faith in the constancy and consistency of God. On the surface there is turmoil and revolution, but Matthew is quick to point out that God had planned this long ago.

Matthew obviously loves his Jewish past and wants to see how it fits into his faith in Jesus. We are constantly reminded of Jesus' Jewishness as son of David, son of Abraham. Matthew's Gospel is the rebuttal of any Marcionite desire to replace Judaism with Christianity, to replace the Old Testament with the New. Matthew's Gospel tells us to find our Jewish roots if we are to understand our Christian life.

A century later, the Christian churches will make a concerted effort to reappropriate the Old Testament institutions. The Christian elder will be described as "priest." The Lord's Supper will be seen as "sacrifice." Christian assembly halls will be called "temples." Even much of the Jewish legalism will be imported into the church. Some will lament this development and periodically try to "purify" the church of such elements. Others will exploit this development and find a basis of power to rule. Perhaps a better understanding of Matthew's Gospel with its refrain of "fulfillment" will enable us to find the true balance.

The Jesus of this Gospel, of course, looks much more like the Christ of our faith than did the Marcan Jesus. "All power and authority" are given to him. Soon after this Gospel, we will portray him as the *pantocrator,* the all-powerful one. Jesus in this Gospel loses something of his closeness to our weak humanity, but he gains in his proximity to divine authority. "You heard it said,...but *I* say to you...."

It is God's powerful reign that we contemplate in this Gospel. While we no longer have the kingdom compared to the seed that grows secretly by itself (see Mk 4:26–29 with no parallel in Matthew or Luke), we still have this kingdom likened to the mustard seed (Mt 13:31–32) and the yeast (Mt 13:33), whose insignificant beginnings contrast so starkly with their glorious endings. Matthew wants us to see that glory more clearly. Twice we glimpse Jesus risen from the dead reassuring us of his triumph (Mt 28:9–10, 16–20). The glorious angel rolling back the stone of the grave also helps us overcome the darkness of death (Mt 28:2–3). The apostles are no longer models of

Jerusalem. A Herodian tomb with a rolling stone entry.

blindness, but reflect understanding and faith (Mt 13:51). The glorious Son of Man remains ahead of us, but his triumph is already manifest in this world. We are followers of this king.

EXERCISES

Exercise 1. (see pages 116–117): Read Matthew 5–7, the Sermon on the Mount. What topics in this section would be of great interest to a Jewish Christian and of less interest to a Gentile Christian?

Exercise 2. (see pages 122–123): Read Is 7:14 and compare it with Matthew's citation of the text in 1:23. In what way has the evangelist modified Is 7:14 to insist on the fulfillment of this prophecy? In the same way, compare Mic 5:2 with Mt 2:6; Hos 11:1 with Mt 2:15; and Jer 31:15 with Mt 2:18. Can you find an Old Testament text that corresponds to Mt 2:23?

Exercise 3. (see page 126): Read Matthew 26–27 and carefully compare it with Mark 14–15. What scenes have been added by Matthew? In the scenes common to both Gospels, what details are different in Matthew's version? Can you find a common thread to these differences?

Exercise 4. (see page 130): Read Matthew 24–25 and find the parallel sections in Mark 13. What is different in the Matthean text? Can you spot any differences, perhaps introduced to deal with the problem of "the delay" of Jesus' return?

REVIEW QUESTIONS

1. What is the overall structure of the Gospel of Matthew? What objective literary indications in the text lead to this structure?

2. How does tradition identify the author of the First Gospel? How does the two-source theory pose a problem for this identification?

3. How does Matthew insist on Jesus as the Jewish Messiah? In what way does Matthew change the text of Mark to insist on Jesus as a king?

4. In what other ways does Matthew's christology differ from Mark's? What texts substantiate your answer?

5. How does Matthew break the Marcan association of persecutions and hatred with the end of the world?

6. Which parables of vigilance in Matthew 24–25 suggest a concern for the delay of the end of the world? How else does Matthew's eschatology differ from Mark's?

7. How does Matthew change the text of Mark to insist on Jewish involvement in the death of Jesus?

8. What text is actually cited by Mt 27:9–10? How is this citation a key to understanding Matthew's view of the death of Jesus? What does this

text have to do with the shift in the scope of Jesus' mission? Where is this shift described in the Gospel of Matthew?

FOR FURTHER REFLECTION AND DISCUSSION

1. From very early times, the Gospel of Matthew, placed first, has been the favorite among Christians, cited more and known better than the other Gospels. Why do you think this is so?

2. Compared to Protestant prayer life, Catholic prayer life places more stress on such Jewish elements as priesthood, sacrifice, good works. What else in the very Jewish Gospel of Matthew could tend to make it a favorite of Catholics?

3. Jews today take offense at the anti-Semitic elements in the Gospel of Matthew, especially in its portrayal of the death of Jesus. How would you explain this Gospel to a Jewish friend?

8

The Gospel of Luke and the Acts of the Apostles

I. History and Overview

A. The Author

1. The Traditional Answer

An early tradition identifies the author of the Third Gospel as a man named Luke, a physician and companion of Paul. The earliest extant testimony to this tradition is a document called "The Anti-Marcionite Prologue" dated A.D. 160–180. It reads:

> Luke, a Syrian of Antioch, doctor by profession, was the disciple of the Apostles. At a later date he was the disciple of Paul until the death of the latter. After having served the Lord without fault and never having married, he died, full of the Holy Spirit, at Boeotia, aged eighty-four. As gospels had already been written by Matthew in Judea and by Mark in Italy, Luke, under the impulse of the Holy Spirit, wrote his gospel in the region of Achaia. In the prologue he shows that other gospels had been written before his, but that it was necessary to present to the faithful converted from paganism an exact account of the economy of salvation, lest they should be impeded by Jewish fables or caused to stray from the truth by the deceits of heretics.

Toward the end of the second century A.D., Irenaeus wrote, "Luke, the companion of Paul, wrote the latter's gospel in a book" (*Against the Heresies* 3.1.1).

2. The Critical Answer

(See exercise 1.)

The opening lines of the Gospel tell us a little about the writer. He describes himself as a researcher, using more than one written source. The writer also distinguishes himself from the "original eyewitnesses and ministers of the word" (1:2).

Do we find in the texts any support for the traditional identification of this writer with the companion of Paul? In a critical examination we note three things:

(a) The author of the Third Gospel also wrote the Acts of the Apostles. This is clear from the opening lines of both writings, which refer to a Theophilus as the recipient of the work. The opening of Acts refers to an earlier account that sounds like the Gospel. This is very important, because it tells us to see the Gospel and the Acts as two parts of a whole. The first part describes the life of Jesus; the second part, the work of the disciples after Jesus. In our search for the message of Luke, then, we can examine both the Gospel and Acts. Unfortunately, this continuity is broken by the Gospel of John, now interposed between the two Lucan writings.

(b) Paul names a Luke as one of his companions in the last years of his mission (Phlm 24). Colossians 4:14 describes this Luke as "our beloved physician" and as a Gentile. 2 Timothy 4:11 places Luke with Paul during his final days in a Roman prison; however, nothing in the Third Gospel or in Acts identifies the name of the author. The tradition that associates the author with Paul is the only source for the name Luke.

(c) In 16:10 Acts begins a series of descriptions of Paul from the perspective of a companion: "After this vision, we immediately made efforts to cross to Macedonia." These "we-passages" continue intermittently through the end of Acts (16:10–17; 20:5–15; 21:1–18; 27:1–28:16). Taken together with the conclusion that the author of Acts is the author of the Third Gospel, these passages provide a possibility for the traditional answer identifying the author as Luke, the companion of Paul. The "we-passages," however, admit another explanation, namely, that the author of Luke-Acts used a journal or travel diary of a companion of Paul. Such an explanation would account for the intermittent character of these passages.

As we will see when we compare the contents of Luke-Acts with that of Paul's letters, striking discrepancies exist between the two bodies of writing. These discrepancies involve both information about Paul and also critical points of theology, and they render very difficult any identification of the author of Luke-Acts with a companion of Paul. From a comparison of the texts of Luke and Paul, we see some connection with the apostle Paul, but historical criticism warns us to be ready to see this author again as an anonymous member of the early church, whose real identity we may never know. On this point, however, it would be better to wait until we study the writings of Paul.

Galilee, north of Nazareth.

B. The Original Readers

Luke, as we will continue to call him, appears to be writing for Gentiles. He omits Marcan stories that concern specifically Jewish issues, such as that of Jesus and the traditions of the ancients (Mk 7:1–23). He also tones down statements that would be offensive to Gentiles. They are no longer compared "to the dogs" as in Mk 7:27.

On the whole, this Gospel appears to be representative of the non-Jewish or "Greek" branch of early Christianity, just as Matthew's Gospel represents the Jewish branch.

C. The Date

As was the case for Matthew, Luke's literary dependence on Mark places the Third Gospel roughly in the 80s. The reference in the Gospel to the destruction of Jerusalem, which the author has inserted into his source, requires a date after A.D. 70:

> When you see Jerusalem encircled by soldiers, know that its devastation is near. (Lk 21:20)

D. The Overall Structure

The overall structure of Luke is rather simple. The key element is that of a long journey from Galilee to Jerusalem that occupies the whole mid section of the Gospel—9:51–19:27. It is in this section that Luke places most of his Q material. Before this section, the Gospel describes Jesus in Galilee (4:14–9:50). After this section, the Gospel narrates the story of Jesus in Jerusalem: his final preaching, his passion and death, and his resurrection (19:28–24:53). The introduction to the Gospel includes an infancy narrative as well as an introduction to the preaching ministry of Jesus (1:5–4:13).

The outline, therefore, has four major parts:

Preamble (1:1–4)

I. The Beginnings of Jesus (1:5–4:13)
    A. The infancy narrative (1:5–2:52)
    B. Introduction to the ministry of Jesus (3:1–4:13)

II. The Ministry in Galilee (4:14–9:50)
     (22 episodes)

III. The Journey to Jerusalem (9:51–19:27)
      (12 episodes added to the Marcan story: 9:51–18:14)
      (Marcan stories of Jesus approaching Jerusalem: 18:15–19:27)

IV. The Jerusalem Ministry (12:28–24:53)
     A. Jesus preaching in Jerusalem (12:28–21:38)
     B. The passion narrative (22:1–23:56)
     C. The resurrection (24:1–53)

The Acts of the Apostles picks up were the Gospel leaves off, in Jerusalem at the scene of the ascension. The words of Jesus to his apostles in this scene in Acts in fact describe the structure of the whole book of Acts:

> You will receive power when the Holy Spirit comes down
> on you; then you are to be my witnesses in Jerusalem,
> throughout Judea and Samaria, yes, even to the ends of
> the earth. (1:8)

After two introductory chapters centered on the disciples' reception of
the Holy Spirit at Pentecost, Acts then describes the apostles' work in
Jerusalem (3:1–7:60), then their work in Judea and Samaria
(8:1–12:25), and finally Paul's work bringing the gospel to the world
of that time (13:1–28:31). This long section of Paul's work appears to
be structured around three missionary journeys—13:1–15:35,
15:36–18:22, and 18:20–21:14. The final part of Paul's career
describes his trip to Jerusalem—like Jesus in the Gospel—his arrest
and imprisonment, his trip to Rome as a prisoner (21:15–28:31).

Preamble (1:1)

   I. The Beginnings of the church (1:2–2:47)

   II. Jerusalem (3:1–7:60)

   III. Judea and Samaria (8:1–12:25)

   IV. Paul to the "ends of the earth" (13:1–28:31)
      A. first missionary journey (13:1–15:35)
      B. second missionary journey (15:36–18:22)
      C. third missionary journey (18:23–20:38)
      D. Arrest and journey to Rome as a prisoner (21:1–28:31)

II. The Faith of Luke

A. Luke's Christology

Luke's Gospel ends with the ascension of Jesus to heaven:

> Then he led them out near Bethany, and with hands
> upraised, blessed them. As he blessed, he left them, and
> was taken up to heaven. They fell down to do him rever-
> ence, then returned to Jerusalem filled with joy. (Lk
> 24:50–52)

The Acts of the Apostles begins with the same scene:

> No sooner had Jesus said this than he was lifted up

before their eyes in a cloud which took him from their
sight.... After that they returned to Jerusalem. (1:9–12)

This image of Jesus ascending to heaven thus becomes not only a
literary axis for the writings of Luke but the key to understanding
his christology as well as his soteriology, as we will see below.

The scene of the ascension is so important that Luke provides
us with an explicit interpretation, given in the mouth of Peter. After
the coming of the Spirit (see below), Peter addresses the crowd of
Jews from all parts of the eastern world. In the key section of this
speech, Peter proclaims:

> This Jesus God has raised up, and we are his witnesses.
> Exalted at God's right hand, he first received the
> promised Holy Spirit from the Father, then poured this
> Spirit out on us. This is what you now see and hear. David
> did not go up to heaven, yet David says, "The Lord said to
> my Lord, Sit at my right hand until I make your enemies
> your footstool." Therefore let the whole house of Israel
> know beyond any doubt that God has made both Lord and
> Messiah this Jesus whom you crucified. (Acts 2:32–36)

For Luke, the ascension was not the first walk in space. It was
above all the exaltation of Jesus to the right hand of God, to the
realm of God, the powerful and saving king, whence Jesus acts in a
divine manner. Such a description involves very precise relationships between Jesus and God and between Jesus and the Spirit.

1. Jesus and God

Luke is clear: it is God who makes Jesus Lord and Messiah
(2:36), and it is God who raises up Jesus (2:32). Jesus is clearly in a
subordinate position to God. This picture of Jesus under God is consistent with the Gospel, where we see the beginnings of Jesus in the
womb of his mother. In this Gospel Jesus is a human being. He surpasses any other human being on earth, even the great Caesars and
kings of the time, as Luke carefully suggests. Filled with grace and
wisdom from his youth (2:52), Jesus is the greatest of the great
benefactors of the day. Yet in the Lucan picture, Jesus is still a
human being who begins in time. Nothing in the Gospel suggests an
existence of Jesus before his conception.

In the light of this humanity, the elevation of Jesus to the right
hand of God becomes all the more important. It is an unheard-of

exaltation of a human being. Jesus is called "Lord" frequently during his earthly career (5:8; 7:13; etc.). Yet as Peter in his speech declares, it is from this exaltation that Jesus is truly Christ and Lord.

2. Jesus and the Spirit

According to Peter in this text of Acts, Jesus' relationship to the Spirit is double, "He first received the promised Holy Spirit from the Father, then poured this Spirit out on us" (2:33).

The Gospel of Luke illustrates the first relationship, Jesus as receiving and bearing the Spirit. For Luke as for Mark, that reception took place at the baptism of Jesus. Except for some special touches, Luke reproduces his source:

> Now when all the people were baptized and when Jesus also had been baptized and was praying, the heaven was opened, and the Holy Spirit descended upon him in bodily form, as a dove, and a voice came from heaven, "You are my beloved Son. With you I am well pleased." (Lk 3:21–22; cf. Mk 1:9–11)

For the Lucan Jesus, however, this is not the first contact with the Spirit. In the infancy narrative (Lk 1–2), we see the Spirit presiding over Jesus' conception (1:34) as well as inspiring people in the presence of the infant (1:41; 2:27). All three Gospels speak of the Spirit leading Jesus into the wilderness at the beginning of his ministry (Mt 4:1; Mk 1:12; Lk 4:1). Luke adds that Jesus was "full of the Holy Spirit" (4:1) and afterward "returned in the power of the Spirit into Galilee" (4:14), where he proclaimed, "The Spirit of the Lord is upon me" (4:18). Such a beginning establishes Jesus as a man of the Spirit and places his whole ministry under the Spirit's aegis.

At the end of the Gospel and at the beginning of Acts, we hear of the other relationship of Jesus to the Spirit. Before his ascension, Jesus promises, "See, I send down upon you the promise of my Father" (Lk 24:49), and "you will receive power when the Holy Spirit comes down on you" (Acts 1:8). When the Spirit arrives at Pentecost (Acts 2), we are thus prepared to understand that it is Jesus who pours out this Spirit, as explained by Peter.

The shift in the relationship from receiving to bestowing the Spirit accentuates the importance of the ascension for Luke. It is this elevation to the right hand of God that explains the shift. From the right hand of God, Jesus shares the divine power of bestowing

The Sea of Galilee and the Jordan River.

the Spirit of God. Through his ascension, this human being now enters into a divine function.

(See exercises 2, 3.)

B. Luke's Soteriology

What then is the special significance of Jesus' suffering and death? When we look for clues to the meaning of the cross in the Gospel, we are somewhat disappointed. The most that Luke will say is that it was necessary. "Thus it is written that the Messiah must suffer and rise from the dead on the third day" (Luke 24:46). "Did not the Messiah have to undergo all this so as to enter into his glory?" (24:26). The suffering and death of Jesus appear in Luke merely as a divinely ordained preliminary to Jesus' glory. Luke gives no direct religious significance to that death.

This deemphasis on the death of Jesus as directly saving seems to be reflected in an omission on the part of Luke. Mark, as we saw, includes a simple line—which eventually will be intensely developed in Christian theology—describing the death of Jesus as a "ransom" or "redemption" (in Greek, a *lytron*). Luke repeats almost word for word from Mark the context of this statement, a teaching about authority and service. But where Mark has Jesus describe himself as one who has come "to give his life as a ransom for many" (Mk 10:45), Luke's Jesus simply says, "I am among you as one who serves" (Lk 12:50). Luke apparently saw the idea in his source and chose not to include it in his Gospel.

It would appear that for Luke the great saving event is not the death of Jesus but his ascension. This is the moment when Jesus truly becomes "Lord and Christ" (Acts 2:36). This is the moment when Jesus bestows the Spirit of God on the world.

(See exercise 4.)

On the other hand, the crucifixion scene in Luke contains a touching scene that includes what we would call a promise of salvation. Jesus promises one of the criminals on Calvary, "Truly I say to you, this day you will be with me in paradise" (Lk 24:43). At the sight of Jesus the criminal, like the people gathered on Calvary (24:48), had been moved to some form of repentance. Luke, the Gentile heir of Greek philosophy, clearly has a sense of personal "salvation" immediately after death—something of a "soul" going to heaven—before the public bestowal of the Spirit, long before the public resurrection of the dead. Just as Jesus is "Lord" (Lk 5:8) long before God officially makes him "Lord" (Acts 2:36), so salvation is anticipated before it is official. Luke's God is flexible. The "order" of salvation focuses on the ascension and the bestowal of the Spirit, but love of God reaches out to anyone who through repentance is ready for salvation.

Luke shares with Matthew a view of the Gospel as open to all humanity. Luke's basis for this openness, however, is very different from Matthew's. Matthew, we recall, placed the universality of the Gospel in a historical event, in the death of Jesus seen as the rejection by the Jews of their Christ. Luke, who deemphasizes the death of Jesus, places the universality of the Gospel in the very nature of the Gospel. From the opening chapters, we hear of Jesus as "a revealing light to the Gentiles" as well as a glory for Israel (Lk 2:32). When Luke gives us the genealogy of Jesus, he works back not just to Abraham but all the way to Adam (Lk 3:38). Jesus is thus from the start related to all humanity. Nowhere in this Gospel does Jesus restrict his mission or that of his disciples to the tribes of Israel. We are thus well prepared for the command of Jesus before his ascension to preach "in Jerusalem, throughout Judea and Samaria, yes, even to the ends of the earth" (Acts 1:8).

C. Luke's Eschatology

(See exercise 5.)

One of the most distinctive contributions Luke makes to the New Testament is his view of the end of the world. In effect, Luke's eschatology has become the "standard" for the church down through the centuries.

1. Deemphasizing the Nearness of the End

We see the new thought of Luke first in a careful comparison of his description of the end of the world (Lk 21:5–33) with that of Mark (Mk 13:1–32). This comparison likewise helps us appreciate better what the evangelist does with his sources. As we read the accounts from the two Gospels, we see several significant changes that Luke makes:

Mark 13	Luke 21
[5] And Jesus began to say to them, "Take heed that no one leads you astray. [6] Many will come in my name, saying 'I am he!' and they will lead many astray.	[8] And he said, "Take heed that you are not led astray; for many will come in my name saying, 'I am he!' and, 'The time is at hand!' Do not go after them.
[14] But when you see the desolating sacrilege set up where it ought not to be…then let those who are in Judea flee to the mountains.	[20] But when you see Jerusalem surrounded by armies, then know that its desolation has come near. [21] Then let those who are in Judea flee to the mountains….
[19] For in those days there will be such tribulation as has not been from the beginning of the creation which God created until now, and never will be. [20] And if the Lord had not shortened the days, no human being would be saved; but for the sake of the elect, whom he chose, he	[23] For great distress shall be upon the earth and wrath upon this people; [24] they will fall by the edge of the sword, and be led captive among all nations; and Jerusalem will be trodden down by the Gentiles, until the times of the Gentiles are fulfilled.

shortened the days....

[24] But in those days
after that tribulation, the   [25] And there will be signs in
sun will be darkened, and   sun and moon and stars...."
moon will not give its
light, [25] and the stars
will be falling from heaven...."

The changes follow a consistent pattern. First, Luke clearly identifies the time of great distress with the destruction of Jerusalem and the Temple in A.D. 70. The vague apocalyptic language of Mark is changed to reflect precise historical events. Second, Luke deemphasizes the nearness of the end of the world. He has Jesus warn against those who say the end is near. He introduces "the times of the Gentiles" between the destruction of A.D. 70 (v. 24) and the end with its cosmic catastrophes (v. 25).

On the other hand, Luke does reproduce the Marcan line, "Truly, I say to you, this generation will not pass away till all has taken place" (Lk 21:32; cf. Mk 13:30). To see how Luke handles this paradox, we must examine another aspect of his eschatology, the role of the Spirit.

2. The Spirit

Again, a comparison with Mark helps us understand the special message of Luke. In both Gospels, Jesus begins his preaching immediately after his own baptism. In both Gospels, the opening lines of Jesus form a type of keynote address, giving the tone for the rest of the Gospel. In Mark these opening lines consist of the summary in 1:15:

The time is fulfilled, and the kingdom of God is at hand;
repent, and believe in the gospel.

The exact meaning of these lines still remains a mystery for us today, but it would be easy for a reader, especially one in the first century, to see these lines as a proclamation of the near end of the world.

Luke presents the opening lines of Jesus in 4:18–21. Jesus reads from the book of Isaiah:

The Spirit of the Lord is upon me, because he has
anointed me to preach good news to the poor....

Jesus then declares,

> Today this scripture has been fulfilled in your hearing.

In place of the nearness of the kingdom, Jesus proclaims the bestowal of the Spirit and the preaching of the Gospel. This proclamation in Luke forms the keynote address of Jesus.

Something similar occurs at the opening of Acts. There the apostles ask about the kingdom,

> Lord, has the time come? Are you going to restore the kingdom to Israel? (1:6)

Jesus answers by drawing their attention away from the kingdom and to the Spirit,

> It is not for you to know times or dates that the Father has decided by his own authority, but you will receive power when the Holy Spirit comes upon you, and then you will be my witnesses not only in Jerusalem but throughout Judea and Samaria, and indeed to the ends of the earth. (1:7–8)

This is precisely the same shift we saw when we compared the opening lines of Jesus in Mark and Luke. It is the Spirit along with the spread of the Gospel that occupies the central position in place of an intense expectation of the end.

Luke's use of the Spirit here to develop his eschatology is rooted in the prophet Joel. If we turn to Jl 2:28–32 (or 3:1–5), we see a clear association of the Spirit with the Day of the Lord, that climactic end of history preached by so many of the Old Testament prophets:

> After this I will pour out my spirit on all mankind. Your sons and daughters shall prophesy, your old men shall dream dreams, and your young men see visions. Even on the slaves, men and women, will I pour out my spirit in those days. I will display portents in heaven and on earth, blood and fire and columns of smoke. The sun will be turned into darkness, and the moon into blood, before the day of Yahweh dawns, that great and terrible day. All who call on the name of Yahweh will be saved....

In this Jewish tradition exemplified by Joel, the Spirit was an element of the last days. The Spirit was above all an eschatological gift.

In the Acts of the Apostles, Luke will emphasize the Spirit. This Spirit will animate and guide the early church throughout its expansion as well as confirm the work of the apostles and ministers of the word. In effect, the Spirit will make the ascended Jesus present again to his disciples. That Spirit begins its work with the spectacular inauguration of Acts 2, the description of the first Christian Pentecost.

After describing the descent of the Spirit on the disciples, an event that drew bystanders to the house where the disciples gathered, Luke calls Peter to center stage, where Peter explains the meaning of the events:

> Men of Judea, and all you who live in Jerusalem, make no mistake about this, but listen carefully to what I say. These men are not drunk, as you imagine; why, it is only the third hour of the day. On the contrary, this is what the prophet spoke of: In the days to come—it is the Lord who speaks—I will pour out my spirit on all mankind. Their sons and daughters shall prophesy.… (Acts 2:14–17)

Through the mouth of Peter, Luke explains this gift of the Spirit as the fulfillment of the great eschatological promise. In some way, the great Day of the Lord prophesied by Joel had just dawned. In some unexplained way, with the coming of the Spirit, the end of the world had arrived.

What Luke has done is divide the meaning of the end of the world into two components, a physical component and a spiritual one. Luke displaces the physical aspect to the distant future ("until the times of the Gentiles are fulfilled"). He sees the spiritual aspect, however, as realized with the events fifty days after the first Christian Easter.

In this way Luke can understand how the predictions of Jesus of a near end could be realized. In some way the end did come in "this generation." At the same time, he can understand how Jerusalem could be destroyed while the rest of the world continued to exist.

We see here a remarkable freedom of interpretation, an interpretation that draws new conclusions from the tradition that transmitted the words of Jesus, new conclusions necessitated by the course of historical events. The story of Jesus is modified and retold from the point view of a new understanding.

3. A Theology of History

By this reinterpretation Luke gives us a theology of history. He has identified the religious significance of the present. It is "the time of the Gentiles," the time of the Spirit and preaching. Up to the beginning of Christ's ministry (his baptism) was the time of "the Law and the Prophets." After that beginning is the time of "the good news of the kingdom of God" (Lk 16:16). The time of Jesus is the great turning point, the great axis of history.

Luke thus reminds us that history is an instrument of God's dealings with humanity. Most religions in the Hellenistic world sought God in the timeless interiority of mystical or ecstatic prayer. Obviously, from Jewish teachers Luke learned to look for God's salvation in historical events. It is not surprising then to see in the Gospel repeated efforts to situate the story of Jesus in world history:

In the days of Herod, king of Judea...(1:5)

In those days Caesar Augustus published a decree ordering a census of the whole world. This first census took place while Quirinius was governor of Syria. (2:1–2)

In the fifteenth year of the rule of Tiberius Caesar, when Pontius Pilate was procurator of Judea, Herod tetrarch of Galilee....(3:1)

Bethlehem from the surrounding fields.

III. Theological Reflections

The remarkable approach of Luke to the issue of the end of the world points out several important aspects of our faith. First of all, we note Luke's freedom to reinterpret the text of Mark, which supposedly was presenting the words of Jesus. Luke sees the need to reinterpret these words in the light of his experience—the end did not come with the fall of Jerusalem. He could have approached the problem as did Matthew. He could have simply urged vigilance despite the apparent delay and then just have left it as a mystery (see also 2 Pt 3:8–9). Instead he decides to change the prediction of Jesus, in effect reinterpreting that prediction and then retelling the prediction in such a way as to incorporate the new interpretation. According to Luke, Jesus now warns against those who say the end is near and then makes a clear distinction between the war of A.D. 70 and the end (cf. Lk 21). Luke is concluding that Jesus—for whatever he meant by his prediction—could not have meant that the end would come on the tails of the destruction of Jerusalem. How did Luke know this? His historical experience told him. Luke is willing to incorporate "worldly" experience into his faith. By showing the willingness and perhaps even the necessity of integrating his faith with his experience of life, Luke has begun the task of critical theology.

The approach of Luke to the end results in a paradox. For Luke the end is clearly not yet. Jesus will return only after "the time of the Gentiles." Yet for Luke the end is already. Joel's prophecy of the coming of the Day of the Lord has been realized in the coming of the Holy Spirit. Christians are thus placed in the paradox of a kingdom that is at once future and present. In effect, Christians are warned against placing all their attention on a future realization of the kingdom to the extent that the present is voided of importance. Christianity is not "pie in the sky when you die." At the same time, Christians are summoned to live in hope. Our life is not heaven on earth. We are called to rejoice in the glory and triumph of Christ present now through his Spirit especially in the church. At the same time, we are called to look forward to his glorious coming, living in a transition period that still requires much suffering (Acts 14:6).

Luke's christology with its insistence on the humanity of Jesus might bother Christians today who hold a deep conviction of the divinity of Jesus. As we saw, Luke presents Jesus as a human being who begins in time and who remains subordinate to God. Good Christian theology must agree. Jesus *as human* begins in time and remains always subordinate to God. We have created the specifying phrase *as human*. Luke does not qualify his description with this specification. Luke's christology, therefore, should bother those Christians with a "high christology" only to the degree that they forget the nature of the Gospels.

When we compare Luke's insistence on Jesus' humanity with his equally intense insistence on the exaltation of Jesus to "the right hand of God" (Acts 2:33), an exaltation that gives Jesus power over the very Spirit of God, we begin to perceive a fundamental insight of Luke. This insight is often forgotten in modern piety. God saves us through another human being. God bestows his Spirit through another human being. Human nature has, in fact, been drawn into the very life and work of God. To the extent that we view Jesus as divine, we might not be impressed with his role of bestowing the Spirit. We could see here simply a divine activity by a divine agent. When we approach the gift of the Spirit, however, from the Lucan perspective, we can perceive the fascinating picture of God who can draw his own creature so intensely into his life that the creature functions as a source of divine life.

From Lucan christology, we are at the same time thus directed to God, the Father, as the ultimate agent of our salvation. Jesus is our Lord and Savior only as exalted to God's power. The Spirit which Jesus sends remains the "promise of the Father" (Lk 24:49). The mediating role of Jesus is not one geared to activate God's salvation. The role of Jesus is rather to demonstrate that God not only bestows gifts but also bestows the giving.

EXERCISES

Exercise 1. (see page 139): Read Luke 1–4; Acts 1–2. From these chapters what can we see about the authorship of the Third Gospel and Acts and the relationship of the two books to each other? What persons are common to both accounts? What other common elements can you find?

Exercise 2. (see pages 142–145): Read Luke 1–2. What does Luke recount about the origins of Jesus? Is Jesus pictured "coming down" from heaven or in any way existing before his conception? What grounds does the text give for Jesus being called "Son of God"?

Exercise 3. (see pages 142–145): What powers does Jesus have and exercise during his ministry according to the Gospel? Which stories about this power come from Luke's sources and which from Luke alone? What powers does Jesus have in the Acts of the Apostles?

Exercise 4. (see pages 145–146): Read Luke 22–23 and compare it with Mark

14–15. What details and whole stories has Luke added to the passion narrative? What has he dropped?

Exercise 5. (see page 147): Read Luke 21 and compare it with Mark 13. What similarities do you find? What are the major differences?

REVIEW QUESTIONS

1. What is the traditional identification of the author of the Gospel of Luke and the Acts of the Apostles?

2. What is the overall structure of the Gospel of Luke and Acts? What literary indications exist in the text to divide the Gospel and Acts in this way?

3. Describe the shift in the relationship between Jesus and the Holy Spirit according to Luke. What texts substantiate your answer? How does the ascension of Jesus function in Luke's christology?

4. How does Luke describe the relationship between Jesus and God? Does that relationship change?

5. How does Luke change Mark 13 to express his eschatology? What appears to be Luke's principal concern in making these changes? How else in the Gospel do these concerns appear?

6. What is the role of the Holy Spirit in Luke's eschatology? What is the Old Testament basis for that role? What texts substantiate your answer?

FOR FURTHER REFLECTION AND DISCUSSION

1. Do you ever think about the end of the world? Why? How would you compare or contrast your attitude toward the end with Luke's?

2. Both Luke and Mark emphasize the humanity of Jesus, each in his own way. Which picture of Jesus the human being appeals more to you? Why?

3. Why did Luke write the Acts of the Apostles, when the other evangelists stopped with the death and resurrection of Jesus? Is Acts also a story about the person and work of Jesus?

9

The Literary Form of Gospel

After having examined the Gospels of Mark, Matthew and Luke, we are now in a position to reflect on the kind of literature or *literary form* we are dealing with in these Gospels. The question is important, because it is directly linked to the issue of the truth of the Gospels, the power of these texts to make us react one way or another.

I. The Concept of Literary Form

If we were reading the front page of the evening newspaper, we would expect to find a particular kind of writing. The front page is supposed to provide us with the who, what, where, when, and why of some event. If we shifted to the editorial page, we would expect to find a very different kind of writing, one that would deal with oughts and shoulds, where values and personal positions on issues would predominate over the facts of some specific event. If we shifted to another page and began reading a description of a new automobile, noting the word *advertisement* over the description, we would immediately shift our mental gears, expecting a very different kind of "literature."

These three types of newspaper writing are examples of literary forms (sometimes called *literary genres*). Each form has a different purpose. Each operates according to different norms, evoking a different set of questions on the part of the reader. Each can be truthful or deceptive.

The potential truth of each form is very different. It would be unfair to demand in an editorial the factual, descriptive truth that we expect in a news article. Yet the editor must follow norms guiding even the presentation of opinions and positions to avoid the accusation of *yellow journalism*. We generally expect intensely rhetorical and persuasive language in an advertisement, yet laws forbid deceptive advertising.

Each form has its legitimate purpose and place in the newspaper. To say one is a better form than the other is to compare the proverbial apples and oranges. Only when we lose sight of the literary form, only when we read an advertisement thinking it is a news article, do we run into trouble. At that time we apply the wrong questions to the piece of writing.

The list of the various literary forms in our literature is endless. We can talk about *historical writing* and *fables*. Each—even a fable—contains its particular kind of truth. Within the category of history, we can talk about *modern critical history* and *folk history*. Each has its own purpose and kind of truth. As long as we understand *what kind of writing* we are dealing with, we can understand its particular truth. We know what questions to bring to the text and what questions not to bring.

(See exercise 1.)

A. Literary Forms in Scripture

A serious difficulty arises when we try to apply these considerations of literary form to the texts of scripture. With the Bible, most people are intensely concerned about the issue of truth, which has become a battle flag in discussions. The first question to occupy many people reading a narrative from scripture is, How do we preserve or defend the truth of this narration? The pressing nature of this question frequently obscures the fact that no one has asked, What kind of truth is the narration presenting? What is its literary form?

(See exercises 2, 3.)

Most of us have a particular expectation toward narrative truth. This expectation is healthy but it aggravates the difficulty of understanding scripture. Most of us have an intense desire to know the facts of some event. Factual reporting has long occupied the front pages of our newspapers. We have become very distrustful of personal positions and interpretations as mere expressions of opinion and feeling. Moreover, our scientific model of thinking, where hypotheses are tested against observable facts, has become the dominant model of a "serious quest for truth." This model is, in fact, the one behind most of the chapters of this book. The difficulty lies not with this model or with our desire for facts. Such an attitude has become a great liberating and humanizing force in our culture. The difficulty lies rather with the resulting tendency to relegate all that is not factual and publicly observable to a type of inferior truth.

A religious person imbued with this attitude will read the narrations of the Bible and immediately sense a need to understand the narrations as a kind of newspaper reporting. How else can the hard, factual character of the narration be preserved? And if it is not preserved, what value has such a narration? Such a person is instinctively identifying the literary form of a biblical narration not on the basis of the evidence given by the text but on the basis of a cultural bias about what is *truly true*.

When first raised, the issue of literary forms in the Bible evoked intense controversy among dedicated believers. The mainline Christian churches have taken a stand. Among Protestant churches, as we saw above (see chapter 1), the Presbyterian Confessions of 1967 insist on recognizing the "thought forms and literary fashions of the places and times at which they [the scriptures] were written" (9.29). In the Catholic Church the importance of this position is clear:

> Those who search out the intention of the sacred writers must, among other things, have regard for "literary forms." For truth is proposed and expressed in a variety of ways, depending on whether a text is history of one kind or another, or whether its form is that of prophecy, poetry, or some other type of speech. (*Dei Verbum*, #12)

The Second Vatican Council directly connects the issue of literary form with the issue of biblical truth. As a matter of fact, if one insists that the literary form of the Synoptic Gospels is that of newspaper reporting or some other form of factual history, then the changes found in the accounts present an insurmountable problem. In the Synoptic parallels we saw Matthew, Mark, and Luke describe the same event in the ministry of Jesus. The word-for-word similarities among the Gospels indicate that the authors were aware that they were relating the same events. The differences among the accounts, however, are often irreconcilable as descriptions of the historical events. Were the disciples dumbfounded when Jesus entered the boat after walking on the water (Mk 6:52), or did they understand and confess their faith in Jesus (Mt 14:33)? Did Jesus warn against those who say the end of the world is near (Lk 21:28), or did he predict it as coming shortly after the destruction of Jerusalem (Mk 13:24)? The reconciliation of such narrative discrepancies can take place only when we are willing to look at possibilities of narrative literary form beyond that of newspaper reporting.

The identification of the literary form of gospels should come from literary analysis. Concern for biblical truth may lead us to raise the question of this identification, but determining the identification among the range of possibilities is a matter of intense literary investigations, not a matter of faith or an indication of one's dedication to the Bible. Unfortunately those intensely concerned with identifying the Gospels as factual histories defend their position not by pointing to evidence in the text but by accusing the persons who disagree of having no faith.

II. The Literary Form of Gospel

Our investigations of Mark, Matthew, and Luke give us data to wrestle with the question, What is a gospel? What is the literary form of these writings we have been studying? The primary difficulty we have in answering this question arises from the apparent uniqueness of these documents. No ready-made category seems to exist into which these writings fit. Our task is, therefore, to define a new category.

A. What the Gospels Are Not

One approach to such a task is to decide first what *gospel* is not. *Gospel* does not seem to be *biography,* a more or less complete account of a person's life or part of that life. A striking difference between *gospel* and *biography* lies in the episodic character of our Gospels. In the three Gospels we have studied, we have found a collection of short vignettes about Jesus. The sequence of these episodes in the Gospels comes, as we have seen, from the evangelist, not from the chronology of Jesus' life. Furthermore, small periods of time in the life of Jesus, such as the last few days of his life, occupy a disproportionate place in these narrations. The Gospels really do not give us "a life of Jesus."

Second, gospel does not seem to be *critical history,* the type of historical writing we are familiar with in history texts and monographs. Except for a brief mention at the beginning of Luke's Gospel, no attempt is made to identify or control sources, an essential factor in critical history. Oral traditions predominate as sources for material, but nothing is said about the factual reliability of those traditions. The traditions as sources completely disappear behind the stories contained in those sources.

Third, gospel does not even seem to fit the category of *popular history,* the type found in the writings of Herodotus or Thucydides, writings that narrate in general form some great event or epoch, yet introduce a great deal of subjective evaluation, even a certain amount of fiction in order to capture the sense of the event. Once again, gospels are composed of isolated and independent episodes, strung together by the evangelist. Gospels do not have the historical sequencing necessary even for popular history.

On the other hand, gospel does not seem to be *fiction* of one form or another, like the myths and stories of the gods and heroes of ancient times. The evangelists express great interest in the historical person of Jesus. They see their lives deeply affected by what Jesus said and did. Their narrations about this man, therefore, seem rooted in historical facts.

B. What the Gospels Are

What we seem to have in gospel is a free rendering of the historical events surrounding the person of Jesus. It is a literary form still very much bound up with the dynamics of oral literature, where stories are easily modified, where storytellers look far more into the eyes of the listeners than at the authority of their sources as they recount their tale, where understandability dominates over historical accuracy. Oral tradition develops in freedom and liveliness, and the Gospels reflect that freedom and liveliness.

Gospel as a literary form cannot be understood apart from an understanding of the faith the early Christians had in the resurrection of Jesus. Put somewhat simply, these Christians did not want to write a history of Jesus, because histories are written about dead people. For the Christians Jesus was very much alive. As new situations and questions developed in the early church, Jesus was there for the early Christians, continuing to teach and guide them. For the early Christians, the words of the historical Jesus who taught in Palestine became inextricably woven into the continuing words of the risen Christ.

What we have in a gospel seems to be a combination of memories about historical events and profound interpretations (and reinterpretations) of those events. Mark recalls a memory of Jesus walking on the lake—a memory already the subject of intense interpretation—and then interprets that story in the light of his faith in the mystery of Jesus and the "blindness" of even the closest associates of Jesus. Matthew reinterprets the story in the light of his faith in the apostles as models of faith—which they may have become by the time Matthew was writing.

The principal difficulty for us is the combination of the story with the interpretation. Minimal interpretation is inevitable in the most factual account. Even heavy-handed interpretation is often legitimate in order to keep a tradition alive. The Constitution of the United States is a clear example of this interpretive process; however, we prefer to keep the original experience or document separate from the subsequent interpretations. This separation allows us to recognize and test the subsequent interpretations.

In the Gospels, however, we have the original experience and the interpretations woven inextricably together. As the Christians reinterpreted Jesus, they told the story differently. The closest parallel today is that of an artist who no longer sees his or her work as simply reproducing a photocopy of some visual experience. Even the "realistic" artist deliberately changes the lines and colors—blurring the forms as originally experienced—in order to incorporate an interpretation onto the canvas.

The evangelists, like most artists, were confident that their interpretations of Jesus expressed the truth better than any "photographic reproduction." They were confident that their contact with the truth of Jesus was not just from the memories that linked them to the historical events but was also from their continued processing and reprocessing of those memories. They were confident in a type of revelation that continued long after Jesus' death.

We get a sense of that confidence in continuing revelation in John's Gospel, where Jesus speaks about his earthly teaching and about the future understanding of the disciples:

> I still have many things to say to you but they would be too much for you now. But when the Spirit of truth comes he will lead you to the complete truth, since he will not be speaking as from himself but will say only what he has learned. (16:12–13)

Whether Jesus spoke these words or not, they witness to a faith that there was more to be learned than could be found in the historical instructions of Jesus. More would come but only in the future, a greater truth that was in continuity with the instructions of Jesus, but one geared to the future, not just the record of the past.

Perhaps the idea of "a record of faith in the historical Jesus" best captures the essence of gospel. We have in these documents what an early community believed about Jesus. The object of their faith was a historical person and his historical deeds, yet that object of faith was perceived as containing more than what could be registered by a neutral observer. His historical deeds were perceived as unleashing forces and powers invisible to empirical observation. We have in the Gospels those faith perceptions of Jesus.

LITERARY FORM OF GOSPEL

Is not	Is
biography	reflection of belief
critical history	memories of events
popular history	interpretation of events
fiction	

Figure 20.

C. Gospel and Community

Gospel therefore cannot be understood apart from the community that produced it. The Gospel records the faith of that community. It registers the modifications and interpretations introduced by the preachers and storytellers of that first generation.

Any reliability that Christians today place in the Gospels, therefore, is inseparable from the reliability they place in that community. Today we can read the modifications of the Jesus traditions effected by the early Christians either as deviations from the truth of Jesus or as deeper insights into that truth. The position we take depends entirely on how we accept the early community as reliable. To insist on the Gospels as normative for the faith of any generation of Christians is to insist on the faith of the first Christians as normative for following generations.

From another point of view, any faith today in the "inspiration of the Bible" is inseparable from a faith in the "inspiration of the early community." An "inspiration" that governs the final product must affect the whole community and the individuals of that community to the degree they contributed to that final product. Understanding the Gospels as issuing from a multitude of eyewitnesses, storytellers, preachers, and writers, themselves influenced by their listeners and readers, means seeing inspiration as affecting a whole community.

A Christian imagination today has a harder time picturing

such a "communitarian inspiration" than picturing the inspiration of a few witnesses and their secretaries. A Christian imagination today must picture inspiration in perhaps a far less miraculous mode than it does with the image of one or more authors being guided to express the truth. Yet ease for the imagination or simplicity for human understanding has never been a criterion in theology searching to express divine possibility.

(See exercise 4.)

The "Inn of the Good Samaritan" on the Jerusalem-Jericho road. Christians turned a parable into an historical account.

EXERCISES

Exercise 1. (see pages 155–156): List the various writings—scribbles and printed matter—you can find in one room of your house. Briefly identify the literary form of each and the truth we expect from each.

Exercise 2. (see page 156): Read a few pages of Paul's Letter to the Romans. What are the most obvious differences between the literary form of this letter and that of the Synoptic Gospels?

Exercise 3. (see page 156): Read Luke 10:29–37. What is the literary form of this text? What kind of truth can we look for in this form?

Exercise 4. (see pages 158–162): Among the various narrative literary forms used and developed in our culture today, which comes closest to that of *gospel*? What differences still remain?

REVIEW QUESTIONS

1. What is the meaning in general of *literary form*? Give examples.
2. What is the literary form of *gospel* as we find it in the New Testament? What data from the texts of the Gospels are relevant for answering this question?

FOR FURTHER REFLECTION AND DISCUSSION

1. What would a Gospel look like if it had the literary form of a television documentary? Of a Broadway musical?

2. Does the truth about Jesus and preached by Jesus lend itself to some literary forms more than others? Are there some literary forms that are incapable of expressing divine revelation?

10

Historical Background— A Sketch of Hellenistic Culture

As we saw earlier, the cultural background of the New Testament begins with the attempt of Alexander the Great to unify the world by fostering and imposing the Greek way of living and thinking. In fact, the conquered peoples seem to have welcomed the Greek way of life, blending it with their own Oriental ways. Today historians call this resulting blend of Greek and Eastern patterns *Hellenism* or *Hellenistic culture*. This term is meant to distinguish this culture from the pure Hellenic culture of classical Greece centuries earlier. From Greece, Hellenism assumed a love of the rational, a love of order and definition, a willingness to think and speak in abstract terms. From the Eastern world, this culture blends in the love of the imaginative—the concrete and mysterious, the paradoxical and even contradictory—along with a desire to speak not in abstractions but in dramatic story.

Despite the widespread acceptance of the Greek language and manners, Hellenism betrayed an underlying attitude of unrest and alienation. People were looking for something better, something more in life. The world under the Hellenistic rulers, and then under Rome, was unified but much too vast for the average individual to feel a sense of belonging. In the old city-states people lived in a unity of perhaps five or ten thousand citizens, in which they knew a significant part of that population, even the kings and rulers. In the empires after Alexander, people were thrown into a world civilization. A king or an emperor, whom they never saw or knew, had life-and-death control over them. It was a world that was not theirs. They lived and worked in it, but did so as aliens.

The Parthenon at Athens.

This background helps us understand better the intense religious dynamism which characterized that world. Movements sprang up promising a better existence, promising salvation. The old religions, those of the Greek and Roman mythologies, simply celebrated the *status quo*. For the most part, the farther away the Greek or Roman gods stayed from you, the better off you were. In the new philosophies and religions, however, people sought help from the gods. People sought communion with the divine. The earth seemed too bleak a place in which to place one's hope. This search for salvation appears in several Hellenistic movements ranging from the intensely rational to the bizarre and mythical.

I. Platonism and Neoplatonism

To understand Hellenism, we must briefly review an earlier philosophy that profoundly shaped the mentality of the subsequent centuries. This was the philosophy of Plato (ca. 428–347 B.C.). Developing the views of his teacher Socrates (ca. 470–399 B.C.), Plato speculated on the basis or ontological status of such values or ideals as justice or truth. From this speculation, he developed a whole view or philosophy of the universe and of human life.

Plato started with the lived experience of "justice" or "truth," an experience that is much like ours. These concepts mean a great deal to us, especially when they are absent. In fact, we get to know them mostly by their absence—or at best by their limited presence. All this means that we know of them before we experience their deficiency. Their basis in reality must be other than this deficient experience of them. Furthermore, such "ideals" seem to be more than human thoughts. If we are deeply upset by the absence of justice, our concern is not simply with our thinking. Some *thing* is wrong. If nowhere in this world do we find such ideals in their full reality, these ideals must be independent of any concrete realization in our earthly experience. Plato then reasoned to the need to base these ideals in a separate world, a spiritual world, a world of all ideals and essences.

This world on earth in this line of reasoning thus appears as a place where the ideals are reflected in limited and temporary ways. But the spiritual world "above" is the place where reality has its permanence and perfection. Plato thus developed what would be called a *cosmic dualism,* a view that reality is not one universe but two, a heavenly spiritual world of standards and ideals, eventually under God, and an earthly material world where passing shadows of the ideals could be found.

In a logical procedure Plato then developed a view of the human being which echoed this cosmic dualism. Human beings, as Plato saw them, are capable of living in this world and sensing the passing material shadows but at the same time they are capable of reasoning to the existence of the eternal ideals and even of understanding some of those ideals. The human being, therefore, must likewise be not one reality but two: a spiritual mind and a material body, united now but separated at death.

In Plato's logic, this *anthropological dualism* leads to a depreciation of the body, conceived now as a prison of the spiritual mind. Death in this view is a liberation that allows the spiritual soul to return immediately to its natural habitat, the spiritual realm of ideals and essences.

The Platonic school ("the Academy") continued after Plato's death, undergoing various developments as it continued into Hellenistic times, where Christian intellectuals saw in this school a system of thought intensely congenial to the faith of the New Testament. The later developments of Platonic thought became known as Neoplatonism.

Neoplatonism maintains the cosmic and anthropological dualisms of the earlier school; however, it developed a system by which the variety of reality from the eternal and one God appeared as stages in a cosmic process, through the spiritual essences down to the material world. One type of reality came or "emanated" from the other in a continuous descent. Plotinus (ca. A.D. 204–270), the best-known exponent of Neoplatonism, gives us an elaborate and systematic account of this complex vision.

(See exercises 1, 2.)

II. Stoicism

With its roots in classical Greece, a second philosophical movement caught fire in the Hellenistic world. It was called *Stoicism* from the *stoa,* or covered walkways, where the original stoic philosophers first expounded their ideas. Zeno, the one credited with founding the Stoic school, died around 264 B.C. In many ways Stoicism is the ethical child of Platonic dualism.

The basic interest of Stoicism was reason. Like our word "reason," the Greek equivalent, *logos,* connoted both the mental process of thinking and the basic meaning behind an event or action, the reason for something. We hear this meaning in our English word "logical." The word *logos* also meant "word" and suggests the close connection between thought and speaking. When the Fourth Gospel describes Jesus as the eternal Word (Jn 1:1), the author in fact uses the Greek word *logos.* The Stoics marveled at the regularity of nature and saw behind it all a universal *logos,* a kind of world reason or soul, that gave meaning to the whole universe.

The good life, according to the Stoics, communed with this

The reconstructed Stoa of Attalus at Athens interior.

cosmic *logos.* It was one in tune with the supreme reason of nature. Such a communion was possible through each individual's reason, that power in the human person which was part of the cosmic reason and which allowed people to function on the same order as that of the whole universe.

If reason was the key to salvation, then the obstacles to reason clearly were the basic evils of life. According to the Stoics, our emotions and bodily senses prevent us from reasoned activity. We cannot think straight when we are angry or in pain. Even intense pleasure can prevent us from cool reason. Hence, the Stoics developed the ideal of *a-patheia,* a lack of passion or emotion, or at least a state of mind that resists any influence by these forces. This is not the *apathy* signified by our English cognate. *Apathy* generally means a lack of energy and interest. Rather, stoic *a-patheia* meant intense energy, but one directed and lived entirely on the level of the mind. This for the Stoic was the great ideal of *freedom,* which was much more an internal attitude than a political or social condition.

The Stoics developed a characteristic way of teaching called the "diatribe." Again, this word should not be confused with "a prolonged, bitter argument," the sense that our English word *diatribe* has come to mean. Rather, for the Stoics a *diatribe* described a literary form, a way of explaining their lofty message to those uninitiated into the technical aspects of Stoicism. The diatribe was a speech involving many examples, lists of virtues and vices, rhetorical questions, imaginary partners who objected to the matter at hand, and other forms of dramatization that aided a neophyte to understand. It was a literary form probably developed in the Stoic schools of philosophy. Clearly, the Stoics thought of themselves as marketplace philosophers, not ivory-tower academicians.

All these elements of Stoicism are particularly important for the study of Paul, whose letters show hints of Stoic ideals: freedom, conscience, virtue, as well as distrust of "the flesh." His letters, with their lists of virtues and vices, their rhetorical questions, and imaginary interlocutors, likewise reflect the manner of the Stoic diatribe.

(See exercises 3, 4.)

III. The Mystery Cults

At the other end of the Hellenistic spectrum lay the mystery cults. These religions offered salvation to those initiated into these cults through participation in a secret drama. These cults made no appeal to reason or logic. Rather, they summoned the heart and called for an intensity of commitment through the power of images and mystery.

These mystery cults formed around stories portrayed on a stage. These dramas dealt generally with the problem of life and death. Watching the drama unfold on stage, the participant identified with the story and thus began to deal with the perplexing problem of death.

One such cult developed around the story of Isis and Osiris. This was the story of a hero, Osiris, killed by his enemies and hacked to pieces. His enemies then tossed his parts into the Nile, which carried them in its flow down to Hades. At this point of the story, the audience responded with lamentation and dirge, allowing the horror of death to sweep over them. The story then continued with Isis, Osiris's loving wife, finding her way to Hades, where she dutifully collected Osiris's members, enabling Osiris, as it were, to pull himself together. Once he returned to life, Osiris became the lord of Hades. The audience at this point rejoiced with great exultation.

A similar mystery cult celebrated the story of Persephone. This cult, with its center at Eleusis, portrayed the drama of Persephone, a beautiful, radiant girl. Wherever she went on earth, her radiance provoked the birds to sing, the flowers to bloom, the sun to shine. All of nature responded to her beauty and vitality. Pluto, however, the god of the underworld, became jealous of earth and kidnapped Persephone. At this loss, the flowers died, the birds disappeared, and the cold blast of stormy weather replaced sunshine. To the rescue came Persephone's mother, Ceres, who complained to Zeus, the chief god. Zeus then worked out a compromise. Persephone would remain with Pluto six months of the year and return to earth the other six months. The audience responded appropriately at every stage of this drama.

Whatever the story, the theme was similar: the cycle of life and death. By participating in the mythical representation of this cycle, the members of the cult would purge their fears of death and experience the exuberance of life. Participating in the mystery cult constituted a sort of peak experience, giving the cult members courage to face drab reality. To heighten the experience of the drama, members solemnly vowed never to disclose the contents of the drama to outsiders, hence the name *mystery* cult.

Paul describes ancient practices in the early church that echo many of the traits of the mystery cults. In particular he describes baptism (Rom 6:4) and eucharist (1 Cor 9:14–22; 10:17–34) as rituals

Eleusis. The gates of the underworld.

or dramas in which the participant became part of a greater drama of Christ's life and death. The question, therefore, arises about the degree to which these rituals and dramas of the New Testament reflect the contemporary mystery cults? In what ways are these rituals really similar to the mystery cults? In what ways are the Christian rituals different?

(See exercise 5.)

IV. Gnosticism

Somewhat akin to the mystery cults was a religion, or philosophy, called Gnosticism. It flourished in the centuries immediately following the period of the New Testament. Although it existed as a systematic religion or group of religions only after the New Testament, Gnosticism appears to have its beginnings as a general movement in times preceding and coinciding with those of the New Testament.

As a philosophy of life, Gnosticism can be summarized by seven major points:

1. God, the source of all goodness, dwells in a spiritual realm totally apart from this universe and has never had, nor ever will have, anything to do with this universe.
2. This universe is essentially evil. The evil lies in its material

nature, which is directly opposed to spirit. All of reality thus falls into one of two categories: matter or spirit, evil or good, darkness or light.

3. The human person is a spark of the divine spirit entrapped in evil matter, the body. Such an entrapment occurred because of a fall or sin.

4. Redemption consists, therefore, of escaping from this evil body and returning to God.

5. This return to God begins with knowledge. In Greek the word for this knowledge is *gnōsis,* hence the name Gnosticism. This saving knowledge, moreover, is, above all, knowledge of self, knowledge that one is truly a spark of the divine, that one is really an alien on earth.

6. This knowledge comes by way of revelation, a special message from God, sent to rescue human beings from their entrapment. In many forms of Gnosticism, this revelation comes by way of a revealer, a messenger of light who descends into the realm of darkness to bestow the saving message.

7. This knowledge can come in the form of a myth, an imaginary story unrelated to historical events. Historical events, after all, can have no saving significance for a Gnostic. What is of history is necessarily evil because it is of the earth. Only the interior, a-temporal can save. A myth can save simply because it conveys the proper knowledge.

Of all the movements and societies of the Hellenistic world, Gnosticism seems to best embody the blend of Greek rationalism and Oriental mysticism. At the heart of the Gnostic aspiration is the drive "to know," especially to know oneself and one's purpose in life. In this movement we see also the Platonic dualism and depreciation of body. But now this dualism is couched in terms of religious good and evil. The Oriental appeal to the heart comes in with the dramatic imagery of light and darkness. The universe is imagined in terms of concentric spheres dominated by evil forces through which the "enlightened" soul must journey on its way to heaven.

The Gnostic soul can now view the problem of good and evil in the world as ultimately resolved. This problem is, of course, the experience of a world that embodies moments of beauty yet crushes that beauty in its ultimate power of death, the experience of people who are somewhat good but capable of horrendous cruelty. It is the mixture of good and evil in this world that perplexes. For the Pollyanna, for whom life is all bliss and goodness, there is obviously no problem. And for the soured cynic, for whom life is ultimately absurd and ugly, there is likewise no problem. The cynic accepts life as such and stops being surprised when the absurd and ugly penetrate human defenses. The problem lies in the mixture of good and evil that we experience. Just when we think life is great, it turns sour. Just when we think of suicide, a ray of light appears.

The Gnostic can view this mixture of good and evil in life as the manifestation of the inevitable churning that results from the contact of ultimate goodness and ultimate evil in our human life. The Gnostic resolves the problem of the mixture into two ultimate principles.

The Gnostic thus sees life as incomplete and demanding a serious task, a journey from this world to another. Gnosticism is a way of salvation. The key is thinking correctly about yourself.

(See exercises 6, 7, 8.)

V. Theological Reflections

The similarity on many points between the accounts of the New Testament and Hellenistic movements might cause some concern. Do these parallels relativize Christianity? Do they reduce Christianity to just one more salvation movement within the Hellenistic world?

Our method requires that answers to these questions come from an examination of the evidence, not from preconceived ideas, even if these ideas seem to stem from religious faith. As we search the evidence, however, certain reflections stemming from our faith can at least sensitize us to the data.

First, is it so surprising that the Christianity of the New Testament has parallels with the world in which it developed? If Jesus had lived in the twentieth century and if the accounts of his work had developed during our time, the Christian Gospels would no doubt reflect the currents of our times. If people are offered salvation, the first question they have is, What are we to be saved from? The answer must be thought and expressed in terms of needs that are truly part of our lives.

Second, we might find it difficult to see divine revelation involved in ideas and movements which we often roundly condemn as "pagan." But must we really see God so distant from what is not explicitly Jewish or Christian? If our faith convinces us that God's hand is present in the traditions of Judaism and Christianity, no corollary is to be drawn a *priori* regarding other traditions. God may or may not be present in those other traditions. Only the experience of each tradition allows us to evaluate the possibility of divine presence. However, where in any culture we see love, heroic self-gift, and a sincere desire to understand, our faith suggests that in fact we see the effect of God's presence.

Third, it is only by comparing Christianity with its contemporary culture that we can begin to see what is original and specific to Christianity. Such a distinction between the contemporary culture and the specific character of Christianity allows Christianity to be a prophetic witness and to call a culture closer to God. Christianity thus functions less as an alternative to any given culture than as a leaven that permeates a culture, accepting what is good and transforming what is not. It would appear that the first Christian theologians, Paul and John, functioned this way.

EXERCISES

Exercise 1. (see pages 165–167): Read Phil 1:22–24. Can you find a view of the human person that resembles that of Platonism?

Exercise 2. (see pages 165–167): Read Heb 8:3–5 and 9:23–24. What similarities do you see in this biblical picture with the cosmology of Plato?

Exercise 3. (see pages 167–168): Read Gal 5:13–26 and Rom 7:13–25. Do you find any echoes of Stoic ideas in these texts? What are the similarities and the differences?

Exercise 4. (see page 168): How many lists of things can you find in Paul? How many times does Paul interrupt his writing to pose objections and then to answer them? What other typical elements of the Stoic diatribe can you find?

Exercise 5. (see pages 168–170): Read Rom 6:3–5 and 1 Cor 10:14–22. In what way are the "sacred dramas" described in these texts similar to the dramas of the mystery cults?

Exercise 6. (see pages 170–172): Read "Hymn of the Pearl" from appendix 4. Look for any details that correspond to the typical ideas of Gnosticism.

Exercise 7. (see pages 170–172): The importance of Gnosticism for understanding the New Testament is clear. Can you find echoes of the Gnostic ideas in the New Testament especially in the Fourth Gospel? What are the major differences between the early Christian faith and Gnosticism?

Exercise 8. (see pages 170–172): Read Jn 1:1–17; 17:3, 25–26; Eph 3:1–5. Can you find echoes of Gnosticism in these texts?

REVIEW QUESTIONS

1. What is *Hellenistic culture?* Where did it come from? What are its main elements?

2. What is meant by *cosmic dualism* and *anthropological dualism* as found in many movements or schools of Hellenism? Give an example from one of those movements or schools.

3. Describe a typical mystery cult story. How does the story of Isis and Osiris fit that type? How does the story of Persephone fit that type?

4. What is *a-patheia* for Stoicism? How does this attitude fit into this philosophy? What is its relationship to freedom?

5. What are the main tenets or ideas of Gnosticism? What elements of the Fourth Gospel echo these tenets?

FOR FURTHER REFLECTION AND DISCUSSION

1. Were Jesus born today and the evangelists people of today's culture, how would our culture have affected both Jesus and those who would write about him? How would Jesus have explained "the kingdom of God" for today's culture?

2. What happens to the message when the Gospel crosses cultures, as it did when it moved from the Hellenistic culture to Western culture? What challenge does this crossing pose for missionary preaching?

3. Can the core message of Paul or any other New Testament writer be separated from the Hellenistic culture out of which it appears to have grown?

11

Paul—His Life and Letter Writing

A major part of our New Testament stems from one man and his letters. Turning to these letters, we in a sense start over again. Before Mark recounted the acts and teachings of Jesus, wrestling with the mystery of Christ and his death, before Matthew and Luke needed to come to grips with the delay of Jesus' return, Paul of Tarsus was developing his understanding of Jesus, of Jesus' death, and of the end of the world. Decades before the Gospels, Paul was explaining the new Christian faith in letters to communities of Christians in the eastern Mediterranean world. With Paul's letters we tune in to the earliest stages of Christian theology.

Compared to the other New Testament authors, we know a great deal about Paul. Information about this writer greatly helps for understanding his letters. This information comes to us from two sources. First and most important, Paul frequently speaks about himself and his work in his own letters. Second, we have an extended account of Paul in the second half of the Acts of the Apostles.

The use of Acts as a source of historical information about Paul, however, is problematic. Knowing how Luke used his sources in the composition of his Gospel, we can suspect that his account of Paul in Acts would involve much freedom and reinterpretation in the light of Luke's faith. We should not be surprised, therefore, to find glaring discrepancies between the account of Acts about Paul and Paul's own recollections of himself as given in his letters. Where discrepancies exist, we should probably rely on the letters for historical information. In the letters we have an account "from the horse's mouth," as it were.

On the other hand, we have no reason to disregard totally what Luke says about Paul in Acts. As we will see, the itineraries of the middle part of Paul's career described in Acts correspond well to

those described by Paul himself. Often where details described by Luke clash with
those described by Paul, the
main ideas are basically the
same. We will see this when
we look carefully at the events
of Paul's life as described by
Paul and by Acts.

We must, therefore, con-
stantly remember the source
of any information we want to
include in our life of Paul. For
the most part we must start
with   Paul's   statements.
Where information from Acts
is consistent with explicit
information we have from
Paul as well as the presuppositions and hints we have
from Paul about himself, then
we should cautiously accept
the Lucan account as filling in
gaps in our knowledge of Paul.

The "Gates of Cilicia"
north of Tarsus.

I. Birth and Education (A.D. 10–35)

Paul writes to the Philippians about his earliest days:

[I was] circumcised on the eighth day, from the race of
Israel, the tribe of Benjamin, a Hebrew from Hebrews, a
Pharisee according to the law. (3:4; cf. also Rom 11:1)

A good guess is that Paul was born around A.D. 10; therefore he
was some fifteen years younger than Jesus. Writing to Philemon,
probably around A.D. 65, Paul calls himself "an old man" (*presbytēs,*
v. 9), which could put him around fifty-five or older. Luke felt he
could describe Paul as "a youth" *(neanios)* at the stoning of Stephen
around A.D. 35 (Acts 7:58). That word would describe a boy around
fifteen or older.

It is Luke who names Paul's birthplace as Tarsus in Cilicia
(Acts 22:3), a city that appears to have been at the crossroads of
East and West in the great caravan routes of this time. We can find

no reason why Luke would have invented this birthplace rather than another city, and this location explains Paul's later connection with Barnabas and other prominent Christians in Antioch not far away from Tarsus. Locating Paul's home in a culturally diverse and active city like Tarsus identifies Paul as a "Diaspora" Jew and helps us understand his mastery of the Greek language and his passion for adapting belief in the Jewish Messiah to a Gentile world rather than compelling Gentile converts to conform to Jewish beliefs.

Luke actually goes much further and identifies Paul as "a citizen" *(politēs)* of Tarsus (Acts 21:39). The active "citizens" of a Hellenistic city were more than the tax-paying residents of that city. They were the ones active in the official religious cults of the city. The responsibilities of a "citizen" meant full involvement in the city's cultural and religious life. We do have pictures of renegade Jews of the time as active citizens in Hellenistic cities, but the idea of a devout Pharisee, a detail about Paul which both he himself (Phil 3:4) and Luke (Acts 23:6) mention, as a "citizen" of a Hellenistic city is virtually absurd. Luke desires to portray Paul as a member of the highest class and ranks of society—hobnobbing with governors and kings, frightening jailers who arrest him. Therefore, Paul's Tarsian citizenship is probably a Lucan invention.

LIFE OF PAUL

A.D. 35	The conversion or vocation of Paul
35–38	Sojourn in "Arabia" (Gal 1:17)
38	First visit to Jerusalem, meets Cephas (Gal 1:18)
38–49	Work in the region of Syria and Cilicia (Gal 1:21)
49	Second visit to Jerusalem with Barnabas and Titus meets Cephas, John (Gal 2:1–10)
49–53	Mission to Galatia, Philippi, Thessalonica, Corinth writing 1 Thessalonians
54–58	Mission to Galatia, Ephesus, Corinth writing 1 Corinthians, 2 Corinthians, Romans, and Galatians
58	Trip to Jerusalem
58–60	Two years imprisonment in Caesarea
61	Trip to Rome
61–63	Two years imprisonment in Rome
63–67	A return to Ephesus? writing Philippians, Colossians, and Philemon
67	Paul's death

Figure 21.

Although Paul eventually joins the tent makers to work for a living, he was probably born into a wealthy family. We see this in his education, using the Stoic diatribe to develop his thought, citing Greek poets, and above all drawing with ease from the Greek Old Testament to compose scriptural homilies, to refute opponents, or simply to translate the agrarian message of Jesus into almost metaphysical concerns of life and death. Education was virtually a monopoly of the wealthy at the time of Paul.

We see his wealthy background in the examples Paul uses. He refers in a matter-of-fact way to the family "pedagogue," the household slave whose job was to babysit the small children of a wealthy family (Gal 3:23–25). He refers to the parents' role of giving money to the children rather than receiving money from them (2 Cor 12:14), an example well understood in rich circles but incomprehensible among the working class.

One last matter about Paul's education: Luke portrays Paul as studying in Jerusalem as a boy—most likely an older teenager—at the feet of the famous Gamaliel (Acts 22:3). Paul is silent about this. This silence is all the more expressive in those texts where Paul wants to vaunt his Jewish background, a technique he uses to defuse his judaizing opponents (see Phil 3:5; 2 Cor 11:22). More than likely, this picture of Paul going to Jerusalem to learn the Law is part of Luke's desire to make Jerusalem the true center of salvation. When Paul says he was not known to the Judean churches at the time of his conversion (Gal 1:22), he is probably telling us that he was a real stranger in that part of the country.

The name Luke gives Paul up to Acts 13 is Saul. After Acts 13:9, his name is Paul. Paul probably had two names, one Jewish, *Shaul,* the name of the first Israelite king, the other Greek, *Paulos,* the only name Paul uses in his letters. As with other "bi-national" names, for example John Mark, one or the other name dominated, depending on whether the person was speaking with Jews or Greek-speaking Gentiles.

II. Paul's Conversion/Vocation (A.D. 35)

(See exercise 1.)

Both Paul and Luke agree. Paul hated Christians and persecuted them (Gal 1:13–14; Phil 3:6; 1 Cor 15:9; Acts 9:1–2). Paul never explains why or exactly what that meant in terms of hostile action. Luke fills in some gaps and describes Paul armed with the authority of the Jerusalem high priest to arrest and extradite Jewish Christians from Damascus, the capital of the province of Syria. After Archelaus, son of Herod the Great, was deposed from ruling Judea, the Sanhedrin's authority was limited to Judea. Luke's details fleshing out the picture of Paul the persecutor are probably not historical.

Using the time spans described by Paul to space later events, we need to specify A.D. 35 as the year when Paul's life changed. Paul describes the key event in Gal 1:15–17:

> When [God], the one setting me apart from my mother's womb through his grace, was pleased to reveal his Son to me, in order that I might preach the good news about him among the nations, immediately I did not consult flesh and blood nor did I go up to Jerusalem to the apostles before me, but I left for Arabia and again returned to Damascus.

In effect this description is a development of Paul's self-identification as "an apostle not from human beings nor through human beings but through Jesus Christ and God the Father" (Gal 1:1). Given without any further details, this "revelation" of God's Son to Paul, is the basis of his being an apostle (1 Cor 9:1). This is a revelation *in the same order* as the appearances of the risen Jesus shortly after his death to his disciples (1 Cor 15:5–9).

The language Paul uses to describe this encounter with Jesus is close to that of the prophet Jeremiah, who describes his calling:

> Before I [God] formed you in the womb I knew you, before you were born I dedicated you, a prophet to the nations I appointed you. (Jer 1:5)

The similarity of vocabulary and the many other resemblances Paul draws between himself and Jeremiah suggest that Paul saw the event that changed his life as a prophetic "calling." He was not the same afterward. He reversed course in his attitude toward the church of Christ. In that sense we might call the event a "conversion." But Paul generally speaks of his new direction not as a "change of religion"—what we would consider a conversion—but rather as an introduction into the mysterious council and plan of God, with all the suffering and compulsion that characterized the "calling" and "sending" of the great prophets before him. Paul never left Judaism. For him the encounter with Christ meant understanding and living this religion with the power of the Spirit, not simply observing the letter (see 2 Cor 3). He had entered "the mystery" that was there—although hidden—all along (Col 1:26–27).

On the other hand, Luke fleshes out the event with apocalyptic strokes: in Acts 9:3–7 light flashes and Paul falls to the ground. A heavenly voice speaks to him, tells him to stand, and commissions him. The same pattern can be found in Rv 1:10–19 and Ez 1:26–2:3. The most important difference between Galatians and Acts lies in Jesus' instructions to Paul: "Go into the city [Damascus], and it will be said to you what you must do" (Acts 9:6). According to Acts, Paul goes to Damascus, where Ananias, a leader of the Jewish Christian community, baptizes, heals, and instructs Paul (9:10–19). Through Ananias and later Barnabas, Paul is introduced to the Jerusalem church (9:19–28).

On this point Paul is emphatic: "I did not consult flesh and blood" (Gal 1:16). Paul is pointing out his authority to write to the Galatians. It comes directly from Jesus. That origin puts Paul on the same level as the other apostles.

For Luke also, Paul is a great authority. Luke dedicates about half of Acts to the work of Paul; however, Luke portrays the authority of Paul as coming through the church of Jerusalem. In broad strokes Luke agrees with Paul; in details they are miles apart. We are probably safer restricting our reconstruction of the event to the little Paul says about it: it was a revelation of the risen Christ, and it changed Paul forever.

III. The Years Leading to the Second Meeting in Jerusalem (A.D. 35–49)

Paul gives only brief information about the fourteen or so years that follow his conversion/vocation. He does so in the continuation of the Galatian text we examined:

> Then after three years I went up to Jerusalem to confer
> with Cephas and remained with him for fifteen days. But
> I did not see any other of the apostles, only James the
> brother of the Lord.... Then I went into the regions of
> Syria and Cilicia. (Gal 1:18–21)

The trip to Jerusalem described here by Paul accords fairly well with the description in Acts of Paul's introduction to the church in Jerusalem by Barnabas (Acts 9:23–30). Luke mentions a second trip by Paul to Jerusalem with Barnabas which cannot be fitted at all with Paul's descriptions (Acts 11:29–30; 12:25). However, the elaborate journey Luke describes in Acts 13–14 more or less corresponds to the sojourn in Syria and Cilicia that Paul describes. Luke skews Paul's location a bit to the west and includes Cyprus; otherwise, the geography is similar. As he will say, Paul engaged in evangelizing activity during that sojourn. Luke's desire for order, especially in ordered threes, probably led him to structure this period into a circuit that would eventually lead to the picture of "the three missionary journeys" of Paul.

This "first missionary journey" in Acts 13–14 takes Paul with Barnabas to the island of Cyprus, to the cities of Salamis and Paphos. Up to now the cousin of Barnabas, John Mark, has accompanied them; however, once the group moves on to what is now southern Turkey (the ancient city of Perga), John Mark leaves and returns home. Paul was quite upset by this, as Luke will later describe. Paul and Barnabas now head inland over the Taurus mountains. The route is dangerous because of highway robbers. They stop in Antioch of Pisidia, near central Turkey. They then travel east to Iconium (modern-day Konya), then on to Lystra and Derbe. As Luke tells it, the story in each town is similar: the group first preaches to the Jewish community—the presence of which probably dictates the itinerary—then, after resistance from this group, they preach to Gentiles with great success. Retracing their route, the group returns to Antioch (see figure 22).

The sequence of cities in this journey corresponds to nothing in Paul's own descriptions of travels connected with his letter writing. Whether this period in Paul's life included a systematic journey, as Luke recounts, or series of trips during an early period of missionary activity, we do not have any writings from Paul from this time.

IV. The Meeting in Jerusalem (A.D. 49)

(See exercise 2.)

Paul continues the narration of his life from his sojourn in Syria and Cilicia:

Then after fourteen years I went up again to Jerusalem with Barnabas, taking also Titus. I went up according to a revelation and laid out to them the gospel I preach to the Gentiles—privately to those of high standing, lest in any way I run or have run in vain. But not even Titus

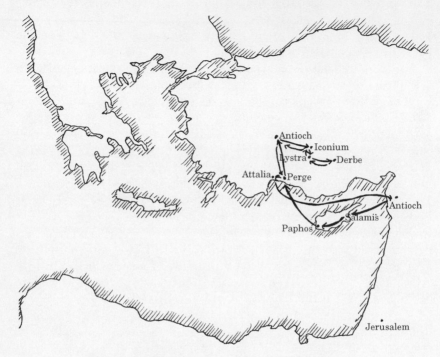

Figure 22. **Paul's First Missionary Journey.**

who was with me, being Greek, was forced to be circumcised.... On the contrary, seeing that I was entrusted with the gospel of the uncircumcision just as Peter with that of circumcision, that the one working in Peter for an apostleship of circumcision also worked in me for the Gentiles, and knowing the grace given me, James and Cephas and John, those esteemed to be pillars, gave me and Barnabas the right hand in sharing, in order that we go unto the Gentiles, while they unto the circumcision. The only stipulation was that we remember the poor, the very thing I was also eager to do. (Gal 2:1–10)

If we date the conversion/vocation of Paul to around A.D. 35, then fourteen years later becomes A.D. 49. Paul describes an important meeting with the leaders of the church in Jerusalem, dealing with the issue of the Gentiles' role in the otherwise Jewish community. Paul has apparently taken the position that Gentiles need not become Jews first in order to become Christians, that they are not obliged to observe the Abrahamic Law regarding circumcision nor probably most of the cultic elements of the Mosaic Law. The issue has apparently arisen again with the Galatians, and Paul needs to make the point here that he had the full approval of the most esteemed leaders of the Jewish Christian community for his gospel of freedom. He is with Barnabas and Titus. He meets James, Cephas [Peter], and John.

The only stipulation is to "remember the poor." The phrase may very well designate the Jewish Christians of Jerusalem (cf. Rom 15:26). In the next century, the Jewish Christians—having fled from Jerusalem—will call themselves "the poor," the Ebionites. The Qumran community of Jews at the time of the New Testament used that term for themselves as the faithful remnant. In Judaism the significance of the term developed in connection with the theme of the faithful but humble remnant, as found for instance in Zep 2:3; 3:12–13. Paul is thus agreeing gladly to remember the Jerusalem church as "the mother church," as having a key role in the whole church of God. Paul is agreeing to the unity of Gentiles with Jews in this new people of God.

Luke's account in Acts 15 agrees in the substance of the meeting but differs greatly in details. In Acts the meeting is held in Jerusalem and deals with the freedom of the Gentile Christians. Paul is with Barnabas and meets Peter, James, the apostles, and also "the presbyters" of Jerusalem. What strikes us as different in the Lucan account is first of all the general tenor of the meeting. In

Paul's account, it was a private meeting. Here it is a large council with speeches and consensus building. In Paul the agreement was simple. In Acts the agreement has several parts:

> Namely to abstain from meat sacrificed to idols, from blood, from meats of strangled animals, and from illicit sex. (Acts 15:29; cf. also 15:20)

We never hear of these food laws regarding blood again in the New Testament. The prohibition generally disappears from history. Paul discusses the issue of meat offered to idols in his letter to the Corinthians some six years later (see 1 Cor 10:14–23); however, he does not even mention this agreement.

More than likely, Luke is embellishing the story he has about Paul. He knows that some agreement was reached, that Gentiles retained their freedom, and that they as Gentiles joined Christian Jews as one people. If we look for background regarding the food laws about blood, we find it in the Noah covenant (Gn 9:3–6), the last covenant God made with humanity as a whole. While miles apart in the details of the event, Luke again is remarkably close to the substance of the agreement, that Jews and Gentiles together form a unity under God.

Because of our ability to compare the two accounts, our understanding of the accuracy of Acts 9–15 can become a test case for our understanding the rest of Acts in terms of historical information. We should therefore summarize again on the points of agreement between Galatians and Acts:

(a) Both speak of a radical change in Paul from being a persecutor of the church to being an energetic exponent of the faith as a result of an encounter with Jesus near Damascus. In both Paul's account and Luke's, Paul's authority is unquestioned. For Paul this authority comes unmediated from Christ; for Luke it comes through the church of Jerusalem.

(b) Both accounts describe the first trip to Jerusalem, where Paul is introduced to the leaders.

(c) Both authors speak of an extended stay in the northeast corner of the Mediterranean world. Luke describes this period as the first missionary journey; Paul gives us no details.

(d) Both describe a type of summit meeting in Jerusalem, where there was agreement on the basic freedom of the Gentiles in the church, a symbol now of all humanity in covenant with God. The main persons at this meeting are the same for both Paul and Luke.

The discrepancies we have noted above indicate that Luke did not read Galatians or get his information from Paul. The agreements indicate that Luke did have some historical sources. He is not simply making up his story, although he may well be filling in the gaps with his own imagination and reflection.

It would appear rash, therefore, to dismiss Acts altogether as an unreliable source of information about Paul. We must be aware, however, of the limits of this source. From the test case examined above, Acts appears to give us a general picture of the major events in Paul's life. The details about Paul in Acts, on the other hand, look suspect. The words of Paul, the particular incidents, and the exact people involved may well stem from Luke's theological imagination rather than from his sources of historical information.

We will rely on Acts for the next ten years of Paul's life, because there is a very close correspondence between Paul's descriptions of his travels and those found in Acts. By comparing itineraries, we will be able to situate a good part of the letter writing of Paul in the next two "missionary journeys" described in Acts. This comparative approach will be easier if we start with Luke's description and then search the letters of Paul for correlations.

V. The Second Missionary Journey (A.D. 49–53)

Acts 15–18 describe a second journey, this time with Silas (Silvanus of the letters) and Timothy (from Lystra). This journey takes the missionary group into Galatia in northern Turkey, and then westward to the Aegean Sea, where, according to Acts, Paul receives a vision of a Macedonian appealing to Paul to come to Europe. After this revelation, Paul sails for Macedonia (northern Greece), where he founds Christian communities in Philippi, Thessalonica, and Beroea. Paul then travels to Achaia (southern Greece), where he preaches in Athens and founds a community in Corinth before returning to Antioch (see figure 23).

The stay in Corinth as described by Luke gives the one date that we need to estimate all the other dates we are attaching to Paul's life. Up to the stay in Corinth we have only lengths of time, either explicitly indicated or requiring our estimation: fourteen years from the conversion to the meeting in Jerusalem, a trip through Turkey and Greece that would take three or four years. Now in Corinth we have Paul described as appearing before the tribunal of Gallio (Acts 18:12), an office that we can date rather securely to A.D. 51–52. Paul's arrival in Corinth around A.D. 52 fits well also with Luke's description of Paul's meeting with Priscilla

Figure 23. Paul's Second Missionary Journey.

and Aquila, Jewish Christians expelled from Rome by Claudius around A.D. 49 (Acts 18:2).

A. Writing 1 Thessalonians

In 1 Thessalonians, Paul describes his founding the church in that capital city of Macedonia. He had come from Philippi (2:2). Both he and the Christians of Thessalonica had suffered severe opposition (1:6; 2:2). He had recently left that city and had tried several times to return (2:17–18). Timothy, whom he had sent to them from Athens, has just returned with encouraging news of the Thessalonians (3:1–6). In response Paul writes this letter.

These details fit well into the end of Paul's second journey as described in Acts. Paul is probably in Corinth. 1 Thessalonians would be dated, therefore, around A.D. 52, about eighteen years before the writing of Mark's Gospel, which makes this letter the oldest Christian writing in existence.

VI. The Third Missionary Journey (A.D. 54–58)

Acts 18–22 describes the third journey. At this time Paul revisits the Galatian churches and then heads to Ephesus, where he spends about two years. After a detailed description of Paul's Ephesian ministry, Luke then briefly mentions a visit to Macedonia and a three months' stay in Achaia. The rest of this section in Acts details the portentous return to Jerusalem, where Paul will be imprisoned (see figure 24).

A. Writing 1 Corinthians

Writing 1 Corinthians, Paul states that he is in Ephesus (16:8). He has already founded the church in Corinth and hopes to come again shortly and spend the winter in that city (4:19; 16:5). Hence, this letter correlates easily with Acts' description of Paul's third journey, and particularly with his extended stay in Ephesus. The year would be around A.D. 55.

B. Writing 2 Corinthians

Although we cannot presume that this letter was written after 1 Corinthians just because it is called 2 Corinthians, an instruction

Figure 24. **Paul's Third Missionary Journey.**

in the letter assures us that in fact the present order in our Bibles corresponds to the actual writing. In 1 Corinthians Paul instructs the community to begin a collection of money for the church of Jerusalem (1 Cor 16:1–4). In 2 Corinthians the collection is much further along (2 Cor 8–9). In Romans, Paul has the collection and is on his way to Jerusalem (Rom 15:25–27).

2 Corinthians poses special problems that we can only sketch in this study. In its present form, 2 Corinthians seems to be at least two letters of Paul later edited together: chapters 1–9 and chapters 10–13. The tone of chapters 1–9 is conciliatory. Paul alludes to a major "falling out" between him and the church, during which an angry letter was written, a "letter in tears" (2 Cor 2:3–4; 7:8). The description of that angry letter does not match 1 Corinthians. On the other hand, the tone of 2 Corinthians 10–13 is sarcastic and angry. These chapters do not seem to fit well in their present place just after an intense appeal for money (chapters 8–9). We may, therefore, have at least a part of "the letter in tears," now placed in chapters 10–13 by a later editor who removed an ending and an opening in the two letters and sewed the two into their present form.

2 Cor 6:14–7:1 also appears as a "lump" in the letter as we now have it. With 6:14 we have a sudden shift to the topic of not associating with unworthy people. Nothing in the preceding text explains why Paul would introduce that topic at this point. Furthermore,

**Corinth. The tribunal building with the
Acrocorinth in the background.**

7:2 picks up practically the very wording of 6:13 and continues the preceding topic of accepting Paul. If a reader jumped from 6:13 to 7:2, a listener without the text would have no hint of omission. In 1 Cor 5:9 Paul refers to a letter written by him earlier about not associating with immoral persons. Evidence thus suggests that we have at least an excerpt of that first letter now in 2 Cor 6:14–7:1.

In the first part of 2 Corinthians (chapters 1–9), Paul names Macedonia as the place from which he is writing (8:1). Paul encounters serious problems with the Corinthians sometime after writing 1 Corinthians. To deal with these problems, he sends Titus to this church (12:18). Paul eventually travels to Macedonia to rendezvous with Titus, who reassures Paul of a change of heart in Corinth. Paul then writes this letter.

Paul would have written 2 Corinthians 10–13 somewhat earlier before he left Ephesus, and he would have written 2 Cor 6:14–7:1 much earlier from Ephesus, even before he wrote 1 Corinthians. In all, then, we have four letters of Paul written to the Corinthians.

For all its complexity, 2 Corinthians fits into the Lucan itinerary of Paul's third journey. The earlier sections would have been written during his stay in Ephesus, the later part as he was traveling from Ephesus to Corinth (Acts 20:1–2). That voyage would have been in late fall, A.D. 57.

The Temple of Augustus in Galatia (Ankara).

C. Writing Galatians and Romans

Writing to the Galatians, Paul says almost nothing about his situation. This letter, however, strongly resembles Romans in its theme, in its structure, and even in the images and expressions used by Paul to develop his thoughts. On the other hand, nothing suggests that one is a copy of the other. No significant verbatim strings link the two together. Shifts in the details of the imagery suggest a creative mind still playing with his associations. These comparisons persuade us that the two letters were written by Paul very close to each other.

Romans was written from Cenchreae, the eastern port of Corinth, where Paul was about to embark for Jerusalem (Rom 15:31–16:1). He is writing this letter, as he explains, to prepare for his coming to Rome, which he hopes to use as a base of operations for a trip to Spain (15:23–24). Romans appears as a careful exposition of Paul's thinking. He apparently felt the need to introduce his main thoughts to the Roman community, perhaps to refute certain misunderstandings that they may have developed about him.

Romans fits very well into the picture Luke draws of Paul in Greece at the end of his third journey (Acts 20:2–3). We are probably now in the spring of A.D. 58.

Many of the ideas expressed in Romans appear in Galatians, in less developed form. What appears in Galatians as an angry polemic against any use of the Law shows up in Romans as a more balanced view of the freedom of Gentiles compared to the privilege of Jews, who have the Law. A reasonable hypothesis sees Galatians as an early draft of the ideas Paul was working on in his exposition for the Romans, but which he sent to the Galatians to answer a severe crisis that broke out in that church. We can imagine Paul working on his letter to the Romans when he hears of the Galatian desire to adopt Jewish practices. Paul sees that the radical answer to the Galatian crisis lies precisely in the proper understanding of justification by faith and the freedom that results from that justification, themes he is developing for the Romans. He pulls his thoughts together and applies them specifically to the Galatian crisis, sends off the letter, and then continues his composition of Romans.

We can therefore place the writing of Galatians also in Corinth in the spring of A.D. 58.

VII. The Last Years of Paul (A.D. 59–67)

The remainder of Acts (chapters 23–28) recount the five-year imprisonment of Paul, first in Caesarea for two years, then on

Malta, where Paul was shipwrecked on a trip bringing him to Rome, and then in Rome for two years. Here Acts abruptly concludes the story of Paul. The year would be around A.D. 63. Acts ends with Paul's two-year house arrest in Rome, leaving some four years before the traditional dating of his death in Rome in A.D. 67.

If we wish to see the final chapters of Acts as roughly historical and hold to the traditional date of Paul's death, we can envision a release from prison in Rome in A.D. 63 and either a trip to Spain as Paul had planned (Rom 15:24) or a return to the Near East as indicated by later traditions (1 Tm 1:3; 2 Tm 4:20; Ti 1:5). A release from prison would accord with the ancient Roman law of releasing a prisoner after a maximum of two years if an accuser failed to file a formal complaint.

It is also possible that Acts 22–28 give us little historical information about Paul. From what we know about Roman citizenship at the time of Paul, it is highly unlikely that Paul would have *inherited* such a privilege as Luke describes (Acts 22:25). As we mentioned above, from what we know of citizenship in a city like Tarsus and the religious implications of such citizenship, this status would be almost impossible for a Pharisee (cf. Acts 21:39). In general, the picture of Paul discoursing before kings and governors (Acts 26) as well as his aristocratic treatment on the prisoner ship (Acts 27) corresponds to a Lucan desire to portray Paul as one bearing the highest social rank, one who has integrated intense Christian faith with noble citizenship. Such a picture does not fit well with Paul's complaints about his beatings and laborings (2 Cor 11:23–28).

A. Writing Philippians, Colossians, and Philemon

Three letters—Philippians, Colossians, and Philemon—stand out from Paul's writings as having been written from prison. These three letters resist any easy correlation with Acts. Traditional exegesis places their writing in Rome, where Acts describes a two-year house arrest (28:30–31). Close examination of the texts, however, makes Rome an improbable location for the writing of at least Philippians. Philippians 2:25–26, for example, presupposes at least four recent trips by someone between Paul and Philippi. Such communication suggests rather an imprisonment somewhere in the Aegean basin, at Ephesus, for example, which was about a week's travel from Philippi. Philippi to Rome was at least a month's travel.

Ephesus would be a likely place for Paul's writing to the Colossians and to Philemon, also an inhabitant of Colossae. Colossae was

Philippi. The central market place (Agora).

about 150 miles east of Ephesus. A study of the companions of Paul in both Colossians and Philemon shows that the two letters were probably written together, and in Philemon Paul tells his reader that he hopes to be coming to him soon (Phlm 22).

The Ephesian hypothesis for these letters makes specifying a time for the writing of these letters difficult. Important theological shifts in both Philippians and Colossians suggest a late date, although it is not impossible to see Philippians as written from Ephesus even before 1 Corinthians.

If we hold to Luke's story of Paul's imprisonment and trip to Rome, then we need to place these letters after Paul's presumed release. In this hypothesis, Paul found himself *again* in prison during the last four years of his life. Through the help of friends and secretaries, he continued his instructions and exhortations in letter writing.

If Acts 22–28 does not portray the historical trip of Paul to Rome and his imprisonment there, then we have even greater possibilities for locating Philippians, Colossians, and Philemon in the last years of Paul's career in the Near East—about which we know virtually nothing.

B. The Authenticity of Colossians

Among these three letters, Colossians stands out with a different writing style and some significant shifts of theological imagery.

In Colossians we are already "resurrected with Christ" (2:12; 3:1). Christ is "the head of the body" now identified explicitly with "the church" (1:18). Such differences have led many to think of this letter as written by someone other than Paul after his death, like the "Deutero-Pauline" letters we will briefly discuss in chapter 16. It is very difficult to decide this question. Writing style may be a function of how dominant Paul's secretary was in penning the letter (cf. Rom 16:22). The shifts in theology appear to be rooted in positions already taken earlier by Paul (e.g., living a "new life" now by baptism in Rom 6:4). Most important, unlike the other Deutero-Pauline letters we will look at, this letter remains very comprehensible as a late stage of Paul's thought. Pragmatically it matters little for our understanding of this letter whether we view the author as Paul in a mature stage of his own thinking or as a Pauline disciple incredibly skilled at taking Paul's thought to the next stage of development.

Thus we will consider eight letters as representing Paul's authentic thought. In these eight letters we will look for consistency and some development. Figure 12 summarizes how we place these letters in Paul's writing career, along with possible correlations with Acts.

VIII. After Paul's Death The Deutero-Pauline Letters

We have not spoken of 2 Thessalonians, Ephesians, 1 and 2 Timothy, or Titus. Strong evidence suggests that these letters were not written by Paul, although they name Paul as their author. Ephesians is in large part copied from Colossians. Paul did not write his letters in this way. 1 and 2 Timothy and Titus clearly reflect the situation of the church in the last decades of the first century.

2 Thessalonians is more difficult to judge. It does not contain such evident marks of pseudonymity as do the others mentioned here. If it were written by Paul, 2 Thessalonians would have to have been penned almost immediately after 1 Thessalonians. Such a supposition causes many problems, such as a seeming denial of having written an earlier letter (2 Thes 2:2) and the striking shift of eschatology expressed in this letter from his position in 1 Thessalonians. Many other problems long associated with 2 Thessalonians simply disappear when we think of it as written long after Paul, by a person speaking in Paul's name, interpreting Paul's earlier writings for a new situation. Considering 2 Thessalonians as Deutero-Pauline "works better" than considering it an authentic letter of Paul. Although we must always be prepared for the possibility that we

are wrong, we will consider 2 Thessalonians to be Deutero-Pauline in accord with the scientific method of holding to the hypothesis that "works best" until a better one comes along.

We will treat these letters in chapter 16, where we will also treat the theological problem of those letters that say they are written by Paul but may not be.

IX. Theological Reflections

When we catch a glimpse of Paul's divine calling to be an apostle, we are confronted with a mind-boggling mystery. We recall Jesus' work preparing his Twelve presumably to continue Jesus' mission. Through instruction after instruction, disappointments and victories, for perhaps three long years, Jesus works with his personally chosen disciples. Yet it is one of the adversaries who carries the witness "to the ends of the earth" as Jesus commanded his apostles (Acts 1:8). Is this divine irony? Is this the reminder of God's ways as being far beyond human ways? Is this a warning not to second guess God's future for humanity?

Christians have long reflected on the manner in which Paul's background made him the ideal bridge over which the Gospel passed to the Gentile world. Paul was both devout Jew and educated Hellenist. He could understand the importance of Jesus from his Jewish background. He could relate Jesus to concerns and questions of the Gentile world by his Greek background. None of the Twelve seemed capable of doing this. It was through Paul that the agrarian message of the Palestinian Jesus—with his images of fields and flocks—became the Gospel of the urban world—with its concern for freedom and slavery, riches and poverty, life and death.

We need to reflect also on the discrepancies regarding Paul's life that we noted between Acts and the letters of Paul. How do these discrepancies relate to the theological position about the inerrancy of scripture? Are the inaccuracies of Acts also part of the word of God?

Obviously we are dealing with the issue of literary form and the *kind* of truth proposed by the form we have discovered in the Acts of the Apostles. The situation here is parallel to the problem of "errors" in the Gospels. If Acts were of that literary form which we see in critical histories today, then those discrepancies in Acts as compared with the parallel descriptions in Paul would be simply Luke's errors about Paul. If, on the other hand, Acts deliberately proposes to combine memories and factual reports about Paul with imaginative reenactments that dramatize theological understandings, then the discrepancies become instances of interpretations different from Paul's understanding of himself. Luke sees God's calling of Paul differently than Paul does. The object now is not simply historical events but a divine mystery where diversity of human understanding is probably the only way of overcoming an unavoidably limited view.

EXERCISES

Exercise 1. (see page 178): Read Acts 9–15 and Galatians 1–2. Make a list of the events in the Acts dealing with Paul. Then try to match that list with the events mentioned in Galatians.

Exercise 2. (see page 181): Compare specifically the meeting in Jerusalem in Acts 15:1–29 with the meeting described in Gal 2:1–10. Does this look like the same meeting? What is similar? What is different?

REVIEW QUESTIONS

1. What are our sources for knowing about the life and work of Paul? What special care do we need to exercise in using these sources?

2. What do we know about Paul's education and background?

3. What are the most important things Paul writes about his "conversion"? Where does he write this?

5. Where does Paul say he is when writing 1 Thessalonians, 1 Corinthians, 2 Corinthians (1–9), and Romans? What journey in Acts would best fit the description of Paul's situation?

6. How many letters did Paul write to the Corinthians? Explain what we may have of each of these letters.

7. What clues in Galatians help us guess at where and when Paul is writing this letter?

8. What are the problem and the possibilities of situating Philippians, Philemon, and Colossians in Paul's writing career? What do we know and what don't we know about when and where he is writing these letters?

FOR FURTHER REFLECTION AND DISCUSSION

1. *Parallel to Paul's task, missionary work today faces the challenge of crossing cultural borders and translating the gospel from one side to the other. Where in the world today is this challenge most evident? What kind of "Paul" do we need today to do the job?*

2. *Paul bases his status as apostle on his experience of the risen Christ. Can apostles exist today? Are there any?*

12

Paul—His Letters

As we saw in the last chapter, Paul's letters give us a glimpse into the earliest stages of Christian theology. In this chapter we turn now to the content of Paul's letters and to their major lines of theology, especially as they fit the principal developments in the New Testament.

We need the Gospels to understand Paul, who was clearly assimilating and reacting to the oral traditions about Jesus. We need to have a feel for the general work, death, and resurrection of Jesus if we are to understand Paul. Our studies of the Synoptics should help us understand Paul. Yet at the same time, we need to set aside the theological developments we have learned from our study of Mark, Matthew, and Luke. Paul was not influenced by these developments. Our task will be to let Paul speak for himself.

I. Overview

A. Letters in General

(See exercise 1.)

Our first task in examining Paul's writings and thought is to understand that his thought comes to us in the form of letters. In fact, twenty of our twenty-seven "books" of the New Testament are letters. Two others, Acts and Revelations, contain letters. Letter writing continued through the centuries as a major form of Christian theological discourse. Evidently in its simple and social character, letter writing was from the start a congenial way for Christians to express their faith.

We usually write letters for one purpose: to speak to someone with whom we cannot converse in person. Letters are generally poor substitutes for a face-to-face conversation. In this respect, letters are quite different from essays. We write essays in order to put our thoughts down in writing. An essay is writing for the sake of writing. We may not know exactly who is going to read our essays. Our concern is first of all to articulate our thinking as best as we can, to preserve the thought for the future, and to fix the word in a permanent form. Our letters, on the other hand, usually have as their purpose communication with particular people in particular situations. Once the communication is made, a letter is often thrown away. As a letter it has served its purpose. Only when it takes on a new function—such as documentation or souvenir—is a letter saved.

Paul's writings are letters, not essays. They are very close to the oral mode of communication. As letters, Paul's writings are basically written conversations. They respond to questions asked and problems exposed. In this they maintain the dialogical characteristic of oral communication. When Paul includes travel plans in these writings, he is in effect reminding his readers that these letters are poor substitutes for personal presence. He hopes to explain things better when he arrives in person.

As letters, Paul's writings reflect a crucial stage in early Christianity, its shifting from an oral to a written form of its traditions. As letters, Paul's communications maintain the liveliness and creativity of the early oral tradition. Paul wrestles with grave crises. He does not always have the final solution, but he is willing to offer stopgap measures. Often his words have the tone of an emergency solution. Sometimes he probes in directions that are later discarded. By reading these letters, we tune into the most creative period of Christianity's history. We listen to an apostle rejoicing and agonizing with his communities, not having all the solutions, but risking new visions of a dynamic, powerful faith.

Paul's instructions are very much bound to concrete situations. They are not timeless statements of abstract truths. Through a very delicate process of critical interpretation, we can find consistent themes running through Paul's correspondence, themes that allow us to understand our faith. But we distort Paul's work if we just transpose the propositions from his letters into our world.

To muddy the waters a bit, two qualifications must be made as to what we have said above about Paul's writings as letters. First, a great diversity exists within the writings of Paul. Some, like his writing to Philemon, clearly appear to be personal letters. Others, like his writing to the Romans, begin to take on at least some characteristics of an essay. At the turn of the twentieth century, the German scholar G. A. Deissmann made the distinction between a letter and an epistle. Scholars today question any rigid use of this categorization, yet the classification of Deissmann is useful. A letter, as we have described, is simply written conversation. An epistle, on the other hand, is something of an essay with the form of a letter, that is, with a letter opening and greeting, and with a letter closing. Most Christian "letters" of the late first century appear to be essays in letter form. They appear to be epistles. Paul's Letter to the Romans may partially fit this category. Writing to the Romans, Paul appears to be introducing himself and his main teaching. He is interested, therefore, in a careful expression of his positions. What comes from his pen in Romans is quite different from his letters to Galatia or Corinth, where he appears to be writing in haste and deep emotion.

A second qualification of our understanding of Paul's letters lies in the way Paul always maintains a certain public and official tone to his writings. Even in his letter to Philemon, Paul does not write as one private individual to another. Rather, he associates Timothy with himself in the writing, and he addresses not only Philemon but also Philemon's wife Aphia, Archippus, and the whole church that meets in Philemon and Aphia's house (Phlm 1–2). This naming of others may be a technique of putting pressure on Philemon to do something. In any case, it lifts the letter out of any classification of private correspondence. Similarly, Paul asks that his letters be read by the whole communities (cf. 1 Thes 5:27); he asks that the letters be exchanged with other churches (Col 4:16); and he frequently identifies himself as an apostle, that is, as an authority in the Christian community.

These two qualifications, nevertheless, leave intact the basic literary form of Paul's writings as that of letter, the first move of Christianity from the oral to the written mode of tradition. They are lively and creative expressions of Christianity in a critical hour of its history, groping for ways of dealing with overpowering forces at play.

B. The Authentic Letters of Paul

Unlike the Gospels we have examined, the eight letters of Paul show some important diversities of theology among themselves. They span probably some fifteen years. Paul adapted his message to the specific group he was addressing. He developed his thought progressively and even seemed to change his mind on some points. The ideal study of Paul would examine each letter independently for its major ideas.

For our study here we will simply glance at each letter and its special purpose. We will then pick the most expressive texts to bring out the Pauline contribution to the themes we have been tracing through the New Testament. We can find enough consistency in Paul's letters to permit us to articulate a Pauline christology, soteriology, and eschatology. But first we need an overview of Paul's letters in their chronological order.

1. 1 Thessalonians

As we saw in the last chapter, 1 Thessalonians responded to Timothy's report of that church, a report that seems to have included several questions from the Thessalonians. Writing this letter, Paul follows the general format of Jewish Hellenistic letters in the opening. He starts with an identification of himself, the writer, an identification of the readers, a greeting ("grace and peace...") and a prayer. In the body of the letter we find two sections. Paul first establishes his personal connection with the church by recalling his work there and by recounting his own experiences after departing. He then answers the questions of the Thessalonians. The outline of the letter in broad lines thus follows a "newsy" part and an instructional part:

I.   Opening and Thanksgiving Prayer (1:1–10)

II. Paul and the Community (2:1–3:13)
     A. The foundation of the community (2:1–16)
     B. After Paul's departure (2:17–3:10)
     C. Prayer (3:11–13)

III. Response to Questions and Other Instructions (4:1–5:22)
     A. The moral duties of holiness and charity (4:1–12)
     B. Eschatology (4:13–5:11)
     C. Various directives (5:12–22)

IV. Conclusion: Blessing, Greetings, Prayer (5:23–28)

It is the eschatology of 1 Thessalonians that dominates this letter. It must have been a major issue in the church. Paul deals with two specific questions: What will happen to those who have died? When will the end be? He answers: the dead will rise, and we should not even try to calculate the end times. This letter will be important when we outline Paul's eschatology.

2. 1 Corinthians

From the "newsy" sections of 1 Corinthians we learn of two delegations that either informed Paul of problems in the Corinthian church or carried questions from that community (see 1:11 and 16:17). This rather long letter thus moves through a wide variety of topics as presented to Paul. Paul introduces these topics often with a formula, "And now concerning...." A technique of incorporating precomposed essays or homilies likewise appears for the first time in this letter and contributes to its unusual length. Unusually dense clusters of Old Testament citations will often mark these homiletic sections, now integrated into answers to specific problems or questions.

The overview of the letter shows the following organization:

I. Opening Address and Thanksgiving (1:1–9)

II. The Problem of Disunity in the Church (1:10–4:21)
—A homily on the cross and the spiritual wisdom (1:18–2:16)

III. Three Other Major Problems (5:1–6:20)
A. Incest in Corinth (5:1–13)
B. The use of pagan courts (6:1–11)
C. Illicit sex (6:12–20)

IV. Response to Questions and Other Problems (7:1–15:58)
A. Marriage and virginity (7:1–40)
B. Food offered to idols with digressions (8:1–11:1)
C. Conduct at church worship (11:2–34)
D. The spiritual gifts (12:1–14:40)
—Hymn on charity (13:1–13)
E. The resurrection of the dead (15:1–58)

V. Concluding Remarks (16:1–24)

This letter is practical in its orientation, yet draws from profound theological insights to explain and motivate the practical instructions. For instance, in the opening chapters Paul urges the Corinthian Christians to unity. In this exhortation Paul draws from his understanding of the cross and the role of the Spirit in this understanding to point out that a contentious and divisive attitude in the church implies a lack of understanding of the cross and a lack of spiritual life (see 1:10–3:4). Paul tells the Corinthians to stop envying each other's gifts and functions in the church, and he does this by drawing on his understanding of the church as the body of Christ (12:1–31). This letter thus becomes a profound meditation on life in the "church of God" (1:2), a reflection on both human failings within the church and divine assistance.

The number of topics touched by this letter, however, has made it a gold mine for understanding a wide variety of theological topics. We will return to texts of this letter when we look at Paul's view of the resurrection of the dead.

3. 2 Corinthians

As we saw briefly in the last chapter, 2 Corinthians is most probably an edited form of at least three letters, with all but 6:14–7:1 written shortly after 1 Corinthians. The angry letter (chapters 10–13) involves intense reflections by Paul on his own ministry. He dwells here on the paradox of divine strength and human weakness working so well together. The conciliatory letter reflects on Paul's ministry. Here Paul drifts from views of his work as a ministry of "the new covenant" (3:6) to a sense of his ministry as part of a cosmic "reconciliation" operated by God (5:17).

Given that we have two letters here in inverse chronological order, 2 Corinthians has the following structure:

I. The Letter of Reconciliation (chapters 1–9)
    A. Opening greeting and divine praise (1:1–7)
    B. Paul's ministry (1:8–7:16)
       1. Review of recent events—part 1 (1:8–2:17)
       2. The new covenant (3:1–4:6)
       3. Paul's afflictions and hopes (4:7–5:10)
       4. Divine reconciliation (5:11–7:4)
       —Fragment of earlier letter (6:14–7:1)
       5. Review of recent events—part 2 (7:5–16)
    C. Instructions for collection (8:1–9:15)

II. The Angry Letter (chapters 10–13)
    A. Defense against accusations (10:1–18)
    B. Paul and the false apostles (11:1–15)
    C. Paul's sufferings as an apostle (11:16–31)
    D. Paul's visions and revelations (12:1–10)
    E. Concerns for the Corinthian church (12:11–21)
    F. Final Warnings (13:1–10)

III. Conclusion (13:11–13)

Because of the occasion that provoked these letters, we have here profound insights into ministry and church. Unlike the practical orientation of 1 Corinthians, Paul in 2 Corinthians seems to have pondered more and probed deeper into God's reconciling action. The thought races from point to point. Paul reflects on the role of the Old Testament scriptures in Christian life (3:4–18), the light of God in our hearts (4:6), and the new creation of God as now in Christ (5:16–21). Paul pours it all out in a passionate outburst of concern for his beloved Corinthians.

4. Galatians

Galatians is a strange mélange of Paul's anger and his systematic thought. Paul is clearly angry. This is the only letter that does not include some prayer for blessing or thanksgiving for something good in the community to which he is writing. Instead of a thanksgiving, Paul starts with an expression of astonishment (1:6–10). The intensity of Paul's feelings comes through in the sections expressing his personal concerns. Yet alternating with these sections are symmetrical cycles and systematic portrayals of the plan of God leading through the Law to Christ. Paul here draws on pre-composed scriptural homilies (see 3:6–14; 4:21–31).

In the hypothesis explained in the last chapter, such a mélange of anger and theology makes sense. Paul is preparing a systematic presentation of his thought for the Romans. He hears of disastrous developments in the Galatian churches and tries to apply what he has prepared for the Romans to the Galatians. The result of this effort is a letter in the following structure:

  I. Opening Address and Expression of Astonishment (1:1–10)

 II. Autobiographical Defense of His Authority (1:11–2:16)
      —Transition (2:14–16)

III. Instruction on Justification through Faith (2:17–4:31)
      A. Summary of his position (2:17–21)
         —Personal concerns for the Galatians (3:1–5)
      B. Abraham and the Old Testament (3:6–22)
         1. First cycle: Blessing, curse, Christ (3:6–14)
         2. Second cycle: Promise, the Law, Christ (3:15–22)
      C. Before and after Christ (3:23–4:31)
         1. First cycle: The pedagogue and Christ (3:23–29)
         2. Second cycle: The baby and the son (4:1–7)

    —Personal concerns for Galatians (4:8–20)

    3. Third cycle: Abraham's two sons then and now (4:21–31)

  IV. Christian Living: The Antithesis of Flesh/Spirit (5:1–6:10)
    A. Freedom, not slavery (5:1–12)
    B. Freedom, not works of flesh but works of love (5:13–6:2)
    C. Maxims (6:3–10)

  V. Conclusion (6:11–18)

Galatians gives us the first attempt to see justification through faith. Paul's perspective is that of history. The period of salvation before Christ—what we would call the Old Testament—has its positive role in relationship to Christian faith, as childhood is related to adulthood. Paul's scriptural homilies here—with all the allegorical whimsy typical of such homilies of the day—draw especially from the Torah.

In the later ethical section of the letter, Paul shows how such soteriological adulthood leads to a way of living. This adult life is a life of freedom and love. It is a life according to "the Law of Christ" (6:2).

5. Romans

Paul's letter/epistle to the Romans repeats many of the issues and even the examples of Galatians but does so without the anger. The result is a more balanced and extensive view. Paul keeps the cyclical development of the earlier letter, but shifts to a historical perspective. The cycle now rotates among sin, Christ, and Israel.

In the second cycle, Paul develops a long section on the present place of Israel in God's plan. Paul is probably dealing with Gentile–Jew relations (as he perceived them) in the church of Rome. From the beginning of the letter, Paul prepares us for this development by the repeated refrain, "Jew first and then Greek" (1:16; 2:9, 10).

Paul also keeps the main division between an instructional section and an ethical section that he had in Galatians. The result is the following structure:

  I. Opening Address and Prayer (1:1–15)

  II. First Cycle: Justification (1:16–4:25)

A. Summary presentation (1:16–17)
B. The need: All humanity as sinful (1:18–3:20)
C. Justification by faith (3:21–31)
D. Example from Israel: Abraham (4:1–25)

III.   Second Cycle: Salvation (5:1–11:36)
A. Summary presentation (5:1–11)
B. The need: Sin, death, and the Law (5:12–7:25)
C. Life in the Spirit (8:1–39)
D. Example from Israel: Israel today (9:1–11:36)
1. The glory of Israel (9:1–5)
2. God freedom in his election (9:6–29)
3. Israel's unbelief and Christian faith (9:30–10:21)
4. The chosen remnant (11:1–10)
5. The Gentiles' salvation through Israel (11:11–32)
6. Concluding doxology (11:33–36)

IV.   Ethical Concerns (12:1–15:13)
A. The renewal of mind and spiritual worship (12:1–2)
B. Humility and charity within the community (12:3–13)
C. Charity to all, even to enemies (12:14–21)
D. Submission to civil authority (13:1–7)
E. Fulfilling the Law by love (13:8–10)
F. Vigilance (13:11–14)
G. Charity toward the scrupulous (14:1–15:6)
H. Welcome one another (15:7–13)

V.   Conclusion (15:14–16:27)

Romans gives us the most thorough presentation of God's plan of salvation as Paul understood it. The epistle has its somber and glum side: salvation means little without a sense of sin. It also has its glorious side in its presentation of God's love and gift of the Spirit. All of this is set within the issue of Israel and the gospel. This writing is not the whole of Paul's theology, but it is a major presentation of it. An understanding of Romans goes a long way toward our grasping Paul's faith.

6. Philippians

Paul's letter to the Philippians is basically a letter of thanks. It is his warmest letter. Paul's gratitude for the Philippian's help in his imprisonment leads him to describe his situation and plans. Paul appears to have no worries about misconduct in the Philippian church—apart from the bickering of a few individuals (4:2). But the theological engine is running too fast in Paul's mind not to pour out intense reflections about his own hopes in life and death as well as general encouragements to the Philippians to maintain their struggle for the faith.

Philippians gives us a good example of Paul incorporating pre-composed material. We will return to chapter 2 of this letter in our discussion of Paul's christology. Here we find one of the most expressive texts in Paul regarding the identity of Christ.

Because it is a letter—less concerned with symmetrical and systematic presentation than with personal communication—Philippians is difficult to outline, without listing all the topics touched on. Breaks in the flow of the material (2:19; 3:2; 4:10) suggest that Paul wrote this letter over an extended time. At these breaks Paul plunges into a new topic. As an overview we can list the following sections:

I. Opening Address and Prayer (1:1–11)

II. News of Paul's Situation (1:12–26)

III. Exhortations (1:27–2:18) [break]
   —Christological hymn (2:6–11)

IV. Plans Concerning Timothy and Epaphroditus (2:12–29) [break]

V. Exhortations (3:1–4:9) [break]

VI. Paul's Gratitude (4:10–20)

VII. Closing (4:21–23)

The letter shows a depth of thought and a development that would make more sense as a letter written later in Paul's career. Not only are the insights about Christ the clearest presentations in letters; his view of death goes far beyond what he wrote to the Thessalonians and Corinthians. When he speaks of his own great achievements, Paul in this letter shows a calmness of spirit that may be the direct result of his imprisonment, where all is stripped away and his life in review takes on its full meaning. He can talk of "achievements" as "horse manure" in the light of "knowing Christ Jesus my Lord" (3:8).

7. Philemon

The letter to Philemon, one chapter long, is Paul's simplest personal letter. This letter contains virtually no theological agenda. Paul is dealing with the practical problem of returning a runaway slave to a Christian master. Yet the love that moves Paul's words—"I am sending him, that is my own heart, back to you" (12)—reveals the apostle to us, and in that revealing picture we see Paul's faith. The letter also helps us understand Paul's relations with wealthy patrons such as Philemon, the sense of "partnership" Paul wanted with these people (6), as well as the need Paul had for their support (22).

The letter exhibits the clearest parallel in Paul to the typical Jewish Hellenistic letters of the day:

I. Opening (1–6)
   A. Identifications (1–2)
   B. Greeting (3)
   C. Letter prayer (4–6)

II. Body (7–22)

III. Conclusion (23–24)
   A. Greetings from those with Paul (23–24)
   B. Prayer (25)

To a large degree, the similarity of this letter to Colossians in terms of the situation and people with Paul and those addressed supports the traditional idea of Colossians' authenticity.

8. Colossians

Like Romans, Colossians is addressed to a group that was not founded nor even personally known by Paul. Epaphras, apparently a disciple of Paul and the leader of the church of Colossae, comes to Paul with the problems of the church there—problems that look like superstitious fears of cosmic powers.

Paul—or somebody very close to Paul—answers in a typically Pauline fashion. He avoids a moralistic exhortation, as if to tell the

Colossians simply to shape up. Rather, he goes deeper to what Paul sees to be the real problem: not understanding the role of Christ in the universe. The letter incorporates the second hymn we will look at in our examination of Paul's christology, 1:15–20. This is a hymn composed before the writing of this letter and inserted into the text by Paul. Paul may have written the hymn. If he did not, he at least agreed with it well enough to make it part of his own writing.

Not only in this hymn but through the rest of this letter we find an intense focus on the person of Christ. He is the great "mystery" present through ages past but only now revealed to Christians (1:26), Christ is the one in whom "dwells the whole fullness of the deity" (2:9). The instructions of this letter as well as its ethical exhortations revolve around Paul's christology.

The following can serve as an outline of the letter:

I. Opening (1:1–20)
    —Christological hymn (1:15–20)

II. Instructions (1:21–2:23)
    A. Transition (1:21–23)
    B. Review of Paul's work (1:24–2:5)
    C. Life in Christ (2:6–15)
    D. Application to the errors in Colossae (2:16–23)

III. Ethical Exhortations (3:1–4:6)
    A. Basis: Life with the risen Christ (3:1–4)
    B. Vices and virtues (3:5–17)
    C. Duties in the Christian home (3:18–4:1)
    D. Various exhortations (4:2–6)

IV. Conclusion (4:7–18)

Compared to the earlier letters of Paul, this letter shows several shifts in theological imagery. Colossians speaks of Christians already risen (2:12; 3:1). But if Paul earlier wrote of this resurrection as future (Rom 6:5), in the same breath he spoke of our "new life" as present now (Rom 6:4). Colossians speaks of Christ as "the head" of his body, which is clearly "the church" (1:18; 2:19). But Paul spoke of the local community already as "the body of Christ" (1 Cor 12:12, 14; Rom 12:4) and occasionally spoke of "the church" as a single encompassing reality (1 Cor 12:28; see also 1 Cor 1:2). None of these shifts takes us out of Pauline theology, but they do take us to its furthest developments. They make good sense as representing the last thinking of Paul in the trajectory that began with 1 Thessalonians.

Letter	Place of Writing	Date	Correlation with Acts	
1 Thessalonians	Corinth	A.D. 52	Acts 18:1–17	2nd journey
1 Corinthians	Ephesus	A.D. 55	Acts 19:1–40	3rd journey
2 Corinthians	Ephesus & Macedonia	A.D. 57	Acts 19:19–20:1	3rd journey
Galatians	Corinth	A.D. 58	Acts 20:2–3	3rd journey
Romans	Corinth	A.D. 58	Acts 20:2–3	3rd journey
Philippians	Ephesus	A.D. 64?	————	
Philemon	Ephesus	A.D. 64?	————	
Colossians	Ephesus	A.D. 64?	————	

Figure 25. **A Summary of Paul's Letter Writing.**

II. The Faith of Paul

Forcing Paul into the schema we have used to survey the faith of the New Testament authors does a disservice to his theology. Paul's thought touches a wide range of matters. But our purpose here is to see Paul in the context of the New Testament and how his thought compares to others.

A. Paul's Christology

(See exercise 2.)

In Paul's letters we have the earliest testimonies of faith in Jesus as unique in God's plan of redemption for humanity. Written some thirty or forty years after Jesus and recalling Paul's earlier preaching, these letters echo the faith of the first generation of Christians.

Who then is Jesus for Paul? One aspect of Paul's christology becomes clear quickly in our reading. Paul is interested above all in Jesus' work or functioning in God's dealing with humanity. Paul is more concerned with what Jesus does than with what Jesus is. Yet especially in the later letters, Paul presses the implications of his christology to describe Jesus' being.

In this functional portrayal of Jesus, Paul consistently portrays Jesus under God. The subordination of Jesus to the Father is all the more striking in descriptions meant to depict the ultimate stage in God's triumph over evil. As Paul states in 1 Corinthians:

> When everything is subjected to him [Christ], then the Son himself will be subject in his turn to the One who subjected all things to him, so that God may be all in all. (15:28)

Two texts, probably among Paul's last writings, begin to speculate on the ontological presuppositions of this functional subordination of Jesus to the Father. Both texts appear to have a literary history independent of the letters in which they now exist. Both texts may have been composed by Paul at an earlier time, or may even have been written by writers other than Paul. In any case Paul sees these texts as close enough to his christology to use them in his attempts to instruct his churches by letter.

1. Philippians 2:6–11

Writing to the Philippians, probably in the last years of his career, Paul introduces a Christian hymn. It describes Jesus in three stages, as preexisting, as a human being, and as exalted after his death. The movement from one stage to another is consistent with Paul's christological statements in earlier letters.

> 6. Who existing in the form of God
> did not consider being equal to God a matter of robbery
> 7. But he emptied himself taking on a form of a slave
> becoming in the likeness of men.
> and being found in the state of a man.
> 8. He humbled himself becoming obedient unto death,
> death on a cross.
> 9. Therefore God highly exalted him
> and gave him the name above all names
> 10. So that in the name of Jesus every knee bend
> in the heavens and on earth and below the earth
> 11. And every tongue confess that Jesus Christ is Lord
> To the glory of God the Father.

Verse 6 of the text describes Jesus before he became a human being. It makes two statements about him. First, he was "in the form of God," and second, he did not consider equality with God something he should rob or had robbed. The second statement is ambiguous in the Greek, describing this equality either as something Jesus does not have and refuses to snatch or as something he has and has legitimately. The English translation usually refuses to transmit this ambiguity and makes a choice between the two possibilities.

What is Paul saying here? Is he declaring Jesus to be divine? The expression "form of God" is not clear. It may be describing Jesus as the "image of God," since for Paul the Greek word for "form" *(morphē)* is very close in meaning to the word for "image" *(eikōn)*. As Paul writes, "Let us be trans*formed (metamorphoumetha)* in the same *image (eikona)"* (2 Cor 3:18).

What is clear here is Paul's insistence on Jesus as more than a human being. Jesus exists before he becomes a man, and he exists with specific personal attitudes. Paul pictures a person existing in a heavenly realm before becoming human. Such a description harmonizes with and explicates Paul's earlier statements, which now can be seen to describe the transition between the heavenly and earthly realms:

> Though he was rich, he became poor for your sake. (2 Cor 8:9)

> Though he did not know sin, God made him sin for our sake. (2 Cor 5:21)

The description in Phil 2:6 also explains further Paul's descriptions of Jesus' being sent by the Father as more than a prophetic sending (Rom 8:3; Gal 4:4).

Verses 7–8 then describe the earthly career of Christ. We are struck by the somber and grim aspects. Paul insists on this incarnation as a thorough humiliation, Christ's "emptying" of himself. Nothing glorious appears here, nothing joyful. The whole description is dominated by Christ's death. The two virtues that Paul specifies here are humility and obedience, the virtues characteristic of a slave.

This description fits well with many other Pauline allusions to the earthly career of Jesus: coming "in the likeness of sinful flesh" (Rom 8:3), becoming "a curse for us" (Gal 3:13), being "born under the Law" (Gal 4:4), becoming "sin" (2 Cor 5:21). Paul sees very little positive in the earthly career of Jesus. He says nothing about the miracles or extended teachings of Jesus recorded in the Gospels. Occasionally Paul refers to "a word of the Lord," probably referring to a teaching of the earthly Jesus. However, in general, Paul seems to view the life of Jesus on earth only as a preparation for his death. Paul focuses on Jesus' coming in mortal, weak flesh. He likewise focuses on Jesus' intense solidarity with humanity in its sinfulness, a theme echoed in the Synoptic Gospels with the stories of Jesus' baptism and table fellowship.

Verses 9–11 then describe the Christ who dominates Paul's theology. This is the risen, glorious Lord, whom Paul met near Damascus. Paul describes this exalted Christ with several significant statements. God gives him "the name above all other names," very probably a reference to God's own name, Yahweh. Christ receives universal adoration, and every tongue proclaims him as "Lord."

The connection between the title Lord and "the name above every other name" is clear to anyone familiar with the late Jewish manner of referring to God. Although the name Yahweh appears frequently in the Hebrew Scriptures, Jews developed the practice of using a substitute for that name, whenever they read aloud. The most common substitute was *Adonay,* Hebrew for "my Lord(s)."[1] Hence "Lord" and "Yahweh" became closely connected in the Jewish mind, even in languages other than Hebrew.

What then is Paul saying with these descriptions of the exalted Jesus? Is he saying that Jesus is God? After all, for Paul and for others of his culture, to bear a name meant more than having an attached label. The name expressed who the person really was, what role God has given that person. For Jesus to receive the divine name, meant for Paul that Jesus was in some way divine. But what does Paul mean by saying that Jesus *received* the name and specifically as a recompense for his humiliation and death?

Furthermore, we might ask how Paul sees this final stage (vv. 9–11) in comparison with the first stage (v. 6). Is this exaltation a return to the same level as the first? Or is it a higher level? The hymn as a whole describes the movement to the third stage as a recompense for Jesus ("because of this"). Does that imply a higher level at the end? Readers who would deny that vv. 9–11 refer to a higher level usually argue that v. 6 already describes Jesus as God—and you cannot rise any higher than that.

But is v. 6 so clear about Jesus' divinity? An interesting parallel to Jesus as in the form of or as the image of God appears from the Old Testament. The parallel is the description of Adam, created in the image of God (Gn 1:26–27). The serpent's temptation of Adam and Eve was "to become like God" (Gn 3:5). Their sin was, therefore, one of pride as well as disobedience to a specific prohibition of God (Gn 2:16–17). If the parallel was on Paul's mind, then it provides a clue to Paul's meaning. When Paul describes Jesus "in the form of God," not thinking about robbing equality with God, and becoming both humble and obedient, Paul may well be thinking of Jesus as a "new Adam," undoing the damage of the first Adam, an image Paul earlier used in an explicit manner (1 Cor 15:45–49). Paul is still thinking of Jesus in his saving function, hence again in his role under God.

This understanding of v. 6 clarifies vv. 9–11. The exaltation of Jesus is a recompense for his humble life and death. This exaltation is thus an act of God for someone under God. God goes to the extent of sharing his very name with Jesus, sharing his very identity. Yet God does this for Jesus. This is not an attribute Jesus has by divine nature. In fact the exaltation does not place Jesus on the same level as God, for all this is done precisely "to the glory of God the Father."

2. Colossians 1:15–20

Colossians 1:15–20 is also very probably a christological hymn composed prior to the letter to the Colossians. In this hymn we have several important statements about Christ:

> 15. Who is the image of the invisible God,
> the first born of all creation
> 16. Since in him was created all things
> in the heavens and on the earth
> things visible and things invisible
> Whether thrones or dominations or princes or powers
> All things were created through him and for him,
> 17. and he is for all things
> and all things stand together in him.
> 18. And he is the head of the body, the church.
> Who is the beginning, the first born of the dead,
> in order that in all things he may have primacy,
> 19. So that in him all the fullness was pleased to dwell
> 20. And all things are reconciled for him
> making peace through the blood of his cross
> whether things on the earth or things in the heavens.

The first half, vv. 15–17, describes Jesus related to all of creation. The second half, vv. 18–20, describes him related to redemption and the church. The combination of the two aspects again reminds us of the functional concern dominating Paul's description here. We will look especially at the first half, where Jesus is again described as "the image of God."

The description is ambiguous. Jesus is called "the firstborn" of creation. That description appears to place Jesus within creation. The following lines, describing God creating "in him," "through him," and "for him," imply a position outside of creation, above creation. This position is even clearer where Paul states, "he existed before all else."

Very important is the way this hymn relates Jesus to creation. All things are created "in" and "through" him, implying a role of Jesus as a kind of instrument or means by which God creates. More striking is the statement that all things are created "for him." Earlier Paul wrote,

> There is only one God, the Father, from whom all things
> come and for whom we exist. (1 Cor 8:6)

In this earlier text Jesus is also the one "through whom" all things come to be, but in true Jewish fashion Paul applied the "for whom" to God. "For whom" expresses the ultimate purpose of the universe, its final goal, the source of its deepest meaning. In Colossians, Paul is placing Jesus in this divine spot.

The description of Jesus as the "firstborn" reminds us of similar descriptions of "wisdom" in later Jewish writings (Prv 8:22). There too Wisdom is described as involved in creation (Prv 8:27–29). In these writings, Wisdom preexists creation, has divine functions, is not identified with God, and yet does not appear as a "second God." In these writings, the Jewish theologians were engaged in poetic personification. They were describing an aspect or attribute of God as though it were a person. The word of God was similarly described (cf. Is 55:10–11).

Paul and others with him may have read these Jewish texts and have seen in them the means by which they could express their faith in Christ. They saw Jesus as more than a human being. They saw him having divine functions, even preexistence. But they did not want to identify him with the Father, nor did they want to speak of him as a second God. Normally such an apparent contradiction of judgments would have led to an unsolvable impasse. But the poetic personification of Wisdom provided a way. Here was the vocabulary by which Paul could think the unthinkable. If the Jewish writers could say these things about Wisdom, Paul could say them about Christ.

In this way Christians learned to speak about Jesus as divine-like, as preexisting his birth, as sharing in the divinity of God. Yet such language did not compromise their monotheism. Especially by describing Jesus as personally preexistent in the heavenly realm of God, the door was open to the next step of identifying Jesus with God. But Paul does not seem to be at that point.

B. Paul's Soteriology

Paul's soteriology, his teaching about salvation, is his burning interest. Paul's vision centers on the work of the Father. It is the Father who saves us. It is the Father who reconciles us. It is the Father who shows us his love. But for Paul the Father saves us through Christ, and specifically through the death and resurrection of Christ. Following the theme we examined in the Synoptic Gospels, we will focus on the death of Jesus and how that death can be used by God to save.

To develop such views, Paul had to overcome an enormous paradox. As a historical factual event, the death of Jesus was the bloody execution of a convicted criminal. There was nothing religious, nothing holy about it. Paul and the early Christians needed to see this event as life-giving. To do so they had to interpret this death, they had to find some mediating image, through which the connection between a horrible death and the gift of salvation could be drawn. In effect, we can distinguish three such interpretations or mediating images in Paul. At different times, Paul saw that death as (a) an act of obedience, (b) a purchase of our freedom, and (c) a religious sacrifice.

1. An Act of Obedience

In Rom 5:19 Paul states,

Just as through one man's disobedience all became sinners, so through one man's obedience all shall become just.

Here Paul is mediating the death of Jesus through the interpretive image of an act of obedience. As an act of obedience, this death can be understood as life-giving, as counteracting the disobedience of Adam.

Paul has chosen an image from interpersonal existence, the attitude of obedience of one person toward another. The focus is on the internal attitude of Jesus, not so much his physical death.

If one could put the horrible physical death of Jesus aside and focus only on the spiritual attitude, this image of "one man's obedience" would go far to assist the early Christians to accept the crucifixion of Jesus. Yet from his constant references to "the blood" of Jesus as the means of justification (Rom 3:25; 5:9; 1 Cor 11:25), Paul apparently does not want to "spiritualize" the action by which we are redeemed.

2. A Purchase of Freedom

The physical death of Jesus for all its painfulness becomes more prominent in both Gal 3:13 and 4:4, where Paul describes Jesus' death as an act of "buying back":

> Christ bought us back from the curse of the law by becoming a curse for us. (3:13)

> When the fullness of time came, God sent his son, born of woman, born under the Law in order to buy those who were under the Law.... (4:4)

In both places Paul uses the word *exagorein,* translated often as "to redeem" or "to deliver," but which literally means "to buy back."

In this case Paul is using an economic image or category to say how the death of Jesus can bring forth life. As "a price paid" for us, that death can be understood as saving. Such an image expresses well the great value we are worth, the enormous "cost" of our redemption. The image also expresses the seriousness of the sinful condition. This condition is not trivial even in the eyes of God. It demands great "effort" or a great "cost" to be remedied.

A difficulty arises when we push this image beyond what it is meant to express, when for instance we ask, To whom was the price paid? Paul does not intend to express any other partner in the deal, and efforts to identify such a partner lead to serious distortions of Paul's thought. Early Christian writers after Paul, for instance, suggested that Jesus paid the price to the devil, presumably the one who held us in slavery, from whom we could be ransomed if the price were right. The difficulty with this idea, of course, lies in the image of the devil that it conveys, suggesting a devil with real bargaining power with God, one who could demand a particular price. The other early suggestion saw Jesus paying the price to the Father. Again a serious difficulty arises with the image of God that this suggestion conveys. Now it is the Father who plays the role of the slave master, who has to be bought off. Paul, as we will see, would never subscribe to such a picture of God.

In effect, the interpretive image of Jesus "buying us back" by his death simply does not express anything further than the action of Christ, for all its importance, for all its "cost." There is no one from whom we are purchased. There is no one to whom a price is paid. To pose the question is to push the image beyond what it can express.

3. A Sacrifice

It is in the third image, however, that Paul homes in on the redemptive death of Jesus precisely as bloody death. In 1 Cor 5:7 Paul writes,

Christ our Passover [lamb], has been slaughtered.

In Rom 3:25 he describes Jesus as the "propitiatory," the golden plate on the top of the Ark of the Covenant, which was sprinkled by the blood of sacrificed animals on the Day of Atonement:

God presented him as a propitiatory through faith in his blood for a manifestation of God's justice.

In these and other texts Paul likens the death of Jesus to the bloody deaths of the sacrificial animals in the Temple. Here Paul has found a mediating image through which the death of Jesus as death can be seen as life-giving. This time the image is drawn from religion, from the Temple practices still going on as Paul was writing.

Like the animal deaths, with all the ugliness involved in slaughtering and burning an animal, so the death of Jesus, with all its obscene horror, could be envisaged as a way of worshiping God. The sacrifice represented the ones offering it to God. So Jesus dying on the cross represented humanity to God in some sort of atoning worship.

The difficulty with this image—with bloody sacrifice in general, but all the more with Jesus as the sacrifice—lies in the picture of God it implies. God appears as a Moloch-like, bloodthirsty God, a

God who is so angry that he demands death, someone's death—if not our death, then Christ's. Such a picture of God easily arises from the notion of bloody sacrifice.

While the image of bloody sacrifices inevitably carries this difficulty, Paul explicitly rejects such a picture. In effect Paul takes the representative value of Christ's death and turns it around:

> God proves his love for us in that while we were still sinners Christ died for us. (Rom 5:8)

Hence, whatever Paul wants to say with the image of the "sacrifice of the cross," he does not want to imply that this action of Jesus changed God from an angry to an appeased God. Rather he insists that the cross originates in the love that God already has for us.

At this point we could press the question further. Why would God choose the death of his Son to manifest his love and thus to redeem us? Paul must have wrestled with this question, not in the sense of second-guessing God or of trying to decide how God had to act. The question really asks about how we can understand such a decision of God in the light of other aspects of his dealings with us.

Paul's answer would lie in his notion of sin, a notion he inherited from his apocalyptic background. Echoing apocalyptic writings of his time, Paul describes the universality of sin in Romans 1–3 and the objective power of sin in Romans 7. Here Paul speaks of "the slavery of sin" (7:14) and the "power of death" (7:24). Although Paul insists that sin entered the world "through one man" (Rom 5:12), once it entered, it became a sort of cosmic force larger than human beings.

The sacrificial death of Jesus thus expresses a divine decision to deal with sin on its own level. Had sin, in Paul's eyes, been simply a matter of bad attitudes, of stupid decisions, or a sick mentality, then salvation could come as a form of a great moral instruction. The savior could work as a great moral philosopher or cosmic psychiatrist. In this view of sin, there is no need, indeed no sense at all, for a savior to die for us. But Paul sees sin as no less than the power of death itself through which sin operates. In dealing with sin on its own level, redemption would have to wrestle with the very powers of death, where the corruptibility of "flesh" would be manifested for all its weakness. Paul sees this in the death of Christ. In the crucifixion, Paul attains a clear vision of sin.

C. Paul's Eschatology

(See exercise 3.)

To understand Paul's eschatology we must remember the dating of his writing. We are prior to Mark's connection of the end with the destruction of the Temple, prior to Matthew's concern with the delay, and prior to Luke's resolution of the delay by means of the Spirit. We are in fact close to the early simple faith that the end must be near. If Jesus has destroyed the power of sin and death, then full salvation in the form of resurrection of the dead must be near.

Paul wrote about the end of the world more in his earlier letters than in his later ones. Three letters in particular are important for understanding the eschatology of Paul: 1 Thessalonians, 1 Corinthians, and Romans.

1. 1 Thessalonians

Paul expresses his views about the end of the world most explicitly in 1 Thessalonians. The Christians in Thessalonica had apparently begun to worry about the members of their community who were dying off. Were these dead going to miss the joy of Jesus' return in glory? Paul answers that they will not miss out on anything because they will rise from the dead and thus we will all be "with the Lord" forever:

> The dead in Christ will rise first, then we the living who are left will be caught up in the clouds to meet the Lord in the air. And thus we will be with the Lord forever. (4:16–17)

This consoling instruction to the Thessalonians follows a mini-apocalypse or a visualized scenario of the end detailed with symbolic elements.

> We say to you, from a word of the Lord, that we the living who are left at the return of the Lord will have no advantage over those who have fallen asleep. That the Lord himself at a command, at the voice of the archangel, at the sound of the trumpet, will come down from heaven.... (4:13–16)

As we read these descriptions of the end of the world, however, we should also keep in mind a much older description of God's appearance in Sinai as given in Exodus:

Now at daybreak on the third day there were peals of thunder on the mountain and lightning flashes, a dense cloud, and a loud trumpet blast, and inside the camp all the people trembled. Then Moses led the people out of the camp to meet God; and they stood at the bottom of the mountain. The mountain of Sinai was entirely wrapped in smoke, because Yahweh had descended on it in the form of fire. Like smoke from a furnace the smoke went up, and the whole mountain shook violently. Louder and louder grew the sound of the trumpet. Moses spoke, and God answered him with peals of thunder. Yahweh came down on the mountain of Sinai, on the mountain top. (Ex 19:16–20)

The similarities of the two scenes are striking. Both speak of clouds and a trumpet as accompanying the appearance of the Lord. Both speak of the Lord descending. Both speak of the people going out to meet the Lord. The similar images and wording lead us to conclude to some sort of dependence of Paul on this well-known text of Exodus. Paul either was consciously thinking of this text or was sharing a common way of thinking that depended on this text. We see in other descriptions of the end the frequent appearance of trumpet blasts and clouds. These had become part of the stereotype for an apocalyptic description of the end.

Paul could be relying directly on the Exodus text, or he could be sharing a common stereotype that depended on the Exodus text. In either case this dependence on the Old Testament text here leads us to see the details of Paul's description of the end as stemming from a literary form rather than from special knowledge about the future events. These details tell us more about the literary forms and stereotypes of Paul's time than about the end events. Paul uses these details because that is what the end was "supposed" to look like—according to the human norms at Paul's time.

A reading of Thessalonians according to the intention of the author thus requires us to search beyond the individual details of this description and seek the purpose of Paul. What is he trying to say? What is his main point? The last lines of Paul give us the clue. Basically, Paul is exhorting the community to be comforted by the prospect of the end. He is insisting on a living relationship between the believers and the Lord, a relationship that not even death can prevent, a relationship that will last forever. "So we shall stay with the Lord forever" (4:17).

It is interesting to note here the presupposition expressed in vv. 15 and 16 in the words, "we the living who are left." Paul seems to be considering the real possibility that he himself might be alive at the time. If the general presupposition were to picture the end far off in the future, this attempt of Paul to be vivid would sound strange. He seems to see it coming within his lifetime. This expectation of a speedy end continues through most of Paul's writing.

On the other hand, Paul discounts any possibility of calculating the time of the end: "About times and seasons, brothers, you have no need of me writing to you, for you know well that the day of the Lord will come like a thief in the night" (5:1–2). The end of the world is totally God's work. Hence, there is no way we can know its timing; it is to come suddenly. According to Paul, no signs will forewarn us.

2. 1 Corinthians

Paul's confidence about the nearness of the end is not based on calculating the future. Rather it is based on what God has already done in the past, namely, raising Jesus from the dead. In 1 Corinthians, Paul makes this connection between the general resurrection at the end of the world and the particular resurrection of Jesus.

Chapter 15 of 1 Corinthians is dedicated to the resurrection of the dead and the eschatological triumph of God. He begins his considerations, however, by recalling a tradition from the past:

> First of all, I handed on to you what I received: that Christ died for our sins according to the scriptures, that he was buried, that he rose on the third day according to the scriptures, and that he appeared to Cephas and the Twelve, then he appeared to over five hundred of the brothers at one time—most of whom are still alive, although some have died—then he appeared to James and all the apostles. Last of all he appeared to me as one born out of due course. (15:3–8)

Paul, we must note, associates his experience of Jesus on the way to Damascus with that of the earlier apostles. Paul insists that what he saw was the Lord in his risen body (1 Cor 9:1), not some spiritual flash of light (contrast Acts 9:3–8). When Paul then describes the characteristics of the risen body, we must remember that he is the only one in the New Testament to have seen a risen body and personally to have written about it.

For Paul, the resurrection of Jesus is "the firstfruits" of the general resurrection (15:20). It is not simply an isolated event. It is the beginning of a whole series. Just as the firstfruits of a season signal the beginning of the harvest, so the resurrection of Jesus indicates that final triumph of God over death has begun. Because the resurrection of Jesus and the general resurrection of the dead belong together, Paul would inevitably conclude that one should soon lead to the other. Christ's resurrection begins the end. But the series must follow a divine order:

> Just as all men die in Adam, so all men will be brought to life in Christ; but all of them in their proper order: Christ as the firstfruits and then, after the coming of Christ, those who belong to him. (15:22–23)

In the remaining part of this chapter, Paul makes two very important points about the end of the world: first, he describes this end as the ultimate triumph of God through Christ. It will be the moment when all "enemies" are overcome. The last enemy is death itself.

> Then will come the end, when Christ will hand over the kingdom to God the Father....When all things are subject to Christ, then he the Son will be subject to the one who subjected all things to him, so that God may be all in all. (15:24–28)

Paul is thinking of all things, human and nonhuman, when he considers this ultimate submission to the Father. It will be a kingdom involving the whole of creation.

Second, Paul insists on a radical transformation of material reality as it becomes part of God's final triumph. Paul speaks specifically of the human body and describes the contrast between the mortal body we experience now and the risen body we will have then. He makes this contrast by a series of antitheses:

> | What is sown in the earth is subject to decay, | what rises is incorruptible |
> | What is sown is ignoble, | what rises is glorious. |
> | Weakness is sown, | strength rises up. |
> | A natural body is put down | a spiritual body comes up. |
>
> (1 Cor 15:42–44)

With this description Paul is trying to say two things. First of all, he insists on a continuity between ourselves as mortal and as risen. What is sown is what rises. This continuity is located in our body (*sōma*). At the same time, however, Paul insists on a discontinuity between the manner of our existence before death and after the resurrection. The resurrection is not simply the return to our earthly way of living. It is not simply the resuscitation of a corpse. The shift is from a "natural" mode to a "spiritual" mode. As Paul states in other texts, this discontinuity is located especially in our "flesh" (*sarx*). "Flesh" is left behind. "Flesh" does not inherit the kingdom (1 Cor 15:50). "Body" does.

Of course, after all this insistence by Paul, we still do not see what the resurrection of the dead or the end of the world is supposed to be like. Paul has told us mostly what it will *not* be like. It will not be simply the resuscitation of dead corpses. Paul cannot tell us much more than that. If we can live with the mystery of a seed germinating into a plant, as Paul points out (1 Cor 15:36–38), then we can live with the mystery of God's final triumph.

3. Romans

While the early texts of 1 Corinthians 15 and 1 Thessalonians 4–5 contain Paul's most vivid pictures of the end, a more mature presentation of Paul's eschatology occurs in his letter to the Romans, where in general he tries to lay out his theology in some balanced form. The text is chapter 8, which in many ways could be considered the most important chapter in all of Paul's writings.

This chapter begins with a description of salvation, referring to both Jesus and the divine Spirit as the media through which God brings his creatures from death to life:

> There is no condemnation now for those who are in
> Christ Jesus, for the Law of the Spirit of life in Christ
> Jesus freed you from the Law of sin and death. (8:1–2)

For Paul in some way this salvation is already accomplished. We have been freed from death. Typical of a person thinking in apocalyptic dualism, Paul describes this liberation in terms of two superhuman forces, "the Law of the Spirit of life" and "the Law of sin and death." Paul is thinking of sin not so much as an ethical problem but rather as the very power of death.

In the next verses Paul develops this dualist drama in terms of

"Spirit" and "Flesh." Again he is thinking less in anthropological terms than in cosmic terms:

> The mentality of the Flesh is death; the mentality of the Spirit is life and peace. Thus the mentality of the Flesh is hatred of God. It is not subject to the Law of God; it cannot. Those in the Flesh cannot please God. (8:6–8)

Were Paul speaking of anthropological elements here, his words would betray a Gnostic dualism. Perhaps he is flirting with this Hellenistic position because of the sympathy he knows his readers would have for this dualism. But for Paul coming out of a Jewish apocalyptic perspective, the flesh *(sarx)* is not the human body *(sōma)*. As we saw in his letter to the Corinthians above, the human body for Paul is capable of redemption, of resurrection, of spiritual transformation. Flesh is not. Flesh, apparently for Paul, is corruptibility, mortality, the face of sin. There is no resurrection of the flesh.

Rescue from this power of sin and death is outside the capacity of a human being. No effort, no good work can free us from death. Rescue is a gift of God mediated through Christ and the divine Spirit. This is a rescue begun now but still future in its full realization.

> If Christ is in you, the body is indeed dead through sin, while the Spirit is life through justice. If the Spirit of the one raising Jesus from the dead dwells in you, the one raising Jesus from the dead *will* bring to life also your mortal bodies, through the Spirit dwelling in you.... All who are led by the Spirit are sons of God. (8:10–14)

In the climactic section of this chapter Paul ties together the elements of (a) prayer, (b) future salvation, and (c) all of material reality in an intricate chiastic structure:

A. You did not receive a spirit of slavery again leading you into fear, but a spirit of adoption through which we cry out, "Abba!" "Father!" The Spirit itself gives witness with our spirit that we are children of God.

B. If furthermore children, then heirs, heirs of God, co-heirs with Christ, if indeed we suffer with him in order to be glorified with him. (I do not consider the sufferings of the present time, to be worthy of comparison with the future glory to be revealed in us.)

C. For the expectation of creation awaits the revelation of the sons of God.... Because that same creation will be freed from the slavery to corruption and given a share in the glorious freedom of the children of God. We know that up to now all of creation groans with labor pains. In fact not only that but we ourselves having the firstfruits of the Spirit groan awaiting the adoption as sons, namely, the redemption of our bodies.

B´. For we are saved in hope. But hope seen is not hope. Can one hope for what is seen? Rather if we do not see, we hope in patient longing.

A´. In the same way the Spirit assists our weakness. For we do not know what to pray for as we should. But the Spirit itself supplicates with ineffable groaning. And the one searching the hearts knows the mentality of the Spirit, for the Spirit supplicates in God's way on behalf of the holy ones. (8:15–27)

The chiastic structure ties together Paul's theology.

C: The resurrection of our bodies for Paul is the meaning of salvation. It is the ultimate triumph of God by his Spirit over death and sin. But here Paul points out how this resurrection of the body is part of a bigger picture. God intends to "resurrect" all of material creation. Salvation is not simply getting one's soul to heaven. It is the structuring of all creation.

B–B´: Surrounding this central thought is the constant reminder that this salvation is future. We are not "saved" yet. We may be justified, reconciled, set at peace. But salvation is nothing less than this future eschatology. Hence we are confronted with the fundamental Christian challenge of a patient hope, an assurance to live by, yet a dissatisfaction in not seeing.

A–A´: Surrounding the whole development is the reason why we can live now in assurance. We have the Spirit in our hearts. Our life toward this eschatological future is, therefore, a life of prayer. This prayer is very simple. It may not even involve a human striving but rather allowing the Spirit to address God. The address is summed up in one word, *Abba,* an Aramaic word, probably rooted in Jesus' own instructions about prayer, a word which in its "endearment" form is proper to that of a young child addressing its father. In effect, the elaborate eschatology of Paul as lived now, as influencing our mentality now, condenses to one simple word addressed to God, *Papa.*

III. Theological Reflections

These insights of Paul into the meaning of Christ's death, into the identity of Christ, as well as his view of the coming triumph of God have earned Paul the title of "the theologian." Very probably Paul received much from his fellow Christians, especially in the Antioch community. Yet it is Paul who writes these insights down and therefore to Paul we give the credit for this work.

Some have objected that this theological work of Paul does not sound much like the preaching of Jesus, at least as we understand it from the Synoptic Gospels. Did Paul corrupt the Gospel of Jesus? Or did Paul succeed in translating that Gospel, originally spoken in agrarian Palestinian terms, into an urban Hellenistic vocabulary? Every translation and every interpretation involve changes and shifts. Did the substance remain the same?

The debate may never be over, but we should note some striking similarities between Jesus and Paul, especially in Paul's view of God and God's offer of salvation. Although Paul uses a lot of ink writing the names Jesus and Christ and describing this person in his letters, the real protagonist in his descriptions is God the Father. It is God, as we have seen, who takes the initiative to save humanity. It is the love of God that begins the drama of the crucifixion and manifests itself in that terrible death. And it is God the Father who raises Jesus from the dead and thus begins the chain of events into which all of humanity is to be drawn.

When Paul insists on justification by faith, he is not—as many today suppose—introducing a creedal criterion and restriction of what Jesus described as God's unconditional love. Paul is answering those who would say that the religion of the Law is the way of salvation. Paul is protesting against any who would say that we are saved by good or law-abiding deeds. Justification by faith for Paul means salvation by grace or gift (see Rom 3:22–24). Faith in this context is not the one good work everyone is required to do in order to somehow force God's love. Rather faith is simply receiving the gift, letting the gift be gift. And the gift is God's justifying and saving love. Paul is in effect saying that no law, no religion, no creedal posture or confession can ever be a way of salvation. Such religious elements might be responses to the earthly stages of salvation. Only God's love brings about salvation. God loves us while we were his enemies (Rom 5:8). Fundamentally Paul is as "iconoclastic" as Jesus. He too breaks the sacred icons of religion as any basis of spiritual hope. Like Jesus he places all hope in the almost insane love of God for his children. For Paul, like Jesus, a religion confessing the love of God though Jesus is a privileged response to that divine love, but it is never a way of salvation.

It is true that, unlike Jesus, Paul says little about "the kingdom of God." Maybe he just never heard of the Lord's Prayer and its petition for the coming of the kingdom. Or maybe he just couldn't get beyond the first word, *Abba*. With the Spirit in our heart, that simple one-word prayer said it all. Our life, our salvation is in the hands of a Father who performs the greatest irrationality of the cosmic age: he sends his loving Son, the reflection of himself, to die for his hate-filled children. This is the act of a father—or a mother—who is watching his or her children die and reacts vigorously, in love, for it all to stop.

Paul and Jesus are, in fact, remarkably similar in this vision of God as loving Father. The difference between Jesus' gospel and Paul's instructions lies more in the philosophical form of Paul's discourse. Jesus tells a story of a father's irrational love for his prodigal son. Paul tells of an eschatological transformation from the power of "flesh" to that of Spirit. Perhaps many of us feel more comfortable with the stories of Jesus. But the philosophical instructions of Paul made the gospel understandable to a world deeply concerned about the power of evil and death and struggling to articulate the principles of any rescue from this power.

Paul's letters, originally meant as preliminary communications with the Christian communities of the area, now are an object of study and a source of understanding for Christians today. These letters give us a glimpse of the most dynamic period of Christian history. These are the earliest documents we have from early Christianity. In these letters are the seeds for the later theological development within the church. As Platonic thought and other Greek philosophies entered into this rational endeavor, Christian theology tended to lose sight of the original stories of Jesus and consequently to suffer in quality. Paul's letters call us back to the original effort, still close to the poetic images, yet expanding the context of thinking to include the philosophical probe.

NOTE

[1] This substitution was so regular, that the vowels of *Adonay,* a-o-a, were incorporated into the Hebrew text, which originally held only the Hebrew consonants. Westerners, unfamiliar with this substitution, continue to mistake the divine name for *Yahowah,* combining the consonants from one name with the vowels from the other.

EXERCISES

Exercise 1. (see page 197): Recall the last letter you wrote to a friend or acquaintance. Why did you write it? How well did you prepare and organize the writing? If the letter were picked up by another, what difficulties would that person have understanding your statements?

Exercise 2. (see page 209): Read Phil 2:6–11 and Col 1:15–20. What are the most important statements about Jesus found in these texts?

Exercise 3. (see page 219): Read 1 Thessalonians 4–5 and l Corinthians 15. Describe the main elements of Paul's eschatology.

REVIEW QUESTIONS

1. Distinguish a letter from an essay. Why does the literary form of a letter pose special problems for the interpretation of its meaning?

2. What are the major parts of 1 Thessalonians, 1 Corinthians, 2 Corinthians, Galatians, Romans, Philippians, and Colossians?

3. What text(s) in Paul best describe Paul's faith in the preexistence of Jesus? What does Paul say and presuppose about Jesus in this stage? What Old Testament figure may help Paul describe Jesus as preexistent?

4. What is Paul's basic approach to the earthly Jesus? What for Paul is important and what does not appear to be important about this earthly ministry of Jesus?

5. What text(s) in Paul best describe Paul's faith in the risen and exalted Jesus? What does Paul say and presuppose about Jesus in this stage?

6. Where does Paul describe or presuppose Jesus' death as a "sacrifice"? What problem does this image of "sacrifice" pose for a picturing of God? How does Paul handle this problem?

7. What other images does Paul use to see the death of Jesus as saving? What expressive value do these images have? What problems arise with these images?

8. Where does Paul describe the second coming of Jesus? What Old Testament text is similar to Paul's description?

9. What does Paul say about the nature of the risen body? What does Paul say about the transformation of all creation at the end of the world? How do these descriptions fit into Paul's general view of salvation?

FOR FURTHER REFLECTION AND DISCUSSION

1. What has Paul done to the preaching of Jesus? Compare what Jesus preached in the Synoptics and what Paul writes about sin and salvation. Do you think Jesus would like Paul's rendition of the gospel?

2. Paul views salvation as a transformation of reality from a "corrupt-

ible" existence to a "spiritual" existence. How does this view differ from our view of salvation as getting our souls to heaven?

    3. If salvation and justification is the work of God, and if the triumph of God's work is assured, why does Paul get angry in his letters?

13

The Gospel of John

I. History and Overview

The Fourth Gospel in our New Testament, the one tradition-ally named "The Gospel of John," could call to mind the vivid stories about Jesus we read in the Synoptic accounts. Moving to this Gospel, we could anticipate returning to the simplicity of the story-telling and teachings characteristic of Matthew, Mark, or Luke. After all, we are talking about a *gospel* again, aren't we?

From the first verse of this Fourth Gospel, however, something strikes us as different. We begin with a poetic and mysterious description, "In the beginning." We hear the name Jesus Christ (1:17), but only after we are introduced to "the Word" existing with God (1:1) and some spiritual contrast between "light" and "dark-ness" (1:5). This writing does not represent the same literary form we defined as "gospel" from studying the Synoptic Gospels. Instead of short snatches of oral tradition, we have carefully composed essays placed in the mouth of Jesus, representing carefully written reflections on the meaning of God's action to save the world through Jesus. Speeches are longer and far more unified in their topics. Nar-ratives of Jesus' action flash with intense symbolism and prepare us for later teachings. Like Paul's writings, the text of this Gospel is primarily theology. Unlike Paul's letters, however, this theology is couched in the stories of Jesus. If we continue to call this writing a "gospel," we are going to use the term in a different sense.

This Gospel includes several stories not found in any form in the Synoptics: the miracle at Cana, the story of Nicodemus, that of the Samaritan woman at the well, the raising of Lazarus, and the foot washing. Other stories echo a Synoptic narration but only from the broad strokes in which they are told: the royal official's child, the cure of the paralytic on the Sabbath, the cure of the man born blind, and the anointing at Bethany. This Gospel does contain a few stories

Jacob's Well in Samaria.

common to the Synoptics: the story of John the Baptist, the cleansing of the Temple, the feeding of the five thousand, the stilling of the storm, the anointing and triumphal entry into Jerusalem, the Last Supper, and the passion story. Yet in their wording, their details, and their order, these stories appear in a very different way.

The uniqueness of this Gospel appears above all in the longer, well developed discourses of Jesus. These sections are not secondary collections of short independent instructions, but are carefully developed, extended essays, the result of literary effort rather than oral tradition. For almost a chapter, Jesus explains to Nicodemus the requirements for "seeing the kingdom of God." For another chapter Jesus explains to the Samaritan woman the meaning of "living waters." In contrast, the Sermon on the Mount and the other discourses in the Synoptics appear to be only collections of related sayings of Jesus.

A new way of speaking likewise appears in this Gospel. We see an abundance of paired opposites: light and darkness, truth and lies, love and hate, life and death. This "dualistic" type of language links this Gospel to a Hellenistic form of Judaism, a form quite different from the Judaism behind the other Gospels.

(See exercises 1, 2.)

A. Background of Ideas

Since the discovery of the Dead Sea Scrolls at Qumran, we know that this Hellenistic form of Judaism flourished within Palestinian Judaism. The echoes of Johannine themes ring in the dualistic language of Qumran:

> God created man to govern the world and has appointed for him two spirits in which to walk until the time of His visitation: the spirits of truth and falsehood. Those born of truth spring from a fountain of light, but those born of falsehood spring from a source of darkness. All the children of righteousness are ruled by the Prince of Light and walk in the ways of light, but all the children of falsehood are ruled by the Angel of Darkness and walk in the ways of darkness. (1QS 3:17–21)

The exact relationship of John's Gospel to Qumran remains obscure, but the common style suggests a common theological movement, desiring to push religious questions to an almost metaphysical base. The religious question of good and evil is pushed to the level of Satan in conflict with God, the power of darkness in conflict with the power of light. Such a movement excited a good part of the Jewish world. It became the background for the Fourth Gospel.

Dualistic thinking becomes full blown in the Gnosticism of the next centuries. This religious movement, with its stress on "knowledge" as the key to salvation, must have had its roots in New Testament times and before. Questions arise about the influence of these Gnostic roots on the Gospel of John. In this Gospel Jesus is clearly the messenger who descends from the realm of heavenly light and enters the darkness of this world (1:1–14). In this Gospel eternal life is defined in terms of knowledge: "Eternal life is this: to know you, the only true God, and him whom you have sent, Jesus Christ" (17:3). Yet the descriptions of Jesus in this Gospel as the word of God become flesh (1:14) or descriptions of the word's role in creation (1:3) set this Gospel apart from any Gnostic writing.

B. The Dating of the Gospel

Several clues in this Gospel point to the 80s or 90s as the time of its writing. The Jewish authorities, for instance, are no longer distinguished as Sadducees, chief priests, or Herodians, along with the Pharisees. For the most part, in their conflict with Jesus these

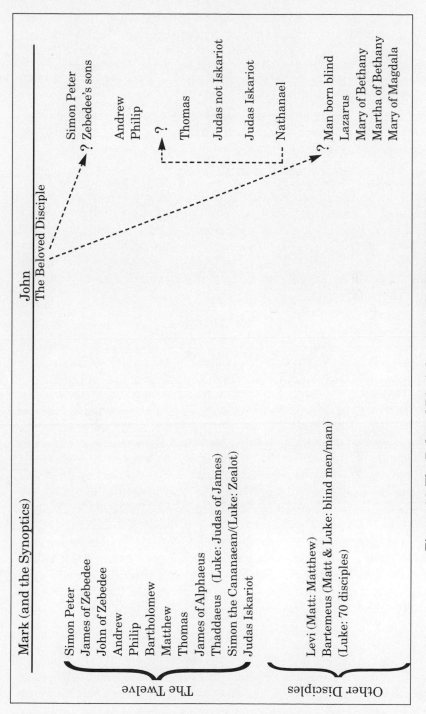

Figure 26. **The Beloved Disciple among the Disciples of Jesus.**

diverse groups have all been absorbed by "the Jews" or "the Pharisees." Such descriptions of the Jewish authorities recall the situation decades after the destruction of Jerusalem in A.D. 70 when the rabbis and Pharisees had regrouped the Jewish people under their leadership. The Gospel of John seems to be so late that the earlier authorities have been more or less forgotten.

It was also during the period of the 80s and 90s that the Pharisees led the Jewish people through an effective purging of the synagogue of believers in Jesus. To be excommunicated from the synagogue *(aposynagōgos)* was the frequent fate of Jewish Christians in this period. It was a period of hatred between the synagogue and the church. With its extremely harsh language against the Jews, the Gospel of John seems to reflect this late-first-century situation. The fears of becoming *aposynagōgos* expressed in this Gospel (9:22) and the descriptions of Jewish authorities throwing out believers in Jesus (9:34) again lead us to see the stories in this Gospel as taking shape in this period of Jewish–Christian hostility.

C. The Author

1. The Traditional Identification

Ancient tradition has identified the author of this Gospel with John the Apostle, the son of Zebedee (see Irenaeus, *Against Heresies* 3.1.1). The Gospel itself links its writing to a person known only as "the disciple whom Jesus loved" (Jn 21:20, 24). Although the Beloved Disciple is never named, he has a central role throughout the Gospel. He reclines "in Jesus' bosom" (13:23), just as Jesus reclines "in the bosom of the Father" (1:18). He follows Jesus all the way to the crucifixion (19:26). He is the first to believe in and to recognize the risen Lord (20:8; 21:7). The prominence of the Beloved Disciple in the Fourth Gospel and the prominence of John the Apostle in the Synoptics suggests that the two are in fact the same, that the ancient tradition identifying the author of this Gospel with John is correct. If the Beloved Disciple were not John, then how did the Beloved Disciple disappear in the Synoptics, and how did John the Apostle disappear in the Fourth Gospel? (See figure 26.)

2. The Critical Problems

Problems arise with the identification of the Beloved Disciple with John, the son of Zebedee. First of all, Acts 4:13 describes John as "uneducated" *(agrammatos)*. While this description allows a wide range of meanings, it suggests an educational background typical of a Galilean fisherman. It does not suggest the education and literary skill presupposed by the Fourth Gospel, a literary masterpiece. This objection vanishes if we see authorship in a broad sense involving many persons, where the originator of the tradition (the apostle) can be different from the composer (a literary master with strong Hellenistic leanings). The objection also vanishes if we wish to appeal to a special miracle, by which the author's inspiration also provided extraordinary literary skills. However, appeals to miracles could explain every problem away. An attempt to wrestle scientifically with the data of a text must reserve an appeal to miracles as a last resort.

Actually, the most significant problem for identifying the author and Beloved Disciple as John the son of Zebedee arises from the way the Beloved Disciple appears in the Gospel, especially in one story. The story is that of the anonymous disciple and Peter at the court of the high priest:

> Simon Peter in company with another disciple, kept following Jesus closely. This disciple, who was known to the high priest, stayed with Jesus as far as the high priest's courtyard, while Peter was left standing at the gate. The disciple known to the high priest came out and spoke to the woman at the gate, and then brought Peter in. (18:15–16)

This "other disciple" looks like the Beloved Disciple for two reasons. In a persistent way, he goes unnamed. This appears to be an example of the deliberate anonymity shrouding the Beloved Disciple. Second, he is in the company of Peter and exhibits a distinct advantage over Peter, a frequent situation of the Beloved Disciple. The description certainly does not match that of a Galilean fisherman. This disciple appears to be part of the priestly power circles of Jerusalem. Such a person does not fit the description of any of the twelve apostles and thus would appear to be another disciple outside of the Twelve.

Throughout this Gospel, the Beloved Disciple does all the right things. Acting in a way very different from the ambitious son of Zebedee (Mark 10:35–37), the Beloved Disciple really typifies what it means to be a disciple. Perhaps the very name by which he is designated indicates the role model he is meant to be in this Gospel. What disciple, after all, is not loved by Jesus?

On the other hand, the Beloved Disciple in this Gospel does not appear to be a mere symbol for discipleship. In 21:20–23, a discussion about his death takes place. A supposed prophecy about his not dying until the end of the world is vigorously rejected as misunderstood. Such a discussion presupposes the death of this Beloved Disciple. He was a real person.

All of these considerations leave scholarship in a state of perplexity. The Beloved Disciple may in fact be John, the son of Zebedee, without the warts. The arguments against this identification are not overwhelming. The Beloved Disciple may be a person other than any of the Twelve, around whom gathered a community independent of the "apostolic communities." The Beloved Disciple may also be an amalgam of several persons, beginning with the apostle John, but including traits of other persons, including a very talented writer from the priestly circles of Jerusalem, the evangelist who actually wrote this Gospel.

(See exercise 3.)

D. The Editing of the Gospel

Clearly more than one person had a hand in the final form of this Gospel. Some rough connections in the text show the work of a rather timid editor. At the end of chapter 14, for instance, Jesus appears to bring his farewell discourse to an end and to invite the disciples to leave the supper room with him:

> I shall not go on speaking to you longer; the Prince of this world is at hand. He has no hold on me, but the world must know that I love the Father and do as the Father has commanded me. Come, then! Let us be on our way. (14:30–31)

The next verse, 15:1, does not seem to follow. Jesus begins a new discourse which continues through chapter 17. Chapter 18, however, follows very well from the end of chapter 14:

> After this discourse, Jesus went out with his disciples across the Kidron Valley. (18:1)

A similar roughness appears at the end of chapter 20, where the Gospel comes to an eloquent conclusion:

Jesus performed many other signs as well—signs not recorded here—in the presence of his disciples. But these have been recorded to help you believe that Jesus is the Messiah, the Son of God, so that through this faith you may have life in his name. (20:30–31)

What follows in the next chapter again looks out of place. Jesus continues to appear to his disciples and instruct them. Chapter 21 must, therefore, lead to a second conclusion for the whole Gospel:

There are still many other things that Jesus did, yet if they were written about in detail, I doubt there would be room enough in the entire world to hold the books to record them. (21:25)

Such "lumps" in the Gospel narration lead us to see a later editor adding material to the text after it had been finished, someone other than the person who composed the earlier, shorter edition. The rough transitions make sense only in view of an editor who was afraid to touch the original text, except to add the material. The original author may be dead or somehow unavailable to authorize a modification of the lines written.

Several editions of this Gospel may, in fact, have shaped it to its present form. When we speak, therefore, of "the author" we may be describing several persons who had a hand in this text. We see in this Gospel, then, an expression of faith by several persons, eventually an expression of faith by a whole community. At the origin of this community is the Beloved Disciple.

E. The Outline of the Gospel

Of all the Gospels in the New Testament, John's appears to be the most carefully organized. Despite the stories added later, the final product of all the editing appears to be an artistic unity. The portrayal of Jesus is highly stylized. The descriptions appear to suggest abstract ideas, patterns, and relationships. For instance, one dominant pattern involves Jesus revealing himself and others reacting to that revelation. This combination of revelation and reaction is what John identifies as "the judgment" (see 3:19). The pattern appears from the early figures of the Gospel reacting to Jesus showing who he is, all the way to the Jews reacting to Jesus presented to them by Pilate.

The structure of the scenes woven together continues the

stylization. Perhaps more for this Gospel than for any others, understanding its structure or outline is the key to understanding the faith of the author.

This Gospel begins with a poetic overture. The first eighteen verses introduce us to many of the major themes of the whole Gospel. These verses are known today as the Prologue.

The Jordan River.

The first major part extends from the Prologue to the end of chapter 12. The opening days of Jesus' ministry fill out the rest of chapter 1, forming another introduction to the Gospel. The rest of this half of the Gospel then describes Jesus' ministry with outsiders, people from Galilee, Samaria, and Jerusalem, who listen to him and either accept or reject his message. The subdivision of this part generally follows the dominant pattern of the Gospel: Jesus reveals himself by significant acts; people then respond. This pattern happens twice. In chapter 2 he reveals himself first at Cana, acting like the Messiah, providing abundant wine at a wedding feast. Then he reveals himself in the temple at Jerusalem, referring to the building as "my Father's house" (2:16). Immediately following these manifestations of Jesus, three persons one after the other approach Jesus and function in the Gospel structure as three distinct responses to him. Nicodemus, the theologian, comes at night and is baffled (3:1–21). The Samaritan woman does much better, eventually testifying to the villagers about

Jesus (4:1–42). However, the royal official is the model for those accepting Jesus. He believes "in the word Jesus spoke to him" without yet seeing any sign (4:46–54).

Chapter 5 begins this cycle of revelation and response again, yet in a more intense way. The manifestation of Jesus at the pool in Jerusalem (5:1–15) is followed by a discourse explaining the significance of Jesus' work (5:16–47). Similarly, the manifestation in Galilee with the bread (6:1–15) is followed by the Bread of Life discourse (6:25–71). Chapters 7–10 include descriptions of various responses to Jesus, some accepting him, others rejecting him. The vigor of the response follows the intensity of the manifestation.

Chapters 11–12 stand somewhat outside this pattern of manifestation and response. The thrust of this section lies in the movement of Jesus to his "hour." The arrival of this moment is solemnly proclaimed in 12:23 when the Gentiles respond to Jesus.

The second major part comprises chapters 13–20. This part includes the extended discourses at the Last Supper (John 13–17), the passion narrative (John 18–19), and the resurrection (John 20).

The Last Supper (at which there is no supper) is made up of six parts, including two distinct farewell speeches of Jesus. These farewell speeches were probably written independently of each other. Some discrepancies exist between the two. For instance, in the second farewell speech Jesus states, "Not one of you asks me, 'Where are you going?'" (16:5). However, in the first, Thomas implicitly asks that question when he complains to Jesus, "Lord, we do not know where you are going. How can we know the way?" (14:5).

As now found together, these farewell speeches sandwich two other discourses which do not deal at all with Jesus' departure, but which together form a vivid contrast: a discourse on the life and love of one living as a branch on the vine of Jesus (15:1–17) and a discourse on the hatred of the world toward the followers of Jesus (15:18–27). On the outside of these farewell speeches are the descriptions of Jesus' foot washing (chapter 13) and of Jesus' "priestly" prayer to the Father (chapter 17). These two scenes are related to each other by an important Johannine theme—namely, the relationship of disciple to Jesus parallels that of Jesus to the Father. Hence, as it now has been edited together in its final form, the whole Last Supper section forms a six-part chiasm:

    A. The foot washing
      B. The first farewell speech
        C. The life and love on the true vine

            C´ The hatred of the world
        B´ The second farewell speech
    A´ The prayer of Jesus to the Father.

The narrative of Jesus' suffering and death (chapters 18–19), likewise, appears in a carefully composed literary structure:

A. The garden of the arrest (18:1–11)

B. The Jewish "trial" (18:12–27), developed by a contrast:
   a. Peter's denial outside
     b. Jesus' public proclamation inside
   a´ Peter's denial outside

C. The Roman trial (18:28–19:16), composed of seven scenes centered around the "crown" of Jesus:

      a. The initial accusation, outside
        b. The kingship of Christ, inside
          c. The preference for Barabbas, outside
            d. The crown of thorns
          c´ The rejection of Jesus, "the Man," outside
        b´ The power of Pilate, inside
      a´ The moment of judgment: Jesus, "the king," is rejected, outside

D. Calvary (19:17–37) is composed of five scenes, perhaps centered on the "mother" scene—although the chiastic correspondence of the other scenes is not clear. The themes are unity, the disciple, the mother, the Spirit:
   a. The inscription on the cross
   b. The undivided garment of Jesus
   c. The mother of Jesus and of the disciple
   d. The delivering of the Spirit
   e. The blood and water from the side

E. The burial garden (19:38–42) recalls the garden of the arrest.

The appearance narratives of the risen Jesus, found now in chapter 20, moves from the discovery of the tomb by Peter and the Beloved Disciple, to the appearance of Jesus to Mary Magdalene, and finally to the appearance of Jesus to his disciples, repeated for

Thomas. The narratives end with a solemn conclusion to the whole Gospel (vv. 30–31).

As it now stands in the Gospel, chapter 21, with a complex appearance narrative in Galilee, forms an Epilogue balancing the Prologue of this Gospel.

Pulling all this together we can organize the Gospel as a whole according to the following outline:

Prologue (1:1–18)

I. Part One (1:19–12:50)
   A. Historical introduction: The opening days (1:19–51)
      1. John the Baptist (1:19–34)
      2. The first disciples of Jesus (1:35–51)
   B. Two signs of revelation and the responses of faith (chapters 2–4)
      1. The sign at Cana and the sign at the Temple (2:1–22)
      2. Nicodemus, the Samaritan woman, and the official at Cana (2:23–4:54)
   C. Two signs of revelation and diverse responses (chapters 5–10)
      1. The cure of the sick man and the sign of the bread (chapters 5–6)
      2. Belief and disbelief in Jerusalem (chapters 7–10)
   D. Movement toward the hour of Jesus (chapters 11–12)

II. Part Two (chapters 13–20)
   A. The farewell discourses (chapters 13–17)
      1. The foot washing (13:1–32)
      2. The first farewell discourse (13:33–14:31)
      3. The true vine and the hostility of the world (15:1–16:4)
      2′.The second farewell discourse (16:5–33)
      1′.The prayer of Jesus (chapter 17)
   B. The passion story (chapters 18–19)
      1. The arrest in a garden (18:1–11)
      2. The hearing before Annas (18:12–27)
      3. The trial before Pilate (18:28–19:16a)
      4. The crucifixion (19:16b–37)
      5. The burial in a garden (19:38–42)
   C. The resurrection appearances (chapter 20)

Epilogue (chapter 21)

II. The Faith of John

This Gospel is particularly rich in its theological content. We see a depth and development here far beyond the earlier Gospels. We will look particularly at this Gospel's christology, soteriology, and eschatology.

A. John's Christology

(See exercise 4.)

The Prologue introduces us to the main figure of the whole Gospel. In the opening line, we have him identified as "the Word" who is both "with God" and is "God" (1:1). The last line of the Prologue repeats the same thoughts, forming an inclusion of these eighteen verses: "It is God the only Son,[1] who is in the bosom of the Father, who has revealed [him]" (1:18). In both verses, 1:1 and 1:18, we see a description of Jesus (finally named in 1:17) as God, as related to God, and as revealing.

1. Jesus as God

The paradox of Jesus as both God and related to God is expressed in the opening verse by a switch in the Greek. As God, Jesus is identified with the single Greek word *theos*. As related to God, Jesus is described as "with *ho theos*." The little Greek word *ho* is just the definite article, like our English *the,* but it is never translated. With the definite article, evidently John intends *ho theos* to designate the Father, from whom Jesus is always distinguished. Without the article, John apparently intends *theos* here to designate a reality broader than the Father, what we might today name "the Godhead," or "the divine substance," or some other term that designates God as more than the Father. John is stretching the concept of *theos,* a term that has been practically a proper name of the Father and therefore a name that could never be applied to Jesus. John is stretching that word to include something more, with which Jesus can be identified. In this shift of meaning, we see the roots of Trinity developing: only one God, but more than one divine person.

The paradox of a simultaneous identification and distinction from God is expressed in v. 18 by naming Jesus "God the only Son" and then speaking of him as "in the bosom of the Father." The image here is probably that of a baby son carried by his father. The title God in this verse forms an inclusion for the Prologue.

The theme of Jesus as God runs through the Gospel. The explicit confession of Thomas, "My Lord and my God!" (20:28), forms a great inclusion for the whole Gospel. In other places the theme appears more subtly: for instance, in chapter 5 Jesus is accused of "making himself God's equal" by speaking of God as his own Father (5:18). This dispute was provoked by Jesus' healing a person on the Sabbath and declaring, "My Father is at work until now, and I am at work as well" (5:17). In the first century, rabbis discussed the nature of God's Sabbath rest. These scholars came up with a difficulty. How could God take a day off if people go on dying and being born or conceived on the Sabbath? A person who has died must be judged. There would be no "cold storage" until the next day. A person beginning life must have a soul created by God the day that person begins to live. Hence the scholars of the Law were willing to allow God to judge and to give life. But only God was allowed to do that! When we look at Jesus' answer to the charge, we see that he claims the right both to judge and to grant life (5:21–22) and to do this in perfect unity with the Father (5:19–20). Jesus' answer here is clear. He is not *making* himself God. He *is* God, in perfect operative unity with the Father.

A model of the pool of Bethesda. See John 5:1–9.
The Fortress Antonia is in the background.

The "I Am" declaration at the feast of Tabernacles (8:58) may be the clearest claim to divinity in the whole Gospel. The expression seems to reflect the story of God revealing himself to Moses:

> God said to Moses, "I am who I am." And He added, "You will say to the sons of Israel I Am sent me to you." (Ex 3:14)

The name "I Am" for God is then found in the book of Isaiah (43:25; 51:12; 52:6). But in case the reader would miss the literary allusions, the author has the adversaries in the story function to interpret the event. They see it as blasphemy. They do not dispute the meaning, they reject the truth of the claim.

Since Jesus is not the Father, it would at first sight appear that this Gospel is proposing a faith in two Gods, God the Father and God the Son. This would be a radical break with the foundation of all Jewish faith, "Hear O Israel, the Lord our God is the one Lord" (Dt 6:3).

2. Jesus as the Revelation of God

The second major aspect of John's christology allows him to avoid this conclusion. Jesus is God, not as a second God but as the perfect manifestation of God the Father. What is true of God is true of Jesus because Jesus expresses what God is. Jesus is the very revelation of God.

The Prologue orchestrates this theme from its first line. "In the beginning was the Word" (Jn 1:1). This "Word" is the spoken word of God, speaking himself, expressing his very identity, revealing himself. The image of the word of God here is taken from the Jewish prophetic traditions, where the Word is the message of God given to the prophet to be spoken again publicly with the authority of God.

The symbolism of "light" continues the theme of Jesus being the manifestation of God (see 1:4–5 and 8:12). The last verse of the prologue then explicitly describes Jesus' role as revealer, "This one revealed" (1:18).

The mention of the Word becoming flesh (1:14) in this context, then, functions to show how this revelation of God becomes available to human beings. Becoming flesh is the way in which the word of God becomes a human word, the way of letting the divine light be seen by human eyes. The first result that John mentions is our seeing: "We have seen his glory" (1:14).

The point made here is that Jesus is the revelation of God. He does not just reveal God the way the prophets revealed God, pointing away from themselves to God. Rather, Jesus reveals God by who and what he is. As he says to the confused Philip at the Last Supper, "He who sees me sees the Father" (14:9). In this sense, likewise, Jesus not only tells the truth, he is the Truth (14:6). "The Truth" in John's Gospel is precisely the revelation of God, shining in the world, offering God's life to humanity.

Almost every chapter in this Gospel contains some allusion to the revealing function of Jesus. The sign at Cana "revealed his glory" (2:11). He is identified as "the teacher" by Nicodemus (3:2). Jesus announces the crucifixion as the moment when "you will know that I Am" (8:28). The whole Gospel is written

That you may believe that Jesus is the Messiah, the Son of God, and that through this belief you may have life in his name. (20:30)

B. John's Soteriology

(See exercise 5.)

As indicated in this conclusion to the Gospel, *life* is intimately connected with revelation. The Prologue identifies *light* with *life*. "The life was the light of human beings" (1:4). *Life* in John's Gospel is the regular substitute for *salvation*. Over and over in the Gospel, Jesus offers life through revelation:

I have revealed your name to them and I will continue to reveal it so that your love for me may live in them and I may live in them. (17:26)

This life offered by Jesus is the life of Jesus himself, and it is the love that defines the very essence of God.

The revelation that he is becomes life when it is believed, when it is known, when it is accepted into the human heart. In a line that could be taken right out of a Gnostic document, the Gospel defines eternal life as knowledge itself.

Now this is eternal life: that they know you the only true God and the one whom you sent, Jesus Christ. (17:3)

This "knowledge," of course, is not a head trip. This is not some secret information that will save the initiated. Rather "knowledge" here is the broad personal relationship expressed by the Hebrew word for knowledge, *da'at,* a word that could even refer euphemistically to sexual intercourse. In this meaning John differs from his Gnostic contemporaries.

From beginning to end, the Gospel plays on the words, "to know," "to see," "to believe," and even "to come to." In relative interchangeability, these words are closely associated and even placed in synonymous parallelism—all in the context of Jesus' offer of eternal life.

> This is the will of my Father, that anyone seeing the Son
> and believing in him may have eternal life. (6:40)

> The one coming to me will never hunger, and the one
> believing in me will never thirst again. (6:35)

The availability of life or salvation begins with the dawn of this revelation. This dawn includes the entire revealing life of Jesus. More specifically, this availability begins with the light and word of God entering our world. For John salvation begins at Christmas:

> The Word became flesh and dwelt among us and we saw
> his glory, the glory of an only begotten of the Father, full
> of grace and truth. (1:14)

Unlike Paul, John insists on the glory and joy of the incarnation. This is not a moment of emptying and humiliation. It is a moment of God manifesting himself in the darkness of our world, and with that manifestation comes the glory of eternal life. (See figure 27.)

For John the crucifixion is also of great importance, but not as a sacrifice offered to God, as Paul would describe. It is not so much a moment of terrible suffering and degradation, as Mark would describe. On the contrary, little is said here of Jesus' suffering. Rather, Jesus carries his cross serenely and goes majestically to his death. For John the crucifixion is the high point of saving revelation. For those looking at this revelation of God with the eyes of faith, the end is realized and eternal life begins.

This significance of the crucifixion is clear from an examination of Jesus' first prediction of the event. Referring to this event as a "lifting up," Jesus in this Gospel explains its meaning by a reference to the story of Moses and the bronze serpent. A careful comparison of the Old Testament text with that of John shows the significance. In the Old Testament story, the people sinned, God punished them by a plague of deadly snakes, and then God relented and offered a rescue from that punishment:

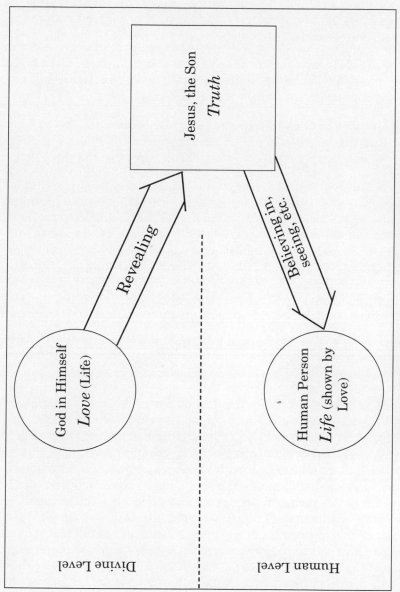

Figure 27. The Schema of John's Soteriology.

> The Lord said to Moses, "Make a seraph and mount it on
> a pole, and if anyone who has been bitten looks at it, he
> will recover." Moses accordingly made a bronze serpent
> and mounted it on a pole, and whenever anyone who had
> been bitten by a serpent looked at the bronze serpent, he
> recovered. (Nm 21:8–9)

In the Gospel's allusion to this text the key phrase "to look" is
replaced with the phrase "to believe." As this interchange shows,
the two phrases are relatively synonymous for John.

> And just as Moses lifted up the serpent in the desert, so
> must the Son of Man be lifted up, so that everyone who
> believes in him may have eternal life. (Jn 3:14–15)

When John thus portrays the passion and death of Jesus
(chapters 18–19), his emphasis is not on the suffering and humiliation of Jesus. Rather, his stress lies in the public and even glorious
character of these final events in the life of Jesus. Pilate repeatedly
manifests Jesus to the crowd: "Behold the man" (19:5), "Behold your
king" (19:14). The crucifixion takes place "near the city," where
many can see the event (19:20). An eyewitness testifies to the event
"so that you may come to believe" (19:35).

C. John's Eschatology

(See exercise 6.)

Matthew, Mark, and Luke had their one or two chapters
detailing the end of the world. We read in vain for a similar description in John. This Gospel describes no Son of Man coming on the
clouds, no gathering of the elect, no final triumph over evil.

John does, however, speak of "the judgment," stressing its
uniqueness so as to indicate that he is speaking of the final judgment. John also speaks of the dead being raised and the bestowal of
eternal life. This is the language of definitive salvation. He even
speaks of the appearance of the great "glory" of God in terms that
suggest the great light and splendor proper to the final triumph of
God and the return of the Lord.

The clearest portrayal of "the judgment" occurs in the story of
Jesus' discussion with Nicodemus. Here Jesus has spoken of the
new life that is at once connected with "being begotten of water and
the Spirit" (3:5) and with seeing/believing in "the Son of Man lifted

up" like the bronze serpent Moses lifted up (3:14–15). Jesus then speaks explicitly of "judgment" *(krisis)* and the action "to judge" *(krinein)*. While the words in themselves could have a positive or negative meaning, John uses the words in this text only to express negative judgment, "condemnation" and "to condemn."

> The one believing in the Son is not judged. The one not
> believing, however, is already judged, for not believing in
> the name of the only begotten son of God. This indeed is
> the judgment: the light came into the world and men
> loved darkness more than the light. (3:18–19)

The Synoptics and Paul gave us images and a notion of a judgment in which people appear at the end of the world before a judge who declares salvation or condemnation as a result of past behavior. If we approach John's text with this typically apocalyptic notion, the description here is perplexing.

To make sense of this text, we must observe the two elements or moments John insists on as constituting judgment. From these two elements we can also see the broader view of judgment as either definitive salvation or condemnation. The one dominant element here is that of human response—believing or rejecting Jesus as the Light. However, a second prior element or moment is briefly mentioned which alone makes the other possible: the light comes into the world, the moment of revelation and action on the part of God. These two elements together constitute the event of "judgment" for John: God reveals his Light, and human beings respond. The text stresses the negative response, "not believing," "preferring darkness to light." The resulting judgment is thus really condemnation. Implied here and briefly alluded to, however, is the positive response, "believing in the Son." Such a response to revelation would result in salvation. In this text John just says such a person "is not judged" in the sense of condemned.

John's portrayal of judgment turns the apocalyptic portrayal upside down. Instead of people passively waiting for the verdict of the divine judge, people actively judge themselves. Instead of the outcome of judgment being a future uncertainty, this outcome is clearly known. It is simply the flip side of one's reaction to God's revelation. Instead of this judgment taking place in the eschatological future, it takes place whenever revelation takes place.

The Gospel dramatizes this theme of judgment at the trial of Jesus. At this trial Jesus appears to be judged. The people appear there as the accusers. On a deeper level, however, something else is

taking place. In his narration, John insists on the trial and the crucifixion as a moment of revelation. Pilate, the highest official of the
land, twice presents Jesus to the people, "Behold the man!" (19:5),
"Behold your king!" (19:14). Twice the people reject Jesus: "Crucify
him!" (19:6, 15). Pilate appends a sign to the cross written in three
languages proclaiming Jesus to be king, "read by many of the Jews,
since the place where Jesus was crucified was near the city"
(19:19–20). The response is, "You should not have written 'king of
the Jews.'" According to John this is a moment of judgment, but
ironically, it is not the judgment of Jesus. It is the judgment of the
people who were shown the light and who refused it.

When writing of "the judgment," John is thinking specifically
of the moment when Jesus comes as the word of God made flesh,
accepted by some, rejected by others. John's description of judgment
as the confluence of divine revelation and human response allows
us to say the moment of judgment occurs at any moment in which a
person perceives the Light of God. John has taken an event traditionally placed in the future and made it present. If God is speaking
to me, this is the moment of judgment. This present moment is thus
charged with all the significance normally reserved for the future
eschaton in the traditional apocalyptic portrayal. To use a modern
theological term, we can describe the posture of this Gospel as *realized eschatology*. The events of the end are happening now.

A similar transformation occurs in the Johannine presentation
of the the resurrection of the dead. The speech following Jesus' work
on the Sabbath, vividly presents this resurrection as a present
event, once again associated with the moment of divine revelation.

> Just as the Father raises the dead and gives life, so also
> the Son gives life to whom he wills.... Amen, amen, I say
> to you, the one hearing my word and believing in the one
> sending me has eternal life and does not come to judg-
> ment but has moved from death into life. (5:21, 24)

The resurrection of the dead is happening in the present. It
happens as one hears and accepts the revelation of Jesus. John
appears to be talking of a spiritual reality, one that happens apparently within the heart of a person.

Curiously, as this text continues, the position shifts to the
future and the resurrection of the dead appears in a more traditional
form of moving out of one's tomb. The following verses are as close as
John comes to an apocalyptic scenario of the end of the world:

> Amen, amen I say to you that the hour is coming and is
> now when the dead will hear the voice of the Son of God
> and those hearing will live.... Do not be surprised at this,
> that the hour is coming in which all those in the tombs
> will hear his voice and come forth, those who were doing
> good to resurrection of life and those who were doing evil
> to the resurrection of judgment. (5:25, 28–29)

John, in effect, is holding to both realized and future eschatology. Perhaps these two contiguous sections of chapter 5 have different literary histories; perhaps one was added after the other was written. The final product, however, contains both.

The third element of the eschaton mentioned by John, the vision of the divine glory, appears only in the Prologue of the Gospel. Once again, the allusion is to a magnificent light characteristic of the special presence of God. This light recalls the power and glory associated with the coming of the Lord as described by the Synoptics and by Paul. In John, however, this glory is associated with the divine Word becoming flesh, the scene we portray at Christmas:

> And the word became flesh and dwelt among us, and we
> saw his glory, a glory as that of the only begotten of the
> Father, full of grace and truth. (1:14)

For the most part, then, this Gospel is not concerned with any association of the end of the world with the war of A.D. 70. Nor is it in any way concerned with the apparent delay of this end. The cosmic fireworks are removed from the Johannine sky. Instead the focus is on the present meaning of this eschaton and especially on how this end is anticipated in the present. John shows no concern with future life or the world to come. His concern is with eternal life, a life that begins in this world, a life that must start in the present or it never begins.

III. Theological Reflections

John's Gospel immediately stirs up important theological reflections as the reader attempts to apply this Gospel to life in the present. First of all, this Gospel presents a remarkably simple picture of Christian life. The principal and almost unique challenge of Christian living is to see and believe in Jesus. Accepting this revelation into one's heart is accepting the seed of life into oneself, a seed that then transforms itself into the very life of God. Just as God, who is Life in itself, reveals himself in the Truth, who is Jesus, so by internalizing this Truth, human beings engender Life within themselves.

Very rarely does this Gospel speak of good (or bad) works (see 3:19; 5:29). Now and then a hint is made about something we today would call "a sacrament" (see 3:5; 6:53–58). Otherwise, this is a Gospel of "faith alone," Jesus. The crucifixion of Jesus calls us simply to look and believe.

The result of that faith-filled contemplation is eternal life. This is the very life of God. Christians are thus not simply "adopted children" of God, as Paul would say, but are truly engendered children. The Father has indeed communicated his life to them as surely as a natural father communicates his life to his natural children. Jesus' words to Nicodemus, in Greek *gennēthē anōthen,* should read in English, "begotten from above" (3:3). Jesus is talking about the communication of life by a Father on high. If the allusions to Christian praxis and Christian sacramentality are in fact later additions to soften a rather "Gnostic" approach, the result of all this possible editing remains clear. The foundation of Christian life is the communication of life from God to the believer, and it comes through the heartfelt gaze of the Christian on Jesus. All Christian activity then flows from and manifests this life.

Second, the reflective reader today is directly confronted with John's "high christology." Jesus is presented as God. We are invited to join "doubting" Thomas in his confession, "My Lord and my God!" (20:28). Is the reader called upon to worship Jesus? Interestingly, this is exactly what the cured blind man does as his "illumination" becomes complete. "And he worshiped him [Jesus]" (9:38). The action word is the same as that used otherwise in this Gospel to describe the worship of God (see 4:20–24; 12:20). Neither the apostles nor the Beloved Disciple, on the other hand, is ever described worshiping Jesus.

Perhaps the key to understanding our religious relationship to Jesus, according to this Gospel, is to understand how this Gospel sees Jesus' divinity as a reflection or manifestation of the Father's divinity. "The one seeing me sees the Father" (14:9). The worship of Jesus is of its nature the worship of the Father.

Yet, there is a necessary flip side of this christology. The Father really does not figure as prominently in this Gospel as he does in Paul and the Synoptics. In the earlier theologies, the Father is the one who raises Jesus. In John, Jesus rises by himself. In the earlier writings, Jesus obediently and in full anguish engages himself in the plan of the Father, who alone knows fully this plan (cf. esp. Mark

13:32). In this Gospel, Jesus is in full knowledge and in full command of the situation. The Father necessarily recedes behind the
power and majesty of Jesus himself. To see Jesus is to see the Father,
but we are first seeing Jesus and "it's all there." The theocentrism of
Paul and the Synoptics has ceded to a christocentrism in John.

Flipping the picture one more time, an interesting thing happens in John to our picture of the Father. Philip wanted to be shown
the Father (14:8). He represents the desire for the magnificent theo-
phany. Jesus says, "Look at me and you see him." John breaks the
stereotypes of the religious imagination of God, stereotypes that are
rooted all the way back to the story of Sinai. We expect the flashing
light, the thunderous rolls and trumpet blasts. Instead we see a
human being, one nailed to a cross—albeit calmly and serenely
nailed. This is the image of love, the image of the act of giving life.

Third, John's view of realized eschatology, and in particular
his view of "the judgment," raises several concerns. Since our first
"encounter" with Jesus, have we all now been judged? Are we now
divided like the crowds in the Gospel into those saved and those
condemned (see 5:29; 7:12)? As is clear from this Gospel, "encountering" Jesus or being otherwise the recipient of God's revelation is
a very dangerous thing. After such an encounter, we will not be the
same. The chances of getting seriously bruised are fairly great.

On a theological level, John has given us the deepest significance of revelation. He has pointed out the seriousness of this event,
the responsibility we must assume for our eternity.

But John is not a "pastoral theologian." He is not considering
the complexities that occur once this simple schema of revelation/
judgment is understood in relationship to the convolutions involved
in concrete human life. For instance, he does not even consider the
question, What happens if you change your mind about Jesus? We
know we can change our minds about anything. Here on earth our
commitments are always limited. We never succeed in bringing our
whole selves to any decision. There is always a reluctant residue that
remains outside the commitment—a saving element when it comes to
finding leverage to back off bad decisions. In his desire to give us the
basic theological schema of eternal life, John simply passes over this
complication. However, in our inevitable need to deal with concrete
human life—our own or others—we must consider this complication.
Any attempt to classify lives as definitively "saved" or "condemned"
is to pretend we live in the simpler world of angels.

The "pastoral" concern likewise surfaces when we ask about
the exact form in which a person might "see" the life-giving light of

Christ. In his theological simplification, John again proposes a simple schema. The light shines in the historical Jesus, the Word made flesh. To see Jesus and accept him is to come alive. To reject him is to die. The theological point is clear: there is no other source of eternal life available to human beings outside of Jesus.

But must a person psychologically recognize Jesus in this "seeing"? If this were a theological necessity, we would necessarily rule out all babies from the possession of eternal life. Is it possible that Jesus enters the life of many in a form that remains anonymous? Philip gets into trouble by insisting on traditional religious stereotypes. We are warned that God is bigger than our images and expectations. The history of church mission is filled with the inane struggle to make people accept our stereotypes of things divine, our names for the One who really has no name. The Light shone in the world long before we ever wrote about it—even in the Gospel—and gave it names.

Finally, the differences and developments of John's Gospel raise the serious issue of reliability. This Gospel presents Jesus quite differently than do the Synoptics or even Paul. The Gospel is clearly the result of a development in the religious reflection of a group of Christians. Given our knowledge of Jesus from the Synoptics, it is unlikely that Jesus expressed himself and his work in the dualistic terms found in John and with John's great stress on life-giving revelation. Chapters in this Gospel appeared to be composed more or less from scratch in Greek. For instance, Jesus' discussion with Nicodemus in chapter 3 turns around the ambiguity of a Greek word *anōthen,* which can mean either "again" or "from above." The chapter is structured around Jesus' correction of Nicodemus's misinterpretation of the Greek word.

That John and the community for which John wrote were conscious of this development, that they understood how they exceeded the words and actions of Jesus himself is clear in the very lines of the Gospel proposed as Jesus' very teaching:

> There is yet *more* I have to tell you, but you are not able
> to bear it at this time. When that one comes, the Spirit of
> Truth, he will guide you into all truth. (16:12–13)

This line reflects the consciousness of the evangelist and the community that the historical teachings of Jesus were not the final word. There was *more* that would come later, that would come through the Spirit.

We are directly confronted with that "more" in the distinctive "realized eschatology" of John and above all in his high christology, the christology that became the standard for Christians from the Council of Nicea in A.D. 324. Whether they understood this or not, the mainline Christians who accepted the Nicean description of Jesus as "God, from God...consubstantial with the Father" were placing their reliance on the "Spirit of Truth" guiding a community in its faith development. Declaring the Fourth Gospel to be a reliable norm of faith, Christians today are relying on that early community, believing that the early Johannine community was "on target" in its understanding of Jesus. Any attempt to oppose belief in Jesus and his Gospels to belief in church community is simply a misunderstanding of our unique access to the historical Jesus. The New Testament becomes a critic of church teaching only in the sense that the earliest positions of the community become a critic of the later positions.

What the Fourth Gospel does, furthermore, to the New Testament is to demand an eventual radical reinterpretation of the other writings. While each earlier document must retain its own integrity on the level of literary expression, the Fourth Gospel requires a theological synthesis of the earlier writings into its perspective, as some sort of "higher" view. The issue here is the unity and coherence of truth. This is not an issue from a purely literary or historical perspective. From the literary and historical perspective we *must* read Mark, Matthew, Luke, and Paul through their own eyes, not through John's. If we ask the question, Who is right? then the issue of unity appears and *contradictory* positions must be deemed "wrong." If we ask the question, How can all these writing be right? then the issue of coherence demands some level of integration, in which usually the broader perspective becomes the matrix of coherence for the more restrictive. In this way the Fourth Gospel apparently must assume a dominating and controlling role in the New Testament—for one who would believe in the New Testament as a canonical whole. But this introduces questions that perhaps are best reserved for our final reflections on the New Testament.

NOTE

[1] Today the study of manuscripts (textual criticism) has generally, although not unanimously, shown the preference of this reading over variants such as "the only begotten" or "the only begotten Son of God." English translations still differ because of their choice of Greek manuscripts.

EXERCISES

Exercise 1. (see pages 230–231): Read the story of the cleansing of the Temple as given in Mk 11:15–17 and Jn 2:14–22. What details are the same? What details are different? Among the contrasts, which details in John seem to say something special about Jesus? What significance can you find in other details?

Exercise 2. (see pages 230–231): Compare and contrast the crucifixion and death of Jesus as given in Mk 15:22–41 and Jn 19:17–37. What significance can you find in the contrasting details in John?

Exercise 3. (see pages 234–236): Imagine the community or church of the Beloved Disciple and its relationship with the communities which developed around the apostles (see Acts 1–12). How much of the relationship between the Beloved Disciple and Peter could be a reflection of the relationship between the communities?

Exercise 4. (see page 242): Read Jn 1:1–18. How is Jesus introduced? How does this text identify Jesus? What is said about him?

Exercise 5. (see page 245): Read the Passion story in John 18–19. What is said about these events fitting into God's plan of salvation? What details carry special stress in this narration? Can you determine what is the special significance of these details?

Exercise 6. (see page 248): What are the events typically associated with the end of the world in Mark, Matthew, Luke, and Paul? Where in the Fourth Gospel do we find references to these events?

REVIEW QUESTIONS

1. Describe the overall structure of the Fourth Gospel.

2. What does the Fourth Gospel say about its authorship? What are the difficulties with identifying the author of the Fourth Gospel with John the son of Zebedee? Which difficulty is the most important?

3. List the texts in the Fourth Gospel where Jesus is called "God." List other texts that imply that Jesus is God.

4. List the texts in the Fourth Gospel where Jesus is described as "the revelation" of God. What images and names are used to describe this relationship with God?

5. What is the relationship between revelation, life, and the death of Jesus in the Fourth Gospel? How does the crucifixion of Jesus fit into this relationship?

6. Describe the general eschatology of the Fourth Gospel. What is "judgment" for this gospel? When does it occur?

FOR FURTHER REFLECTION AND DISCUSSION

1. Protestant theology insists on salvation received by faith alone. What in the Fourth Gospel could make it a favorite of Protestants?

2. What does it mean in practical living to say that Jesus is God? The later church used philosophical categories, such as "person" and "nature," to say what this affirmation means. What does the affirmation mean to someone who hasn't the foggiest idea of these philosophical categories? Would such a person necessarily conclude from John that there are two Gods?

3. Few of the arguments for oral tradition found in the Synoptics are found in John. If we defined the literary form of gospel from our study of the Synoptics and especially from the role of oral tradition in the Synoptics, is calling the Gospel of John a "gospel" stretching the word to the breaking point?

14

The Letters of John

I. History and Overview

Associated with the Fourth Gospel are three smaller writings which tradition describes as also written by the apostle John. These writings are known as the letters 1 John, 2 John, and 3 John. Actually, 1 John is not a letter. It is an essay or treatise instructing Christians on the importance of loving one another in some form of community and of believing in Jesus as "come in the flesh," the source of spiritual confidence. 2 John is a short letter, but neither the writer nor the reader is named. The writer identifies himself as "the Presbyter" or "the Elder." The reader, designated as an "elect Lady and her children" may well be a church or a series of churches if this letter is mean to circulate. 3 John is also a short letter from "the Presbyter" to an individual named Gaius.

(See exercises 1, 2.)

These writings are closely related to each other and to the Gospel of John. 1 John seems to allude frequently to passages in the Gospel, sometimes almost citing them. Note the similarity, for instance in the comparison of the two endings:

> I have written these things to you that you might have eternal life for those believing in the name of the son of God. (1 Jn 5:13)

> These things have been written that you might believe that Jesus is the Christ, the Son of God, and that those believing might have life in his name. (Jn 20:31)

Since 1 John appears to reflect a time in the church later than that reflected by the Gospel, we can conclude that 1 John is a sequel to the Gospel and is dependent on that Gospel.

In turn, 2 and 3 John seem to reflect expressions and ideas of 1 John. For instance, we read in 2 John:

> Now I ask you, Lady, not as though writing to you a new commandment, but what we have heard from the beginning, that we love one another. (5)

1 John includes the lines:

> Beloved, I do not write you a new commandment, but an old commandment which you have from the beginning.... The one loving his brother remains in the light. (2:7, 10)

> This is his command: that we believe in the name of his Son Jesus Christ and that we love one another. (3:23)

Examples of such verbal similarities run through all three documents, indicating that 1 John, 2 John, and 3 John do, in fact, belong together and belong with the Fourth Gospel. A real possibility is that 2 John is a circulating cover letter for 1 John, which in turn is an attempt to summarize and reinterpret the Gospel in the light of later developments and shifts of emphasis. 3 John seems to stand on its own as dealing with specific practical needs. Its similarity with 2 John may be simply a result of common authorship.

It is difficult to determine whether such affinity among all the Johannine writings indicates the same author for all or simply the same "school" of Christian teaching. As we will see, enough significant shifts exist between the Gospel and the letters to suggest that a person other than the author of the Gospel is involved in the writing of the letters. If this is the case, then the letters represent a church development somewhat beyond the Gospel—a development, however, within the basic framework of Johannine theology. On the other hand, we can understand the differences among the letters in large part by the different literary forms each letter represents: an essay, a letter to a community, and a letter to an individual. Nothing in the letters urges us to see a shift in authorship.

As communications among Christian communities in the Johannine idiom, the letters indicate that "Johannine Christianity" has spread beyond a single dominant community. We see in Demetrios of 3 John a traveling preacher, apparently moving from one community to another in the service of the Johannine gospel. We see in Diotrephes, also of 3 John, the bureaucratic struggles of a network spread out to the extent that issues of authority now surface.

Especially, however, in the warnings about false teachers, teachers who have arisen *within* the community, mentioned in both 1 and 2 John, we see reflections of a movement grown to such an extent that it must struggle vigorously with issues of continuity with its origins. These are not the struggles expressed in the Gospel, where Jewish adversaries from outside are putting pressure on the believers in Jesus. The struggle in the letters is an intramural struggle concerned with who best represents the original teachings of Jesus. The importance given to a confession of Jesus "having come in the flesh" (1 Jn 4:2; 2 Jn 7) suggest that the adversaries are Christian Gnostics of some form, for whom "flesh" is essentially evil and could have nothing to do with our salvation. The exhortations to "confidence" that run throughout 1 John (2:28; 3:21; 4:17; 5:14) indicate that the community is discouraged.

The basic picture we receive from these writings leads us to place them toward the end of the first century. At this time correct teaching was understood to be the key to continuity with Jesus and his gospel. The dominant struggle of the churches was from within. The churches were groping for some form of authority structure that would pull the group together, structures such as the presbyterate that appears in the Acts and, as we will see, in the Pastoral Epistles.

1 John is not easily divided into clear structural units. The theme of correct faith in Jesus (christology) is woven closely with the theme of correct living (*parenesis*) in circular or repetitive patterns. Some units stand out by chiastic and parallel structures. Other material, more or less homogeneous around a theme, falls between these structures. On the basis of such observations, we can study 1 John with the following outline:

I. Prologue (1:1–4)

II. Christian Living and Divine Light (1:5–2:17)

III. The End Times and the Anointing (2:18–28)
    A. Eschatology—the antichrist (2:18–19)
    B. The anointing in our hearts (2:20–21)
    C. The antichrist, denying "Jesus is the Christ" (2:22–23)
    B´ The anointing in our hearts (2:24–27)
    A´ Eschatology—the final revelation of God (2:28)

IV. Being Begotten of God and Sinlessness (2:29–3:10)
    A. Being begotten of God (2:29–3:3)
    B. Sinlessness (3:4–8)
    A´Being begotten of God (3:9a)
    B´Sinlessness (3:9b–10)

V. Love and Confidence (3:11–24)

VI. The Two Spirits and Confession of Jesus Come in the Flesh (4:1–6)

VII. Our Love and God's Love (4:7–21)
    A. Exhortation to love (4:7–8)
    B. God's love (4:9–10)
    A´Exhortation to love (4:11–13)
    B´God's love (4:14–16)
    A´´Exhortation to love (4:17–21)

VIII. Our Faith and the Testimony of God (5:1–12)

IX. Conclusion (5:13–21)

The structures of 2 and 3 John are less complicated, since we can identify the typical parts of a Hellenistic letter and some obvious shifts of topics in the letter body. 2 John appears in the following structure:

I. Opening Salutation and Letter Prayer (1–3)

II. The Body
    1. The commandment to love (4–6)
    2. Warning against false teachers (7–11)

III. Conclusion (12–13)

Similarly, 3 John:

I. Opening Salutation and Thanksgiving (1–4)

II. Body
    1. Compliments to Gaius (5–8)
    2. Concern about Diotrephes (9–10)
    3. Recommendations for Demetrios (11–12)

III. Conclusion (13–15)

II. The Faith of the Johannine Letters

A. The General Shift

We can trace the same three themes of christology, soteriology, and eschatology in these "letters" as we did in the Gospel and note both deep similarities with some differences. What characterizes the message of the "letters," however, is a distinct pastoral concern. Unlike the Gospel, these Johannine writings focus on the difficulties and challenges of Christian living and acting. The background and foundation from which this pastoral concern arises are deeply Johannine. "To remain in the Son and the Father" (1 Jn 2:24) is the foundation of all. However, the stress is on the practical exercise of that communion in human conduct:

> The one saying he remains in him ought *to walk* just as
> he walked. (1 Jn 2:6)

And this is love, that we *walk* according to his commands (2 Jn 6). The perspective has shifted from that of encountering Jesus as the Word of Life (the Gospel) to living out one's faith in a community of shared life and preaching the word of life (the letters).

(See exercise 3.)

The expression "fellowship" *(koinōnia),* occurring in the first chapter of 1 John, is most likely a reference to the Johannine church community. The Fourth Gospel, on the one hand, almost hides its ecclesiology behind its christology. The vine, often a symbol of God's people, is identified with Jesus himself, the True Vine, but one in which the branches together are to live and draw life (Jn 15:1–8). 1 John, on the other hand, sees "the fellowship" explicitly as the goal of the proclamation of life: "And we proclaim [this word of life] to you in order that you might have fellowship with us" (1 Jn 1:3). This fellowship is connected with forgiveness of sins and acting out our life in the light:

> If then we walk in the light, just as he is in the light, we
> have fellowship with one another and the blood of Jesus
> his son cleanses us from all sin. (1:7)

The perspective is basically the same as that of the Gospel. The concern has shifted to practical living out of one's faith. The author is translating the lofty theology of the Gospel into the difficult demands of life. Similar shifts appear in the three themes of our study.

B. Shifts in Christology

The christology of 1 John resembles closely that of the Gospel of John. In typical Johannine vocabulary, 1 John proclaims Jesus repeatedly as "God's Son" or "his Son" (1:3, 7; etc.) or simply as "the Son" (2:22–24; 4:14; 5:12; cf. 2 Jn 9). Moreover, this Son is the one whom the Father has "sent into the world" (4:9). Like the Gospel, 1 John also insists on Jesus as the word and revelation of God. In a verse that echoes Jn 1:1–4, the author proclaims,

> Concerning the Word of life—life appeared and we saw and we witnessed and we proclaimed to you as the eternal life, which was with the Father and has appeared to us. (1 Jn 1:2)

One phrase at the end of 1 John may proclaim a faith in Jesus as God, "He is the true God and eternal life" (5:20). The pronoun most probably refers to Jesus Christ, the name that immediately precedes. This verse, however, has suffered a great deal in the manuscripts, and the phrase might refer to the Father. Nowhere else in the letters is there a concern to affirm Jesus as God.

The absence of a great stress on the divinity of Jesus in this writing may be the result of a shift to a greater theocentrism than exists in the Gospel. 1 John speaks often of the Father, of "the Father's love" (2:15), of what "comes from the Father" (2:16), of the importance of doing "God's will" (2:17), of "his holiness" (2:29), of "the love the Father has bestowed on us" (3:1), of being "confident before him [God]" (3:19), of being sure "that God is with us" (3:21), and of God defined as "love" (4:8, 16).

In this writing, God the Father, not Jesus, is "the light" (1:5). The shift implied in this phrase is more than just a loose use of a metaphor. The principal focus of the Gospel's christology was to identify Jesus as the perfect revelation of the Father, "the light" radiating from God. To identify God the Father as the light now is to lose that christological focus. Both the Gospel and 1 John start with the affirmation, "No one has ever seen God" (Jn 1:18; 1 Jn 4:12). The Gospel uses the affirmation to insist on the importance of the revelation of God by God the Son (1:18b). 1 John uses the affirmation to stress the importance of loving one another (4:12), that is, of loving our brother whom we have seen (5:20).

(See exercise 4.)

A new christological stress in 1 John lies in affirming that Jesus "has come in the flesh" (4:2). The thought also dominates 2 John (see v. 7). The same emphasis probably occurs in the importance given to the affirmation that Jesus came "in the blood" (1 Jn 5:6). For the author, each affirmation is the criterion for discerning the true Spirit of God. Together "flesh and blood" is a way of referring simply to human existence (cf. Mt 16:17; 1 Cor 15:50; Gal 1:16; perhaps Jn 1:13). The stress given to these affirmations suggests a crisis in the church around some Gnostic-like denial of Jesus' humanity or at least of his human death.

C. Shifts in Soteriology

In its view of salvation and the death of Jesus, 1 John again shows its roots in the Gospel of John and its development beyond the Gospel. As in the Gospel, "life" in 1 John is the equivalent of "salvation." This treatise begins as the announcement of "the word of life" (1:1). It ends with the summary where typically life is connected with faith:

> I wrote you these things in order that you might know that you possess eternal life—you who believe in the name of the Son of God. (5:13)

The parallel with life is "remaining" in God and God in oneself. As in the Gospel, such indwelling is the result of accepting the word of revelation into our hearts:

> Let what you have heard from the beginning remain in you. If what you have heard from the beginning remains in you, then you will remain in the Son and in the Father. (1 Jn 2:24)

What strikes us in 1 John is the realism of this indwelling and life. Dealing with the "impeccability" of the believer, this treatise describes this life as a result of divine "impregnation":

> Any one begotten of God does not sin, because God's seed
> remains in him, and he cannot sin because he is begotten
> of God. (3:9)

The description here is more than being "of God's seed" or being "of
God's stock" (cf. the NAB translation). This is a description of God's
seed "in him"—precisely in the description of being "begotten"
(gegennēmenos) of God. The image is almost sexual in its realism.
One is truly a child of God. One is truly begotten of this Father—
because God's seed has been planted within and has engendered a
new life just as—especially in ancient physiology—the seed of a
human father engenders a new life in a mother's womb.

The "seed of God" is identified by its parallel with the word of
God. The seed remains in us (3:9). The word of God remains in us
(2:14). What we have heard from the beginning remains in us (2:24).
This is the same message as that of the Gospel, but the imagery is
far more vivid.

The pastoral shift characteristic of 1 John appears in the way
this treatise now links practical action to this life begotten in us. In
both the Gospel and 1 John the new life engendered in us through
the Word leads to love. The "new commandment" which is "to love
one another" runs from the Gospel (13:24) through 1 Jn 3:23 and
even 2 Jn 5. In 1 John, however, this "love" becomes a matter of
sharing "life's wealth" with a needy brother:

> Whoever has life's wealth of this world and sees his
> brother in need and closes his compassion to him, how
> can the love of God dwell in him? (1 Jn 3:17)

For both the Gospel and 1 John, this love is a divine reality; it
is God's love within us germinated as a result of "the Truth" entering our hearts. Yet for 1 John, this love must show up in human
deeds, not just fancy talk. 1 John presents this stress with an interesting comparison:

> Children, let us love, not in word or tongue, but in deed
> and truth. (1 Jn 3:18)

The words of this admonition are very carefully selected. The contrast we see at first is simply that between a love which is only "in
word" and one which is "in deed." But connected with that is the
other part of the comparison. The "tongue" (glōssa) is the possession
defined as the power that brings forth the word. Thus "truth"
(alethēia), which in Johannine theology is the revelation of God in

Jesus, now appears almost defined as a power to bring forth deeds of love. The sign of possessing the revelation that produces eternal life is the fact "that we love the brethren" (3:14). One who would refuse to love in a practical way, not only is wrong. Such a one directly contradicts "the truth." Such a one becomes "a liar" (cf. 1 Jn 2:4).

A significant shift in the soteriology of 1 John appears also in the presentation of Jesus death as "atoning" or "sacrificial," as if we had here an influence of Pauline theology. In the Gospel of John the crucifixion of Jesus brings salvation by its revelatory character. "When you lift up the Son of Man, then you will know that I AM" (Jn 8:28). 1 John, on the other hand, refers to Jesus as "an offering *(hilasmos)* for our sins...and for the sins of the world" (2:2). The idea and the vocabulary come close to Paul's descriptions of Jesus as the *hilastērion* (Rom 3:25). 1 John sees this sacrificial death of Jesus as a proof of God's love:

> In this is love, not that we loved God, but that he loved us and sent his Son as an offering for our sins. (4:10)

This idea echoes Paul's written some thirty years earlier:

> God establishes his own love for us, in that, while we were still sinners, Christ died for us. (Rom 5:8)

Paul is concerned with establishing the evidence of God's love, as if he were in some forensic debate. 1 John is concerned with identifying the exact place of a revelation of God's love through Jesus, a revelation that begets life. The Gospel has already announced the same idea (Jn 3:16). 1 John adds the nuance of cultic sacrifice.

This insistence on the "sacrificial" character of Jesus' death may be connected with 1 John's insistence on Jesus come "in the flesh" (4:2) and come "in the blood" (5:6). A Gnostic-like denial of Jesus' humanity would reject, likewise, any view of Jesus' very death as having any redemptive value.

D. Shifts in Eschatology

The Gospel of John turned the apocalyptic views of judgment, resurrection, and glory upside down and described these eschatological realities as present now in the act of faith and knowledge of the Truth. Eternal life in John had replaced any future life that supposedly would come after a cataclysmic end time.

1 John retains the emphasis on eternal life as present, yet

unexpectedly brings back the apocalyptic picture of future anguish
and glory. 1 John interprets the adversaries that his church must
face precisely in terms of "the antichrist" (2:18; 4:3), a typical anti-
God figure who appears by other names in traditional apocalyptic
literature (cf. Dn 7:19–25; 2 Thes 2:3–4; Revelation 13). The struggle with these false teachers is, for 1 John, the sign of "the final
hour" (2:18). Our vision is directed to the future. We are told to
"remain" in God now with a view to a future revelation:

> Remain in him, now, children, so that when he is
> revealed, we might have confidence and not be ashamed
> before him in his coming. (*parousia,* 2:28)

The Greek expression "in his coming" *(en tē parousia autou),*
used for the return of Jesus at the end of the world, was a favorite of
Paul and is found outside of this text only in Paul (1 Cor 15:23; 1
Thes 2:19; 3:13; 4:15; 5:23). Again, we could have here a way in
which the Pauline and Johannine traditions are coming together.

When 1 John speculates on the exact nature of this end time,
he returns to Johannine themes of revelation and divine life. In this
way he also unites the realized eschatology of the Gospel with the
new view to the future. 1 John insists eternal life is now. We are now
children of God, but the future holds an intensification:

> Now we are children of God, but it is not yet revealed
> what we will be. We know that when it is revealed we will
> be like him, because we will see him as he is. (3:2)

The Johannine theme of now sharing God's life through revelation
remains the basis of this future eschatological hope. The future will
bring more because the future will bring greater *vision*. And this
vision will make us more "like God." The present and the future
thus form a continuum of revelation and sharing of divine life. We
are not to evacuate the present of saving significance, since this revelation and life are now. But we are to look to the future for a
greater intensification.

III. Theological Reflections

Whether written by the author of the Gospel of John or by
another author of the same school, the "letters" of John are important evidence of the way early Christian theology was willing to
develop. The Gospel had developed a symmetrical synthesis, yet

circumstances had changed. Perhaps contact with other Christian churches had occurred. The results are the shifts we note in these later Johannine writings.

At the same time, these writings stand firm on the permissible parameters of development, rejecting some changes as evil. For the author of these writings, "getting it right" about Jesus is very important. While this author never makes one's christology the determining factor of one's salvation or eternal life—as do many fundamentalist preachers today—this author does see one's christology as a sign or symptom of spiritual health or sickness. A correct christology is a sign of the Spirit of God; a false christology, that of a spirit not from God (1 Jn 4:2–3). The *antichrist* is identified by his denial of Jesus as the Christ (1 Jn 2:22). Much of this manner of impugning the character of the adversaries is part of the polemical rhetoric of the time. People were used to hearing an attack on some messages in terms of an attack on the messenger, much as we are used to the hyperbole of persuasive advertising. But the point remains that the author sees one's theological position as a very important part of one's relationship with God.

Given even greater importance, especially in 1 John, is the believer's responsibility to express love toward others. The writings here speak only about "one another" and "the brother" as objects of this love. The scope appears limited to the members of the Christian community. However, the importance given to this "commandment" is a significant development from the Gospel. The Gospel stressed accepting the light of Jesus, coming to him, looking on him, and believing in him as Truth. Very little else is required for eternal life. 1 John brings up the problem of illusion and deception that one might fall into with this simple presentation of the Gospel:

> The one claiming to be in the light and hating his brother
> is still even now in the darkness. (2:9)

> If anyone says, "I love God," and hates his brother, that
> one is a liar. (4:2)

Conversely, the reliable sign of passing from death to eternal life is the simple fact "that we love the brothers" (3:14). The language here is as strong as that warning against false christologies.

The perspective is clearly that of a pastor who must translate "lofty" theology into practical terms. What does this faith mean in terms of living today in this world? In effect, we have here an important theological hermeneutic: if you cannot see a difference an idea makes in your life, you do not understand the idea. However abstract, the meaning of the idea involves an "application" to life.

In their insistence on the practical, these later Johannine writings draw close to the Gospel of Matthew. It was this Gospel that identified the wise disciple as the one who, unlike the fool, not only hears the words of Jesus but "puts them into practice" (Mt 7:24–27). It was this Gospel that insisted on the final judgment as one based on practical acts of love—even if those acts are lacking a specifically Christian understanding. "As often as you *did* it to the least of my brothers, you did it to me" (Mt 25:40).

In addition, we have seen ways in which these later Johannine writings draw close to the Pauline perspectives. These "letters" thus show the tendency of faith to synthesize. Rooted squarely in a Johannine perspective of Truth and Life, these writings appear open to the viewpoints of other churches. Perhaps it was the crises faced by the Johannine community that forced it to look beyond its own theological horizons. The crises—denials of Jesus' humanity, ethical quietism—perhaps pointed out the limits of these horizons and the need to look beyond, to listen to what other Christians were saying. The sense of "catholicity" was developing.

EXERCISES

Exercise 1. (see page 258): Read 2 John and Paul's letter to Philemon. Abstracting from the content, what similarities do you see in the form of these letters? What differences in detail do you find?

Exercise 2. (see page 258): Read 1 John. Why do you think an author would have written this essay? From the points the author stresses, can you figure out what problems he intended to address? Can you figure out the adversaries he was writing against?

Exercise 3. (see page 262): What was the church of 1 John like? What does this writing say about activities that would be those of a community of believers? What would be the identifying signs of a member of that community?

Exercise 4. (see pages 263–264): Read 1 John and note everything it says or implies about God the Father. According to this writing, what is the relationship of Jesus to God?

REVIEW QUESTIONS

1. What are the literary forms of "the Letters of John"?
2. What similarities link these writings to one another and to the Fourth Gospel?

3. Compared to the Fourth Gospel, what shifts of emphasis do these writings show in their christology, soteriology, and eschatology?

FOR FURTHER REFLECTION AND DISCUSSION

1. The author of 1 John is harsh against those who propose an apparently Gnostic christology. Rather than calling the other camp "antichrists," wouldn't a greater tolerance of other views be more in line with Christian charity and even a more effective way to the truth?

2. If the author is not the apostle John, if—as probable—the author is of a later generation of Christians, what is he referring to when he writes in the opening of the treatise about proclaiming "what we have heard, what we have seen with our eyes...and touched with our hands"?

15

Historical Development— A Sketch of the Late First Century

As the first century drew to a close, the early Christians faced daunting challenges. The first generation of leaders had passed away. The empire with its incredible power had turned against them. Jewish leaders, who had managed some form of coexistence with the Jewish Christian branch of Christianity, now became adamant to separate themselves from the followers of Jesus. Christians were no longer welcome...anywhere.

Within the church, divisions began to develop and harden. Gnosticism, with its hostility to body and rejection of anything human in Jesus, began to organize. With groups professing contradictory positions, it became difficult to identify the real Christians.

The New Testament books written during this period reflect these challenges. We have seen how the Gospels of Matthew and John reflect hostility toward Jewish leadership. Even later writings—the Deutero-Pauline epistles, the Johannine and general epistles, and the book of Revelation—not only show the marks of these historical challenges but at times are understandable only against the backdrop of this history. We therefore pause again to survey briefly the events of these decades.

I. The Passing of the Apostles and Early Leaders

Our information about the apostles of Jesus and the other leaders of the early church at this time is sketchy. The Acts of the Apostles describes events to about A.D. 62. After that, we rely on popular traditions, implications in the New Testament texts, and brief comments from historically minded writers of the time.

		EVENTS IN THE EARLY CHURCH
	A.D. 27–30	Public ministry of Jesus
	30	Death of Jesus
	35	Death of Stephen
	44	Persecution under Herod Agrippa I death of James, the brother of John
	49	"Council" of Jerusalem
Nero	54	
	62	Death of James, the brother of the Lord
	67	Death of Paul
	70	Destruction of Jerusalem
Domitian	80	Christians expelled from synagogues
Trajan	98	

Figure 28.

A. Paul

The last letters we studied of Paul left him in prison. But we were not sure where that prison was, nor did we have any information about the outcome of that imprisonment. He expected to be released (Phlm 22; Phil 1:25).

Tradition places the death of Paul in Rome in A.D. 67. Apparently he was beheaded under Nero. St. Jerome, writing in the fourth century, gives us this information, and the descriptions and implications of 2 Tm 1:17 and 4:6–7 support this tradition. As we will see, this letter probably attempts a realistic fiction of Pauline authorship and thus witnesses to an accepted tradition of Paul's death in Rome.

After his death, Paul remained a thorn of controversy but was quickly considered by many to be a great Christian theologian and leader. On the other hand, some Christians rejected Paul, perhaps mostly because Marcion chose Paul's writings as the heart of his Gnostic New Testament. Jewish Christians may have continued for several decades in their opposition to Paul. This hypothesis finds some support in the Jewish Christian writings now known as the *Pseudo-Clementines,* where the lawless teachings of Simon Magus appear to represent the "lawless teachings" of Paul. Yet any need to camouflage Paul instead of openly opposing him would itself indicate Paul's prestige among other Christians. Despite the controversies, a significant group of Christians collected his letters and placed them on the same level as scripture, as is implied in 2 Pt 3:15–16.

B. Peter

The last events of Peter that we read about in the New Testament start with a sudden departure from Jerusalem under the persecution of Herod Agrippa I (Acts 12:17). This persecution probably took place around A.D. 44. Peter then appears in "the council" of Jerusalem around A.D. 49 (Acts 15:7–11; cf. Gal 2:1–10), and finally at Antioch in a significant argument with Paul apparently sometime shortly after the meeting in Jerusalem (Gal 2:11–14).

Tradition places the death of Peter also in Rome at the same time as that of Paul. Some archaeological evidence supports this tradition:

(a) The names of both Paul and Peter appear in graffiti scratched on the walls of catacombs in Rome. Both are singled out as the object of intercessory prayers.

(b) The ancient Constantinian basilica of St. Peter, now forming the foundation of the present basilica in the Vatican, is built over an ancient Roman cemetery. Moreover, it is built on the slope of a hill. Both the cemetery and the slope would make this location architecturally awkward for a church. Even the emperor would have faced serious opposition against disturbing a Roman cemetery. Constantine thus must have had an important reason for selecting this site.

(c) Under the main altar of the present basilica of St. Peter are the remains of a first-century Christian tomb that contained the bones of a middle-aged man. The remains seem to correspond to a second-century description of the "monument of Peter," which was found on the Vatican Hill.

If Priscilla and Aquila were expelled from Rome because of their Jewish Christianity, a significant Jewish Christian community must have been established in Rome by A.D. 49 and perhaps as early as A.D. 44, depending on how we date the edict of Claudius. As leader of the Jewish Christian branch of Christianity, Peter would have an important reason for coming to Rome, although the image of him "founding" the church of Rome as the first "bishop" is clearly a later religious simplification.

C. The Two Jameses

James the Apostle, the son of Zebedee and brother of John the Apostle, died at the hands of Herod Agrippa I. His murder, mentioned in Acts 12:2, took place around A.D. 44.

James the Brother of the Lord appears as a leader of the

Jerusalem church toward the middle of the first century (see Acts 15:13–21; 21:18). Apparently he functioned as a skillful diplomat and buffer between the Christian Jews in Jerusalem and the Orthodox Jews in power there. The Jewish historian Josephus recounts his murder in A.D. 62, provoked by the jealousy of the high priest.

D. John the Apostle

John the Apostle and son of Zebedee, whom tradition identifies as the author of the Fourth Gospel (see chapter 13 above), has two very different fates, depending on which tradition we follow. One, the more widespread, places him in Ephesus, where he lived to be an old man and died a natural death. The other tradition is based on a liturgical tradition celebrating his death along with that of his brother, James. This tradition seems to place John's death in Jerusalem, where presumably he would have died a martyr with his brother.

Ephesus. The Curetes' Street.

E. Thomas and Andrew

Other apostles attracted legends that are difficult to evaluate. One legend describes Thomas traveling to India, where he founded Christian communities. Today in India the Christians of St. Thomas trace their origins back to this apostle.

According to a tenth-century legend, Andrew traveled to Greece and was crucified on an X-shaped cross in the city of Patras. The popularity and timing of this legend, however, are connected to the rivalry of Constantinople with Rome over church leadership.

Gradually the *office* of apostle—as in the "twelve apostles"—died out. Even in the 80s, Luke recognized that the apostles who were martyred were not replaced—except for Judas, whose death occurred when twelve apostles were still necessary to ensure the symbolic transition from the "twelve tribes of Israel" to the new twelve patriarchs. (For this conception, see Lk 22:3; Mt 19:28.) Paul of course arose in an "untimely" manner, with a new claim to the role of apostle, redefined in Pauline terms. In a loose relationship with the apostolic role of Paul but unconnected with the nature and requirements of the twelve followers of Jesus, a new role or office arose in the late decades of the first century—that of elder or presbyter. To follow this development, we must first glance at a related development, the importance of precise teachings about Jesus and his work.

II. The Rise of Orthodoxy

With the passing of the first generation, a special challenge faced the Christians. How did they know that they were in continuity with the first group that followed Jesus? How were they to know who were the real Christians and who were fake?

The earliest disciples knew the answers to these questions by reference to their personal relation to the Lord. They were disciples of Jesus because they literally followed him. The next generation referred to the apostles in the same way. These Christians knew they were in continuity with the movement Jesus started because of their personal relationship with the apostles.

When the apostles died off, Christians could no longer be assured of their apostolicity and identity as Christians by such a personal relationship. In place of the presence of the apostles, the key factor became the teaching of the apostles. One could be assured of continuity with the apostolic group by adherence to the apostolic teaching. One could know who the real Christians were by testing for this same teaching. Correct teaching or "orthodoxy" became an essential foundation for Christian life.

(See exercise 1.)

The very existence of the New Testament shows the importance of orthodox teaching. Collected and preserved, the writings would function as a test to evaluate the later positions of church authorities. Within the New Testament, the importance of this correct teaching progressively mounts as the writings appear. In Paul snatches of creedal formulas appear. At the other end of the spectrum, 1 John makes adherence to a specific christology the distinction between having the Spirit of God and having the spirit of the antichrist (see 1 Jn 2:18–23; 4:2–3). In the Pauline tradition, 1 and 2 Timothy along with Titus will transform the Pauline concept of faith into correct teaching (see 1 Tm 6:3–10).

The struggles presupposed by this insistence on orthodox teaching appear to be struggles within the Christian community. The adversaries seem to be "brothers" rather than outsiders. A century later, Irenaeus will identify the great "heresy" as Gnosticism, described by him as a full-blown religion within Christianity. Shortly after the turn of the second century, Ignatius of Antioch suggested that this Gnostic movement was vigorous much earlier (see *Smyrneans* 5:2–3). It would appear that some form of Gnosticism within the Christian community was the backdrop against which this great insistence on correct teaching arose.

An interesting corollary to this insistence on correct teaching was the need for each community to have an authoritative teacher. A community needed one who could identify the true from the false teaching, one who could insist on conforming one's confession of faith to orthodox doctrine. Such a teacher would control membership on the basis of orthodox confession.

We can trace the important development of this teaching office and situate it in the historical needs of the church provided we see the letters 1 and 2 Timothy and Titus as written not by Paul but by someone in his name writing decades after his death. We will examine the plausibility of this hypothesis in the next chapter.

Using this hypothesis, we can see the concentration of power in local leadership beginning with documents from the 80s. At this time ministry within the church begins to look more like an "office" rather than a "gift." Ministers are clearly designated. Their function becomes more permanent. Symbols of power, such as "laying on of hands," help in the public designation of the ministers.

It is particularly the office of "elder" (in Greek, *presbyteros*) that seems to have filled this need for an authoritative teacher in the church (see Ti 1:9). The office was something like Paul's own role as "apostle" except that it was local. Paul was out in the field.

He functioned almost like a military officer with his lieutenants—Timothy, Titus, and others. He was out traveling somewhere to be contacted for help in resolving crises. But he was not a resident leader. At his death a void appeared, and the local leadership stepped into that void.

Most probably this local leadership sprang up in the hands of the "household heads," the wealthy men and women who owned property large enough to host the Christian gatherings. Socially these were powerful people—naturals for church leadership when hard decisions had to be made. The letters of Paul frequently mention their invaluable collaboration. Somewhere, sometime between the last letter of Paul and the writings of Luke in the 80s, these household heads known by Paul as "administrators" and "leaders" became the "elders" or "presbyters" of the church, gradually absorbing the role of "the teachers" and "the prophets." Just as Paul seemed to embody the spectrum of gifts in order to exercise his power, so these local leaders assumed other functions in order to govern the church.

Luke gives us the first indication of Christian "elders" or "presbyters" in the church. He first speaks of them in Jerusalem (see Acts 15). Although Luke is writing in the 80s and tends to anachronistic retrojection, the office may in fact have begun in Jerusalem as an imitation of the Jewish elder. Luke's description of Paul and Barnabas, however, appointing "presbyters in each church" (Acts 14:23) conflicts with the ecclesiology we have from Paul's own letters. Luke appears to be using an institution of the 80s to describe Paul's work in the 50s.

Diotrephes of 3 John illustrates such a powerful, albeit misguided, local authority. As a household head, he clearly has the local "power of the keys," and his use or misuse of hospitality is considered a very serious matter. He appears in a teaching role and has the power to expel from the church. Although not called a "presbyter," like the itinerant author of this letter, he appears to function much as the "elders" or "presbyters" of 1 and 2 Timothy and Titus, where we have elaborate descriptions of this office, presumably from the same late period.

(See exercise 2.)

III. Conflicts with Judaism

The late first century likewise marks the definitive split between Christians and Jews. What begins as a Jewish movement becomes a new religion by the end of the century. The antagonism leading to this split marks the later New Testament writings. We can sketch this development by looking at the major events.

A. Early Persecution

The Acts of the Apostles describes the stoning of Stephen (Acts 7) and the beheading of James the Apostle (12:2). Stephen's death must have occurred around A.D. 35; James's, around A.D. 44. These killings mark the sporadic hostilities of the earlier period.

From the evidence at our disposal, it appears that the Jewish hostility was directed not so much at the Christians as such but at the Hellenistic-Jewish Christians. This group, of which Stephen was a leader, apparently posed serious cultural threats to the powers of Jerusalem. The Jewish Christians, however, seemed to have been tolerated within Judaism as one more diverse sect, along with the Sadducees, Pharisees, Zealots, Essenes, and others.

B. The Execution of James the Brother (A.D. 62)

A more ominous development occurred in A.D. 62 with the murder of James the Brother. This person, who guided the Jerusalem church along the difficult path of Jewish Christianity, was removed from the scene. At this point hostilities worsened.

C. The Destruction of Jerusalem (A.D. 70)

At this time forming a distinct group within Palestinian Judaism, the Zealots were becoming more active in fomenting armed revolt against the Romans. Within a few years, war broke out against Rome, and groups such as the Jewish Christians became even more intolerable for Jewish leadership.

Tradition speaks of a general move at this time of the Jewish Christians out of Jerusalem up to Syria, according to the words of Jesus, "When you hear about wars and threats of wars, do not yield to panic...those in Judea must flee to the mountains" (Mk 13:7, 14). Later, the Jewish Christians in Syria will be known as the Ebionites, "the Poor."

In A.D. 70 the army of Titus stormed the city of Jerusalem, burning the Temple and destroying the city. The revolt against

Rome was thus brutally suppressed. The one city that formed a bond between Jew and Christian disappeared.

D. The Excommunications of the Christians (80s–90s)

The rabbis and Pharisees together formed the only powerful group to survive the disaster of A.D. 70, and they rallied the nation around their brand of Judaism, that of synagogue service and fervent dedication to the Law.

This period of Jewish restoration after the destruction of Jerusalem was marked by intolerance toward heterodox views, particularly those of the Christians. It was a period of systematic excommunications of Christians from the Jewish communities.

A prayer written at this time, part of the "Twelve Benedictions" to be recited before the synagogue services contains a curse on the Christians. Any Christian Jews wishing to participate in the synagogue service, as they had done all their lives, would in effect have to curse themselves. It reads:

> For the renegades let there be no hope, and may the arrogant kingdom soon be rooted out in our days, and the Nazarenes [Christians] and the *minim* [heretics] perish as in a moment and be blotted out from the book of life and with the righteous may they not be inscribed. Blessed art thou, O Lord, who humblest the arrogant.[1]

We see echoes of these excommunications especially in the Gospel of John, where an entire chapter deals with the excommunication of a man cured of blindness (John 9).

In the end the Christian church and the Jewish synagogue became hate-filled enemies, with subsequent history recording the brutalities. Christianity became predominantly Gentile. The Jewish Christian community faded into obscurity. Ironically, the followers of Jesus became a religion in themselves distinct not only from "paganism" but also from Judaism.

IV. Conflict with Rome

The earlier writings of the New Testament record serious attempts by the Christians to find an accommodation with Rome. Paul upholds the authority of the civil government and its taxes as founded on God's will (Rom 13:1–7). Mark emphasizes the teaching of Jesus in the "render to Caesar" episode (Mk 12:17). Rome had provided the civil peace and security in which the Gospel could be preached.

A. The Persecution of Nero (A.D. 64–68)

Nevertheless, suspicions were growing that the Christians were evil people, hating life, eating babies, and in general acting strangely. The secrecy with which some Christian communities shrouded their services no doubt contributed to these suspicions.

In A.D. 64 when the emperor Nero was facing a riot in Rome for his failure to act properly during a terrible fire in the city, these suspicions were exploited. Nero blamed the Christians for the fire and initiated the first of a long series of state-sponsored persecutions.

In Rome, Christians were arrested and tortured to death to the delight of the populace. For the entertainment of Romans, Christians were placed in the arena with hungry wild animals. One writer describes Nero himself illuminating his evening parties with patio torches consisting of Christians covered with tar, being burnt alive.

This type of torture was not unusual; it was common for slaves to be brutally killed. This type of persecution under Nero thus seems to indicate that the Christians arrested were mostly of the slave and lower classes.

The Colosseum at Rome.

B. The Persecution under Domitian (A.D. 81–96)

About thirteen years later, alarmed at the presence of Christians in his Pretorian Guard and among the nobility, the emperor Domitian again triggered a persecution of Christians. Historians today have a difficult time understanding the nature and extent of this persecution. Christian writings, however, speak of courageous soldiers who chose to be frozen to death rather than renounce their faith. Flavius Clemens exemplifies the nobility put to death at this time.

One factor behind this persecution was Domitian's desire to be worshiped as a god. Previous emperors were divinized after they died, and special cults were developed for their worship. Domitian, however, wanted to enjoy divine status while he was alive and therefore commanded all subjects to worship him or be considered disloyal and treasonous, liable to death.

Whether or not it accurately portrays the actual persecution of Domitian or simply presents a slanted perception of that persecution, the book of Revelation almost certainly reflects this Roman hostility. The author speaks of men who worshiped "the beast" who "was allowed to wage war against God's people" (Rv 13:7–8) and also of the whore who sits upon seven hills and "was drunk with the blood of God's holy ones" (Rv 17:6, 9).

The statue of Domitian.

C. The Persecution under Trajan (A.D. 98–117)

Under Trajan, who became emperor two years after Domitian, the insanity of the persecutions died down. In his correspondence with Pliny, Trajan outlined a policy to be followed for the persecution of Christians: (a) Christians were not to be searched out. (b) If, however, denounced as a Christian, a person was to be arrested, interrogated, and if found to be a Christian given the chance to renounce his or her faith. (c) If a Christian renounced Christ, that person was to be set free; if not, killed.

This was the policy that would be generally in force through the next two centuries. This was the policy that would confront countless Christians with the question of how firmly they believed in Christ. Many Christians did renounce their faith. Many, however, did not and died.

(See exercise 3.)

V. Theological Reflections

Several reflections come to mind when we review this background for the New Testament. First of all, we see again the way the New Testament reflects its own historical background and how that background assists us in understanding the meaning of the texts.

Second, we are struck by the predominance of struggle in this period. For the most part, the earliest leaders of the church did not die natural deaths. The community found itself quickly in a struggle with its own membership. Hostile political and religious forces surrounded the church for the next centuries. Struggles seemed almost a natural part of Christian community life.

Third, the church survived and adapted. When strong leadership was needed, when charismatic exuberance did not seem to provide a recipe for survival, "official" catholicism seems to have arisen. We today tend to distrust and disdain powerful office, especially in religious matters. Yet that official power within the early church guided it through rough waters.

The fact that this survival took place through the adaptation to historical pressure is a challenge not only to those who would demand a constant return to pristine forms but also a challenge to those who would freeze the late-first-century forms into something that now is unchanging. The church of the late first century was very different from the Pauline church of the mid-first century, yet both seemed to be fully "church." This diversity within the New Testament argues against inflexibility.

It is particularly interesting to see how the powerful authority within the local church developed. If we are correct in seeing its origins in the adaptations of the household heads, then we must revise the traditional picture of "apostolic succession"—which comes to us mostly from Irenaeus fighting the Gnostic threat. The local elders

or presbyters, the ancestors of our modern bishops, were not themselves successors to the twelve apostles but in fact seemed to
develop from the "charism" of household administration and leadership (see 1 Cor 12:28). Whatever conceivably could be deemed a
requirement for being "an apostle" as Jesus chose them—for example, being male—simply is not relevant to the discussion of continuity of modern church leadership with early forms. Many of the
household heads mentioned by Paul were in fact women—presumably widows who would have succeeded to the positions of their
deceased spouses.

Such a conclusion naturally presupposes the hypothesis of
authorship which we alluded to above regarding the letters of 1 and
2 Timothy and Titus. It is to those letters and others in the category
of "Deutero-Pauline" letters that we must now turn.

NOTE

[1] Text from C. K. Barrett, *The New Testament Background: Selected
Documents* (New York: Harper & Row, 1961), p. 167.

EXERCISES

Exercise 1. (see page 275): The Apostles' Creed is a statement of orthodox
    teaching intended to identify true Christians. What diverse teachings
    can you find in this creed? The Nicean Creed is recited in church
    every Sunday. Can you identify other teachings in that creed?
Exercise 2. (see pages 275–277): Who are the most important leaders in your
    church? What specific functions and authority do they have in the
    community? How do these leaders compare in their functions to
    church leaders of the first century?
Exercise 3. (see pages 279–282): Where are Christians persecuted today?
    What similarities and differences can find between modern persecu-
    tions and those of ancient Rome?

REVIEW QUESTIONS

1. What literary or archaeological evidence provides information
about the deaths of Paul, Peter, James the Son of Zebedee, James the
Brother of the Lord, and John?

2. Why did correct teaching become so important among Christians of
the last decades of the first century A.D.?

3. Who are the presbyters or elders in the early church? How did they
arise? What was their principal function?

FOR FURTHER REFLECTION AND DISCUSSION

1. If you had to organize the leadership offices in the church today, how would they function? What would you require of anyone holding an office?

2. What would Jesus think of church developments of the late first century? Of our century?

3. In light of your responsibilities, do you think it would be better to deceive a persecutor about your faith in order to stay alive or to confess your faith if it meant death?

16

The Deutero-Pauline Epistles

The New Testament contains thirteen letters which claim to be written by Paul. These thirteen together constitute the *Pauline corpus*. We have looked at eight. Where are the other five?

The ones we have skipped thus far are Ephesians, 1 and 2 Timothy, Titus, and 2 Thessalonians. Our approach to these five will contradict a tradition extending from the second to the nineteenth century. That tradition held these letters to be written by Paul, just as they say in their opening verses that they are written by Paul. Our examination will conclude that these epistles are written by someone other than Paul, probably after Paul's death, and that these letters make much more sense in the light of this approach.

We will have a significant theological task if we are to uphold the "inerrancy" of these letters which say they were written by Paul. We will also have to amass some rather persuasive data if we are to run counter to the obvious statements of authorship that show up in the first verse of each of these writings. The result will not be conclusive proof, but a reasonable hypothesis supported by strong probability.

Today we call such use of another's name fraud, a concept that for some seems incompatible with divine revelation. The question of whether we can conceive of God using fraud to mediate his message remains intriguing. But to categorize this ancient-world practice of using another's name by this modern concept of fraud is really to oversimplify the phenomenon we are dealing with.

The practice of an author writing in the name of another is known as *pseudo-epigraphy*. Examples of pseudo-epigraphy abound in both Jewish and Christian literature. Jewish examples begin to appear around the second century B.C., about the time that Jewish authorities were telling the people that prophecy had been suspended for the time being (see 1 Mc 4:46), when the idea of closing the canon of scripture was gaining ground. Writers convinced that they had a Spirit-filled message for the people tended then to ascribe their writing to someone living during the "accepted" times. Thus, the author of Daniel, an Aramaic-speaking Jew writing around 169 B.C., ascribes his writing to a man supposedly living in the sixth century B.C. Similarly, the author of Qoheleth clearly hints in the first verse that he is King Solomon, yet the book appears almost certainly to be a third-century B.C. writing.

Christian examples of pseudo-epigraphy are numerous in the second century A.D. From that period we have the *Gospel of Peter,* the *Acts of Paul,* the *Protevangelium of James,* and many others. Behind these Christian writings was apparently the idea of making the dead heroes of the preceding generation come alive and speak again to the new situations.

The complexity of the pseudo-epigraphy can be seen even in the way people of the first centuries looked upon a person's name. The name of a person represented that person; it somehow made that person present. To know the name of someone and to call on that person meant to have some power over that person. For people of this time, invoking a person's name as the author of a document was a way of making that person present as author.

Letter	Principal Reason for Doubting Pauline Authorship
Ephesians	Extensive copying from Colossians
1 and 2 Timothy, Titus	Reflects church authority and church problems of the last decades of the 1st century
2 Thessalonians	Makes better sense as responding to the late 1st-century problem of the *delay* of the End

Figure 29. **The Deutero-Pauline Letters.**

We, at least in the Western world, will never fully understand this mentality in which the past was never really past, in which persons whose names were known were never really absent. We will never fully understand the phenomenon of pseudo-epigraphy which stems from this mentality. Our culture revolves around the perceived uniqueness of the individual human subject. We are intensely jealous of our "property." We are programmed from early childhood to find a role in life where we can "be ourselves" in the fullest possible way. We want our artistic creations above all to express our unique and personal dynamisms. For this reason artists sign their works. Such a culturally determining interest in the unique human subject was simply absent from the classic world we are studying.

For us then the most appropriate attitude toward this manner of writing is respectful observation with a prudent hesitation to apply culturally conditioned systems of values as a precondition for the meaning of the text. This means we need a certain detachment that lets the writing be what it is, that refuses to impose blanket condemnations.

When we ask the question of authorship, we are asking about *authenticity* in the literary sense of the word. This question of authenticity should not be confused with the ethical question, where the adjectives *authentic* and *unauthentic* connote values. If we speak of a New Testament book as "unauthentic," our concern is uniquely about authorship. We are not suggesting the churches made a mistake in "canonizing" the book. We are not even intending to demote the book to some lesser rank than the authentic works of Paul. Our deep concern is to understand the historical, psychological, and literary horizon in which a book was written. Recognizing a book in the Pauline corpus as unauthentic is recognizing that the work must be understood in its own horizon, not that of Paul. Conversely, the mind of Paul must be understood apart from these unauthentic books. To refuse this recognition is to cause enormous and unnecessary confusion.

I. Ephesians

With these thoughts in mind, we turn to the writing commonly known as Paul's Letter to the Ephesians. This title is full of problems. The work is not a letter, and it is probably not to the Ephesians. The expression "in Ephesus" appears to have been added to the manuscripts in the fourth century. Before that, the address in 1:1 read something like "to the holy ones and faithful ones in Christ Jesus." In this form, the writing addresses a very general audience, more or less as do James, 2 Peter, and Jude. For the sake of convenience, however, we will continue to refer to this writing as "Ephesians."

In its literary form, Ephesians appears to be a letter only in its opening and closing lines. It begins like a letter with the usual salutation of Paul (1:1–2) and it ends like a letter with the usual final greetings of Paul (6:21–24). In between, this writing is a theological essay. Thus, we should call this writing an "epistle," an essay in letter form.

Is it written by Paul?

A. The Question of Authorship

Several aspects of this epistle argue against Pauline authorship. Perhaps most important is the way this writing depends on Colossians. At times the author of Ephesians simply copied sentences and expressions from Colossians making small changes, as seen in the following comparisons:

Ephesians	*Colossians*
[1:1] Paul an apostle of Christ Jesus through the will of God to the holy ones who are... and faithful ones in Christ Jesus [2] Grace to you and peace from God our Father and the Lord Jesus Christ Blessed be the God and Father of our Lord Jesus Christ...	[1:1] Paul an apostle of Christ Jesus through the will of God and Timothy the brother [2] to the holy ones in Colossae and to the faithful brothers in Christ. Grace to you and peace from God our Father We thank the God, the Father of our Lord Jesus Christ...
[15] Therefore, I also, hearing of your faith in the Lord Jesus and of your love to all the holy ones...	[4]...hearing of your faith in Christ Jesus and the love which you have to all the holy-ones
[2:5] And you being dead transgressions were brought to life to Christ Jesus...	[2:13] And you being dead to transgressions and to the foreskin of your flesh, were brought to life with him...
[3:7]...the gospel, of which I became a minister according to the gift of the grace of God given to me... [3:1] the dispensation of the grace of God given to me for you...	[1:25]...the church, of which I became a minister according to the dispensation of God given to me for you to fulfill the word of God,
[4] the mystery of Christ which was not made known to other generations of the sons of men as now revealed to his holy apostles and prophets...	[26] the mystery hidden from ages and from generations now, however, manifested to his holy ones.

[4:2]...with all humility and meekness, with patience, bearing with one another with love, [32] forgiving one another, just as God in Christ forgave you.

[3:12]...humility, meekness, patience, [13] bearing with one another and forgiving one another, if one should have a complaint against someone just as the Lord forgave you.

[5:5] No fornicator or unclean or lustful person, which is an idolater can have inheritance...
[6] For through such comes anger of God on the sons of disobedience

[3:5] Put to death...fornication, uncleanness, passion...that lust which is idolatry,

[6] Through which comes the the anger of God on the sons disobedience

[15] Walk, not as unwise but as wise [16] redeeming the time

[4:5] In wisdom walk with outsiders redeeming the time

[19] speaking to one another in psalms and hymns and spiritual songs praising and singing psalms in your heart to the Lord, giving thanks always for all things in the name of our Lord Jesus Christ to the God and Father.

[3:16] admonishing one another with psalms, hymns, spiritual songs in grace praising in your hearts the Lord. [17] And all that you do in word or work, do all Christ in the name of the Lord Jesus, giving thanks to God the Father through him.

[6:21] In order that you might know news about me, what I am doing, Tychikos, the beloved brother and faithful minister in the Lord, will make all known to you matter concerning me and comfort your hearts.

[4:7] All the news about me Tychikos, the beloved brother and faithful minister and co-slave in the Lord, will make know to you matters concerning me and comfort your hearts.

Some of the similarities could be explained by letter formulas or common Pauline phrases. Most of the verbatim similarities, however, spread throughout Ephesians require a literary dependence of one writing on the other. Even the differences in the above parallels do not seem possible without a direct modeling on the corresponding Colossian text. We note phrases in Colossians that are used several times in Ephesians. We note also that the differences in the wording seem to be Ephesians' attempt to improve the text, to drop some strange language ("the foreskin of your flesh," Col 2:13) or to make the text ring more Pauline ("and the Lord Jesus Christ," Eph 1:2).

Such copying is foreign to Paul. Even letters as close as Romans and Galatians do not show evidence of copying. Paul was too much a master of his own thought to need to copy in this way.

Furthermore, attempts to reverse the situation and see Colossians as copied from Ephesians run into several difficulties. In effect, Ephesians expands on Colossians at several points, often adding a more Christian perspective (see the advice to husbands and wives, Eph 5:22–33 compared with Col 3:18–19). It is difficult to imagine why the supposed author of Colossians would have dropped these ideas. Ephesians likewise, as we will see, includes several shifts in theology that move away from the more typical Pauline perspectives as found in Colossians. Such a development suggests again that Ephesians developed as a spin-off of Colossians rather than vice versa.

We can only speculate about why the author of Ephesians would have written the way he did. One theory suggests that the author of Ephesians is the same person who gathered and edited the letters of Paul. A reference to the letters of Paul as a whole occurs in 2 Pt 3:16, which suggests the existence of collections at that time. The author may have written Ephesians as a kind of cover letter, representing what he thought to be the synthesis and final stage of Paul's thought. He would not have addressed such a letter to any one church, but would have left the salutation general enough to refer to any church.

B. The Structure of Ephesians

The involved structure of Ephesians indicates the essay character of this writing, even though it begins and ends as a letter. Today most scholars prefer to use the term "epistle" for this literary form.

The epistle has two major sections. After the epistolary greeting (1:1–2), the first major section (1:3–3:21) begins and ends with a hymn of praise (1:3–14 and 3:20–21). The first part of this inclusion thus functions as the typical letter prayer. Sandwiched between both these hymns are two prayers of petition (1:15–23 and 3:14–19). The inclusion has become a chiasm. The heart of the chiasm (2:1–3:13) contains the principal doctrine of the epistle, the great mystery of the church.

The second major section (4:1–5:20) is exhortation. The previous doctrine is applied to Christian living. Four aspects of Christian life follow each other to center stage for a comment by the author: diversity and unity of function within the church (4:1–16), personal Christian renewal (4:17–5:20), the Christian household (5:21–6:9), and the battle with evil (6:10–20). The letter conclusion draws the epistle to a close (6:21–24).

Outlined, this epistle would appear as follows:

I. Opening Address (1:1–2)

II. First Part: The Mystery of the Call of the Gentiles (chapters 1–3)
    A. Blessing and praise (1:3–14)
    B. Prayer for knowledge (1:15–23)
    C. The unity of Christians in Christ (2:1–3:13)
      1. All saved through Christ (2:1–10)
      2. The unity of Jew and Gentile through Christ (2:11–22)
      3. Paul's office as servant of the mystery (3:1–13)
    B´. Prayer for knowledge (3:14–19)
    A´. Doxology (3:20–21)

III. Second Part: Exhortations (chapters 4–6)
    A. A call to unity: faith, love, the gifts (4:1–16)
    B. The new life in Christ (4:17–5:20)
    C. Duties of the Christian home (5:21–6:9)
    D. The spiritual battle (6:10–20)

IV. Conclusion: Recommendations and Blessing (6:21–24)

C. The Faith of Ephesians

This writing does not develop a distinctive christology. As in the Pauline letters, Jesus here is named Christ, Lord, and Son of God. The one distinctive title, shared with Colossians, names Jesus as "the head," especially "head of the church" (1:22; 4:15; 5:23; cf. Col 1:18; 2:10, 19). This description leads us to the soteriology and ecclesiology of Ephesians.

1. Soteriology

Echoing Paul, Ephesians mentions many of the Pauline motifs of soteriology. Salvation is accomplished by the blood of Christ (1:7;

2:13). Christ's death is briefly mentioned as "an offering and a sacrifice" (5:2). Generally evil is described as "sins" (2:1), "trespasses" (1:7; 2:1, 5), or "evil deeds" (5:11). Drawing especially close to the themes of Colossians, Ephesians gives special emphasis to hostile cosmic powers, "dominions" (*kyriotētos,* Eph 1:21; cf. Col 1:16), "principalities" (*archai,* Eph 1:21; 3:10; 6:12; cf. Col 1:16; 2:10, 15), "authorities" (*exousiai,* Eph 1:21; 3:10; 6:12; cf. Col 1:16: 2:10, 15), "power" (*dynamis,* Eph 1:21), and "the prince of the power of the air" (Eph 2:2).

Unlike Paul (but like Colossians), however, Ephesians does not include any description of "sin" as a power of death or corruptibility that dominates us in the interior of our life, from whose bondage we need liberation. In Ephesians the hostile powers seem exterior. The "principalities" and "authorities" dwell in the heavens (3:10; 6:12).

These cosmic powers serve as the backdrop for the description of Christ's victory. Seated now at God's right hand, Christ is "above every principality, authority, power, and dominion and every name named not only in this age but in the one to come" (1:21). The victory of Christ, however, still leaves "the devil" (6:11), "the evil one" (6:16), at work attacking the followers of Christ. We are in the midst of an intense battle, requiring an elaborate panoply of weapons and defenses supplied by God for the present time (6:10–17). Christ in heaven is positioned for the final destruction of evil but has not yet fully subdued evil.

The immediate effect on earth of Christ's death appears to be the church. The church is the reconciled entity, involving especially the reconciliation of Jews and Gentiles. As seen in the outline of this epistle, its central focus is the church. Such a heavy emphasis is given to the church in this writing that any analysis of the theology of Ephesians demands a look at its ecclesiology.

2. Ecclesiology—The Apostles and Prophets in the Church

The christological emphasis in Colossians becomes ecclesiological in Ephesians. We can better understand this shift in emphasis if we look at two aspects of Ephesian's ecclesiology, first the role of "the apostles and prophets" in the church, and second the relationship of the church to Christ as his wife.

Colossians speaks of the Christians "rooted and built up on Christ" (2:7). The thought is similar to that in 1 Cor 3:11:

> No one can lay a foundation other than the one that has been set, namely, Jesus Christ.

Ephesians shifts this image to the church:

> You are built up on the foundation of the apostles and prophets, with Christ Jesus as its cornerstone (2:20).

The foundation has shifted from Christ to the apostles and prophets. A group of people within the church now appear with specific offices, on whom the rest of the church depends for its existence. Christ has not really been displaced, since he holds the preeminent position in the building. The shift is significant, however, and reflects a perspective different from that of Paul, who walked among the apostles and prophets of the church and looked back to Christ. The perspective of Ephesians is that of a period that could look back not only to Christ but also to the first followers of Christ for its origins.

The author makes another reference to the "apostles and prophets" in his description of "the mystery" (3:1–6). Here we have a clear parallel with Colossians, where Paul mentioned "the mystery":

> I became a minister of this church according to the dispensation of God given to me for you, to fulfill the word of God, the mystery hidden from ages and from generations, now however manifested to his holy ones, to whom God willed to make known the richness of the glory of this mystery among the Gentiles, which is Christ in you, the hope of glory. (Col 1:25–27)

The thought is not far from the concluding doxology of Romans, which praises God

> who strengthens you according to my gospel and the preaching of Jesus Christ, according to the revelation of the mystery, silenced in ancient ages, now however manifested.... (Rom 16:25–26; cf. also 1 Cor 2:6–7)

In Ephesians the reference to the mystery reads as follows:

> By reading what I briefly wrote to you, you can learn my understanding of the mystery of Christ, not made known to other generations of the sons of men as it is now revealed to his holy apostles and prophets in the Spirit,

that the Gentiles are co-heirs, co-members, and sharers of
the promises in Christ Jesus through the gospel. (3:3–6)

The additions in Ephesians have significantly shifted the
meaning of the mystery. Instead of being the very person of Christ,
as described in Colossians, the mystery in Ephesians is about the
inclusion of Gentiles into the church. What was a christological
mystery now is an ecclesiological mystery.

Instead of being revealed to "the holy ones," a expression Paul
uses for Christians as such (cf. Col 1:1; Phil 1:1), the mystery in Ephesians is revealed to a special group of church authorities, "the holy
apostles and prophets." Eventually the mystery is "made known" to
"other generations of the sons of men"; however, a distinction is
being drawn between the revelation as such and the publication of
this revelation. As an illumination from God, Ephesians limits the
revelation to "the holy apostles and prophets." This group becomes,
as it were, the channel by which God's grace of revelation passes on
to the rest of the church and humanity. The consequences of this new
perspective on later ecclesiology will be enormous and will stand in a
real contrast to the more "democratic" picture drawn by Paul.

3. Ecclesiology—The Church as the Wife of Christ

Part of the exhortatory section in Colossians consists of a household instruction. Colossians 3:18–4:1 expresses brief instructions
directed to three pairs of groups, basically constituting the Hellenistic
household. Paul begins with "wives" (3:18) and then addresses "husbands" (3:19), "children" (3:20), and "fathers" (3:21). A longer section
instructs "slaves" (3:22–25)—perhaps reflecting this letter's connection with Philemon—and finally a line to "masters" (4:1).

Similar household instructions appear in 1 Pt 2:18–3:7; 1 Tm
2:8–15; 6:1–10; and Ti 2:1–10. These later instructions follow different orders and address different groups. The diversity yet frequency
of this type of instruction tells us that the authors of these letters
along with Paul writing Colossians were all following a general literary form of instruction popular among the Christians at that time, a
form that permitted a great deal of freedom in its application.

When we examine Ephesians, we find there too a household
instruction, 5:22–6:9. In Ephesians, as we might now expect, the persons addressed and the order of the address is exactly the same as in
Colossians. The household instruction in Ephesians in comparison
with that in Colossians, however, is rather striking. For one thing it

contains far more Christian themes than does that of Colossians. We see far more theological motives adduced for accepting these instructions and far more allusions to Christ and other Gospel themes.

The instructions to husbands is particularly interesting for us. Here the motivation following the instruction reveals the author's understanding of the church:

> Husbands, love your wives, as Christ loved the church. He delivered himself for her that he might make her holy, purifying her in the bath of water in the word, that he might present to himself a glorious church, without stain or wrinkle or anything of that sort but rather holy and immaculate. Thus husbands should love their wives as they do their own bodies...as Christ cares for the church, for we are members of his body. "For this reason a man shall leave his father and mother, and shall cling to his wife, and the two shall be made into one flesh." This is a great mystery; I say that it refers to Christ and the church. (5:25–32)

Echoes of the Old Testament resound in this text. The prophet Hosea saw in his unhappy marriage a revelation of the relationship between God and Israel. In the intimate love a husband has for his wife, Hosea saw the type of love God wanted with his people. In the sin of marital infidelity, he saw the evil of Israel's refusal to accept Yahweh as its God (see Hosea 1–3). The prophets Jeremiah and Ezekiel both use the image of the unfaithful wife to dramatize Israel's sin (Jeremiah 3; Ezekiel 16; 23). Although it does not even mention God in its songs celebrating sexual love, the Canticle of Canticles was included in the Jewish canon because religious authorities could recognize in this writing an allegory about God's love for his people.

The author of Ephesians thus takes the simple instruction that Paul gave to the husbands of Colossae and expands it with the Old Testament idea that conjugal love, with its intimacy and passion, expresses the love that God wants to have with his people. The author, however, shifts the image from God and Israel to Christ and the church.

As describing the church, the image of the wife of Christ expresses the intense love Christ has for his church. It also expresses a certain autonomy of the church in regard to Christ. The image of the church as "the body" of Christ (5:23; cf. 1:23–24; 2:15; 4:4, 12, 16) does not leave much room for the church's independent personality.

Depicted as wife, the church appears in Ephesians as being in need of purification as well as the object of a divine love affair.

By incorporating his ecclesiology into this household instruction, the author of Ephesians has likewise given us a theology of marriage. He is saying in effect that Christian husbands and wives manifest in a visible way the love that Christ has for his church. The love of Christian spouses becomes more than just a personal or civil affair. For better or for worse, the world can look upon their love and see the love of Christ.

(See exercise 1.)

4. Eschatology

As an important parallel to its ecclesiology, Ephesians develops its distinctive eschatology. Again, Ephesians expands on Colossians:

> You were buried with him in baptism, in which you were also raised with him through faith in the power of God, who raised him from the dead. (Col 2:12)

In Ephesians this "realized resurrection" is taken a step further:

> God, who is rich in mercy, because of the great love he had for us, even when we were dead in our transgressions, brought us to life with Christ—by grace you have been saved—raised us up with him, and seated us with him in the heavens in Christ Jesus. (Eph 2:4–6)

Not only are we dead and resurrected, but we are also ascended into heaven. Whereas in Colossians, Paul still looks forward to the time "when Christ your life appears" (Col 3:4), in Ephesians there is only one brief mention of "in the ages to come" (Eph 2:7).

This heavenly perspective, as the perspective for the present, appears to dominate the letter, from the opening praise of God "who has blessed us in Christ with every spiritual blessing in the heavens" (1:3) to the glowing picture of the spotless, sanctified church that dominates chapter 5. Christians not only are in the light, but constitute "light" itself and therefore must live as "children of the light" (5:8).

The concern for the delay of the end has disappeared; the end is now a spiritual reality in the life of the believer. A future development of salvation still appears on the theological horizon of this writing.

The author still distinguishes between "this age" and "the one which is to come" (1:21). The "kingdom of Christ and of God" is for the author still a future inheritance (5:5). But with the author's focus on the church and what Christ has already accomplished in his church, Ephesians still appears as the most consistent proponent of "realized eschatology" of all the writings in the New Testament.

II. The Pastoral Epistles: 1–2 Timothy, Titus

Three letters, 1 and 2 Timothy and Titus, form a special group in the Pauline corpus. They are addressed not to churches but to heads of churches. They are less concerned with doctrine than with church order. They exhibit a vocabulary and literary style very different from the earlier letters of Paul. Since the eighteenth century, these writings have been known as the Pastoral Epistles.

Two letters address Timothy as presiding over the church at Ephesus. He is supposedly the companion of Paul recruited at Lystra, the son of a Jewish mother and a Greek father. Paul frequently associates Timothy with himself in the salutations of his letters. In 1 Timothy, Paul supposedly is working in Macedonia. In the second letter, Paul is in prison in Rome, preparing for death.

The third of the Pastorals addresses Titus as presiding over the church of Crete. Titus is not mentioned in Acts, but Paul refers to him frequently, especially in 2 Corinthians, where he played a key role in restoring order to the church in Corinth. Titus appears to have been a stronger personality than Timothy. Paul is presented as traveling toward Nicopolis, a city on the west coast of Greece.

A. The Question of Authorship

In the nineteenth century, when critical Pauline scholarship began asking seriously the question of authenticity, it was the Pastoral Epistles that first fell under deep suspicion. Since then the controversy about Pauline authorship has not ceased.

More conservative scholars point to the personal elements in 2 Timothy (see 1:15–18; 4:9–21) along with the loose train of thought typical of Paul's exhortations as arguments in favor of authenticity. Pseudo-epigraphers generally do not write about such things in another's name. Similar traits, however, are generally absent from the other two letters, particularly by from 1 Timothy, which is noticeably lacking in personal elements.

The liberal scholarship of the nineteenth century pointed

especially to the vocabulary of the Pastorals as arguing against authenticity. Thirty-six percent of this vocabulary is not found in other Pauline writings; that is about two and a half times the normal frequency of new words in Paul. Words that are used in other Pauline letters have shifted their meanings: for example, *faith* has shifted from an attitude of trust to a rule of doctrine.

The most persuasive argument against authenticity, however, lies in the background presupposed in these letters. We glimpse a church being torn by internal forces. The issue of "false teaching" is of first importance, particularly that of "falsely called 'knowledge'" (1 Tm 6:20). As in 2 Thessalonians, apostolic authority, particularly that of Paul, is viewed not as a link in the chain of tradition (cf. 1 Cor 11:23; 15:3) but as the source and guarantee of truth. Teaching and discipline within the church are falling increasingly under the powerful authority of local church leaders. These clues suggest the situation of the church at the end of the first century.

It was at that time that Christian doctrine became critically important. The apostles had died. Continuity with that first generation could no longer be based on personal association or acquaintance. The unity of a community could no longer be cemented around an apostle like Paul, present either by his letter or by his spoken word. In place of personal association, doctrinal conformity became the source of apostolic identity and church unity. A Christian could identify other Christians by what they professed, by their understanding of the traditions. Such doctrinal conformity demands doctrinal authority. Thus, this period of the church was also the period of ecclesiastical offices, particularly that of the teacher, the one who could expound orthodoxy and refute heresy.

Such a situation lurks behind the descriptions and admonitions of the Pastoral Epistles. In the 50s or 60s, these writings would have been out of place. It is not clear why Paul would have written lengthy and detailed instructions to Timothy and Titus at all. In 1 Timothy Paul has supposedly just left Timothy in Crete. In 2 Timothy and in Titus, Paul expresses his hopes to see them both soon. The extensive regulations appear not as emergency instructions but as orders for a considerable length of time. On the other hand, as documents of the 90s, the Pastorals make a great deal of sense. The author is pointing out how the new developments are rooted in apostolic authority, how if Paul were alive, seeing the crises around him, he would be making such an appeal to doctrine and tradition.

The pseudo-epigrapher may have incorporated fragments of Paul's own notes, particularly in 2 Timothy, adding the personal details and greetings typical of Paul. In this way the writer shows greater skill than other Deutero-Pauls. Apart from the short patches of the personal, however, even 2 Timothy bears the earmarks of a work calling Paul by name back from his grave to speak to a new situation, recording the memories of Paul's destiny in Rome, giving tribute to the apostle who wrote with such authority.

B. The Structure of the Pastorals

1 and 2 Timothy and Titus appear to have been composed around two great and interrelated concerns: harmful heresies and offices in the church. Personal matters are then woven into treatments of these concerns. The structure of these letters is fairly loose and would seem to follow the following outlines:

1 Timothy

   I. Salutation (1:1–2)

  II. Exhortation to Fight Heresy (1:3–20)

 III. Church Order (2:1–3:16)
        A. Prayer, especially for authorities (2:1–8)
        B. Instructions about women (2:9–15)
        C. Instructions about bishops (*episkopoi*, 3:1–7)
        D. Instructions about deacons (*diakonoi*, 3:8–13)

  IV. Refuting Heresy (4:1–6)
        A. The heresies (4:1–3)
        B. Correct teaching (4:4–11)
        C. Personal example (4:12–16)

   V. Church Order and the Care of Others (5:1–6:2)
        A. Men and women in general (5:1–2)
        B. Widows (5:3–16)
        C. Presbyters (*presbyteroi*, 5:11–22)
        D. Miscellaneous personal advice (5:23–25)
        E. Slaves (6:1–2)

  VI. Refuting Heresy (6:3–16)
        A. Heresies and venality (6:3–10)
        B. Personal example (6:11–16)
        —Hymn (6:15–16)

C. The Heresies Combated

(See exercise 2.)

1 Timothy introduces us quickly to the problems facing the community. The letter issues a stern warning:

> Remain in Ephesus in order to warn certain people there against teaching strange doctrines, absorbed in interminable myths and genealogies, which promote only speculations rather than the dispensation of God, realized in faith. The goal of this warning is love from a pure heart, a good conscience, and a sincere faith. Some have missed the target and have turned to meaningless talk, wanting to be teachers of the law but not understanding either what they are saying or what they are asserting with such assurance. (1:3–4)

We have not seen reference to "myths and genealogies" before in Paul. On the other hand, the judaizing element is familiar, particularly in its dilettantish form (cf. Gal 5:3). The issues in this epistle, however, clearly center on teachings. The appeal to faith over idle questions indicates an intensely defensive posture against an intellectual attack on orthodoxy.

The author later warns against "things taught by demons in hypocritical lies" (4:1–2). He mentions "forbidding marriage and abstaining from foods which God created" (4:3). Such antimaterial asceticism reminds us of Gnosticism, as does the final warning against "falsely called knowledge *(gnōsis)*" (6:20).

In 2 Timothy we find again the warning against "idle talk," this time connected with the idea that "the resurrection has already taken place" (2 Tm 2:16–18, 23). Titus again warns against "Jewish myths and rules invented by men" (Ti 1:14).

The adversaries here seem to represent a combination of several positions, including judaizing elements. The stress in these letters clearly lies on what these adversaries are teaching. The situation provoked by these false teachers is apparently serious and dangerous. The author advises only avoidance of any discussions. There is little effort to show where the error lies in this teaching. There is no attempt, as in earlier letters of Paul, to argue against the positions. In the Pastoral Epistles, rather, the positions are summarily dismissed as coming from evil men, who should simply be avoided.

D. The Faith of the Pastorals

These letters are not great sources for understanding the faith of the early Christians in terms of the major themes we have been following throughout this book. The content of these letters is geared far more toward the practical work of the church, and we will look especially at the way the church appears to be developing at the time of these letters. When we search for the christology, soteriology, and eschatology of these letters, we find positions we have already seen stated, without emphasis and therefore evidencing general acceptance. Coming from a Pauline tradition, these letters show the convergence of other schools.

1. Christology

A brief comment in Titus suggests that Johannine christology had spread to the Pauline churches toward the end of the first century. The comment is an expression of eschatological hope, and it appears to describe Jesus as God:

> The grace of the saving God has appeared to all human beings, teaching us...that we might live temperately, justly, and devoutly in this world, awaiting the blessed hope and appearance of the glory of our great God and savior Jesus Christ. (Ti 2:11–13)

The expression "great God and savior" is grouped under one article and one possessive pronoun in the Greek. The expression as written applies to one person who is then named, Jesus Christ. No explanation is given. We may have here the remnants of a creedal formula, which the author could presuppose as understood among the intended recipients of this letter. It would appear then that for this author and his community, Jesus is God.

The Pauline view of Jesus' preexistence is hinted at when the author says that "Christ Jesus came into the world" (1 Tm 1:15). A more Johannine approach may be evidenced when the writer says that Christ "was manifested in the flesh" (1 Tm 3:16). Thus, the drama of God saving us "in Christ Jesus before the times of the ages" (2 Tm 1:9) appears as the action of two principal agents, saving humanity before humanity exists and then demonstrating that salvation in time when one of those agents, Christ Jesus, appears in time (see 2 Tm 1:10).

2. Soteriology and Eschatology

Salvation is clearly the action of God. It is willed by God for all people (1 Tm 2:4). Jesus is involved as "the place" in whom salvation takes place—perhaps following the Pauline idea of Jesus being redeemed (2 Tm 1:9). Jesus is "the mediator (*mesitēs*)" of God's salvation for the whole human race (1 Tm 2:5), and this mediation involves the death of Jesus as "a ransom" (*antilytron,* 1 Tm 2:6). Although salvation stems from God, Jesus is active in a vigorous way: "He gave himself for us *(hyper hēmōn)* in order that he might redeem *(lytrōsētai)* us from our iniquity" (Ti 2:14).

What are we saved from? The author does not speak of "sin" in the singular as an apocalyptic power, but rather focuses on "sins" as actions of various people (1 Tm 5:22, 24; 2 Tm 3:6). This ethical sense of sin appears especially in the list of sins and vices found in these writings (e.g., 2 Tm 3:2–5). Paul had his lists of vices (see Gal 5:19–21), which were manifestations of a basic power of corruptibility, "the flesh." The sins and vices of the Pastorals seem to be more the result of perverted "desires" in our hearts which have to be rooted out (see 2 Tm 2:22; Ti 2:12; 3:3). The author here stands in a moral tradition that embraces both the Jewish wisdom traditions and Greek moral philosophy. One's attitude is the key to the good life. "To the clean all things are clean" (Ti 1:15).

The author is not clear how God's salvation in Jesus accomplishes this change of attitude. Rooted in Paul, the author rejects "good works" as the cause of salvation (Ti 3:5). Following Paul, the author describes the saving work of Jesus as something that "abolished death and brought life and imperishability to light" (2 Tm 1:10). Yet faced with the pastoral task of guiding weak people, the author's attention drifts far more to the concrete actions and attitudes of people.

God's work has already been accomplished by Christ's death and resurrection. God has "saved us" (2 Tm 1:9; Ti 3:5). Yet we await "the blessed hope, the appearance of the glory of the great God and savior Jesus Christ" (Ti 2:13). "Eternal life" is something we hope for (Ti 1:2; 3:7).

(See exercise 3.)

The real importance of the Pastorals lies in their picture of the church. What is said about Christ and salvation serves mainly as a backdrop for instructions about the challenges of living out one's faith in a community of believers. Several aspects of the author's faith about the church have deeply affected the ecclesial traditions of Christianity through the centuries—for better or for worse.

3. Faith as Doctrine

The Pastorals speak frequently of "guarding the deposit" (1 Tm 6:20; 2 Tm 1:12, 14). The author is referring to the faith now considered as *something* to be conserved. Faith is something to be held on to (1 Tm 1:19; 3:9). The opposite of "the faith" are "things taught by demons" (1 Tm 4:1). The "words of faith" are in effect the same as "sound doctrine" (1 Tm 4:6).

We see in these letters, then, a shift in the meaning of faith from the earlier Pauline sense of an openness to God's power and a trust in his grace to a sense of faith as a teaching. This doctrinal faith appears in the faith confessions that we see in this letter, such as the following:

> God is one. One also is the mediator between God and humanity, the man Christ Jesus, who gave himself as a ransom for all. (1 Tm 2:5–6)

A statement like this was probably memorized as a formula by which Christians could recognize one another. If you could recite this formula or at least say "Amen" to it, you were a Christian. If you could not, you were probably not a Christian.

This "sound doctrine" or authoritative teaching has thus become the key element in Christian life. Orthodoxy and adherence to orthodoxy become the key to membership in the Christian community. A good minister is one "nourished on the words of faith and of sound teaching" (1 Tm 4:6). Paul is portrayed as a "preacher and apostle and teacher" (2 Tm 1:11), who then is pictured as challenging Timothy:

> Take as your norm the sound words that you heard from me, in the faith and love that are in Christ Jesus. Guard

this rich deposit with the help of the Holy Spirit that dwells within us. (2 Tm 1:13–14)

4. Authoritative Teachers

Such an important role for authoritative teaching involves an important role for authoritative teachers within the community. Someone would have to decide what the "correct teaching" was. Someone had to decide with authority that a particular doctrine reflected the teaching of Paul and the apostles while another doctrine did not. These decisions were of vital importance. According to these decisions, membership in the community was determined.

The Pastorals speak of such an authoritative teacher in the "presbyter-bishop." The Letter to Titus includes an important description of this officer. We hear an instruction of Paul:

> For this reason I left you in Crete: that you might straighten out what had been left undone and that you might appoint presbyters in every town. As I instructed you, a presbyter must be irreproachable, the husband of one woman, having children who are believers and are known not to be extravagant or insubordinate. For the bishop as God's steward must be blameless, not arrogant, not irascible, not a drunkard, not violent, not greedy. Rather he should be hospitable, a lover of goodness, temperate, just, holy, and self-controlled. He must hold fast to the sure word with doctrine, so that he will be able both to encourage with sound instruction and to refute those who oppose it. (Ti 1:5–9)

Although two names are used for this official—presbyter and bishop—it is clear from their connection ("for") that the author is speaking about only one office. High moral demands are placed on this person, but his principal responsibility is teaching. He is the authoritative teacher who determines and defends orthodoxy. The author speaks, however, about several presbyter-bishops in every town. Hence, they do not rule as monarchs, but as colleagues.

A decade or so later, a writer named Ignatius of Antioch will speak of an individual bishop in a city, ruling in the name of Christ, surrounded by presbyters and deacons (see Ignatius's letters: *To the Magnesians* 6:1; *To the Philadelphians,* preface). In this later period, we see the structure of the church with which history is familiar: the monarchical bishop as an office distinct from that of the presbyters. Such a development is far from the "charismatic" church of Corinth to which Paul wrote in the late 50s. The Pastorals function precisely as the link between this earlier congregational type of church and the later episcopal form.

5. Laying On of Hands

Similar to Acts, the Pastorals speak frequently of the laying on of hands. This was a gesture used in Judaism to designate an authorized rabbi. In the Pastorals we hear of the presbyters laying hands on Timothy (1 Tm 4:14), of Timothy laying hands on others (1 Tm 5:22), and of Paul laying hands on Timothy (2 Tm 1:6).

Also as in Acts, this gesture is generally associated with the gift of the Spirit. Hence, we have another aspect in the consistent picture drawn by the Pastorals, an aspect of a visibly structured church as a sacrament of grace. Paul spoke about the Spirit giving gifts "as it wills" (1 Cor 14:11). In the Pastorals, as in Acts, the Spirit is a bit more domesticated. Leaders of the church have a better handle on it. In human gesture, the Spirit's gifts can be somewhat controlled.

6. Antifeminism

From the perspective of twentieth-century sociology and psychology, one of the most unfortunate aspects of the Pastorals is their antifeminism. For the author, woman is secondary in creation and primary in sin. This view was supposed to justify her silent, subordinate role:

> A woman must receive instruction silently and under complete control. I do not permit a woman to teach or have authority over a man. She must be quiet. For Adam was formed first, then Eve. Further, Adam was not deceived, but the woman was deceived and transgressed. (1 Tm 2:11–14)

We should understand the insistence here against the crisis of false teaching in the church. Women were associated with household management, a role that wealthy women frequently held in the classical world, and false teaching was associated with the household, which frequently gave rise to new cults. 2 Timothy brings these elements explicitly together in its polemic against false teachers:

> For some of these slip into households and make captives
> of women weighed down by sins, led by various desires,
> always trying to learn but never able to reach a knowl-
> edge of the truth. (2 Tm 3:6–7)

The author apparently is sharing a widely held perception of upper class women as irresponsible religious innovators. In fact, archaeological evidence does not support this perception. The list of patrons of new cults contains far more men's names than women's. But the perception was real. Apparently in his fear of irresponsible developments within Christianity, this author lashes out and provides an important building block in the next centuries' trend to exclude women from all roles of responsibility within the church.

III. 2 Thessalonians

Of all the writings in the Pauline corpus, the small letter known as 2 Thessalonians, has developed more commentaries and explanations than any other. The fascination with this letter lies in its mini-apocalypse nestled in the middle of frightening warnings and grouchy admonitions.

A. Authorship

To interpret the eschatology of this letter, it is absolutely necessary to decide whether to read it as written by Paul to the Thessalonians or as written by someone long after Paul to anyone but the Thessalonians. The apocalyptic section describes a great "apostasy," the evil workings of a "man of lawlessness," and a temporary "restrainer" now holding that man back. The letter then adds:

> Do you not recall that while I was still with you I told you
> of these things? And now you know what is restraining,
> that he may be revealed in his time. (2:5–6)

If such a line were written by Paul, then the modern interpreter would be faced with figuring out what particular things Paul could have meant. The line would presume that some specific instruction was given about these elements of the end of the world. Scholars and pious writers have attempted to identify these images with realities in the lifetime of Paul such as the Roman Empire or some of the evil emperors of the time. Other writers have attempted to identify these realities with future events and things. Among the candidates for the "man of lawlessness" have been Muhammad, the pope, Martin Luther, even the Jesuits—depending on whom the modern author disliked. The list goes on because the text would presuppose that Paul had something specific in mind.

If such a line were not written by Paul, then the designation of the details of the apocalypse would be simply part of the literary device. We would no longer be directed to a specific reality, but to the functions of those details in the literary drama of this letter. We could appeal to apocalyptic stereotypes as well as general eschatological concerns at the end of the first century. The line "you know what I am talking about" would then be just a clever way of piquing the readers' interest. Outsiders always want to hear more of what the insiders are saying.

Unfortunately, the evidence for or against authenticity is not compelling. The case against authenticity is stylistic. The letter is far less personal than 1 Thessalonians and also contains a strange warning not to be fooled by any letter "as if written by me" (2:2). It would appear that Paul would have just written 1 Thessalonians. When Paul wants to "reinterpret" an earlier letter, he does so by referring to the letter and acknowledging it (cf. 1 Cor 5:9). But the eschatology of 2 Thessalonians, with its insistence on an observable program of God, warning believers well in advance of the end, is hardly compatible with the "thief in the night" eschatology of 1 Thes 5:1–3. But no one has ever accused apocalyptic literature of being consistent.

The case for authenticity is *prima facie*. At its beginning, the letter says it is from Paul, and the ending of this letter (3:17) indicates that the author really wants the readers to think he is Paul. To avoid many of the difficulties mentioned above, some have suggested that 2 Thessalonians was written before 1 Thessalonians and that the "letter of ours" mentioned in 2:15 is in fact this very letter of 2 Thessalonians. That argument would help with the earlier letter repudiation, but it really does not fit the context of 2:15 very well.

If we can put aside theological objections to pseudo-epigraphy, one line of reasoning seems to tilt the argument heavily against authenticity. This line of reasoning is thoroughly pragmatic: it works better. Read as a letter of Paul, most probably written shortly after 1 Thessalonians to reinterpret that letter, 2 Thessalonians remains an enigma. Read as Deutero-Pauline, written most probably in the 80s when the delay of the Parousia was beginning to demand an explanation, 2 Thessalonians makes sense, and we will read 2 Thessalonians this way.

B. The Literary Structure

The structure of 2 Thessalonians is fairly simple. The letter begins with the typical epistolary salutations and prayer, a thanksgiving and a petition (1:1–12). In this prayer, the author is thinking more of the impending eschatological scenario rather than of his readers, for whom he is supposed to be thanking God. The prayer is very vindictive.

The main section of the letter consists of the teaching regarding the end of the world (2:1–14). The last two verses of this section are another prayer (2:13–14), seemingly a prayer for any occasion with little connection to the church of the Thessalonians.

The next section, 2:15–3:16, shifts to exhortations, more prayers, and more exhortations. An insistence on Paul's writing the letter forms a conclusion (3:17–18).

In outline form the letter can be described as follows:

    I. Opening (1:1–12)
        A. Greeting (1:1–2)
        B. Prayer (1:3–12)

   II. Instructions (2:1–14)
        A. The Day of the Lord (2:1–12)
        B. Prayer (2:13–14)

 III. Exhortations (2:15–3:16)
        A. Encouragement (2:15–17)
        B. Request for prayers (3:1–5)
        C. Dealing with the idle (3:6–12)
        D. Final admonitions (3:13–16)

 IV. Conclusion (3:17–18)

C. The Faith of the Author

1. The Eschatological Plan of God

The main concern of this letter is the end of the world and in particular its delay. The author warns vehemently against those who say "the Day of the Lord is at hand" (2:2). The following details concerning the man of lawlessness and the great apostasy seem to draw on stereotypical elements of contemporary apocalypses, where an anti-God figure is almost always featured, along with his success in leading believers astray. In themselves, these elements function as an alarm to "man the ramparts" and, above all, not to be seduced by attractive teachings.

In this letter, however, these elements function to explain why we must not think that the Day of the Lord is at hand. These elements are not yet on stage but are part of God's program preliminary to the end; they have not yet occurred. The author is making an appeal to the theme common to most apocalypses: God has a script already written out. In God's design certain things must happen first. In this insistence on a step-by-step progression to the end, "the restrainer" (2:6–7) might be simply a dramatic way of referring to the delay itself. The end is apparently delayed. We have seen this theme in Matthew. The author of 2 Thessalonians, probably contemporary with Matthew, is simply insisting that whatever is delaying the end, that thing is in God's plan. Sooner or later it will be "removed," but that removal has not happened yet. So please "cool it!"

2. The Apostolic Authority of Paul

Running throughout this letter is a portrayal of Paul laying down authoritative instructions on behavior and faith, being at the origin of binding traditions, himself modeling Christian conduct. All of these aspects of Paul's authority have roots in the authentic letters of Paul, but the emphasis here goes beyond what we have seen earlier. The iron tone of "Paul" here rings in a way never heard before:

> If anyone does not obey our word as expressed in this letter, take note of this person not to associate with him, that he may be put to shame. (3:14)

For those less than sympathetic to Paul, these lines confirm the picture of Paul the dogmatic grouch. But for those willing to see here an expression not of Paul's self-understanding but of a later author looking back to the apostle, these words echo the dogmatic insistence we have seen in the Pastorals. The church was in crisis. Its original leaders were dead. It therefore invoked what seemed to be the bedrock of safety, the authority of apostolic teaching.

(See exercises 4, 5.)

IV. Theological Reflections

Our theological reflections can start with the very fact of pseudo-epigraphy. The last lines of 2 Thessalonians still trouble, "This greeting is in my own hand, Paul's" (3:17). If this author is not Paul, he really wants to "pull the wool over the eyes" of his readers. Granted, authorship and personal ownership did not mean the same then as they do now, but this writer—if not Paul—comes awfully close to looking dishonest. This poses some sort of theological problem.

The real question, I suppose, is, Whose problem? Our faith and the faith of the church are in the inspiration of these writings and in the accuracy of "that truth which God wanted put into the sacred writings for the sake of our salvation" (*Dei Verbum*, #11). Could God communicate infallible truth through some sort of pious fraud? The truth of the Old Testament is often conveyed through sordid actions presented as models. The New Testament is centered on a murder that God used to save the world. One could say that such depictions are simply biblical presentations of human sinfulness. But the general impression we get from these narrations is that God is incredibly flexible (and skillful) in using our sinfulness for his purposes. Refusing to admit that pseudo-epigraphy could take place in scripture because it is distasteful to us might be a crude way of forcing these ancient documents into our frame of mind. Refusing to admit such a practice because it would be unworthy of God to incorporate "deceitful" practices into his plan might be a forgetfulness of the amazing flexibility of God.

It is probably useless to speculate on what befits God's manner of acting, what can or cannot be used by God for his purposes. Theology that tries to second-guess God is usually bad theology. Thus, we are directed back to the evidence of the text and ultimately to the appropriateness of the scientific method for understanding scripture. If we are willing to use this methodology, then our only concern should be to use it well, not how the results will integrate with the rest of our faith.

Ephesians, 1 and 2 Timothy, Titus, and 2 Thessalonians were canonized because they were thought to be written by Paul. Since the establishing of the canon occurred well after the chosen writing was what it was, we can handle this historical error basically as one more "providential mistake." However, we tend to think of inspiration and authorship in parallel form. In fact church writers and authorities concluded that these writings must have been inspired because they were written by Paul. If we reject this presupposition about authorship but do not wish to retreat from the conclusion regarding inspiration, then we must revise our theology of inspiration to focus far more on the final product, the inspired book, rather than the inspired author. However it was composed, whatever the human dynamisms that accompanied the writings, the final product *somehow* is inspired. And we must probably forgo any attempt to imagine how.

On a much more positive note, the hypothesis of pseudo-epigraphy among the Pauline writings alerts us to the flexibility and dynamism of the early church. We have in the Deutero-Pauline letters the witness of how Paul's thought was developed. Faced with questions and crises that Paul did not have to deal with, these Deutero-Pauline writers applied Paul's writings in an innovative and daring way. Instead of simply repeating the words of Paul along with some "interpretation," these writers made Paul speak again. Their attitude toward the authentic writings of Paul, it is clear, was not so much to defend and preserve the words of Paul as to unleash the creativity in those words. Such daring innovation is all the more ironic in the author of the Pastorals—for all his insistence on "guarding the deposit." The mentality here is that of Christian origins and sources which continue into the new eras. It is a mentality that sees "the beginning" accompanying us into the future. This mentality differs from the one that refuses a change because it was not that way in the beginning. The Deutero-Pauline mentality is one of incredible self-confidence. These authors were convinced that their adaptations to new problems and crises, their ways of seeing things, and their new words were exactly what Paul would have said were he alive to say it.

Our theological reflections can also revolve around the content of these Deutero-Pauline writings. If some brief reflection can be made about the eschatology of 2 Thessalonians, it probably can best be made about the historical pessimism of this letter. The letter warns of a great "apostasy" as a result of a power of evil released on earth. The warning is simply the warning we have seen in the Gospels about the permanence of the crucifixion. The "kingdom" Jesus has begun on earth does not appear to be a progressive growth in goodness and happiness. It is a dialectical kingdom, where evil seems to grow also. Resurrection and crucifixion remain linked. Yet 2 Thessalonians also links this historical pessimism to an eschatological optimism. It is with "the breath of his mouth" (2:8) that the Lord Jesus destroys evil in the ultimate triumph of God. What is the point of these ups and downs? Perhaps it is simply the admonition to place our hope in God's power, not in human progress.

On the other hand, future eschatology is almost totally absent from Ephesians and is certainly not the focus of the Pastorals. For these letters the emphasis is the church. Any theology of the church must deal with these writings.

It is relatively easy to dwell lovingly on the picture that Ephesians gives us of "the wife of Christ." A certain modest thrill can enter our hearts at the thought that Christ loves us faithfully and passionately. Ephesians draws this perspective into the future made present and interior. We are seated as church in the heavens. Christ has already sanctified and cleansed this church and we should humbly enjoy that glory.

The ecclesiology of the Pastorals may leave some of us a little cold. These letters have such an emphasis on authority and defensive adherence to tradition. They give us a picture of a structured, hierarchical church. In another culture at another time, these letters might appear far more attractive. Ours is something of a rebellious culture. We are very tired of the abuses of church authority. Yet constant rebellion can be fatiguing. To hear a call to guard a sacred past can be heard as a call to rest a while. The great achievements of the past, often won by great suffering, are still ours. They are our traditions, our doctrines, our link to those before us. Were it not for those, we would not be who we are. The Pastorals call us to mix reverence with criticism, love with analysis.

Still, perhaps the most intriguing theological question is posed by the presentation of "apostolic succession" in these letters, apparently not written by Paul. The matter can be put simply: the Pastorals portray the passing on of church authority from Paul the Apostle, to Timothy or Titus, to the local presbyters, who then presumably continue this tradition of authority. In the battle with Gnosticism in the next century, the church—through writers like Irenaeus—would appeal to this "apostolic succession" as a sign of its continuity with Jesus.

But the writer—in our hypothesis of pseudo-epigraphy—is not Paul, and he is not writing to Timothy or Titus. Writing from his imagination, the author is creating this scenario of the letter. He is reflecting on the office of presbyter in the church, an office that appears to have in fact sprung up spontaneously—that is, through the combined energies of the Spirit and of historical society—from the authority of the household heads and their roles within the early Pauline churches. The household heads were men and women. But Paul, as we know from the clearly authentic Pauline writings, did not "ordain" these household heads. He did not pass anything down through his hands to their heads and out their hands again. In this sense, there is no "succession" among the presbyters of the church. Furthermore, the role of apostle died out. The twelve apostles functioned to guarantee continuity with the twelve tribes of Israel. The Pauline apostles founded churches and left those churches to organize themselves and govern their own lives. Thus, among the presbyters of the later church there was no "apostolic" succession. The use of the twelve apostles as embodiments of the job of modern church ministers and priests is simply a mistake—if, of course, we follow the hypothesis of pseudo-epigraphy.

So the theological issue posed by the Pastorals (and the other pseudo-epigraphical writings) is whether to place more emphasis on the historical reconstruction of the writings following a scientific method of evidence and hypothesis or to place more emphasis on the content of the writings as autonomous entities now independent of their historical origins.

EXERCISES

Exercise 1. (see pages 294–296): Compare the Ephesian images of the church with those in 1 Corinthians 12–14. What differences and similarities do you note? Do the differences of imagery suggest a different conception of the church?

Exercise 2. (see page 301): Read 1 Tm 1:3–20; 4:1–3; 6:3–21; 2 Tm 2:14–3:9; Ti 1:10–16. Do you see any consistency in the presentations here? What kind of a problem seems to be lurking in the background of these letters?

Exercise 3. (see pages 303–304): In 2 Timothy, the author speaks from the perspective of Paul awaiting his death. Read this letter carefully and identify the references to Paul's death. Basing your answer on these texts, what does the author think about salvation immediately after death?

Exercise 4. (see page 310): Reread the Pastoral Epistles and 2 Thessalonians and list the personality and character traits of Paul implied in these texts. By adding the traits drawn from these letters, do we change the portrait of Paul that was developed from those letters more commonly accepted as written by him?

Exercise 5. (see page 310): Write a brief letter in the name of Paul to your parish or diocese. Invoke Paul's help and write what you are convinced he would say today.

REVIEW QUESTIONS

1. What is *pseudo-epigraphy*? What cultural values and attitudes does it embody?

2. What are the main reasons some scholars think that Ephesians was not written by Paul?

3. What is the principal topic or theme in Ephesians? How does this topic compare to that in Colossians?

4. How does the implied eschatology of Ephesians compare to that in Colossians? How does it compare to other letters written by Paul?

5. What are the main reasons some scholars think that the Pastoral Epistles were not written by Paul?

6. What are the topics and themes that run through the Pastoral Epistles? What is the meaning of *faith* in these writings?

7. How does the interpretation of the description of the end in 2 Thessalonians change if we shift from reading this letter as written by Paul to reading this letter as written in the name of Paul after Paul's death?

8. How does our understanding of the personality and character traits of Paul change if we shift from reading the writings studied in this chapter as written by Paul to reading them as written in his name after his death?

FOR FURTHER REFLECTION AND DISCUSSION

1. Compare and contrast the descriptions of the church and church activity found in the Pastorals with your experience of the church today. Do the descriptions of church in the Pastorals come closer to your experience than do the descriptions in 1 Corinthians?

2. What do you think Paul would write today about women's roles in the church? Do you think he would differ from the position of 1 Timothy? Why or why not? Do you think Jesus would differ from this position of 1 Timothy?

3. Do you know of any group that appears to be overly concerned about the approaching end of the world? What would you write to such a group? What do you think Paul would write to such a group?

17

Hebrews

I. Background and History

"St. Paul's Letter to the Hebrews," as it is often introduced in church, is almost certainly neither a letter nor written by Paul. The original readers do appear to be Christians with deep connections to Judaism, particularly to the Temple liturgy and to Jewish scriptures. Hence, there is some accuracy in the description stemming from the second century, "to the Hebrews." Apart from this identification, we know very little of where this letter comes from, who wrote it, or why it was written. Like the Melchizedek described in this writing, Hebrews appears by itself without clear "ancestry."

A. Literary Form

The "newsy" paragraph at the very end of the writing, probably appended at a later stage of the composition, is the only element that suggests Hebrews could be a letter. Everything else in this writing clearly points to it as a homily, a prayerful commentary on scriptural texts, in the style of the contemporary rabbis. Such a literary form was typically read aloud in the synagogue, and Christian leaders would read such homilies in Christian assemblies. The task of such a homily would be to apply the scriptural texts to the present needs of the listeners. The homilist picked from the texts of the day, wove together other texts, and blended these scriptural snatches together with practical admonitions and allegorical applications—usually in total disregard for the intention of the author or other historical considerations.

The author of Hebrews develops this treatise by continually selecting snatches of the Old Testament, mostly from the Psalms and from the Torah with a few significant texts of the Prophets. In typical rabbinic style, the homilist sometimes strings a long series of texts together often on the basis of a common word or image (see chapter 1). Sometimes he uses a long text and refers to various words or expressions in it (see Heb 8:7–13). Sometimes he combines two texts on the basis of a common word—regardless of any shift in the meaning of that word (see Heb 4:3–4). In this treatise we find some fifty-two direct citations of scripture—including repeated references to the same text—and about one hundred other allusions to scriptural texts. The author weaves these citations and allusions together to produce a practical application for living in the present, to produce "a word of encouragement" (Heb 13:22).

The last paragraph (13:22–25), which alone reflects the letter style, looks like a postscript. Apart from this paragraph, the author never refers to "writing" to the recipients. What precedes appears to have been addressed orally to listeners. The last paragraph may have been added when this oral homily was then passed on to another group or circulated among several other churches.

AUTHENTICITY OF PAULINE LETTERS

Authentic	*Doubtful*	*Not*
1 Thessalonians	2 Thessalonians	Hebrews
1 Corinthians	Ephesians	
2 Corinthians	1 Timothy	
Galatians	2 Timothy	
Romans	Titus	
Philippians		
Colossians		
Philemon		

Figure 30.

In many ways this treatise is a "fire and brimstone" sermon. It includes terrifying warnings against falling away from the faith, admonishing the readers against any hope of later repentance (see 6:4–6; 10:26–31). If taken as a careful theological analysis of the meaning of sin and repentance, the message here contradicts the message of Matthew or Luke, for whom God is constantly ready to forgive. The identification of this treatise as a practical homily, therefore, is crucial if we are interested in dealing with the issue of "inerrancy." We have here the rhetoric of persuasion, where a conceptual fuzziness, perhaps even deliberate, contributes to the emotional commitment sought—at the expense of precise intellectual understanding. For example, the description of "falling away" (6:6) blends the description of doubting one's faith here on earth with that of a definitive rejection of God in hell. The effect is electrifying in terms of commitment, but inaccurate in terms of theology.

(See exercises 1, 2.)

B. Author

Nothing except the reference in the postscript to a man named Timothy (13:23) in any way connects this letter with Paul the Apostle. The vocabulary is very different from Paul's. The style of composition, alternating instructions with exhortation, is very different from Paul's. While sharing some thoughts with Paul, the theology of this writing is unique in its focus on Jesus "the high priest" offering priestly intercession now in heaven. The ascription to Paul, which appears as early as the second century in some churches, may have simply been an attempt to "round off" the letters of Paul into a neat fourteen.

All we know of the author is from the footprints of his writing. The author is clearly a highly educated Christian who speaks Greek. He cites the Old Testament consistently from the Greek Septuagint translation. His interest in and knowledge of Jewish practices, his ability to understand the temptation of a glorious Jewish past, his ability to draw relationships between Jesus and the Temple liturgy—all suggest that he himself is a convert from Judaism, the Judaism of the Diaspora. Not without merit, some commentators suggest the name Apollos as a possible identification of the author (see Acts 18:24–28).

C. Date of the Writing

The dating of Hebrews is very difficult. The clear outside limits of any dating are fairly wide. Cited by *1 Clement* in A.D. 96, Hebrews must have been written years earlier than that date for it to have garnered the authority with which it is used without argument by the church leader in Rome. On the one hand, the author addresses his readers as second generation believers, distinguishing between "us" and "those who have heard" the salvation announced by the Lord (2:3). That would require a date somewhere after the 60s.

Commentators today see the references to the sacrificial liturgy as an indication that Hebrews was written before A.D. 70, the year of the destruction of the Temple in Jerusalem. At times, Hebrews describes the liturgy of sacrifices as still in existence:

> The Law…is not able to perfect those coming to offering sacrifices. Else the offerings would have stopped since the worshipers cleansed once and for all would have no consciousness of sin. (10:1–2)

The only real difficulty with this argument lies in the way the author consistently refers to "the Tabernacle," that is, the portable sanctuary carried by the Hebrews during the exodus, rather than the Temple of Jerusalem. The sense in which this Tabernacle is described as contemporary with Christ indicates that the author is dealing more with a religious idea expressed by a concrete image—an icon, as we would say—rather than with historical buildings and practices. It is not clear that the author would have seen the destruction of A.D. 70 as the epoch-making cessation of sacrificial liturgy.

The theology of Hebrews, especially its "high" christology and its eschatological synthesis, suggests a later date. However, dating a writing from its theology is putting the cart before the horse. In effect, we must be ready to shift the historical horizon of this writing back and forth to see which hypothetical dating works best.

D. Structure

The structure of the writing appears in the movement from one theme to another. When we look for literary indications of structure, we find two: first, the alternations between teachings and exhortations and, second, the contrasts between the old sacrifices and that of Jesus. The two appear as repeated loops in parallel cycles. Hence, the following outline for the whole epistle:

   I. Introduction (1:1–4

  II. The Son, Exalted yet Compassionate (1:5–2:18)
        A. Jesus above the angels (1:5–14)
        B. Exhortation to listen (2:1–4)
        A´ Jesus' exaltation and abasement (2:5–18)

 III. Jesus, Faithful and Compassionate High Priest (3:1–5:10)
        A. Jesus and Moses (3:1–6)
        B. Exhortation to listen (3:7–4:14)
        C. Jesus, compassionate high priest (4:15–5:10)

IV. Jesus' Eternal Priesthood and Sacrifice (5:11–10:39)
    A. Exhortation against falling away (5:11–6:12)
    B. God's immutable oath (6:13–20)
    C. Jesus and Melchizedek (7:1–28)
    D. Jesus' heavenly priesthood (8:1–13)
    E. The earthly and heavenly sanctuaries (9:1–10:18)
       a. Worship of the first covenant (9:1–10)
       b. The sacrifice of Jesus (9:11–17)
       a´ The first covenant (9:18–22)
       b´ The sacrifice of Jesus (9:23–27)
       a´´The ineffectiveness of the Law (10:1–4)
       b´´The sacrifice of Jesus (10:5–18)
    F. Exhortation against falling away (10:19–39)

V. Examples of Faith and Disobedience (11:1–12:29)
    A. Living by faith (11:1–40)
    B. Exhortation to accept paternal discipline (12:1–12)
    C. Exhortation not to reject God's gift (12:13–29)

VI. Conclusion (13:1–25)
    A. Various admonitions (13:1–19)
    B. Concluding prayer (13:20–21)
    C. Letter postscript (13:22–25)

II. The Faith of Hebrews

Hebrews focuses on the redemptive work of Christ. The faith expressed here concentrates on soteriology. Yet we can cull certain statements and presuppositions made about Jesus, and we can collect the brief statements about the end of the world to pursue further our systematic survey of the three major themes we have been following.

A. Christology

For Hebrews who is this Jesus who has achieved definitive salvation through his death? The opening lines of the treatise give us an answer. Writing out these lines according to their grammatical structure helps us keep track of the elements expressed here:

In these last days, God spoke to us through his Son
   whom he has appointed heir of all

through whom he also made the ages
who
    being the refulgence of his glory and mark of his substance
    carrying also all things by his powerful word
    having achieved purification from sins
took his seat at the right hand of the majesty on high (1:2–3).

In this dense opening statement, we see Jesus identified first as the Son of God, the place of definitive revelation—similar to the descriptions of Jesus that run through John. Jesus is then described as the heir of all creation and the instrument by which God creates—imagery that recalls the "in whom...through whom...for whom all things were created" of Col 1:16. Jesus as "the refulgence" and "mark" of God recalls Paul's way of describing Jesus as "the image of God" (Col 1:15; 2 Cor 4:4), which in turn was an appropriation of the Old Testament descriptions of divine Wisdom (cf. Wis 7:25–26). Like this divine Wisdom, Jesus appears as sustaining the universe. This description of Jesus' cosmic role is the only language in the treatise that suggests some preexistence for Jesus. The language, at least, approximates describing Jesus as divine; however, with a reference to Jesus' role in cleansing us from sins, the soteriological emphasis immediately enters. At the end this introduction incorporates an image of the exaltation of Jesus after his death, again recalling the vocabulary of Col 3:1 as well as earlier Paul (Rom 8:34) and Deutero-Paul (Eph 1:20).

(See exercises 3, 4.)

1. Jesus as Divine

Is Jesus God for the author of Hebrews? The closest we get to such an affirmation lies in the application to Jesus of the "royal court hyperbole" of Psalm 45. This psalm was addressed to the king—probably of the northern kingdom of Israel. In v. 7 the king is addressed as "God" (Hebrew *elohim;* Greek *ho theos*). He is addressed again in the same way in v. 8 (although in most translations a particular placement of commas changes the direct address to a curiously redundant reference to Yahweh). The psalmist was using the style current in Egypt and other kingdoms to address the king as a god, yet clearly understanding that the king was as human as any sinful human being. Hebrews, however, takes these two verses of Psalm 45 and explicitly applies them to Jesus:

> However to the Son (he says): Your throne, God, is for-
> ever.... Therefore, God, your God has anointed you. (Heb
> 1:8–9)

Did the author of Hebrews see this as courtly hyperbole? In all his
other uses of scriptural texts—in the manner of the rabbinic
homily—he completely disregards the historical context of his citations. We can doubt that he would be concerned here with the original meaning of the words.

Nowhere else in Hebrews does the author speak of Jesus as God.
He concentrates rather on the solidarity of Jesus with human beings
and on Jesus' great exaltation at the end of his life. The use of Psalm
45 here without commentary may be a cautious probing in applying
the term *God* to Jesus, one protected by the citation. The application
of the term *God* to Jesus is consistent with the divine-like qualities of
Jesus described in the opening verses of this treatise.

To express this divine-like quality of Jesus, the title that the
author prefers, however, is not *God* but *Son*. As *Son,* Jesus is the
place of the final and definitive revelation of God (1:2). As *Son,*
Jesus is at once distinguished from God, the "founder of the house,"
and exalted above Moses, "the servant in the house" (3:4–6). As *Son,*
Jesus is also superior even to the angels (1:5).

2. Jesus as Human

The rest of the treatise focuses on one description from the
opening verses, "having achieved purification from sins," where the
author underlines the human character of Jesus. As the author
insists, to function in this saving manner, Jesus "had to become like
his brothers in every way" (2:17).

Jesus' solidarity with weak and suffering humanity is central to
the soteriology of Hebrews. This solidarity does not involve an "emptying" or abasement on the part of Jesus, as Paul would say. This is not
the Pauline sense of a solidarity in corruptibility and even sinfulness
but only in weakness and suffering. Speaking of Jesus, the Son of God,
the author instead insists on both weakness and sinlessness:

> For we do not have a high priest incapable of sympathiz-
> ing with our weakness, but one who has similarly been
> tested in every way, yet without sin. (4:15)

Central to the soteriology of Hebrews is the view of Jesus "in the flesh," a view that insists on suffering and even reluctant submission to the will of God:

> In the days of his flesh, he offered prayers and supplications with loud cries and tears to the one able to save him from death, and he was heard because of his reverence. Son though he was, he learned obedience from what he suffered; and when he became perfected, he became the source of eternal salvation for all who obey him. (5:7–9)

3. Jesus Exalted after his Death

The contrast here between Jesus "in the flesh" and Jesus "made perfect" resembles Pauline contrast of Jesus who "emptied himself" and Jesus "highly exalted" (cf. Phil 2:6–11), the earthly Jesus going to his death and the heavenly Jesus risen from the dead. Again there is little concern for the glorious aspects of Jesus' ministry—his teachings, his miracles. The only aspect of interest to Hebrews—as for Paul—is the suffering and death of this earthly Jesus.

The christology of Hebrews includes the glorification of Jesus "at the right hand" of God. With great insistence, the author repeats four times the description of the "ascension":

> He took his seat at the right hand of the Majesty on high. (1:3)

> He took his seat at the right hand of the Throne of Majesty in the heavens. (8:1)

> He took his seat at the right hand of God. (10:12)

> He has taken his seat at the right hand of the throne of God. (12:2)

As for Paul the author has his attention riveted on the risen, glorious Lord who exists now in heaven.

B. Soteriology

This combined emphasis on Jesus on the one hand as suffering and dying and on the other hand exalted after his death supports the soteriology of Hebrews. In this support Hebrews again follows Paul. However, Hebrews adds a color that distinguishes this letter from Paul's approach. For Hebrews Jesus' movements from death to exaltation are acts of cult.

1. Jesus, Priest and Sacrifice

(See exercises 5, 6.)

The soteriology of Hebrews is remarkably focused. Jesus brings salvation by functioning as high priest, offering himself as a sacrifice to God. The author, like Paul, refuses to spiritualize the death of Jesus. We are cleansed by "the blood of Christ" in comparison and contrast with the blood of goats and bulls (9:13–14). We are consecrated through "the offering of the body of Jesus Christ, once and for all" (10:10).

Paul had described Jesus' death as a sacrifice or something like a sacrifice to God (cf. Rom 3:25; 1 Cor 5:7). Hebrews, however, adds a new facet by continuing the image of priestly sacrifice beyond the crucifixion. The image is drawn from the portrayal of the high priest entering the Holy of Holies, presumably on Yom Kippur, the Day of Atonement. The author uses that image to describe the entrance of Jesus to the heavenly realm, where his priesthood and his sacrifice are now eternal:

> When, however, Christ having come as high priest of the good things that have come to be, [passing] through the greater and more perfect tabernacle, not made by hands, that is, not of this creation, he entered once and for all into the sanctuary, not through the blood of goats and bulls, but through his own blood obtaining eternal redemption. (9:11–12)

The heavenly throne room of God is for the author the true place of sacrificial worship, the true Holy of Holies. Jesus' exaltation to that place becomes an eternal cultic act:

> We have such a high priest who sat at the right hand of the throne of Majesty in the heavens, a minister of the sanctuary and the true tabernacle, which the Lord, not man, set up. (8:1–2)

The great interest, therefore, in the exaltation of Jesus is soteriological. It is this state of Jesus—in connection with his preceding death—that makes Jesus truly savior.

The word *savior* is never used for Jesus in this letter, although he is called "the leader of salvation" (2:10; cf. 12:2). To designate the precise functioning role of Jesus here as high priest, the term the author prefers is *mediator (mesitēs),* a term that Paul particularly rejects in his view of Jesus' work (cf. Gal 2:19–20). Again and again the author of Hebrews describes Jesus as "the mediator of a New Covenant" (8:6; 9:15; 12:24). In Hebrews the term *mediator* has somewhat of a legal sense, describing the function of the priestly human representative in the establishment of the covenant. The word apparently blends here with the term *leader.* Jesus functions this way precisely as dying and entering the heavenly "sanctuary." Nowhere in Hebrews does Jesus, as mediator, function as a "relay" somehow receiving the prayers and needs of the people and passing them on to the Father as if the Father were not in immediate contact with the people.

2. The New Covenant

(See exercise 7.)

The concept of *new covenant* is an essential ingredient in the soteriology of Hebrews. Like Paul (cf. 2 Cor 3:6), the author of Hebrews draws on Jer 31:31 to introduce the concept of a new covenant. In the longest Old Testament citation found in the New Testament, Heb 3:8–12 reproduces the important text of Jer 31:31–34, where the prophet consoled his people with the promise of restoration in terms of a "new covenant," different from the old not in terms of content but in terms of interiority and effectiveness. The Law would be written in the hearts of the people and they would not break that Law. When Paul alluded to this prophetic text and used Jeremiah's language, Paul's descriptions correspond closely to Jeremiah's. The newness was that of modality, that is, now written in our hearts by the work of the Spirit. For Paul the obsolete element was "the document taken alone" *(to gramma),* read without the Spirit and basically misunderstood (2 Cor 3:6–18).

The development of a new covenant in Hebrews moves beyond Paul to develop the idea of replacement. The new covenant in Hebrews is specifically a "better covenant" (7:22; 8:6), one that makes the old as a whole "obsolete" and "close to disappearing" (8:13). The author drives home this position by comparing the old and the new in terms of a Platonic cosmology, the earthly shadow world compared to the true heavenly world. Those who offer gifts according to the Law "worship in a copy and shadow of the heavenly sanctuary" (8:5).

The difference between Hebrews and Paul is subtle but decisive in forming a Christian understanding of the relationship between Christianity and Judaism. Paul saw the epochal work of Christ as an improvement on the Law. He saw (his own) coming to faith in Christ as a precious gift and advancement. But what occurs for Paul is not so much a replacement of the old as a revelation of the old. What existed under the Law was "hidden in mystery." What is new under faith is not a new Law or system of salvation but a new revelation of what was there from the beginning. What was hidden is now manifest through the gospel (Rom 16:25–26; Col 1:25–26). Christians for Paul, therefore, are truly Jews, grafted onto the stock of Judaism as wild branches are grafted onto a life-giving trunk (Rom 11:17).

In Hebrews the split between Judaism and Christianity has moved to the form of two religions, one replacing the other, two covenants one replacing the other. The author is engaged in persuasive rhetoric, trying to encourage the readers to stay the course of their faith and to avoid the apparent temptation of returning to Judaism.

On the other hand, while insisting on a break from the old covenant, the author of Hebrews continues to cite the scriptures of that covenant. In his extensive use of even the Torah (chapter 11), the author presupposes some continuing validity to the old. The author is not a Marcionite. Yet without the "Spirit/document" theology of Paul (2 Corinthians 3), Hebrews leaves the relationship of "new" to "old" hanging in deep ambiguity.

C. Eschatology

(See exercises 8, 9.)

Hebrews begins with a dramatic emphasis on eschatology:

Formerly God spoke in partial and various ways.... In the last of these days [these last days?] he spoke to us through a Son. (1:1–2)

Later in the treatise, the author will describe the historical events of Jesus in eschatological terms:

Now, however, once and for all, at the completion of the
ages, he has appeared to annul sin through his sacrifice.
(9:26)

We can thus read all that follows in the treatise as a description of
"these last days." The identification of the contemporary period as
"the last days" is not Pauline. We have seen it in 1 John (see 2:18) to
explain the appearance of false teachers. A similar thought and language occur in 2 Tm 3:1. By his citation of Joel, Luke describes the
events of Pentecost as the sign of "the last days." Like Luke, the
author of Hebrews focuses on the blessings, not the conflict, of the
end time in which he sees the world.

We find in Hebrews a few references to future eschatology. The
author does describe a second coming of Christ which will bring perfection to his work:

So also Christ, having offered (sacrifice) once and for all
to remove the sin of the many, will appear a second time
not for sin but for the salvation of those awaiting him.
(9:28)

In the next chapter, as part of his intense exhortation to the readers, the author urges them to good works and endurance "as you see
the day drawing near" (10:25; also 10:36–37). Finally, he urges that
our hearts not seek a permanent city "here" but "one to come"
(11:14).

The eschatology of Hebrews could thus be described as
"both...and." Clearly, however, the stress is not on looking to the
future but on understanding the present moment in the context of
the past. The author is offering an understanding of history in
terms of two covenants, one past and one now. The "now" has very
great importance for him. It is the time of the definitive revelation
of God. It is the time of the eternal priesthood of Jesus.

III. Theological Reflections

Many aspects of Hebrews leap up for recognition as fertile
seedbeds of theological reflection—the picture of the compassionate
human Jesus, the understanding of God's plan in terms of a succession
of covenants, the eternal, once-and-for-all character of Jesus's salvation. Two aspects, however, raise questions of church and Bible, questions that pervade much of the ferment of our own period of history.

A. Christ the High Priest

For a member of the Catholic, Orthodox, or Anglican church, Hebrews is a monumental document. These churches to a large degree have developed their liturgies by reappropriating Old Testament practices: Temple, sacrifice, priesthood. This reappropriation can be documented by developments in the second and third centuries, especially in communities rooted in Jewish Christianity. Theologians will continue to analyze and even debate the value of this reappropriation, but it is clear that the writing of Hebrews was a monumental step in that direction.

Paul had introduced cultic categories into Christian faith by viewing the death of Jesus as sacrifice, or something like a sacrifice, to God. But in his view of "spiritual worship," Paul insisted that our "sacrifices" are "living" and consist of our daily lives, our "bodies" transformed by interior renewal (Rom 12:1–2).

Hebrews takes the important next step. The death of Jesus is thoroughly assimilated to the Temple sacrifices and the role of priest introduced into Christian faith. Jesus became a priest. All of this in Hebrews, of course, exists and functions on a heavenly level. The sanctuary is heaven. The sacrificial liturgy involves Jesus standing before his Father. But the drama of salvation has been cast now in Old Testament terms, in the sense of the Israelite-Jewish institutions we know best by the Jewish scriptures. The author of Hebrews urged his readers not to go back to Jewish practices but to see in Christian life the fulfillment of those practices, and the presence of those practices now by a link to realities in heaven. According to Hebrews, it is all right to see our liberation from sin in terms of a sacrifice. It is all right to see our access to God as via a priest. It is all right to see worship as Temple worship.

The next centuries would take the natural step to draw this imagery closer to home, to find a way in which sacrifice, priest, and temple could be located on earth—relying on the links inherent in our concepts of symbol and sacrament. In the Catholic, Orthodox, and Anglican traditions, the leaders of the assembly took on the title "priest." The Lord's Supper became a sacrifice. In even more traditions, the house of worship became a temple, sometimes imitating even the details of the Jerusalem Temple, as for instance in the iconostasis of the Orthodox sanctuary.

The author of Hebrews—wittingly or unwittingly—gave an important impetus to this last step of terrestrializing the heavenly liturgy. In one brief reference, apparently to the Lord's Supper, the author states, "We have an altar from which those who serve the tabernacle have no right to eat" (13:10).

Hebrews, however, also stands as an admonition to anyone who would separate any Christian liturgy from the action of Christ dying and rising "once and for all." For Hebrews, there is only one sacrifice. It is eternal and never repeated. We are not *adding* anything by our eucharistic sacrifices. The Catholic, Orthodox, or Anglican priest is not *another* priest. If there is to be any theological validity to Christian sacrifice and priesthood as found in concrete earthly realities, that validity must be understood in something like the old Platonic idea of *participation*. Something of an archetypal reality becomes in part present in some "shadow" reality. Naturally Hebrews would not insist on the adoption of a philosophical vocabulary. But this treatise would insist there is only one priest, one sacrifice forever.

B. Penitential Rigorism and Inerrancy

A more puzzling aspect arises in a theological reflection on the rigorism expressed in such texts as Heb 6:4–8 and 10:19–39, the exhortatory inclusion bracketing the central section of the treatise. In these exhortations we are told, "It is impossible for those who have been enlightened and tasted the heavenly gift…and then fallen away to bring them to repentance again" (6:4–6). "If we sin deliberately after receiving knowledge of the truth, there no longer remains sacrifice for sins but a fearful prospect of judgment and a flaming fire that is going to consume the adversaries" (10:26–27).

As a matter of fact around the fourth century, when having to deal with Christians who renounced their faith under Roman persecutions, the Christian church took just the opposite stand. Anybody who said fallen away apostates cannot be reconciled to the church was to be considered a heretic. Since that time, an affirmation of the unbounded mercy of God, his unlimited readiness to forgive any sin, has been the matter of a steady consensus among Christians.

What makes these rigorist texts of Hebrews interesting is the way they speak directly of matters of salvation and are not just presuppositions coming from an outdated cosmology or anthropology used as the vehicle for the specifically religious messages. We have a statement of the seriousness of sin, and it looks very much like something in the text "for the sake of our salvation"—to use the expression of magisterial Catholic theology in order to pinpoint the inerrancy of scripture. What do these rigorist texts in Hebrews say about biblical inerrancy?

Earlier in this chapter, we saw the importance of understanding these statements in the literary form of exhortation and persuasive rhetoric, in which we recognize that an expression such as to "sin deliberately" is not given precise definition and appears here to be equivalent to the definitive choice of hell—although obviously the author wants his readers to see the expression as a horrible option in their lives now. But how are we to know that the "inerrant truth" lies in our "benign interpretation" rather than in the apparently rigorist intentions of the author?

If we had only Hebrews from which to draw our conclusions about sin and the mercy of God, there does not seem to be any way within a serious acceptance of the text to avoid accepting the rigorist view of the author. But we do have more. Above all, we have the other writings of the New Testament (to some degree the other writings of the Bible as a whole) to balance and correct these statements. We are not talking about balancing quotes from Hebrews against quotes from Luke or Paul. We are talking about understanding the statements of Hebrews in an intuitive appreciation of the whole. The picture of God we get intuitively from the whole New Testament—or whole Bible—is not compatible with the rigorist view that appears in Hebrews.

The fact that our understanding of God's mercy as prevailing over the rigorist views of Hebrews took three centuries to crystallize indicates another tool we have for interpretation—the church. This intuitive appreciation of the whole need not be our responsibility alone. We can draw on generations of insightful and Spirit-filled readers who have discoursed on the meaning of the text. Furthermore, we can draw on the discernment of a whole body of present-day faithful, who with their particular gifts enable a healthy view of the whole Bible.

And so we stand on our heads a bit, perform some hermeneutical gymnastics, and find a way in which Hebrews is not really wrong. We are reminded—painfully—that the Bible, for all its inspiration and inerrancy, is not a magic book of answers. God is revealing himself and his plan through the complexities and limits of human nature and intention. We must also work to recognize that revelation.

EXERCISES

Exercise 1. (see pages 316–318): Read Hebrews and locate the quotations and allusions to the Old Testament. What do you note about the use of these Old Testament quotations? What part of the Bible do they come from? How does one Old Testament text lead to another?

Exercise 2. (see pages 316–318): Read Hebrews aloud from beginning to end. How does hearing the text differ in impact from reading the text silently? How long does it take to read this work aloud?

Exercise 3. (see pages 320–321): Select the three texts in Hebrews which in your opinion give us the most vivid description of Jesus as more than human.

Exercise 4. (see pages 320–321): In a similar way select the three texts depicting Jesus like us as a human being.

Exercise 5. (see pages 323–324): Identify the descriptions in Hebrews of Jesus' death and the descriptions of Jesus after his death.

Exercise 6. (see page 324): Does Hebrews ever speak of the resurrection of Jesus?

Exercise 7. (see page 325): Find the descriptions, comparisons, and contrasts of the "covenants" that the author uses to define the bond now between God and believers.

Exercise 8. (see page 326): Where and how does Hebrews speak of the end of the world? In what ways is it present? In what ways is it future?

Exercise 9. (see pages 326–327): What other writings in the New Testament come closest to the eschatological perspective of Hebrews?

REVIEW QUESTIONS

1. How would you identify the literary form of Hebrews? What textual evidence do you have for your answer?

2. Name three major aspects of Jesus described by Hebrews. Substantiate your answer by texts from this writing.

3. According to Hebrews, how does Jesus function as *mediator*? What aspects of Jesus are associated with this function?

4. What is the relationship, according to Hebrews, between the old covenant and the new covenant? How does this relationship differ from that found in Paul (e.g., 2 Corinthians 3)?

5. Describe the importance and meaning of *now* for the author of Hebrews.

FOR FURTHER REFLECTION AND DISCUSSION

1. Is the image of Jesus the high priest as presented in Hebrews important for Christians today? What implications flow from this image regarding how God the Father is to be pictured, regarding the Christian church, regarding sin and forgiveness?

2. Imagine yourself in a dialogue with the author of Hebrews, suggesting that he or she "lighten up" a bit concerning fallen-away Christians who want to return to the faith. What would be your arguments? How do you think the author would counter?

3. According to Hebrews, what is the role of non-Christian Jewish people today in the "economy" of salvation? Would Paul agree with this role? How would you explain this writing to a Jewish group in dialogue with Christians?

18

Four Detached General Epistles

Normally commentators group seven letters together in a category, the "General (or Catholic) Epistles." These are the writings in the form of letters directed to an unspecified or even universal audience. They usually include the three Johannine "letters," which we treated in an earlier chapter as a sequel to the Gospel of John. The four remaining writings, as they occur in our New Testament, are James, 1 and 2 Peter, and Jude. They do not appear to have any special relationship with other major New Testament writings. We will look at these four in this chapter.

These writings have a right to feel acutely inferior. Except perhaps for 1 Peter, these texts do not seem to be anyone's favorites. Rarely cited, except for a few well-known verses, these letters are like those wedding gifts that stay packed away, always acknowledged but never used. Moreover, treating these writings together in this chapter does not help.

In fact—again with the exception of 1 Peter—these writings are not terribly inspiring. They can be downright depressing with their emphasis on human sinfulness and divine anger. These are not the readings people use to celebrate weddings and baptisms. The challenge will be to see a realistic role for them in a Christian faith that accepts the New Testament as a whole.

I. The Epistle of James

A. Historical Background

During the time when the church was developing a consensus about the New Testament canon, the writing we know as the Letter of James almost failed the test of acceptance. It is not in the important

Muratorian Canon of the mid-second century. Eusebius, writing in the third century, describes it as a disputed book. The Syrian Christian churches seemed to have hesitated until the fifth century before accepting this writing as canonical.

The argument focused on authorship. With reason, some early church authorities did not think the author was an apostle. At the time when the church was fighting Gnosticism, tracing a teaching back to an apostle was very important.

The author himself does not claim to be an apostle. He starts simply as "Jacob [anglicized, James], a servant of God and of the Lord Jesus Christ" (1:1). Later in the writing the author implies he is a "teacher" in the church (3:1). Noting this absence of the title apostle, many early Christians identified the author with James the brother of Jesus (Mt 13:55; Mk 6:3), whom we see in Acts as a prominent leader of the Jerusalem church with its intensely Jewish Christian membership (see Acts 12:17; 15:13–29; 21:15–26; Gal 1:18–2:12; 1 Cor 15:7).

The high literary style of the letter convinced the Renaissance scholar Erasmus not to identify the author with this relative of Jesus. Since we know so little about James the brother of the Lord and nothing about his "secretaries," the argument is not terribly weighty.

The real motive in favor of such an identification was theological. This identification was, in effect, the historical grounds for including the writing in the canon. However, we must waive, or at least be ready to waive, these grounds for almost all the writings in the New Testament outside the authentic letters of Paul. If we had no compelling reason to identify the author with one of the first-generation leaders of the church, the name Jacob alone would certainly not lead us to that conclusion. It was one of the most common Jewish names of the time.

(See exercises 1, 2.)

The writing has the form of a letter only in its opening verse. After this verse, the writing appears as an exhortatory treatise, directed to any Jewish Christians willing to read it. It even lacks a letter ending. As such, this writing fits the classification of "epistle."

About the dating of the writing, we can note the following. The administrative office of *elder* has already arisen in the church (Jas 4:14–15). This office in the church apparently started early in Jerusalem and probably spread quickly to other Jewish Christian communities like those in Antioch and Rome. More important for suggesting a later date of this epistle, at the time of the writing the office of elder had assumed the *gift* of healing, a gift in the Pauline churches distinct from that of administrator. (cf. 1 Cor 12:28). On the other hand, James's own office of *teacher* appears to be distinct from that of elder (contrast Ti 1:5–9).

James also knows of the teachings of Paul. The epistle form this author is using looks like an imitation of the highly successful letters of Paul. His polemic against salvation by faith alone, with its appeal to Abraham (Jas 2:14–26), is almost certainly directed against Paul's expressions as found in Rom 3:21–4:25, written around A.D. 58. On the other hand, the author does not seem to know Paul's position about "faith working through love," which Paul wrote to the Galatians (5:6).

A relatively early date for this writing is certainly not out of the question. We might have in this writing an early antagonistic response from the Jewish Christian community in Rome to Paul's letter addressed to this community.

(See exercise 3.)

After its opening the epistle moves from one moral topic to another, much like the wisdom writing in the book of Sirach. At times, the teaching is short, in the form of a proverb. At other times, it is developed into paragraph length. Sometimes the teachings cluster according to inclusions, parallel topics, or related subjects. At other times, the teachings follow one another almost randomly. We can study this epistle with the following outline in mind:

    I. Letter opening (1:1)

   II. Body (1:2–5:20)
       A. Grouping: Trials and God's gifts (1:2–18)
          1. Sufferings and trials (1:2–4)
          2. God's gift of wisdom prayed for (1:5–8)
          3. Riches like grass (1:9–11)
          1´ Suffering and trials (1:12–15)
          2´ God the source of all good gifts (1:16–18)
       B. Be slow to anger (1:19–21)
       C. Be doers of the word (1:22–25)
       D. True religion (1:26–27)
       E. Against favoritism of the rich (2:1–13)
       F. Works over faith alone (2:14–26)
       G. The danger of being a "teacher" (3:1)

    H. The power of the tongue (3:2–12)
    I. True wisdom in humble living (3:13–18)
    J. Problems of life away from God (4:1–10)
    K. Not judging others (4:11–12)
    L. Against boasting and presumption (4:13–17)
    M.Warning to the rich (5:1–6)
    N. Patience for the Parousia of the Lord (5:7–11)
    O. Against oaths (5:12)
    P. Grouping: Church activities (5:13–20)
        1. Prayer and anointing of sick (5:13–15)
        2. Mutual confession of sins (5:16–18)
        3. Fraternal correction (5:19–20)

B. The Faith of James

(See exercise 4.)

Human behavior is very important. This is the message of James. Like the prophets of Israel, James insists on "ethical monotheism." Our belief in God should show in our peace-loving conduct and especially in our care for the poor.

While the christology of James is minimal—apart from a few interesting titles for Jesus—James has an acute sense of the presence of God the Father in the life of the believer. "Every perfect gift is from above, coming down from the Father of lights" (1:17). Injustices against the poor reach "the ears of the Lord Sabbaoth" (5:4). Many of James's moral exhortations lead to some statement about God or result from some theological premise.

When we look for some reflection on God's saving action, we begin to see why Martin Luther suspected that this writing was that of a Jewish scribe who did not know the Christian faith. We find no reference to our being "rescued," "redeemed," or otherwise "forgiven" by God either directly or through Jesus.

The closest texts we can find to a soteriology in James are two brief statements: "God in deliberate decision gave birth to us through the word of truth, for us to be something like the firstfruits of his creation" (1:15). We are therefore to "accept the planted word which has power to save your lives *(psychai)*" (1:18). In Paul these expressions would evoke the thought of becoming a part (firstfruits) of a new creation. In a Johannine context the connection between "the word" and "birth" would suggest the mysterious power of God's word to bring about eternal life. James otherwise shows no inclination toward these apocalyptic and mystic approaches.

The human model of salvation James chooses is Abraham, who by his actions "was justified" (2:21). James draws on the description of Gn 15:6, which describes Abraham's transformation: "It was credited to him unto justice" and in that way Abraham became "a friend of God" (2:23). We too are to seek friendship with God, or at least to avoid "enmity with God" through evil loves (4:4). The state of "salvation" is the state of being "near to God" (4:8). The categories here are those of interpersonal relations. We are called upon to do our part in a budding friendship, and God will respond in like manner. "Draw near to God and he will draw near to you" (4:8). In this we "accomplish the justice of God" (1:20). This way of understanding salvation is very Jewish. It can be found throughout the later wisdom books of the Old Testament.

(See exercise 5.)

James's sense of eschatology is acute. Early in the epistle the author reminds people of God's promises. Those who persevere in trials will receive "the promised crown of life" (1:12). God chooses the poor to be "heirs of the kingdom that he promised to those who love him" (2:5). James's invective against wealth and pride rests on the eschatological reversal of roles. God will exalt the humble, and the rich will fade like grass (4:10; 1:10).

For James this eschatological vindication will be soon. James includes no hint of any need to reckon with a delay. With the words Jesus uses to describe the nearness of the kingdom, James proclaims that the coming of the Lord "is at hand":

> Be patient, brothers, for the coming [parousia] of the Lord. Behold the farmer waits for the precious fruit of the land, being patient with it until it receives the early rains and the late rains. And you, strengthen your hearts, for the coming of the Lord is at hand. Do not blame each other, brothers, in order that you be not judged. Behold the Judge stands at the gate. (5:7–9)

For James this nearness of the end is a call to repentance, much like the message of Jesus recorded in the opening summaries of the Gospels (Mt 4:17; Mk 1:14–15). James must have heard the beatitude "Blessed are those who mourn..." (Mt 5:4), for mourning and dejection, over gaiety and laughter, appear to be the hallmark of appropriate repentance (4:9). If the "good news" preached by Jesus takes on such a depressing appearance for James, it is only because he clings to the future action of God, who will reverse everything:

> Humble yourselves before the Lord and he will exalt you. (4:10)

(See exercise 6.)

II. The Epistle of Jude

A. Historical Background

The short writing tucked away toward the end of the New Testament known as the Letter of Jude is hardly ever read for a church celebration. Again imitating the form of a letter by its salutation, this epistle is an angry denunciation of false teachers.

The letter salutation includes an extraordinary element: the writer identifies himself by a reference to his brother:

> Judas [anglicized, Jude], a servant of Jesus Christ, brother of Jacob [James]. (1)

Tradition has identified the brothers Judas and Jacob as the brothers of the Lord (Mt 13:55; Mk 6:3). Despite the absence of the title apostle in the opening of the letter and despite the writer's later reference to "the apostles of our Lord Jesus Christ" as of another generation (v. 17), another tradition identified the author with the apostle Judas of Jacob, listed only in Lk 6:16 and Acts 1:13. (By way of elimination, Thaddaeus in Mt 10:3 and Mk 3:18 appears as the same apostle under a different name.)

We can deduce few things about the author from his writing. He is highly educated, Greek-speaking, and at least a second-generation Christian. From his use of the Torah and his familiarity with Jewish legends, the author is almost certainly Jewish himself. He is writing at a time when false teaching within the church has become a critical issue, when "the faith" was *something* handed down (vv. 3–4). All this points to the time frame we identified for the Pastorals, namely, the 90s.

Are the names Judas and Jacob pseudonyms? Perhaps. In this case, the author most likely is thinking of the brothers of the Lord.

We must remember, however, that Judas and Jacob were among the most common Jewish names of the time.

The epistle falls into the following structure:

I. Salutation (1–2)

II. Body (3–24)
   A. Reason for writing (3–4)
   B. Lessons from the Torah and legends (5–16)
   C. Exhortation (17–23)
   D. Doxology (24–25)

B. The Faith of Jude

Like the other authors of this period concerned with refuting heresy, Jude has a high estimation of the importance of correct teaching. No separation exists for Jude between one's teaching and one's moral character: you are what you think. The introduction of false teaching into the community, therefore, sounds a loud alarm. Jude calls his readers "to struggle" for the faith (v. 3).

The other elements of Jude's faith that we can detect from this epistle appear as little glimmers here and there. Jude is intensely theocentric, focused on God the Father. Christians are "beloved in God" (v. 1). We must keep our selves "in the love of God" (v. 21). God is "our savior" to whom are owed "glory, majesty, power, and authority." Jesus is the one "through whom" this worship takes place (v. 25).

Yet as "master and Lord" (v. 4) Jesus Christ is also dominant in Jude. The author is first of all "a servant/slave" of Jesus Christ (v. 1). It is some form of denial of this lordship that angers the author into his attack on the false teachers.

No picture of "the last things" appears in this short letter, but from the beginning we are directed to some future saving presence of Jesus. We are now "kept safe for Jesus Christ" (v. 1). We are to "await the mercy of our Lord Jesus Christ, [leading] to eternal life" (v. 21). The ultimate goal is "to stand joyfully without blemish before the glory of God" (v. 24). Jude does not say whether this is a personal goal at the end of one's life or a social goal at the end of history. The author, however, does insist that achieving this goal is the work of God.

(See exercise 7.)

III. The Epistle of 1 Peter

A. Background and Overview

Two shorter writings in the New Testament canon identify themselves as written by the apostle Peter. These writings are elaborate exhortations to Christians facing difficulties. Since we are aware of the practice of attaching a dead hero's name to one's writing, we must keep our mind open to the full range of possibilities for authorship and dating.

Several hints in 1 Peter suggest a date long after the traditional death of the apostle Peter in A.D. 65. This writing echoes a number of Pauline themes from the descriptions of Christian freedom and political authority (1 Pt 2:13–17; cf. Rom 6:12; 13:1–7) to the portrayal of Jesus' death as "once and for all" for sins (1 Pt 3:18; cf. Rom 6:10). 1 Peter also echoes the Johannine theme of salvation as being "re-begotten" by the word of God as seed (1 Pt 1:22–25; cf. 1 Jn 3:9–10). The writing thus seems to stem from a period of synthesis, when the New Testament traditions were merging. 1 Peter also refers to "elders" with their pastoral oversight and authority (1 Pt 5:1–5). Such a picture also reflects the church of the 80s and later.

These hints, together with the polished Greek of the composition, strongly suggest that the author is not the Galilean fisherman but a later writer who wanted to continue the influence of Peter, invoking the authority of Peter to address pressing pastoral concerns of the late first century. At its closing, the writer sends greetings from "Babylon," a code name for Rome at least at the time of the writing of the book of Revelation (see Rv 14:8; 17:5, 18; 18:2). Scholars generally suppose that this work was written by someone in Rome, perhaps the very Silvanus or Mark mentioned by name at the end of the writing.

The writing is addressed to the Christians of five Roman provinces covering what is now central and western Turkey, starting at the north with Pontus, moving south and east to Galatia and Cappadocia, then jumping west to Asia, and back north to Bithynia (see figure 31). The fact that an author would invoke Peter's name to address these Christians—where we have no evidence of Peter ever having gone—suggests that the letter probably stems from a later period, when the authority of Peter had developed along with the view of a church as an interrelated community of Christians spread through the world. The earliest parallel to such an ecumenical concern in Rome can be found in 1 Clement, a work presented as

Figure 31. Churches addressed by 1 Peter.

written by the church of Rome admonishing the church of Corinth, probably written toward the end of the first century.

The general perspective of this writing is Jewish Christian. The readers are reminded that they, like the Israelites, are a "chosen race, a palace priesthood" (1 Pt 2:10; cf. Ex 19:6). They are not replacing the Jews as if in a new covenant. They are united to the chosen people, special only by their faith in Christ. The author refers to the continuity of Christ with the prophets (1:10–12) and frequently alludes to the Psalms and other books of the Jewish scriptures. Peter was historically one of the important leaders of the Jewish Christians (cf. Gal 2:7–14). Rome, along with Antioch, was a center of Jewish Christianity at the end of the first century and into the next.

1 Peter has the form and structure of a Jewish Hellenistic letter, beginning with the salutation, the blessing prayer (cf. 2 Cor 1:3–7; cf. 2 Mc 1:2–6), and ending with the greetings typical of Christian letters, as we know them from Paul. The general readership, however, along with the elevated theological tone of the writing, prevents us from identifying the writing as a "letter." This is another "epistle," a treatise or essay in letter form. The frequent allusions to scripture give this writing the tone of a "rabbinic homily." The one reference to baptism (3:21), along with many other possible allusions to this ritual in this epistle, suggests to many scholars that we possess in this writing an early baptismal homily. It is hard to evaluate such a hypothesis. Many of the exhortations suggest a setting of more experienced Christians now dealing with persecutions. It is clear, however, that this writing is far more a studied attempt to express the general challenge of living one's Christianity in a difficult world—as we would find in a religious essay—than immediate responses to specific questions and occasions—as we would find in a letter.

Between the opening and closing, this epistle combines exhortation in a tight weave with religious reflection. Except for the instruction about "the prophets" (1:10–12), every paragraph or unit of the epistle centers on an exhortation. This instruction about the prophets should, therefore, be seen as an extension of the prayer. From this opening to the concluding section, the exhortations follow one another, each one identified by an imperative verb. For each exhortation—except that to "youngsters"—an instruction about Christian life or about Christ forms its basis. No apparent cyclical structure groups these exhortations into larger units. The only internal structure that clearly emerges deals with the sequence of exhortations connected with household (slaves, wives, husbands) or other social structures (elders, youngsters). Hence, our (reluctant) chain-like structure for 1 Peter:

I. Opening (1:1–9)
    A. Salutation (1:1–2)
    B. Epistolary prayer (1:3–9)
    C. Didactic extension of prayer (1:10–12)

II. Body (1:13–5:11)
    A. Set your hopes on the future (1:13–16)
    —as one called to be holy
    B. Live in reverential fear (1:17–21)
    —as one ransomed by the precious blood of Christ
    C. Love one another (1:22–25)
    —as "re-begotten" by the seed of God
    D. Disrobe evil attitudes and actions (2:1–3)
    —as babies growing toward salvation
    E. Be built into a spiritual house (2:4–11)
    —as a chosen race, palace priesthood, a holy nation
    F. Avoid fleshly desires (2:11–12)
    —as aliens and sojourners in this world
    G. Be subject to political authority (2:13–17)
    —as following the will of God
    H. Slaves, be subject to your masters (2:18–25)
    —as Christ suffered for you
    I. Wives, be subject to your husbands (3:1–6)
    —as holy women of old were subject to their husbands
    J. Husbands, live with your wives in understanding (3:7)
    —since we are joint heirs of life
    K. All, be of one mind, be loving one another (3:8–12)
    —for "the eyes of the Lord are on the just" (Psalm 34)
    L. Do not fear those who punish you for doing good (3:13–22)
    —for Christ suffered for the sake of the unjust
    M.   Restrain yourself from debauchery (4:1–6)
    —for you will give an account to the final judge
    N. Be serious, sober, hospitable, serving each other with your gifts (4:7–11)
    —for the end of all things is at hand.
    O. Rejoice in suffering persecution (4:12–19)
    —for the judgment has begun with the household of God

P. Elders, tend the flock (5:1–4)
   —for you will receive the unfading crown of glory
Q. Youngsters, be subject to the elders (5:5a)
R. All of you, clothe yourself with humility (5:5b–7)
   —for God "bestows favors on the humble" (Prv 3:34)
S. Be vigilant (5:8–9)
   —the devil is like a roaring lion

III. Conclusion (5:10–14)

B. The Faith of 1 Peter

(See exercise 8.)

This epistle is synthetic and at times eclectic. We find here together snatches of religious ideas from many of the other writers we have studied. Much seems borrowed from Paul, and some striking Johannine themes also appear.

Given the exhortatory character of the epistle, we should not be surprised by this fishnet approach to theology. The author is more directly concerned with encouraging his readers and exhorting them to specific lines of conduct. This author is no moralizer, however; he links almost every exhortation to some religious insight. The moral or ethical dimension grows out of and is the natural consequence of the insight—wherever the insight happens to come from.

Jesus, never described as "Son of God" in this epistle, is the "Lord" (1:3; 3:15) who has suffered and died for our sins, has risen and ascended to heaven over all angelic powers (3:18–22). He will be gloriously "revealed" in the future (1:13; 4:13; 5:4). Not much else is said of Jesus. He is "known" before the foundation of the world (1:20), but the author is quiet about any activity on the part of Jesus that would suggest preexistence.

Eschatology in 1 Peter likewise appears as a gathering of the core New Testament position. As mentioned above, the great future event is primarily a revelation of Jesus. The event seems imminent, since it is now "the time of the beginning of the judgment" at least for "the household of God" (4:17). So this is "the last times" (1:20). The author's eschatology is a part of his moral exhortation. We are to live as "strangers and sojourners" (2:11) in this world, although accepting our civic and social responsibilities in order to give a good example and witness to others.

The richness of the epistle appears in its soteriology. Along the lines of earlier New Testament writers, the author of 1 Peter places particular emphasis on Jesus' sufferings, understanding these sufferings from the paradigm of the Suffering Servant of Isaiah 53. Unlike Paul, however, 1 Peter insists it was *our* sins he bore. Jesus himself is sinless: "He committed no sin, nor was deceit found in his mouth" (2:22; cf. Is 53:9).

The author evokes the image of the "ransom" to understand the saving sufferings of Jesus. Like Paul, 1 Peter avoids any mention of a recipient of this "ransom" and insists only on the great price or precious nature of the payment. We are ransomed by the "precious blood of Christ" (1:19).

In a shift to Johannine imagery, 1 Peter then explains salvation in terms of being begotten again. The image is announced in the opening prayer:

> Blessed be God...the one who begat us again *[anagēnnesas]* according to his great mercy unto a living hope through the resurrection of Jesus Christ from the dead. (1:3)

In his exhortation to love one another (section II, C), the author sounds very much like the author of 1 John, linking up this regeneration with the word of God functioning as a seed:

> You have been begotten again *[anagēgennemenoi],* not from a perishable seed but from an imperishable one, through the abiding word of the living God. (1:23; cf. 1 Jn 3:9)

The imagery of divine begetting or regeneration does not appear again in the epistle. Except for a brief reference to inheriting "life" (3:7), the theme of eternal life as salvation here and now does not appear. This brief Johannine strand, therefore, appears as part of the eclecticism of the epistles, drawing from apparently established themes from various origins, according to a conviction that they all cohere in the one mystery of Christian salvation.

Where 1 Peter shows its originality is in its development of Christian life. The vast range of exhortations is itself characteristic of this concern for Christian life. Above all, Christians are to be quiet witnesses and examples even to cruel masters.

> Maintain good conduct among the Gentiles, so that if they speak of you as evildoers, but observing your good works, they may glorify God on the day of visitation. Be subject to every human institution for the Lord's sake

...that by doing good you may silence the ignorance of foolish people....Servants, be subject to your masters with all reverence, not only to those who are good and equitable but also to those who are perverse. For it is a grace whenever, because of consciousness of God, anyone bears the pain of unjust suffering. (2:12–19)

Among its many exhortations is one for which 1 Peter is well known:

Be built into a spiritual household so as to become a holy priesthood to offer spiritual sacrifices.... You indeed are a chosen race, a palace priesthood, a holy nation, an acquired people. (2:5, 9)

This description joins with the cultic descriptions in Hebrews to form yet another step in the Christian reappropriation of an Israelite and Jewish heritage. In his description of Christians as "a chosen race, a palace priesthood, a holy nation, an acquired people," the author strings together descriptions of Israel from the Psalms, from Isaiah, and from Exodus. Christians form the real Israel and exercise a real priesthood—although our sacrifices are no longer bloody but "spiritual." Paul described these sacrifices earlier as "living" (Rom 12:1).

(See exercise 9.)

IV. The Epistle of 2 Peter

A. Background and Overview

The epistle we know as 2 Peter begins with the self-identification of the author as "Symeon Peter, slave and apostle of Jesus Christ" (1:1). The identification is close to that of 1 Peter, "Peter, apostle of Jesus Christ" (1 Pt 1:1). Elsewhere only in Acts 15:14 is the name Symeon applied to Peter, apparently as a variant of Simon.

The author speaks of this letter as his "second letter" (3:1), in an apparent allusion to 1 Peter. He also describes himself as an eyewitness to the "transfiguration" as described in Mt 17:1–8. The author clearly wants us to see this letter as written by the Peter we know as one of the Twelve.

This writing, however, is even less of a "letter" than 1 Peter. Only the first two verses, in the style of a Hellenistic letter opening, accord with such a classification. The rest of the writing is an exhortatory treatise. It has no specifically identified readership. Not even the ending, 3:17–18, suggests a letter. We can call it an "epistle" according to the modern designation of essays with some letter form.

Throughout this epistle we see something of a farewell discourse. This is the type of writing that forms the speeches of Jesus at the Last Supper in John 14–17. This is the writing that describes Paul's somber farewell to the Ephesian elders in Acts 20:17–38. It is a warning about future dangers, a promise of God's help, a cascade of advice, with brave allusions to the speaker's coming death.

Almost certainly we have here a writer pretending to be Peter the Apostle, writing long after Peter's death, retrojecting to Peter's last years the advice that the author would like his readers now to hear. The author occasionally slips up in this literary fiction. He refers to "the apostles" as others (3:2), to "our ancestors" who have died during the period of waiting for the return of Jesus (3:4), to the letters of Paul, now collected and considered to be scripture (3:15–16).

The whole eschatology of this epistle really makes sense only in the late first century. It deals with the problem of the delay of the end. It speaks of scoffers, who have apparently heard of the Christian expectations and ensuing disappointments. Tradition puts the martyrdom of Peter under Nero around A.D. 65. From what we know of that decade, the problem of the delay had not arisen. This delay became and remained a burning problem as the century ticked to an end.

Another curious element about this epistle, which strongly argues against Petrine authorship, is its literary dependence on the Epistle of Jude. We can see a clear pattern of verbal similarities between 2 Peter and Jude, which argues that the author of 2 Peter had a copy of Jude in front of him when he wrote. The improvements in 2 Peter in vocabulary and in the chronological order of references to the ancient persons along with the elimination in 2 Peter of references to noncanonical Jewish books all suggest that the author of 2 Peter used Jude and not vice versa. The verbal similarities are carefully disguised by shifts of meaning and by the addition of other material, while following the order of Jude and the general method of Jude to excoriate his adversaries.

Setting up parallel columns from the two letters helps us see the literary dependence. Here we note the verbal similarities in the identical sequence:

2 Peter 2	*Jude*
[1] There will be false	[4] Some men have intruded...

teachers...denying the master who purchased them...

[4] If God did not spare the angels but delivered them to bonds of gloom, holding them to judgment...

[6] And he condemned the cities of Sodom and Gomorrah making them an example...

[10] They are not afraid to blaspheme glorious beings...

[12] These however like speechless animals, born by nature to capture and destruction...will be destroyed...

[15] They follow the way of Balaam of Bosor, who loved the gain of iniquity...

[17] These are waterless wells and mists driven by storms for whom the gloom of darkness is kept....

[18] Proclaiming empty bombast they seduce by desires of the flesh...

[3:3] Know this first, that there will come in the last days scoffers living according to their own proper desires...

denying our only master and Lord...

[6] The angels too... he kept in eternal chains in gloom unto judgment,

[7] like Sodom and Gomorrah and the cities around them...serve as an example.

[8] Similarly...they blaspheme glorious beings...

[10] What they know by nature like speechless animals, in such things they are destroyed...

[11] In the way of Cain and the error of Balaam they abandon themselves for gain...

[12] These are...waterless clouds driven by the wind...

[13] for whom the gloom of darkness is kept for eternity....

[16] These are grumblers, disgruntled ones behaving according to their desires and their mouths speak bombast...

[18] Remember, beloved,...in the last time there will be scoffers living according to their own desires.

The structure of this short epistle is simple. It is that of a truncated Hellenistic letter:

A. Letter salutation (1:1–2)

B. Body (1:3–3:16)
    1. Exhortation to virtue (1:3–21)
    2. Excoriation of false teachers (2:1–22)
    3. Eschatology (3:1–16)
    4. Final exhortations (3:17–18)

B. The Faith of 2 Peter

The vitriolic excoriation of the false teachers, occupying about a third of this letter, is not exactly the text any of us would want to read at a wedding. As we have seen before, this refutation of false teaching through an attack on the moral integrity of the teachers is fairly typical of this time and culture.

From our historical vantage point, we see the fears and anxieties of the church in danger. We see an early church leader angry at the harm he sees being done to the community he loves. So again the fragile human element surfaces.

As we search for the distinctive elements of 2 Peter's faith, a wide range of ideas appears from the text. For instance, we have a description of Jesus as "our God and savior, Jesus Christ" (1:1). The expression is close to Ti 2:13, "our great God and savior, Jesus Christ," and probably reflects a formula current among some Christians. The absence in 2 Peter of any explanation or defense of such an astounding description suggests general familiarity with calling Jesus "God." Otherwise the favorite title for Jesus in 2 Peter is "our Lord and savior" (1:11; 2:20; 3:2, 18).

Concerning Christian life, a dominant theme in this epistle is the importance of the Christian's "knowledge of our Lord Jesus Christ" (1:8; 2:20; 3:18). The theme is similar to that in the later letters of Paul, where such religious knowledge constitutes the perfection of faith and love (cf. Phil 1:9; 3:10). As in Paul, this Christian quality or activity reflects a comprehensive experience of the whole person rather than an academic head trip. We see here the Hebrew or Jewish sense of "knowledge" rather than the Greek sense. The object is a person, not an idea, and the foundation is love.

Perhaps one of the most well known and discussed descriptions in 2 Peter is that of the goal of life as coming "to share in the divine nature" (1:4). The abstract tone of these words stands out from the rest of the New Testament. Whereas we are now used to reading about "God" (*ho theos*), here we hear of "the divine nature" (*theia physis*). The expression aptly describes what of God can be shared, but only a thinker capable of the delicate abstraction of the consistency and definition of some object of thought would feel comfortable speaking of "nature" rather than of a concrete person. philosophers contemporary with 2 Peter were, in fact, speculating on a type of "divine quality" that could be shared with human beings, especially in the perennial quest for immortality. Greek philosophers (especially in the line of Aristotle) had invented the concept of *physis*. Now a Christian writer seeks to integrate this philosophical concern with his faith. In substance 2 Peter is not far from John's concern of obtaining "divine life," the result of being "begotten of God" (cf. Jn 3:3–16). Closer to home, the expression in 2 Peter might best be rooted in 1 Peter's appropriation of the Johannine theme by its description of "re-begetting" (1:3), especially through "the seed" of God (1:23; cf. 1 Jn 3:9–10).

(See exercise 10.)

The dominant theme of 2 Peter, however, is eschatology. About a third of the epistle is dedicated to dealing with the end of the world and specifically its delay. 2 Peter 3:3–4 introduces us to the "scoffers" who articulate the problem of the delay quite well:

> Know this first of all that in the last days there will come scoffers scoffing according to their own desires and saying, "Where is the promise of his coming? For from the days when our forefathers fell asleep, everything continues as is from the beginning of creation."

For the first time we hear the subject matter of the false teachers who have been the object of the author's scorn since chapter 2 of the epistle. This issue of the eschatological delay may, in fact, have been the only matter of concern for the author as he winds up dealing head on with the actual teaching.

In any case, the author testifies to the existence of scoffers and the embarrassment for Christians. The scoffing itself testifies to the early faith of Christians in a speedy end of the world. The scoffing also testifies to the amount of time that must have elapsed for this expectation to have become an embarrassment. Recall how writers like Paul and Mark could speak so straightforwardly of the nearness of the end.

What follows in 2 Peter 3 are three theological responses to the scoffing. First, the author insists on the creative authority of God to create and destroy:

> Of old the heavens and the earth existed formed out of water and through water by the word of God. Through these then the world was destroyed, flooded by water. Indeed the present heavens and the earth are preserved by the same word for fire, kept until the day of judgment and destruction of the impious people. (3:5–6)

The author then presents a second argument:

> In this matter, beloved, do not be ignorant: one day with
> the Lord is as a thousand years and a thousand years as
> one day. (3:8)

God's time is not our time. We have no way of boxing God into our
schedule. The expressions "soon" and "after a long time" have different meanings for us and for God.

Finally, the author shifts to a third reasoning, quite distinct
from the preceding reflections on the transcendence of God:

> The Lord does not delay his promises as some under-
> stand delay. Rather he is patient with us, not wanting
> anyone to perish, but for all to reach repentance. (3:9)

The delay of the parousia is not a problem because God is flexible. If
he appears to be late, he is just waiting for us all to be ready. Next to
all the fire and brimstone in this letter, this statement is striking in
its affirmation of God's will for universal salvation (see also 1 Tm
2:4). This love on the part of God for all is more important than any
divine plan or structure. Timetables can be stretched and eternal
degrees modified for the sake of people.

While the author then insists on the destructive side of God's
"salvation" (2 Pt 3:10–12)—more so than any other book of the New
Testament outside of the book of Revelation—his final word affirms
"new heavens and a new earth" (3:13).

V. Theological Reflections

It is intriguing to think of the mentality that prompted individuals to write such epistles as we have studied in this chapter.
While not exhibiting the personal involvement of a letter—such as
we found in Paul's writing—these epistles move beyond the imper-
sonal approach of an essay or treatise. They are not just writings for
the sake of articulating ideas; they are exhortations, directed to
somebody, however undetermined. The minimal letter form underlines the social nature of the writing.

The content of these four writings likewise manifests an
intense feeling of responsibility for the faith of others. The authors of
James, 2 Peter, and Jude are clearly disturbed by what they perceive
as errors within the church. 1 Peter, on the other hand, exhibits a
more calm concern to help Christians deal with the pressures of the

world. But in their intense exhortatory manner, all four authors appear to want to do something to correct or help fellow Christians toward an authentic living of their faith.

These writers are pastors addressing Christians elsewhere in the world, not just their own "flock." For them to write this way, they must have had some sense of interconnectedness with the various Christian communities of the Greco-Roman world. The sense of universal church, the sense of one "people of God" that we noted developing already in Paul, is now even more apparent. On the other hand, the writers are not passing down instructions through some structure of authority. They are addressing individual Christians as fellow Christians.

If the writers are in fact using pseudonyms, they do not perceive themselves as having an office or role sufficiently authoritative to speak in their own names. In this supposition of authorship, what holds the church together and provides the vehicle for communication is a common tradition stemming from the apostles and other first-generation leaders. The church evidently feels itself bound together by a fidelity to these leaders and their teachings.

It is also intriguing to see, especially in 1 Peter, the efforts to draw on multiple traditions. 1 Peter is heavily indebted to Paul's thought. Yet we have clear echoes of Johannine theology. James, of course, seems to have problems with what he perceives to be Paul's position and prefers the Matthean teaching of faith in action. Perhaps this synthetic movement is the result of the emergence of new "enemies." the false teachers. In any case, the church seems to be becoming "catholic" in its teaching.

Dominating 2 Peter and Jude is the polemic against false teachers. In 1 Peter we see the struggle with outside social oppression. James testifies to the difficulties of social ranks within the church. Jesus predicted struggle for his followers (Mk 13:9–13). These writings testify to the continuing struggle and pain, flowing from Calvary down through the church extended in history. What Jesus left behind is not yet the kingdom of God.

The pastoral anger and the depressing negativity we find in Jude and 2 Peter are aspects of this struggle. In these two letters we find the refutation of false teachings which consists of an attack on the teachers as morally depraved. We have seen this approach in the Pastoral letters and 2 John.

Seeing such negative campaigning *in writing* generally shocks us. We see this type of writing as a continuing demolition of another's character and also as subject to careful analysis in which excesses are painfully exposed over and over. Thinking more in terms of the fleeting character of oral communication to which they were accustomed, the New Testament authors may have expected less of an impact. Today we often will say things that we will not put in writing.

The challenge still remains for us to proclaim such character assassination in the church—if we ever get around to reading these letters. Of course, we cannot use them as paradigms of our struggle against contemporary error, but we can find in them a sense of the seriousness of religious and especially moral error. It is not enough simply to be sincere. Error destroys. We can see in the theological polemic of these writings the sense that sin infects the whole person, not just the emotions or will. Sin clouds the mind. Truth is liberating, not just intellectual fun. Religious truth heals and is as much a grace as any God-given feeling that strengthens our hearts.

In their concern for "the faith, handed down to us from the apostles" these later letters become something of the buffer between the intensely rich writings of Paul and the evangelists on the one hand and Christians of succeeding generations on the other. These writers felt that the apostles and brothers of the Lord could still speak to successive generations. These writers likewise felt—perhaps naïvely—confident that their own perspectives were legitimate mediums for the continued living voice of the apostles and brothers of the Lord. These writings testify to the legitimate desire to continue the process of inspiration. They testify to a faith that the Holy Spirit does manage to raise up inspired writers and continues to reveal divine light even after "the death of the last apostle."

The very concept of the *canon* of the New Testament precludes our adding new books. The concept is based on some priority of the first generation of Christians as "standards" of our faith; however, the presence of pseudonymity among these last writings, along with the mistaken supposition of apostolic authorship as criterion for including these writings in the canon, tells us something of the artificiality of the concept of the *canon*. The New Testament canon is our human invention, our tool for dealing with God's revelation, which surpasses our comprehension.

EXERCISES

Exercise 1. (see pages 333–334): From the lists of the Twelve (Mk 3:13–19; Mt 10:1–4; Lk 6:12–16), identify the two Jameses who were apostles of Jesus.

Exercise 2. (see pages 333–334): Describe James the brother of the Lord as he appears in Acts 15 and 21 and in Galatians 1–2.

Exercise 3. (see page 335): Read Paul's insistence on justification by faith in Rom 3:21–4:25. Compare this with Jas 2:14–16. How do Paul and James differ? From what you know of Paul's position, would he disagree with James? Why?

Exercise 4. (see page 336): What does James say of Jesus? What titles does he use for Jesus? What would lead a reader of James to think the author was a Christian writing to Christians?

Exercise 5. (see pages 336–337): What does James say of God? What titles does he use?

Exercise 6. (see pages 337–338): Find the number of times James refers Christians to the future for an understanding of the value of various present activities and conditions.

Exercise 7. (see pages 338–339): How does Jude connect teaching and moral character? What does he say about bad teachers?

Exercise 8. (see page 344): Gather together all the statements, titles, and descriptions of Jesus in 1 Peter. Who is Jesus for this author?

Exercise 9. (see pages 344–346): Compare 1 Peter's description of Christians as a palace priesthood with the Old Testament description of Israel in Ex 19:5–6 and Is 61:6. What privileges are implied in such a priesthood?

Exercise 10. (see pages 349–350): Read Jn 3:3–16, 1 Jn 3:9–10; and 1 Pt 1:3, 23 and compare the wording of these texts with 2 Pt 1:4. What common idea runs through these texts? How does 2 Peter differ from the earlier texts?

REVIEW QUESTIONS

1. Who traditionally is identified as the author of the Epistle of James? What are the critical arguments against this identification?

2. What church structure is reflected in the Epistle of James?

3. Who is the Old Testament model of faith for James? What is said of this model?

4. Who traditionally is identified as the author of the Epistle of Jude? What are the critical arguments against this identification?

5. What are the critical arguments against identifying the author of either 1 Peter or 2 Peter as the apostle Peter?

6. Describe the general literary form and organization of 1 Peter.

7. In what distinctive way does 2 Peter describe Christian life?

8. What is the principal eschatological concern addressed by 2 Peter? How does this writing respond to that concern?

FOR FURTHER REFLECTION AND DISCUSSION

1. How would you write a letter warning impressionable people today against dangerous influences? What would be the target of your attack? How do you know which things are wrong? Would you include influences within the church?

2. Pick one by one each of the four writings treated in this chapter as if it were the only source you had for knowledge of the Christian faith. What would you learn from James, Jude, 1 Peter, or 2 Peter? Does any element of your faith appear to be missing from these writings?

19

The Book of Revelation

Perhaps the most intriguing book of the New Testament is the last, the book of Revelation, known also by the Greek form of its name, the book of the Apocalypse. Through history this book has provoked enormously wide-ranged and even contradictory interpretations. Over and over this book has triggered bold predictions for the future, often with very precise timetables calculated from details in the text—predictions, however, that do not come true. These predictions have ranged from the calculations of the end of the world expected to happen around the turn of the first millennium (around A.D. 1000) to predictions of invasions of Israel by Russia calculated to happen sometime in the 1980s.

This experience of misinterpretation strongly suggests that we need to read this book in a special way, that we need first of all to understand the type of truth the author intended to express in this book—put another way, that we understand the literary form of this book before we ask what the book is saying to us. We need, therefore, to give special care to the historical background of this book before we search for its message.

I. Historical Background

A. Literary Form

We touched briefly in chapter 6 on the special Jewish mentality called *apocalyptic* that was contemporary with the New Testament. From this mentality—dealing with the clash of good and evil as cosmic powers, the divine determination of limited evil times, and the ultimate victory of God over evil—there comes a distinctive apocalyptic literary form.

Before the identification of this literary form, the book of Revelation appeared to readers as one more "prophetic" writing, with

special affinity with the book of Daniel. Up to that time the identification of the literary form took place within the larger classification
of "biblical" and "nonbiblical" books. Among the biblical books, Revelation, seemed closest to the prophets.

A special breakthrough took place when the book of Daniel
was studied not so much in terms of its relationship to other
prophetic books as in terms of its similarity to nonbiblical books.
The book of Daniel began to be seen as closer to noncanonical Jewish writings such as *1 Enoch, 4 Ezra,* the *Apocalypse of Abraham,*
the *Psalms of Solomon,* and many others written from around 200
B.C. to A.D. 100. These books engaged intense visual symbols—colors, numbers, and beasts, especially beasts in grotesque combinations. These books portrayed evil as a hellish power dominating the
world, allowed to ravage God's people for a period determined by
God's plan for history. Angels interpreted the symbols for the vision-
aries, often named as persons of the distant past whose work was
only recently discovered. Yet from the vocabulary, from the reference to historical events, even from the musical instruments
named, these works all seemed to have been written during the
Seleucid and Roman periods, periods of great suffering and discour-
agement, as we saw in chapter 5.

In this comparison, which cut across the boundaries of the
canon, the book of Daniel appeared as a representative of apocalyptic literature, written under a pseudonym around 170 B.C., dealing
with the rampant evil loosed on Israel under Antiochus IV. The book
began to make much more sense.

Focusing on the book of Revelation with the same insights,
biblical scholars began to make more sense as they understood this
book to be an example of apocalyptic literature. Of itself the writing
proposed to give a divine-like view of history in terms of a conflict
between cosmic good and cosmic evil. The book attempts to give
coherence and significance to events that on the surface offered only
confusion and despair.

For this reason in Revelation two images dominate. First of all
"the heavens" appear as the perspective from which historical
events are viewed. The heavens either open or invite the visionary
to ascend, where he can see the earthly events as God sees them.
Second, "the scroll," or some image of a predetermined script of history, appears on the scene to assure the visionary (and the readers)
that God has already long ago thought of and planned for the events
ravaging the earth now and in the near future. The script is written.
The play needs only to be acted out. God is in charge.

Various images of good and evil then enter the stage, each with its coded symbolism. The initiate knows the code; hence, anything that appears in "white" is good, but watch out for anything wearing "red." Good things come in twelves and sevens—numbers of completeness; bad things come in sixes and three-and-a-halfs—exactly half the numbers of completeness. Thus, if some crowd numbered twelve times twelve times a thousand, that crowd would be absolutely complete, including everyone. The numbers were ideas, not arithmetic calculations.

Classic images from the Old Testament appear in Revelation as in other apocalyptic writings. In the various punishments depicted in this book, we see clear allusions to the ten plagues of Exodus 7–10. Trumpets in this book reflect the trumpet of Ex 19:16–19 or perhaps that of Jl 2:1. The author appears to be drawing from a storeroom of ready-made images to create a literary effect much like a play director moves stage props onto the scene. The choice, therefore, of hail and fire, of locusts, or of darkness in this book derives from the literary background of the author rather than from special knowledge he might have of the future.

Like the other apocalyptic writings of the time, the book of Revelation appears to be a commentary on its own times, recognized as evil times. The narration appears to be an attempt to understand this evil by two approaches. The first attempt is a resolution of good and evil to two "absolute" sources: the power of God and the power of hell. People on earth belong to one of these sources. We are not given the privilege of being lukewarm. The second approach is to view the final conflict as resulting in the total destruction of the forces of evil. This victory of God is as certain as the final scene of a play in a script already written. This victory, always soon to come, indicates just how temporary the present evil times are.

By analyzing its own contemporary struggles in such symbolic and generalized ways, apocalyptic literature—wittingly or unwittingly—provided the basis for successive generations to read their own "evil times" into the text, to see the text as describing their drama of good and evil. Because the book of Revelation refused to name the Roman Empire as the cause of Christian suffering but spoke of this force as "the beast" armed with the force of hell, successive readers could see in this figure Muhammad, Attila the Hun, the pope, Luther, Ignatius of Loyola, Hitler, Stalin, or George Bush—depending on whom they really disliked.

The power and the weakness of apocalyptic literature become evident. As rooted in the original intention of the author, apocalyptic becomes a powerful meditation on the mystery of good and evil and the call to patient endurance against all despair—in any period of time when such endurance is needed. As detached from this original intention, apocalyptic becomes a tool for capricious absolutizing of our hatreds, allowing us to seize on superficial similarities and thus identify our enemies with the enemies of God. The results are tragic.

As expressing the apocalyptic form of its own time, the book of Revelation is thus not a medium for predicting the future. The author probably had no more information about the future than we do. Revelation, rather, provides us with a perspective to understand the present and the future together. This is the perspective in which historical evil is recognized for the momentous power that it represents. It is also the perspective that recognizes the absolute power of God to correct effortlessly the most horrendous situation. It is the perspective of hope—even in a hopeless situation.

B. The Author and Time

The author identifies himself as "John" (1:1), writing on the island of Patmos (1:9), apparently a penal colony in the first century. Tradition has identified this John with the son of Zebedee, who in another problematic tradition is identified as the author of the Fourth Gospel.

The Island of Patmos.

Almost nothing in the text links this book with the Fourth Gospel or the Johannine letters. The brief reference to Jesus as "the lamb" (5:6–14) is no more an indication of belonging to some Johannine school than is the lamb's "slaying" or "sacrifice" (5:2, 12) an indication of belonging to some Pauline school. At best we can see here the eclectic character of later New Testament writings. In its theology of the imminent and cosmic end of the world, Revelation is at the opposite end of the spectrum from the Gospel of John. Nothing in its style or distinctive vocabulary suggests that Revelation stems from the Johannine traditions.

More than likely we have here an author whom we otherwise do not know. Jewish apocalyptic writers used pseudonyms, and later Christian apocalypses likewise used them. How should we understand the author calling himself John? The use of such a common Jewish name without further identification does not accomplish the general purpose of biblical pseudonyms—to give authority to the writing by connecting it with an easily identified hero. Perhaps this Christian apocalyptic writer is breaking with the apocalyptic tradition and giving us his real name.

Rome as an evil power appears in the symbolism of Rv 17:1–14. The numbering of "kings" (emperors) in 17:9–10 would aptly describe the Roman Empire in the late 60s. The persecution of Nero broke out around A.D. 65 and would explain the author's attitude toward Rome. On the other hand, the reign of Domitian (A.D. 81–96) provides several historical references that would explain symbolic descriptions in the text of Revelation. For instance, Domitian initiated the cult of emperor worship during the life of the emperor. Revelation 13:1–10 describes the evil demands of worshiping the beast. The later date would explain the generalized horror of the Roman authority found in Revelation, an attitude quite different from Paul in Rom 13:1–7, written around A.D. 58.

C. The Literary Structure

Understanding the literary structure of Revelation is also a major challenge but very important for reading this book with understanding. The sequence of scenes is very confusing. We see several series of sevens, interrupted by other visions.

Clearly these septenaries are the key to the structure of this book. If we look carefully, many of the other visions also form sequences of sevens, although not always numbered as such. Within these septenaries, we also find special material that appears something like an extended development of the seventh element or a preparation for it. The septenaries do not simply follow each other but are contained in each other. The seventh of the series contains and introduces the next seven.

The three visions involving the narrator appear to be major breaks in the book, but again these major sections do not simply follow each other. By way of an anticipatory displacement, the third vision begins before the second section ends. The result is an interlocking effect that tightly unites one block of material to the other.

The following outline or structure should help us read Revelation with a sense of the parts fitting into a whole. This structure is based on three major parts, with the second and third overlapping or interlocking. The first part is quite different from the other two and consists of seven letters exhorting seven churches in western Asia Minor (see figure 32). The second and third parts consist of apocalyptic visions. A prologue and an epilogue frame the whole:

  I. Prologue (1:1–8)

 II. First Part (1:9–3:22)
        A. Inaugural vision (1:9–20)
        B. Letters to the seven churches (2:1–3:22)
           1. Ephesus (2:1–7)
           2. Smyrna (2:8–11)
           3. Pergamum (2:12–17)
           4. Thyatira (2:18–29)
           5. Sardis (3:1–6)
           6. Philadelphia (3:7–13)
           7. Laodicea (3:14–22)

III. Second Part: A Cycle of Visions (4:1–11:18)
        A. Vision of heavenly worship (4:1–5:14)
        B. The seven seals on the scroll (6:1–8:1)
           1. The first four seals (6:1–8)
           2. The fifth seal (6:9–11)
           3. The sixth seal (6:12–17)
           —Development: The sealing of the tribes of Israel
             and the nations (7:1–17)
           4. The seventh seal (8:1)
        C. The seven trumpets (8:2–11:18)
           1. Introduction (8:2–6)

2. The first four trumpets (8:7–8:13)
3. The fifth trumpet (9:1–12)
4. The sixth trumpet (9:13–21)
5. The seventh trumpet (11:15–18)

IV. Third Part: A Cycle of Visions (10:1–22:5)
   A. Vision of the little scroll and the two witnesses (10:1–11:14)
   B. Seven unnumbered visions (11:19–15:4)
     1. The woman and the dragon (11:19–12:17)
     2. The first beast (13:1–10)
     3. The second beast (13:11–18)
     4. The lamb and the 144,000 (14:1–5)
     5. The three angels (14:6–13)
     6. The harvest of the earth (14:14–20)
     7. The heavenly liturgy (15:2–4)
   C. The seven bowls (16:1–21)
     1. Introduction and the first four bowls (16:1–9)
     2. The fifth bowl (16:10–11)
     3. The sixth bowl (16:12–16)
     4. The seventh bowl (16:17–21)
     —Development: The evil Babylon in shame (17:1–19:10)
   D. Seven unnumbered visions (19:11–21:8)
     1. The white horse and its rider (19:11–16)
     2. The summoning angel (19:17–18)
     3. The capture of the beast (19:19–21)
     4. The 1000-year chaining of the dragon (20:1–3)
     5. The thrones (20:4–10)
     6. The white throne and the one seated (20:11–15)
     7. The new heavens and the new earth (21:1–8)
     —Development: The heavenly Jerusalem in glory (21:9–22:5)

V. Epilogue (22:6–21)

The thought movement through this structure is cyclical and intensifying. We can take corresponding parts and compare their elements to see the intensifications. For instance, comparisons of the visions in chapters 5 and 10 show deliberate shifts:

Chapter 5
Large scroll

Chapter 10
Little book

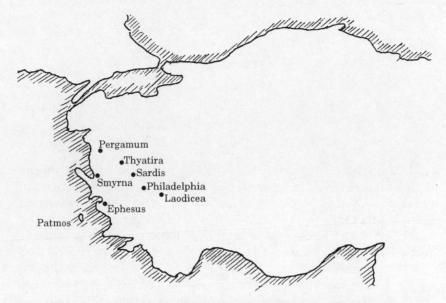

Figure 32. Churches Addressed by the Book of Revelation.

Closed	Opened
Taken by the lamb	Taken by John
In the hand of God	In the hand of the angel
Opened seal by seal	Eaten: sweet and sour

In the punishments that come in explicit sevens, we note the cycles of a series of punishments leading to a moment of victory or salvation. Meanwhile the series themselves follow with repetitions and intensifications:

7 *Seals*	7 *Trumpets*	7 *Bowls*
1/4th the people	1/3rd the people	All
	1st Land	1st Land
	2nd Sea	2nd Sea
	3rd Rivers & Springs	3rd Rivers & Springs
	4th Stars	4th Stars
	Abbadon (5th)	Harmegedon (6th)

The structure of Revelation thus does not seem to reflect any historical concern or temporal sequence. The one thousand years of peace described in chapter 20 do not represent any historical period (supposedly in the future simply because the description is near the end of the book). Rather, these tableaux come one upon the other as faith-filled interpretations of the perennial struggle of good and evil. The numbered septenaries in particular follow the cycle: an initial ominous action of God, an intense punishment and judgment, and finally some form of triumph or salvation. This cycle also describes the whole book.

In this sense the book of Revelation speaks of eschatological events, not historical events. The descriptions are provoked by historical events contemporary with the author. To that degree, knowledge of the historical background of Revelation helps us understand the text. But the descriptions are then broken off from history to describe theological structures.

(See exercise 1.)

II. The Faith of Revelation

The faith of John, the author of Revelation, is a faith absorbed in the opening summary of Jesus' preaching as the Gospels of Mark and Matthew present it: "The kingdom of God is at hand" (Mk 1:15; Mt 4:17). Sometimes described on center stage, most of the time behind the scenes, God dominates the story. It is God's script that is written in the scrolls. God is the transcendent and glorious one whose punishments lead to his victory and glory. It is his kingdom in the form of the heavenly Jerusalem that brings the book to a close. Even in the scenes where God is not described, we sense his power. The lack of descriptions of God simply underlines his transcendence.

For all his transcendence, God is not aloof. He is intensely active in his creation. He is deeply concerned about earthly events and he reacts to rectify the disorders. The action of God happens according to a plan that emanates from the divine council, this throne room where God is surrounded by heavenly beings (Revelation 4–5). This is the war room which epitomizes the very mystery of God's secret plan of salvation. In Hebrew the word for council, *sôd*, is also the word for mystery. For the visionary to obtain access to this council is to participate in the mysterious plan of God. All this, of course, reflects Old Testament imagery (cf. 1 Kgs 22:19–22; Jb 1:6–12; Ps 89:8; Dn 7:9–10).

This paradox of transcendence and involvement plays itself out in Revelation through the figures of mediators. Between God and human beings are Christ, other angels, and John the visionary, who speaks with his churches—and with us (1:1–3; 17:7). In the other direction, angels take the prayers of people back to God (8:4). At times the pictures of this mediation depict almost a relay, by which the action of God moves from one point down to another until it reaches us and our prayers move upward in the same manner. Behind the imagery is the basic conception of God not acting alone but involving others in his divine activity.

A. Christology

Of all the mediators between the world and God, Jesus Christ is the principal one. After we exit from the council of God, it is Jesus who then addresses each of the seven churches to reprimand and to praise them (chapters 2–3). Again in the council room of God, it is Jesus as the lamb who moves God's plan into action by opening the sealed scroll (chapters 4–5).

(See exercises 2, 3.)

Revelation provides a very distinctive christology. Jesus carries some divine attributes. Descriptions of God such us "the alpha and the omega" (1:8; 21:6) are also said of Christ (22:13). Jesus appears with typically divine traits such as brilliant white hair (1:14; cf. Dn 7:9) or a roaring voice (1:15; cf. Ez 43:2). Divine titles and praises are directed to Christ (5:12–14). Yet for Jesus, God is also "his God" (1:6). Jesus always appears as carrying out God's plan, as second in the hierarchy between God and us.

The uniqueness of Jesus in this majestic picture, divine-like yet distinct and under God, is captured by the figure of Jesus as "the great angel." In chapter 19 we see the Messiah pictured as warrior angel:

> I saw the heavens opened and behold a white horse and the rider on it, called faithful and true, and he judged in justice and battled. And his eyes were like the flames of fire and on his head many diadems, having a written name which no one knew except himself. And he was wrapped in a cloak dipped in blood and his name was called "the word of God." And the armies in the heaven, clothed in clean white linen, followed him on white horses. And from his mouth there went out a sharp sword, to strike the nations, and he himself will shepherd them with an iron rod [Ps 2:9]. And he will stomp in the press of the fury of the anger of God the all mighty. And on his cloak and on his thigh is the name written, "King of kings and Lord of lords." (19:11–16)

The reference to Psalm 2 tells us the text is speaking of the Messiah, who for the author of Revelation is Jesus, depicted here as the cosmic victor over evil, leading the heavenly armies of angels like a general in battle-stained gear. The title "word of God" along with the "sharp sword" indicates that the author is relying on a text from Wisdom describing the angel of death from the tenth plague in Exodus:

> For when peaceful stillness compassed everything and the night in its swift course was half spent, your all-powerful word from heaven's royal throne bounded, a fierce warrior, into the doomed land, bearing the sharp sword of your inexorable decree. (Wis 19:15–16)

In the first vision of John, in which he is inaugurated into his role as a relay in the chain of revelation, the author hears and sees

Jesus, the one who was dead and is now living, with traits that suggest a mighty angel:

> I was lifted up in the Spirit on the Lord's day, and I heard behind me a great voice like a trumpet.... And turning I saw seven golden lamps and in the midst of the lamps one like a son of man, wearing an ankle-length robe, with a gold sash around his chest. His head and his hair were white as white wool and as snow, and his eyes like flames of fire...and his voice like the voice of many waters.... When I caught sight of him, I fell at his feet as though dead. He touched me with his right hand and said, "Do not be afraid. I am the first and the last and the living. And I was dead and behold I am living for all ages." (Rv 1:10, 12–15, 17–18)

For the author of Revelation, an angel tends to look "like a son of man" (14:14). In the book of Daniel, the human-like angel described in the vision of the Hellenistic wars is portrayed with the same traits we see in the Christ of Revelation:

> As I looked up, I saw a man dressed in linen with a belt of fine gold around his waist. His body was like chrysolite, his face shone like lightning, his eyes were like lamps of fire, his arms and feet looked like burnished bronze, and his voice sounded like the voice of a multitude.... And hearing the voice of his words I fainted my face to the ground. And behold his hand touched me and raised me to my knees and hands. And he said to me,... "Do not be afraid." (Dn 10:5–6)

This angel in Daniel is probably the same angel that was described in Dn 7:13 as "one like a son of man coming on the clouds of heaven," who is interpreted as God's people in a later stage of the Daniel story (7:27). In turn, the author of Daniel may have read the description of the glorious "one like a man" above the throne of God in the inaugural vision of Ezekiel as this great angel (see Ez 1:26–28).

In any case, this "great angel" figure appears later in Jewish writings as a saving or messianic figure. In the similitudes of *1 Enoch* 37–71, a writing probably contemporary with the New Testament, we read of a heavenly "son of man" as a heavenly agent of God. In *4 Ezra* 13 one "like the figure of a man" comes from the sea, destroys the enemies of God, and gathers a people of peace. The Jewish Christians of the second century, whom we know generally as the Ebionites, also saw Jesus as a "super-angel."

These descriptions all suggest that Christ in Revelation appears above all as a great angel of God. He shares in divine glory and attributes but is himself under God. The author has found a way of expressing the unique power and glory of Christ by drawing on contemporary Jewish theology with its interest in a great angel.

If we are correct in this interpretation of John's christology, then other descriptions of an incomparably glorious angel are probably also meant to be descriptions of Christ. For instance, the angel in chapter 10, the one with the "small scroll," is described in the following way:

> I saw another mighty angel come down from heaven wrapped in a cloud, with a halo around his head; his face was like the sun and his feet were like pillars of fire. In his hand he held a small scroll that had been opened. He placed his right foot on the sea and his left foot on the land, and then he cried out in a loud voice as a lion roars. (10:1–3)

Although never given a trait that would clearly identify him as Christ or the Messiah, this angel has many of the traits we saw in the description of Christ in chapter 1: "ruler," "coming with the clouds," "eyes like lamps of fire," and "voice like a multitude."

One image somewhat inconsistent with that of Jesus the great angel is the image of Jesus found briefly in chapter 12. This is the image of the child born to the mysterious mother who then, along with the rest of her children, is attacked by Satan, the dragon:

> And the dragon stood before the woman about to give birth, so that he might eat up her child when she would give birth. And she bore a son, a male who would shepherd all the nations with an iron rod. And her child was taken up to God and to his throne. (12:4–5)

The allusion to the Messiah king of Ps 2:9, shepherding with an iron rod, tells us that the author wants to describe the Messiah, whom he believes to be Jesus. Here, however, we have not an angel figure but a human child born of a woman.

The presence of this image of Jesus tells us that the author wants to identify the great angel with the human being we know from the Gospels. Although we have no moment of Jesus' glorification described in this writing, implicit in this christology may be that of Luke, who also combines the images of Jesus born of a woman (Luke 2:6) and Jesus exalted to divine glory (Acts 2:32–36).

B. Soteriology and Eschatology

(See exercises 4, 5.)

From the beginning of Revelation the focus on salvation is clear. The opening chapter quickly moves to the message of "Jesus Christ the faithful witness, the firstborn of the dead and ruler of the kings of the earth...who loves us and has freed us from our sins by his blood, who has made us into a kingdom of priests for his God and Father" (1:5–6).

1. Eschatological Salvation

Salvation as described in Revelation cannot be treated apart from eschatology. The salvation described in this book is cosmic. Ultimately it consists in nothing less than "a new heaven and a new earth" (21:1). This is a new reality, a new society in which God dwells with his people, in which all pain and sorrow are eliminated (21:3–4). Such is the vision that forms the last septenary of the book.

Moving toward this climax, Revelation presents us with other scenes of salvation, mostly connected with the seventh element in the various septenaries. Just before the seventh seal of the scroll is broken, Revelation describes the marking of the 144,000 elect and the great multitude of those who have survived and stand before God with robes washed by the blood of Christ (7:1–17). With the blowing of the seventh trumpet, we hear the loud proclamation from heaven:

> The kingdom of the world has become that of our Lord and that of his Christ, and he will reign unto the ages of ages. (11:15)

The seventh of the first septenary of visions (chapters 12–15) is a vision of victory:

> And I saw something like a sea of glass mixed with fire,
> and those were victorious over the beast and over his
> image and over the number of his name. They were stand-
> ing on the sea of glass holding the harps of God. And they
> sang the song of Moses the servant of God and the song of
> the lamb:
> Great and wonderful are your works
> Lord God the almighty.
> Just and true are your ways
> O King of the nations.
> Who will not fear you, Lord
> And glorify your name?
> For you alone are holy.
> All the nations will come and worship before you,
> For your just actions are revealed. (12:2–4)

Only in the septenary of the bowls does the seventh element
(16:17–21) continue the punishment. This bowl, however, leads to
the special development consisting of the ultimate destruction of
Babylon. It is here at the end of this development that we hear the
proclamation of salvation:

> Halleluia,
> The Lord began his reign
> Our God the almighty.
> Let us be glad and rejoice and give him glory
> For the wedding of the lamb has come
> and his wife has prepared herself. (19:6–7)

If we look for some chronological development in the repeated
portrayals of this salvation, we become very confused. In effect, the
sequencing here is purely poetic. It is there for the sake of enticing our
attention toward the ultimate triumph of God at the end. These are
not repeated acts of salvation but repeated portrayals of salvation.

2. Salvation through Conflict

The message we get from these portrayals is that of God's
power to conquer evil, God's power to save—but a salvation that
comes through conflict. The victory is cosmic, but so is the conflict.
Part of the act of saving from evil is letting evil run amok.

When we see references to Jesus' role in this salvation we see
echoes here also of the conflict. We are "purchased" by his blood

(5:9). The victorious crowd washed their robes in Jesus' blood (7:14). Victory comes by "the blood of the lamb" (12:11). Jesus is the victorious lamb "slain" even in heaven (5:6). Praise of the lamb continues to refer to him as "slain" (5:9, 12).

The image of the slain lamb could be rooted either in the Old Testament picture of the Passover lamb (Exodus 12) or in that of the Suffering Servant led like a lamb to slaughter (Isaiah 53). If the image is that of the Passover lamb, then Revelation is probably picking up on the "sacrifice" soteriology that we saw in Paul. If the image is that of the servant, then the suffering and death of the lamb appear as a sort of vicarious suffering. He suffers in our place.

Perhaps connected with this "slaying" of the lamb is the "slaying" of the "martyrs," who are told to be patient "until their number is fulfilled by their fellow servants and their brothers who were going to be killed just as they were" (6:11). This description implies that the death of martyrs advances the script. Until some number of martyrs is "fulfilled" the suffering on earth must wait for the glorious victory. In some way their deaths brings about salvation.

3. Salvation as Rescue and Transformation

If we now compare the major parts of the book with each other, we see two different views of salvation. Parts 2 and 3 (chapters 4–22), dealing with the heavenly visions, portray salvation as the rescue of good people from an evil environment. There is no explicit portrayal of a rescue of people from sin, that is, no transformation of bad people into good people. The grouping into bad and good is given; the scenes then describe the suffering of the good people from evil surroundings and finally their rescue from those surroundings. The marking of the elect is based on the fact that these people are already good people and need to be shielded from the punishing judgment of God (chapter 7).

The image of a "book of life" in particular emphasizes salvation as rescue. The image describes a grouping of the good from the bad, those saved from those condemned. Enrollment in this book is required for entering the heavenly Jerusalem (21:27). Those not enrolled are thrown into "the pool of fire" (20:15). This book was written "from the foundation of the world" and therefore is the work of God himself (13:8; 17:8). In this section of Revelation, therefore, salvation as the enabling of a person to become good—what Paul would call "justification"—is totally a matter of God's activity accomplished even before creation.

Somewhat in tension with this image of the "book of life" are the images we have seen of "the blood" of Christ (5:9; 12:11) and of the "redemption" or "purchase" accomplished by Christ (5:9; 14:3–4). The allusion here is to "justification" occurring in and through history, namely, the crucifixion of Jesus. As with the image of "the book of life," however, these allusions to the crucifixion deal with God's act in the past, transforming human beings before any response on their part is possible. The role of God is given such emphasis that little room is left for human responsibility.

In the first part of the book (chapters 1–3)—which does not include the image of the "book of life"—we see stress on the ethical sense of salvation. The churches to whom the seven letters are addressed are called to a life of fidelity. Those who have failed in some way are called to repentance. Those who are succeeding are praised and encouraged to keep up the good work. It is in this first part that we read the description of Christ who "freed us from our sins" (1:5). The focus is now on the transformation of Christians from sinners to good people. Human responsibility—at least in a "maintenance" role—now appears in full color.

In this "ethical" or "pastoral" section of Revelation, however, God calls churches—not individuals—either to repentance or to perseverance in good behavior. Stress is more on the social patterns of good and evil than on individual decisions. The community is reproached for the loss of its "first love" or for its lukewarmness. Some individuals within the community may have been much more saintly, but the pattern within the community, the reality larger than the individuals and which often dominates the individuals, needs reform. Ultimately the call is to individuals to do something, but the concern is church life.

The superimposition of this "pastoral" first part over the apocalyptic second and third parts shows some intention to interrelate the two ideas of salvation. Revelation provides no systematic explanation of how the two levels interrelate. Perhaps no explanation is possible. Uniting the major literary sections within the unity of Revelation, the organization of this book simply proclaims the unity of the ethical and the apocalyptic.

By placing the two levels together, Revelation invites us to see each with a view to the other. We are to look behind the ethical sense of salvation and see the cosmic and apocalyptic. What on the surface is a matter of human decision is on a deeper level the manifestation of a cosmic clash between the forces of evil and good. Human ethical responsibility becomes intensely serious.

Conversely, the apocalyptic picture with all its divine determinations now appears as a form of exhortation. The pictures of coming catastrophes and triumphs are not simply a matter of tantalizing our curiosity about the future. Like the prophetic announcements of the Old Testament, these pictures are meant to function as encouragement for repentance and perseverance.

III. Theological Reflections

1. Salvation through Suffering

The book of Revelation is thought-provoking because it leaves so many questions unanswered. If the book is an inspired reflection on the plan of God to bring about a glorious triumph over evil after a period of conflict and suffering, the book leaves the question we have seen before—only now all the more urgent—Why the conflict and suffering? We are told to meditate on the presence of evil forces—the beasts, the dragon—but we are told that God allows this presence. We are told of ensuing punishments by God that devastate the earth. God's elect are protected to some degree. But we hear the anguish of the martyrs, How long? Life on earth, according to Revelation, is not a good life. It's horrible.

When we studied the Gospel of Mark, we saw the same anguish on the lips of Jesus himself. The author dealt with the mystery by leaving it mystery and simply stating, "It must be." The suffering of the Son of Man was according to some divine necessity, and we as followers of Jesus had to accept the cross.

Does Revelation offer anything beyond the trusting acceptance of God's "mysterious plan," the decree of God's heavenly council? Like Mark 13, the book of Revelation tells us to look to the future victory of God. More than any other writing of the New Testament, however, Revelation emphasizes the power and seriousness of sin. The book focuses the mystery of suffering on the mystery of God allowing sin—if even for a temporary period. God's decision to conquer sin is clear in this book, but God chooses victory through conflict, through the mysterious permission for sin to retain its power. The victory is thus both easy and not easy. It is easy for God. It is difficult for us.

In this way the power and seriousness of sin are revealed. This is a message for a generation that tends to trivialize sin, to see it as

unimportant "if it doesn't hurt anybody" or to see it simply as a
"social or psychological disorder," thus confined to those immediately affected—much like any disease. Revelation portrays sin as
cosmic disorder affecting all the earth, even nonhuman parts,
indeed all the universe, including the world of spirits. Revelation
portrays sin as affecting God.

Ultimately the faith-filled interpretation of suffering and conflict sees these evil moments as also moments of salvation. According to Mark and Paul we are saved by the cross as well as the
resurrection. Revelation as a book about salvation speaks of the evil
moments on earth as clearly under God's saving control. Thus, not
only are the moments of triumph moments of salvation, so are also
the moments of suffering. The scroll is a scroll about salvation. The
moments of devastation and conflict are part of the scroll no less
than the descriptions of the heavenly Jerusalem and the elimination of all tears. The answer does not satisfy our quest for understanding; it simply directs our hearts to hold above all to the unity
of the scroll, the unity of God's saving, albeit mysterious, script.

2. The Signs of the Times

The vivid sequencing of the eschatological events in Revelation has moved believers for centuries to find some way of connecting the historical events of their days with the signs of Revelation, if
not for predicting the future at least for understanding some coordi-
nation of the confusing events of history with the divine plan, seeing
God dealing with us not just in the interiority of our hearts but also
on the public stage of history. Revelation 12 speaks of the "great
signs" that appeared in heaven (12:1, 3), signs of the apocalyptic
battle of good and evil. The final numbered septenary of divine punishments is called also "a great and marvelous sign in the heaven."
In the back of our heads is the reproach of Jesus to those who predict future weather by observing the heavens but cannot understand "the signs of the times" (Mt 16:2–3).

Christians have misused the book of Revelation in their
attempts to predict the future and identify their enemies with the
enemies of God. Yet Revelation is about God's dealings with his universe, God's plan to save through society and history. John read the
political events of his day, the persecutions of Rome (chapter 17),
the monopolization of economic power (13:16–17), as part of this
plan. Is it totally out of order to search for an understanding of "our
day" in the light of Revelation?

A theme of Revelation is that of the sequence of periods of suffering and of salvation. For instance, the "thousand years of peace" (20:1–3) is a vivid image of a period when salvation on earth appears as more than a fleeting foretaste of the final victory. Periods of sin and periods of salvation appear as the ebb and flow of a divinely ordained tide.

Seeing God's saving grace in this historical, social perspective—in contrast to the momentary helps of interior decision making—leads Christians to interpret history. "The times" of God's creation are not meandering flows of temporality drifting aimlessly through the galaxies. They are "seasons" defined by colors and hues of suffering and comfort. They endure for a while and then are replaced—not in an endless cycle but in the directed movement toward the kingdom. "The times" of God's creation are opportunities, crafted by God especially for a particular "generation," as if to underline the unique love God has for every generation. These are the unique opportunities that tell a generation not to look back to "the way it always was," not to look ahead to some "inevitable fate," but to look to the present gift that makes this generation special.

As in all of his dealings with us, God seems to want to remain hidden in ambiguity. His epoch-making gifts are likewise hidden from the natural eye, perceived only in faith. Faith is always an inner strength and ability, but does seem to direct our hearts to what is outside, where it can find confirmation and focus in realities we meet in life. These are the "signs" that confirm our faith. We do not see God, but we see the blessings, the hidden "miracles" that pop up in our life to assure us of his love. We do not see his Holy Spirit, but we see the holiness of the "saints" we meet or learn of. Of course, without the faith in our hearts, the "miracles" are simply accidental coincidences; the holiness of the "saints," merely personality quirks. Without faith even the empty tomb of Jesus was merely evidence of body snatching.

So we ask with the book of Revelation about "the signs of the times." Can we read of the international events of the past decades and see a special gift from God? Could the collapse of the Communist empire have a theological significance? Can we see in the sudden shrinking of a celibate clergy in the active ministry an opportunity from God crafted for this generation? Nothing compels this interpretation. We are also aware how we can project our personal desires into some vast plan of God that does not exist. But the book of Revelation repeats and repeats the admonition, "Whoever has ears ought to hear what the Spirit says to the churches."

EXERCISES

Exercise 1. (see page 364): Read the story of the ten plagues of Egypt in Exodus 7–11. Compare these plagues to the punishments connected with the seven seals, the seven trumpets, and the seven bowls in Revelation. What similarities do you find? Which series comes closest to the Exodus images?

Exercise 2. (see page 365): Cull from the book of Revelation the descriptions of Jesus. What general picture of Jesus do you receive? How does this picture compare with that of the Synoptic Gospels? With that of the Gospel of John?

Exercise 3. (see page 365): How is Jesus related to God the Father in this book? Is he equal to God? Does he have any of God's functions or attributes?

Exercise 4. (see page 369): Develop Revelation's theology of salvation by noting those scenes where God does something good for his people or where somebody cheers over something good God has done.

Exercise 5. (see page 369): Describe the characteristics of the good people in this book. What makes them good? What behavior are they called upon to practice?

REVIEW QUESTIONS

1. What are the general characteristics of apocalyptic literature? What biblical examples of this literature do we have?

2. What is the overall signficance of "the heavens" in the book of Revelation? What is the significance of "the scroll"? How do these symbols fit into the general apocalyptic concern of this book?

3. What events in the history of Rome form possible backdrops for dating the writing of Revelation?

4. How is the Book of Revelation structured? What clues exist in the text for its organization? Describe the major parts and overall progression of the book.

5. How and where in Revelation does Jesus function as a mediator between God and humanity?

6. How is salvation portrayed in Revelation? What are its principal traits? Who is the principal agent of salvation? What are people saved from?

FOR FURTHER REFLECTION AND DISCUSSION

1. Where today are good and evil most intensely in conflict? What could be our role in this conflict?

2. What are the signs of our times? What special opportunities of grace is God apparently offering us today?

Conclusion

In the first chapter of our study, we noted a serious problem in the method of our investigation. We wanted to analyze a sacred text, yet we needed to distance ourselves from the truth claim of the text and investigate what the words meant in the historical context of the authors and first readers. We wanted to understand a book of faith without using our faith as a major interpretive perspective. Granted that such an approach was only the first step in a larger journey, we needed to pause before the question of truth and respond first to the question of meaning.

The question now arises, has our study preserved the power of this text to raise the question of truth? Can we now ask how we must respond to the meaning of the New Testament as a message that summons us? Can we read the text as life-giving, as the Word of God offering us God's love? Can we read the text *spiritually?* Since such a spiritual reading is the purpose of a sacred text, something is basically wrong with our method if it has closed the door to such a reading.

In fact a significant segment of Christians find our method offensive. In their uncompromising commitment to the truth of scripture, Christian fundamentalists look on such a secular, scientific approach to the Bible as blocking the spiritual and life-giving power of the Bible. While formulated in very diverse ways, the objections to the historical-critical method of biblical studies generally focus on three aspects constantly accented by this method: (1) the apparent errors in the teaching of the biblical texts, (2) the thoroughly human character of the Bible, and (3) the wide divergence of positions of biblical authors. In the mind of the fundamentalist, these aspects, highlighted as they are by the historical-critical method, prevent a believer from a faith-filled and reverent reading of the Bible as the sacred Word of God.

In this concluding chapter we can use this challenge of

fundamentalism as way of reviewing the broad lines of our whole study and of asking the question about the openness of our method to a spiritual reading of the Bible.

I. Errors in the New Testament

The prism of the historical-critical method displays several statements of the New Testament that should be regarded as errors in some sense of the word. According to the historical-critical method, we should reject the accuracy of the statement in the Pastoral Epistles and in Ephesians that the writer is Paul the Apostle. Such an identification gives us wrong information. According to the historical-critical method, Jesus in Mark connects the destruction of Jerusalem with the eschatological return of the Son of Man as two events that immediately follow each other. This connection did not happen. According to this method, Gospel writers changed the descriptions of events in the life of Jesus to such an extent that the stories no longer describe what historically happened.

Fundamentalists generally resist these conclusions by rejecting the evidence as insufficient, by allegorizing its meaning, or dealing with it by some other form of mental gymnastics. ("This generation" means "world epoch," and maybe Jesus walked on the water twice and gave us two Lord's Prayers.) Historical criticism urges rather that we accept these expressions for what they are, descriptions arising out of erroneous historical knowledge or even attempts to deceive others.

To a large degree, as we saw in chapter 1, the problem of errors is resolved by an understanding of the literary forms in the New Testament. Truth is expressed in many ways. As a literary form, *Gospel* does not express historical truth as a detailed correspondence between the narrative statement and the event to which it refers. *Pseudo-epigraphy* is a form that attempts to make a dead hero speak again to a new situation. *Prophetic exhortation* involves hyperbole and tentative probing—perhaps even pious fraud.

More important, as we also noted, our faith rests on "that truth which God wanted put into the sacred writings for the sake of our salvation" (*Dei Verbum,* #11). We are talking about truths about God and salvation. Only as saving, only as mediating a communion with God, is this theological information infallible. In effect, this aspect "as saving," provides for an unevenness within scripture. The aspect of saving truth can be more intense in some texts than in others. Some descriptions in the New Testament may be central and others peripheral to the truth about God and salvation. The proclamation of Jesus' resurrection appears central. The naming of a text's author, peripheral.

How can this distinction be made? Clearly not according to the norms of empirical verification. The historical-critical method cannot recognize "saving truth" as such. To make this recognition, a reader must bring faith presuppositions to the text.

Bringing ecclesial or communitarian faith presuppositions to a text reduces the risks of subjectivism and illusion. Thus, by the fourth century the Christian church considered the rigorism of Hebrews (no repentance after a fall from faith) as peripheral. Implicitly it recognized as central the Lucan picture of God, the God who races out to meet his prodigal son while he is still a long way off. Similarly, most mainline churches today refuse to read the apocalyptic messages of either Mark or the book of Revelation apart from the more central pictures of realized eschatology in the New Testament.

The recognition of unevenness of inerrancy in the New Testament and the Bible as a whole is not an attempt to carve up scripture into what is inerrant and what is not, searching for the so-called canon within the canon. Every word of scripture can be accepted in principle as touched by the aspect of saving truth—although we may not always know how. We can distinguish, however, the intensity of an aspect as we read through scripture, relate individual descriptions to larger themes and eventually to the whole of scripture, and read with the sensitivity of an ecclesial community.

We do not disregard the rigorism of Hebrews. It is a reminder of the seriousness of our faith commitment. We do not disregard the Marcan link between the war of A.D. 70 and the return of Jesus. The message of suffering and mystery contained in that link is a reminder to all Christians of our need to follow Jesus to Calvary. The peripheral elements are like the experiences of an artist that give occasion to great art. They must be recognized and if possible echoed in the one who would appreciate that art and understand its message.

II. The Human Character of the Bible

This issue of biblical inerrancy and de facto errors in the New Testament are part of the larger context of the thoroughly human character of the texts. Modern biblical scholarship insists on the human character of the New Testament and the Bible as a whole. Only as such can it be the object of empirical investigation. This scientific method focuses on the limited perspectives of the biblical texts and the historical contingencies that gave rise to them.

This scientific method can examine a person's or a group's faith in God, but it cannot examine God. This scientific method may examine a faith in a miracle but it cannot examine a miracle as such. In a scientific reading we hear no longer an account of the resurrection of Jesus but rather an account of the faith some people had in this resurrection. The writer describing this faith may have intended to point the reader to the object of this faith, but the historical-critical method focuses exclusively on the pointer.

Many of us would prefer to view the miracle. Miracles show God's presence in a dramatic way. In a miracle a gap appears. Something moves from A to B, from sickness to health, without any natural link between the two. In that gap we can point to the presence of God.

What we perhaps forget is the way God can act just as powerfully in and through natural dynamisms. A story is told of a devout person dying of cancer who had a revelation from God. In that revelation God said he would restore that person to health. The next day a radiologist approached the patient to offer radiation therapy. The person politely refused. An oncologist came in and spoke of an effective chemotherapy. The patient explained that he was going to get better. A surgeon then came by to offer an operation. Again the patient declined. Shortly afterward that patient died of the cancer and at his glorious interview reproached God for not keeping his promise. God responded, "But I sent you my best physicians!"

God is a creator. We often forget this. God produces the very being of creatures. He acts from within giving creatures their very status as independent realities. Their actions—even their free actions woven together in a fabric of history—have their independent status precisely by their dependence on God's creative power. God is in control of the free and contingent action. This activity of God in creation is not as evident as his activity in the miraculous, but it is no less powerful and effective. An understanding of creation allows us to seek and perceive the most intense influence of God in the events of this world of history.

If we choose to study the biblical texts in the confluence of probing choices and historical accidents that gave rise to the texts, we are not precluding God's activity. We are in fact studying this divine activity, but as hidden within the autonomy of the creature. God is no less powerfully active in Paul's early education—which left such an important mark on his letters—than in his miraculous vocation and conversion. Nor, decades later when Luke freely developed and expressed his faith in Paul's conversion, was God less powerfully active.

The dissatisfying aspect of this focus on the human aspect of the New Testament is the ambiguity of the subject matter. A nonbeliever may look at Paul and his early education and see nothing divine at all. The nonbeliever may look at Luke's description of Paul's conversion and see a mistaken recollection of some natural event—anything from a psychological breakdown to surviving a bolt of lightning. The action of God is hidden. It can be overlooked. It is susceptible to many interpretations, and nothing compels us to recognize God.

Why does God deal with us in this mode of ambiguity? I do not think we can give any satisfying answer to that question. But Christian faith centers on a particular union of the divine and the human, which becomes an extraordinary analogy to the mystery of the divine and the human in scripture. The Second Vatican Council refers explicitly to the analogy of the incarnation to describe the words of God in the Bible:

> The Words of God, expressed in human language, have been made like human discourse, just as of old the Word of the eternal Father, when he took to Himself the weak flesh of humanity, became like other men. (*Dei Verbum,* #13)

The point of the analogy is to probe the capacity of human reality to express the divine. The words and convictions of Jesus were human words and convictions but precisely as such expressed the words and convictions of God. The divine truth of Jesus' word took form within the limits of the all too human son of Mary. The Gospel of Mark describes these limits as stumbling blocks which Jesus' contemporaries found in him (Mark 6:3).

In the church's classical formulation of the incarnation, the human actions of Jesus are the actions of God, revealing himself in history. Although it insists on the uniqueness of this hypostatic union, this traditional formulation of the incarnation implies the radical possibility of human nature to express the divine. Furthermore, the New Testament identification of Christ with the believing community (1 Cor 12:27; Mt 25:31–46; Jn 15:1–8) almost demands an analogy between Christ and the community of disciples.

The composite picture of Jesus developed in the New Testament likewise warns us against any rigid separation between divine revelation and human response in faith. The New Testament picture of Jesus arises out of two broad strokes. On the one hand, Jesus is the ultimate revelation of God (Jn 14:9; Heb 7:24–26) and of God's love (Rom 5:8). On the other hand, Jesus is the ultimate response to that revelation (Jn 4:34; Heb 7:24–26) in loving obedience (Phil 2:8). Precisely in his response to the love of God, Jesus reveals that love. In the one person of Jesus, divine revelation and faithful response become one.

The image of Jesus thus suggests an inner unity between divine disclosure and human response in faith. God's actions toward human beings and the human response in faith form a unified revelation event. Divine word and religion are inseparable. As the record of the Christian faith and religion, the New Testament is by that fact a record of God's revelation.

III. Diversity in the New Testament

When we read the New Testament with careful attention to each author, the diversity of positions explodes in front of us. Each author has a different faith in Jesus. Some differences appear simply as matters of emphasis. Other differences are important and put the authors in real tensions with each other. For Mark, Jesus is a human being with mysterious power but who suffers and dies feeling abandoned by God. For John, Jesus is God. He becomes flesh and is crucified but is essentially divine and eternal. For Luke, Jesus is Son of God because he was miraculously conceived and gloriously triumphant after death but essentially a human being. We have traced similar differences regarding the authors' faith in the redeeming death of Jesus and in the final return of Jesus at the end of the world. Luke avoids any view of the death of Jesus as directly redemptive. Paul insists that we are saved by the blood of Jesus. In the light of these differences we must hesitate to speak of any one New Testament faith or theology. Many faiths and theologies appear in this collection of texts.

At this point one could ask, Should we bother trying to find a unity? Can we not just leave the writings in their diversity? Our culture is fairly comfortable with irresolvable diversities even in matters of profound values. We have become very skeptical of the great philosophical systems that purported to bring all things into a coherent whole. When we read the New Testament as a guide to faith, however, we are not asking the political questions of how many people with different values can live together. We are asking whether our faith holds together or not. Even if Mark and John personally disagreed with each other, thought the other was wrong, and found it impossible to convince the other to change his mind, we must ask about the coherence of *what* they wrote. We are given both Gospels in the same canon. Does that canon cohere?

A deep drive in our hearts seeks unity. This drive may start with the simple perception of a horizon around our field of vision, a horizon that allows us to situate what we see in a kind of grid where things can all relate to one another. We meet new experiences and intellectual challenges by trying to situate them in a kind of spiritual horizon. When a new thing does not fit, eventually we will do one of two things: either we will reject the new thing, or we will modify our spiritual horizon. If someone referred to the beautiful red print in this book, you would most likely dismiss that person as having bad color vision. If someone even rudely asserted that you needed a stronger deodorant, however, you most likely would re-examine that general view of your hygiene which you had so comfortably held up to the moment of the jolting remark. The point is you will either reject the new idea as wrong or you modify the interpretive horizon so that it can fit with the rest of your knowledge.

Somehow the early Christians saw that New Testament writings belong together. The canon implies this underlying unity. Somehow the early Christians saw a consistency in these accounts. Assuming that these early Christians were not completely ignorant of the inconsistencies which we have studied, can we repeat this early Christian synthesis? How can we today understand this unity?

When Mark describes Jesus as a limited human being and John describes him as the all-powerful word of God, we confront the challenge of pulling the two positions together without detriment to either. As we said in chapter 13, our desire for coherence generally places John's Gospel in a controlling position. Thus, starting with John's Gospel, Christians will describe Jesus in philosophical terms as a divine person who assumes a human nature. Christians started with John's Gospel because its "high" christology made the furthest-reaching claim to truth. Once that claim is accepted, attempts can be made to integrate the more restricted statements about Jesus as a real human being. By declaring Jesus to be God, this Gospel implies the divinity of Jesus in any account—even those speaking only of his humanity. The Jesus who looked weak and limited in Mark's Gospel is the God of John's Gospel.

Yet in a real sense the controlling position is reciprocal. Mark's Gospel tells us that Jesus was a human being—in the way he thought, in the way he loved, in the way he wore out. Christians today would do well to see Mark's insistence when they read the Gospel of John. Without ceasing to be a divine person and without becoming a second person, Jesus is a human person. If the divine Word comes into this world "from above," this Word comes by a human person uniting himself to God in such a way that he is one person with God. Incarnation can be expressed "from below." Furthermore, if to see Jesus is to see the Father (Jn 14:9), then the Father begins to look like the forsaken convict crucified on Calvary (Mk 15:34). If we read John's Gospel in the light of Mark, we see God capable of suffering and dying in his love for us. Theology develops also as anthropology.

By these reflections we have left the particular interpretive horizons of each Gospel and have developed a larger horizon within which both can speak—to us and to each other. That larger horizon is theology, an attempt to get to the truth of the matter. We are no longer simply describing a historical faith. We are now trying to touch the reality of God and his gifts to us. The diversity encountered in the New Testament has forced us to do this—if we accept the need in principle for coherence, at least the need to search for it. By this search we join the writers of the New Testament in the very drive that moved them to write.

We must be careful, however. Theology as this larger horizon is *heuristic,* a programmatic grid for discovery. It is not a vision of things. The synthesis of the biblical theologies remains a movement, not an achievement. The horizon of theology may be simply an openness to the unknown, to a kind of mystery that lies outside our smaller horizons with their materially filled content. Spiritual and theological growth demands an *openness* to truth as the reality that lies within God's infinite horizon—even if we do not see that reality.

The early Christians probably did not see how Mark's and John's views could fit together, but they knew that they could commit their lives to both views and their faith did not split apart. In holding on to both views, the early Christians felt moved toward some truth of Christ or salvation not described by either author.

The tension and resolution resulting from such divergent theological positions are parallel to a problem discussed in high school physics. It is called "vector resolution." Imagine a wagon drawn by two unyoked horses, each pulling the wagon in different directions with different strengths. Figure 33 illustrates an example of conflicting force vectors and their resolution.

The single-line arrows represent the force and direction of each horse (A and B): the longer the arrow, the greater the force. The wagon will in fact not follow either horse, not even that of the greater strength. It will move in a direction between the two arrows, a direction that can be calculated in physics by completing the parallelogram. That direction is represented by the double-line arrow (X). (This vector resolution was very important for moving a barge through a canal where the horses could not directly pull in front of the barge.)

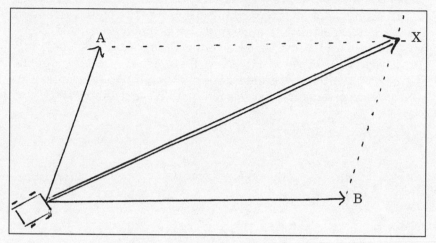

Figure 33. **Vector Resolution.**

The illustration could apply to the diverse positions we find in the New Testament. Mark pulls us in one direction; John, in quite another. If we hang on to both, we move in yet a third direction, somehow between the two, but described by neither. We have no clear picture of either that direction or the goal of that direction. If we let go of either position described in the biblical text, we fail to attain that goal. Our faith holds that the positions are not contradictory. If that were the case, we would be pulled apart like the victims of quartering in merry olde England. We believe in the ultimate compatibility of the diverse positions. That compatibility, however, is not seen. It is only attested by the canon and the vitality of a church holding to that canon.

In our attempt to combine the historical-critical method with a perspective of faith, we have in fact contacted the intense creativity of the New Testament, constantly adapting and reinterpreting, even re-presenting old authors after their death to allow the *apostolic* revelation to continue. Nothing in the New Testament suggests the need "to close the canon" after the death of the last apostle.

If our Christian faith and theology are based on the message of the New Testament, should it not also be styled after the form of the

New Testament? We may need to keep the New Testament canon closed. This is simply a way of acknowledging the importance of those generations closest to the historical Jesus. However, attempts to use the New Testament as an instrument to whip believers into line, to crush innovation, to squash the revelations of God in the present—all this appears very unbiblical.

As a model and standard for our faith, the New Testament stands out especially as a community of people writing to one another with an intense sense of connectedness and responsibility. As viewed in modern study, the New Testament represents a public faith, shared with others and related to contemporary events, constantly reexpressing itself as opened to an inexpressible Mystery.

Appendix 1

Matthew and Mark Parallels

Matthew

1:1–17 Genealogy
1:18–2:23 Infancy narrative
3:1–17 Baptism of Jesus
4:1–11 Temptation of Jesus
4:12–22 Call of first disciples
4:23–25 Summary: teaching
    and healing

5–7 Discourse: Sermon on the
    Mount
8:1–4 Cure of leper
8:5–9:35 Nine other miracles
9:9–17 Call of Matthew and
    question of fasting
10 Discourse: apostles named
    and sent
11:2–19 John the Baptist
    and Jesus
11:20–24 Lament over lake
    towns
11:25–30 Hymn of jubilation
12:1–14 Controversy with
    Pharisees
12:15–21 Summary: crowds
    and cures

Mark

1:1–11 Baptism of Jesus
1:12–13 Temptation of Jesus
1:14–20 Call of first disciples
1:21–28 Teaching and healing at
    Capernaum
1:29–31 Cure of Peter's
    mother-in-law
1:32–39 A number of cures

1:40–45 Cure of leper
2:1–12 Cure of Paralytic
2:13–22 Call of Levi and
    question of fasting

2:33–3:6 Controversy with
    Pharisees
3:7–12 Summary:
    crowds and cures
3:13–19 Call of the Twelve

3:20–21 Relatives set off for
Jesus

12:22–32 Beelzebul controversy
12:33–45 Controversy with
Pharisees

3:22–30 Beelzebul controversy

12:46–50 Relatives arrive
13:1–52 Discourse: kingdom
parables

3:31–35 Relatives arrive
4:1–34 Parables

4:35–5:43 Four miracles

13:53–58 Rejection at Nazareth

6:1–6 Rejection at Nazareth
6:7–13 Sending of Twelve

14:1–12 Herod and John the
Baptist
14:13–21 Feeding the 5000
14:22–33 Crossing lake;
walking on water

6:14–29 Herod and John the
Baptist
6:30–44 Feeding the 5000
6:45–52 Crossing lake; walking
on water

14:34–36 Sick at Gennesaret
15:1–20 Controversy with
Pharisees

6:53–56 Sick at Gennesaret
7:1–23 Controversy with
Pharisees

15:21–28 To Tyre and Sidon
15:29–31 Cures in Galilee

7:24–30 To Tyre and Sidon
7:31–37 Healing of deaf in Galilee

15:32–38 Feeding the 4000
15:39 Crossing to Magadan
16:1–4 Controversy with
Pharisees

8:1–9 Feeding the 4000
8:10 Crossing to Dalmanutha
8:11–13 Controversy with
Pharisees

16:5–12 Loaves understood

8:14–21 Loaves not understood
8:22 Crossing to Bethsaida
8:23–26 Healing of blind man

16:13–20 Peter's confession
16:21–28 First passion
prediction

8:27–30 Peter's confession
8:31–38 First passion
prediction

17:1–8 Transfiguration
17:9–13 Elijah question
17:14–20 Healing of possessed
boy

9:1–8 Transfiguration
9:9–13 Elijah question
9:14–29 Healing of possessed
boy

17:22–23 Second passion
prediction

9:30–32 Second passion
prediction

17:24–27 Peter and the Temple
tax
18 Discourse: apostolic
community

9:33–50 Instructions for
disciples

19:1–2 Journey beyond Jordan
19:3–12 Pharisees on divorce
19:13–15 The children
19:16–30 Rich young man
20:1–16 Parable of laborers

10:1 Journey beyond Jordan
10:2–12 Pharisees on divorce
10:13–16 The children
10:17–31 Rich young man

20:17–19 Third passion prediction

10:32–34 Third passion prediction

20:20–28 Ambition of Zebedee's sons

10:35–45 Ambition of Zebedee's sons

20:29–34 Cure of two blind beggars

10:46–53 Cure of blind beggar

21:1–11 Entrance into Jerusalem

11:1–11 Entrance into Jerusalem

11:12–14 Cursing of fig tree

21:12–17 Cleansing Temple

11:15–19 Cleansing Temple

21:18–22 Cursing and withering of fig tree

11:20–25 Withering of fig tree

21:23–27 Authority of Jesus

11:27–33 Authority of Jesus

21:28–32 Parable of two sons

21:33–46 Parable of vineyard tenants

12:1–12 Parable of vineyard tenants

22:1–14 Parable of wedding feast

22:15–22 Pharisees on tax

12:13–17 Pharisees on tax

22:23–33 Sadducees on marriage in marriage in heaven

12:18–27 Sadducees on marriage in heaven

22:34–40 The greatest commandment

12:28–34 The greatest commandment

22:41–23:39 Attack on Pharisees

12:35–40 Attack on Pharisees

12:41–44 Widow's mite

24:1–49 Discourse: end of world

13:1–37 Discourse: end of world

24:45–25:46 Parables of the end

26–27 Passion and death of Jesus

14 Passion and death of Jesus

28 Empty tomb and appearances

15 Empty tomb

Mark and Luke Parallels

Mark

Luke

1–2 Infancy narrative

1:1–11 Baptism of Jesus

3:1–22 Baptism of Jesus and John's ethical preaching

3:23–38 Genealogy

1:12–13 Temptation of Jesus

4:1–13 Temptation of Jesus

4:14–30 Rejection at Nazareth

1:14–20 Call of first disciples

4:31–44 Day at Capernaum

1:21–39 Day at Capernaum

5:1–11 Call of first disciples and catch of fish

1:40–45 Cure of leper

5:12–16 Cure of leper

2:1–3:6 Controversy with Pharisees	5:17–6:11 Controversy with Pharisees
3:7–12 Summary: crowds and cures	6:12–16 Call of the Twelve
3:13–19 Call of the Twelve	6:17–19 Crowds and cures
	6:20–49 Sermon on the Plain
	7:1–10 Centurion's slave
	7:11–17 Widow of Nain
	7:18–23 John's disciples' question
	7:24–35 Jesus on John the Baptist
	7:36–50 The woman with the ointment
	8:1–3 The ministering women
3:20–21 Relatives set off for Jesus	
3:22–30 Beelzebul controversy	(cf. 11:14–23 Beelzebul controversy)
3:31–35 Relatives arrive	
4:1–34 Parables	8:4–18 Parables
	8:19–21 Relatives arrive
4:35–5:43 Four miracles	8:22–56 Four miracles
6:1–6 Rejection at Nazareth	
6:7–13 Sending of the Twelve	9:1–6 Sending of the Twelve
6:14–29 Herod and John the Baptist	9:7–9 Herod and John the Baptist
6:30–44 Feeding the 5000	9:10–17 Feeding the 5000
6:45–52 Crossing lake; walking on water	
6:53–56 Sick at Gennesaret	
7:1–23 Controversy with Pharisees	
7:24–30 To Tyre and Sidon	
7:31–37 Healing of deaf in Galilee	
8:1–9 Feeding the 4000	[Great Lucan Omission]
8:10 Crossing to Dalmanutha	
8:11–13 Controversy with Pharisees	
8:14–21 Loaves not understood	
8:22 Crossing to Bethsaida	
8:23–26 Healing of blind man	
8:27–30 Peter's confession	9:18 Peter's Confession
8:31–38 First passion prediction	9:21–27 First passion prediction
9:1–8 Transfiguration	9:28–36 Transfiguration
9:9–13 Elijah question	
9:14–29 Healing of possessed boy	9:37–43 Healing of possessed boy
9:30–32 Second passion prediction	9:44–45 Second passion prediction
9:33–50 Instructions for disciples	9:46–50 Instructions for disciples
10:1 Journey beyond Jordan	9:51–18:14 Journey to Jerusalem
	[Great Lucan Addition]
10:2–12 Pharisees on divorce	
10:13–16 The children	18:15–17 The children

10:17–31 Rich young man

10:32–34 Third passion prediction

10:35–45 Ambition of Zebedee's
    sons

10:46–53 Cure of blind beggar

11:1–11 Entrance into Jerusalem

11:12–14 Cursing of fig tree

11:15–19 Cleansing Temple

11:20–25 Withering of fig tree

11:27–33 Authority of Jesus

12:1–12 Parable of vineyard
    tenants

12:13–17 Pharisees on tax

12:18–27 Sadducees on marriage
    in heaven heaven

12:28–34 The greatest
    commandment

12:35–40 Attack on Pharisees

12:41–44 Widow's mite

13:1–37 Discourse: end of world

14 Passion and death of Jesus

15 Empty tomb

18:18–30 Rich young man

18:31–34 Third passion prediction

(cf. 22:24–27 Ambition of apostles)

18:35–43 Cure of blind beggar

19:1–10 Zacchaeus in Jericho

19:11–27 Parable of pounds

19:28–40 Entrance into Jerusalem

19:41–44 Lament over Jerusalem

(cf. 13:6–9 The barren fig tree)

19:45–48 Cleansing Temple

20:1–8 Authority of Jesus

20:9–19 Parable of vineyard tenants

20:20–26 Pharisees on tax

20:27–40 Sadducees on marriage in

20:41–47 Attack on Pharisees

21:1–4 Widow's mite

21:5–33 Discourse: end of world

21:34–38 Summary: Jesus in
    Jerusalem

22–23 Passion and death of Jesus

24 Empty tomb and appearances

Appendix 2

An alternative to the two-source theory:

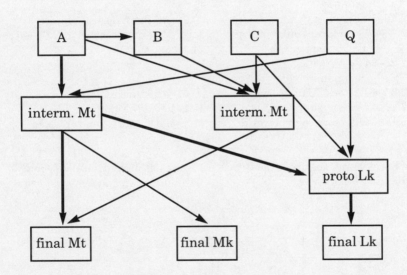

This graph is adapted from that proposed by P. Benoit and M.-E. Boismard in their *Synopse des quatre Evangiles en français* (2 vols.; Paris, 1965). I removed the cells and lines dealing with the Fourth Gospel so that we can compare the graph with the two-source theory.

The top line of lettered sources refer to the earlist documents recording the work and words of Jesus. Through this top level of documents, Benoit and Boismard can gather various traditions—such as those dealing with Peter—now scattered through the Gospels into a single source. The intermediate line allows Benoit and Boismard to speculate how Matthew, Mark, and Luke could mutually depend on each other.

The major drawback of this theory lies in the subtleness with which present texts are assigned to one line or another. The arguments, it seems to me, border on the arbitrary. The assignments thus become so complex that the theory appears too difficult to use.

Appendix 3

The Hasmonean and Herodian Dynasties

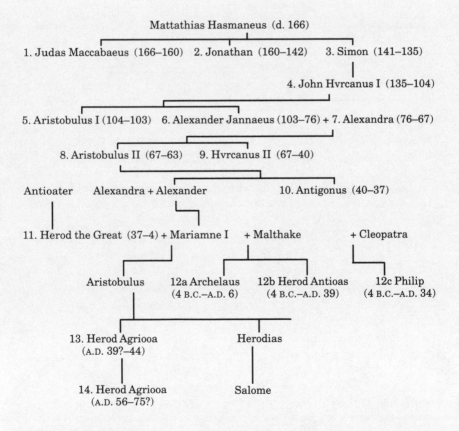

Mattathias Hasmaneus (d. 166)

1. Judas Maccabaeus (166–160)   2. Jonathan (160–142)   3. Simon (141–135)

4. John Hvrcanus I (135–104)

5. Aristobulus I (104–103)   6. Alexander Jannaeus (103–76) + 7. Alexandra (76–67)

8. Aristobulus II (67–63)   9. Hvrcanus II (67–40)

Antioater   Alexandra + Alexander   10. Antigonus (40–37)

11. Herod the Great (37–4) + Mariamne I   + Malthake   + Cleopatra

Aristobulus   12a Archelaus (4 B.C.–A.D. 6)   12b Herod Antioas (4 B.C.–A.D. 39)   12c Philip (4 B.C.–A.D. 34)

13. Herod Agriooa (A.D. 39?–44)   Herodias

14. Herod Agriooa (A.D. 56–75?)   Salome

+ indicates marriage

Appendix 4

"Hymn of the Pearl" from *The Acts of Thomas*

When I was a speechless child, I dwelt in my father's kingdom and constantly enjoyed the wealth and delicacies of those who nurtured me. From the East, our homeland, my parents provisioned and sent me forth. From the wealth of the treasury they gathered for me a load.... They took off the golden clothes which in their love they had tailored for me and the yellow robe woven to my stature. They made an agreement with me, writing it in my mind that I might not forget, saying, "If you go down to Egypt and rescue from there the one pearl which is in the midst of the sea serpent, you will put on your splendid clothes and that robe which goes over it. With your brother, next in rank, you will be herald in our kingdom."

I went from the East and went down with two guides, for the way was dangerous and difficult and I was inexperienced in such travels.... I entered Egypt, and my guides who were journeying along with me left. Rushing to the serpent as fast as I could I stayed near his hole watching for him to become drowsy and fall asleep, that I might seize my pearl. Since I was all alone I washed my face and appeared a stranger to my companions. However I saw there one of my race, a noble out of the East, a youth handsome and attractive, a son of the nobles. Coming to me he conversed with me and I made him my companion, my friend and associate in my affairs. I urged him to guard against the Egyptians and against consorting with those unclean ones. But I clothed myself in their garments that I might not be thought of as a stranger from without, come to take the pearl, lest the Egyptians waken the serpent against me. I do not know how, but they learned of my pretense, that I was not of their country. They dealt with me treacherously. I was given to eat of their food. I thus became ignorant that I was a king's son and began to serve their king. I forgot about the pearl for which my parents had sent me.

While all this befell me, my parents observed and were grieved for me.... They wrote to me, and the nobles stamped their seal thereto, "From your father, the king of kings, and your mother, the keeper of the East, and from your brother, our other son, to our son in Egypt, peace! Rise up and awaken from your sleep and listen to the words of our letter. Remember that you are a son of kings. See the yoke of slavery which you are subject to! Remember the pearl for which you were sent into Egypt. Remember your splendid clothes. Your name is read in the book of life along with that of your brother who waits in succession."

Because I sensed it, I awoke from my sleep. Picking it up and kissing it, I read it. In my heart were written the words that had been recorded. I suddenly remembered that I was a son of kings, and my noble birth began stirring. I remembered the pearl for which I was sent to Egypt. I came as on a war chariot to the dreadful serpent. I overcame him reciting the name of my father. Then I snatched away the pearl and turned about to my father's house. Taking off the filthy garment, I left it in their land. I directed my way to the light of the East, my homeland. I found my awakener on the way. Just as it had awakened me from sleep with its proclaiming voice, so it led me with its light. For then before my eyes were the royal clothes of silk. Leading me and drawing me forward with its love, it passed by Babyrinthos....

Indeed I had not remembered its glory, for as a child and still quite young I had left it in my father's palace. Suddenly as I saw the garment as in a mirror, it become like me. I saw myself wholly in it, knowing and seeing myself through it. In part we were divided from each other, yet again one in single form.... Again I saw that all over it the motions of knowledge were stirring. It was ready to utter a word. Its royal movements rested on me with such a growing force. It strove from his (?) hand, stretched out that I might take it. My desire also spurred me to run to meet it and receive it. I stretched out and was carried off by the colors. I drew completely over myself my excellent royal robe. I clothed myself and mounted up to the place of peace and worship. Bowing my head I worshiped the splendor of the father who had sent the robes to me, for I had accomplished his orders, and he also had done what he promised. At the gate of the royal one, who is from the beginning, I mingled. For he rejoiced over me and received me with him in his kingdom. All his servants praised him with favorable voices. He promised to send me with him to the gate of the king that I could appear with him before the king with my gift and my pearl.

Translated from the Greek text in *Acta Apostolorum Apocrypha,* ed. M. Bonnet (Hildesheim: Georg Olms, 1959), 2.219–24.

Citation Index

I. NEW TESTAMENT

Subject Index